Meeting the Inclusion Challenge in Innovation

De Gruyter Studies in Innovation and Entrepreneurship

Series Editor
John Bessant

Volume 8

Meeting the Inclusion Challenge in Innovation

Giving Voice to Users

Edited by
Tatiana Iakovleva, Elin M. Oftedal and John Bessant

DE GRUYTER

ISBN 978-3-11-124057-2
e-ISBN (PDF) 978-3-11-124103-6
e-ISBN (EPUB) 978-3-11-124190-6
ISSN 2570-169X
e-ISSN 2570-1703
DOI https://doi.org/10.1515/9783111241036

Library of Congress Control Number: 2024939429

Bibliographic information published by the Deutsche Nationalbibliothek
The Deutsche Nationalbibliothek lists this publication in the Deutsche Nationalbibliografie; detailed bibliographic data are available on the internet at http://dnb.dnb.de.

Typesetting: Integra Software Services Pvt. Ltd.
Printing and binding: CPI books GmbH, Leck

www.degruyter.com

Contents

John Bessant, Elin M. Oftedal, Tatiana Iakovleva
Introduction: Meeting the inclusion challenge in innovation —— 1

Elin M. Oftedal, Matthias Kaiser, Tatiana Iakovleva
Back to the future: Reflection on healthcare's past to understand its future —— 21

Nele A.J. De Witte, Annouck De Cat, Hilde Vandenhoudt, Sascha Vermeylen, Vicky Van der Auwera, Leen Broeckx, Ingrid Adriaensen
Sustainable user involvement: Building a user community and fostering high-quality research —— 35

Judy Hong Huang, Elin M. Oftedal, Tatiana Iakovleva
The emergence of a boundary innovation space – the case of Norwegian Smart Care Lab —— 61

Catharina M. van Leersum, Zohrah Malik, Johan van der Zwart, Kornelia Konrad
The creation of a community to engage in innovation processes and citizen science —— 83

Catharina M. van Leersum, Kornelia Konrad, Johan van der Zwart
Ageing in your place: Envisioning healthy, happy, and safe ageing in a neighbourhood with citizen science methods —— 101

Johan van der Zwart, Catharina M. van Leersum, Kornelia Konrad
Climbing the citizen science ladder: Juxtaposing citizens' levels of participation and influence in research analysis and dissemination —— 121

Katherine Neary
Creating new paths: Collaborative challenges in establishing an innovation hub —— 143

Matt Halkes, Nick Peres, John Bessant
Digital futures – enabling innovation through a boundary space —— 163

Maria João Jacinto, Gemma Tria, Luís Correia, Margarida Oliveira, Joana Afonso, Helena Canhão, Pedro Oliveira
Patient innovation as a case-study example of a multisided platform for involving patients in the social innovation process — 173

Misha Gipsman, Denis Yagodin, Ilia Rozovskii
Crisis entrepreneurship: To be a robust link in the chain — 193

Kristian Eiken, Elin M. Oftedal
Superpower or kryptonite? — 209

Anna Szopa
The impact of users on the development of Morphic auto personalization — 229

Thomas Laudal
The dilemma of achieving responsible innovation in regulated markets — 245

Elin M. Oftedal, Tatiana Iakovleva, John Bessant
Navigating towards improved user engagement in healthcare innovation – releasing the power of users — 265

List of contributors — 279

List of figures — 287

List of tables — 291

Index — 293

John Bessant, Elin M. Oftedal, Tatiana Iakovleva

Introduction: Meeting the inclusion challenge in innovation

In the ever-evolving landscape of innovation, the role of the user has transformed from passive recipient to active participant. The success of the innovation process no longer hinges solely on the ingenuity of inventors or the acumen of engineers but increasingly on the integration of user insights and experiences. "Releasing the Power of the User: Meeting the Inclusion Challenge in Innovation" embarks on a journey to explore this pivotal shift, emphasizing the critical importance of user involvement in shaping products, services, and technologies that not only meet market demands but also foster inclusive and sustainable growth.

The inclusion of users in the innovation process marks a significant departure from traditional models that prioritized technical achievements and profitability above user satisfaction and societal impact. This book delves into the myriad ways in which harnessing user input can lead to more effective, efficient, and equitable outcomes. It brings valuable examples of user inclusion across seven countries, exemplifying benefits as well the challenges of the process. By bringing users to the forefront of the innovation ecosystem, we unlock a treasure trove of insights, experiences, and perspectives that can drive more nuanced and context-sensitive advancements.

Through a collection of case studies, theoretical insights, and practical strategies, we aim to illuminate the multifaceted role of users in the innovation process. From co-creation workshops to user-driven research methodologies, the strategies for engaging users are as diverse as the benefits they yield. This book critically examines both the challenges and opportunities presented by this user-centric approach to innovation, offering readers a comprehensive understanding of how to effectively integrate user perspectives for the betterment of technology, society, and the environment.

"Releasing the Power of the User: Meeting the Inclusion Challenge in Innovation" is crafted to address a specific context—the healthcare services sector. Health and care are paramount for every individual, citizen, and nation worldwide. Innovations within this domain are particularly significant, and the extent to which they are designed to serve us, as a society, poses a critical question. In this introductory chapter, we delve into the challenges of the healthcare sector and the imperative need for innovation.

We then ponder the importance of innovating responsibly, which entails innovating for and with society. This necessitates the inclusion of users in the innovation process, prompting us to examine the complex role of users, especially patients, and their behavior towards innovation in healthcare.

While acknowledging that users, and in healthcare contexts, patients, possess invaluable knowledge, the question of how to effectively involve users in innovations remains unresolved. Towards the chapter's conclusion, we introduce the concept of boundary in-

https://doi.org/10.1515/9783111241036-001

novation spaces. These spaces facilitate co-creation with users in a secure environment, thereby unleashing the potential of user involvement in the innovation process.

Innovation needs in the healthcare sector

Healthcare systems worldwide are confronting a significant crisis, driven by the complex interplay of aging populations, escalating expectations, and spiraling costs. This situation, prevalent in both developed and emerging economies, poses a challenge to the sustainability of reliable, safe healthcare services, with public health spending in many countries nearing or exceeding 10% of GDP. These pressures are compounded by the advancing age of populations, the continuous rise in healthcare expenses, and the intricate evolution of medical technologies. Despite the diversity in healthcare financing models across nations, from predominantly public to predominantly private systems, the core difficulties remain universally prevalent.

Historical insights reveal a longstanding awareness of these challenges. For example, a report from two decades ago underscored the limitations of traditional public service reforms in addressing critical societal issues, including environmental concerns, crime, and major public health problems like smoking and obesity. It advocated for a paradigm shift towards "co-created services," where users participate in the design and delivery, emphasizing the urgent need for a radical transformation in the approach to healthcare services (Leadbeater, 2004).

More recent analyses confirm that these issues persist. Projections indicate, for instance, that healthcare spending in the United States is expected to grow at an annual rate of 5.8% from 2015 to 2025 (Keehan et al., 2017. The sector is under increasing pressure to provide high-quality care while managing costs effectively, a challenge intensified by demographic trends, rising prices, and the growing complexity of healthcare technology (Marmot et al., 2012). These challenges are not limited by geographic or economic boundaries, affecting countries worldwide irrespective of their healthcare financing structure.

Innovation is central to addressing these challenges. Beyond developing new products and services, it necessitates a comprehensive re-evaluation of healthcare processes and overarching strategies. The discourse on the significance of innovation is matched by practical evidence demonstrating its potential to effect meaningful improvements.

The rapid expansion of the digital healthcare sector exemplifies such innovation, showcasing how intelligent devices, systems, and the strategic use of data can significantly enhance productivity, quality, and safety in healthcare. This technological advancement offers potential not only for improving primary care through enhanced knowledge and preventive measures but also for facilitating transformative changes in acute treatment processes. To take a simple metaphor, the digital cavalry is gathering on top of the hill ready to sweep down and rescue the beleaguered healthcare system. And its most potent new recruit – machine learning/AI – is still on its way; its deployment could be a game-changer.

Innovation is not just critical; it has become an imperative for the future sustainability and effectiveness of global healthcare systems.

The need for responsible innovation in healthcare

There are considerable grounds for optimism in this smart technology revolution about to take over the sector. But we should be careful; history is littered with examples if technologies which promise much but which do not always deliver. The question of 'responsible innovation' (RI) is central here; the need to think carefully about the potential impacts of technology and work proactively to anticipate and adapt, working with end users to ensure the best outcomes (Owen, Bessant, and Heintz, 2013).

RI emerged as a response to the concerns around technology push and the emergence of unanticipated consequences. Even technologies like the insecticide DDT which were seen as world-changing for good turned out to have negative implications. RI can be defined as . . .*'a transparent, interactive process by which societal actors and innovators become mutually responsive to each other with a view to the (ethical) acceptability, sustainability and societal desirability of the innovation process and its marketable products(in order to allow a proper embedding of scientific and technological advances in our society)* (Von Schomberg, 2013).

Owen and colleagues (Owen et al., 2012) offer a helpful framework (which has been adopted widely by the EU and several major research funding agencies) which sets out some key questions which should be addressed in the development and implementation of innovations. Such principles suggest a broader stakeholder inclusion into the decision-making process, anticipation of societal needs, and reflection of concerns, which calls for new innovation policies to enact it (Kuhlmann et al., 2019)

These principles are particular relevant when it comes to the innovations in healthcare sector. Technology push characterises much of the digital revolution – it is often a solution looking for a problem. The risk here is that the design of innovations, be they wearable devices, smart homes or entire digitally-supported care information systems, does not take on board the perspective of the end user. Smart homes can become a kind of high-tech prison where people feel under surveillance rather than supported, wearables become trackers, robot assistants become policemen supervising nutrition, medication and controlling living structures, etc. (Iakovleva et al., 2021a)

On the positive side digital technologies have a significant advantage in many applications and the new possibilities opened up by artificial intelligence augment this further. Applications are emerging in many directions to help deal with a wide range of challenges, from robot assisted surgery, through patient records management to data mining and AI to help deal with interpretation and diagnosis in mass screening preventative programmes (Barlow, 2017).

Additionally digital technologies offer a higher level of flexibility around core responsible innovation issues – for example, they are 'soft' technologies which can be quickly reprogrammed and adapted, extending the 'responsiveness' dimension to allow for learning and adaptation to suit different contexts.

The challenge in developing and deploying these powerful technologies is to do so in ways which reflect RI principles – anticipating potential problems, using their responsiveness to adapt them to particular contexts and enhance usability by reflecting the inclusion of multiple stakeholder voices (Iakovleva et al., 2019a).

Why inclusiveness matters for innovation

This is not just an ethical question; it is also about effective innovation design. We know from extensive research that engaging with users early on in the innovation process brings two significant benefits. First, it augments the range and depth of solutions because it brings in user knowledge, experience and insight. It can extend the capabilities available to the technical design team only and sometimes bring in valuable tacit knowledge (Von Hippel, 2005).

A second powerful argument for user inclusion is that it helps ensure compatibility of the innovation with the context into which it is designed to fit. Users know what will work in their world (or not) and engaging with increases the potential for faster and more extensive downstream adoption of innovation (Rogers, 2003). There is an extensive library of experience around failed innovations which can be traced back to insufficient understanding or consideration of the compatibility issue (Tidd and Bessant, 2020).

In many cases diffusion of innovation is based on an underlying 'dominant logic', a design which reflects a particular set of interests and viewpoints. There is a risk that alternative designs might be excluded at an early stage as a trajectory emerges, which defines the form and implementation mode of the technology – the challenge of 'technological determinism' (Braverman, 1998).

There are parallels to this in a number of other fields. Early adoption of computer-aided production management systems in the 1970s and 1980s involved an embedded model of how organizations worked and were structured which suited certain kinds of application but limited the effectiveness of the technology in other contexts (Bessant and Buckingham, 1993. Similarly flexible automation technologies during the 1990s often failed to deliver their potential because of the inbuilt design logic, which assumed certain forms of work organization (Leonard-Barton,1988). Indeed the emergence of 'lean manufacturing;' with its emphasis on team working within flexible and autonomous teams owed much to its ability to deliver the flexibility which expensive but rigidly designed technologies could not (Womack and Jones,1996).

Experiences like these suggest that there is an initial 'design space' associated with novel technological opportunities but that this can quickly become colonised by a dominant design and force out other options (Bessant and Buchanan. 1983). A counter-strategy is to engage in extensive engagement with stakeholders who will operate or be affected by these technologies at an early stage (Mumford, 2006b; Trist and Bamforth, 1951).

Even allowing for a degree of user input in this design space the logic of procurement in many healthcare systems is one of centralisation and scale. Although programmable and flexible in theory the nature of this logic argues for one size fits many kinds of solution. Pilots are then rolled out without subsequent tailoring or configuration to suit differing local circumstances.

To summarize, it makes sense to bring in users early in the process and work with them to co-create solutions. Much of the rhetoric around healthcare innovation recognises this as a principle but it is not always followed through. As famously said by Pablo Picasso "*"There is only one way to look at things until someone shows us how to look at them with different eyes"*.

Bringing user insights to bear

But there are problems in taking this inclusive approach. First is the inertia of existing innovation systems which may pay lip service to understanding the needs of the market but which in practice confine this to focus groups and other late-stage testing around polishing a user experience (UX) which has already been 'baked in' by the design team. This could more accurately be termed 'user consultation' since the potential outlined above for drawing on tacit user knowledge about the innovation and its context are largely ignored.

A second point of relevance in the healthcare field concerns who is undertaking the design activity. Unlike consumer markets where the interests of the user are im portant input to early design since this will shape downstream adoption and diffusion, in the medical field there is a multi-layered market in which clinicians and others charged with delivering healthcare are often seen as the primary users. Ideas are often initially developed with the concerns of this group in mind who are assumed to act on behalf of the end-recipient of care – the patient. The risk here is that one group of users is consulted but another is disenfranchised from participating in the design; the result can be a 'doctors know best' solution, which may not meet the underlying patients needs or concerns.

This limits the range of ideas, insights and experience to the practitioner or administrator groups and may exclude the end-user perspective. Centralised procurement processes and pathways can reinforce this perspective; the result is a system which often assumes that it knows what is 'best' for a passive end-user – the patient.

But while such an 'expertise-driven' approach might appear persuasive (not least in terms of ease of implementation) it ignores the fact that end-users have knowledge about what might work (or not) in their context plus a high incentive to contribute towards finding ways to deal with their situation more effectively. There may be limited scope in some areas which require deep clinical knowledge but in many other cases there is much which patients can contribute.

End-users can often influence the outcome of process and system innovations by the ways in which they support the use of those systems. Extensive studies of, for example, the introduction of IT systems has repeatedly shown that their effectiveness depends critically in users working with the system to ensure data integrity (Eason, 1988). Process operators can quickly enhance or retard the operation of new systems; their acceptance is seen as critically dependent on the ways in which such technologies are designed and implemented (Bessant and Buchanan, 1983). Participative design which has its roots in the socio-technical systems design work of the 1950s has become a key element in change management around large-scale process innovation (Trist and Bamforth, 1951; Mumford, 2006b).

This applies particularly in the case of digital approaches which require user engagement such as medical records management. But it is also highly relevant when considering something like a 'smart home' which is widely seen as a policy approach enabling elderly citizens to remain outside the formal acute care system by living a semi-independent life. This relieves pressure on overstretched hospitals and can be both cost-effective and better in terms of health outcomes. But it depends on acceptance and 'ownership' of the smart home by those who will live in it – and that requires their input to its design.

Which brings in the third and most significant challenge – hearing the voice of the user. The principle of user involvement in innovation is well-known across the innovation literature and healthcare has been extensively covered as a use case. Characteristic of user innovators are two significant features: they have a high incentive to innovate and they are tolerant of imperfection, happy to see a prototype which satisfies their needs. They are also often less concerned about wider diffusion; their focus is dealing with their own problem and if others have a similar problem they are welcome to adopt. This is an oversimplification, of course, but there is a well-established pattern here (Von Hippel, 1988).

In the healthcare context these criteria are certainly present; user innovators have a high incentive – at the limit their own survival and the chance to live a dignified life with pain and other discomfort reduced or ameliorated. There is a growing range of innovation, for example showcased on the Patient Innovation platform, which demonstrates the creation of sophisticated solutions to improve lifestyles for patients and their carers (Cennamo et al., 2022). And beyond such active users there are many other innovations which have resulted from insights, ideas and inputs from patients and their carers (Kuenne et al., 2013; Bessant and Maher, 2009)

Users are different . . .

But not every end user (patient or carer) is willing or able to act in this entrepreneurial fashion. As we showed in our earlier work, there is a spectrum of possibility for user engagement. This spectrum ranges from 'passive' users who are simply the recipient of healthcare solutions through 'informed' users who are actively seeking to understand information about their circumstances to 'involved' users who are actively involved in developing the solutions (Bessant et al., 2019). Today's informed patients have unprecedented access to knowledge, from general searches to specialized databases, enhancing their understanding of symptoms and treatments and empowering them to play a more decisive role in their healthcare, challenging traditional dynamics in the health professional-patient relationship.

The shift towards patient-centered medicine is accelerated by involving patients and patient advocacy groups in study design and decision-making processes, embodying the principle "nothing about me without me" and highlighting the importance of organizational responsiveness to patient feedback for responsible innovation in healthcare.

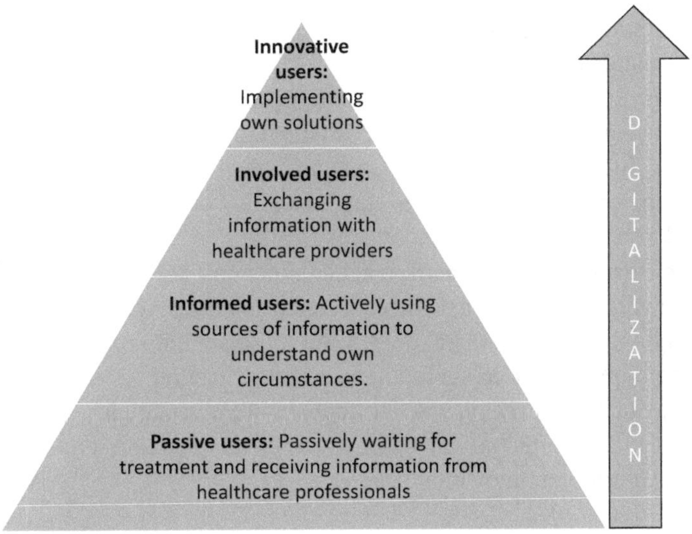

Figure 1: Spectrum of User Innovation Behaviour. Adapted from Bessant et al. 2019.

At the extreme are what we might term 'hero' innovators whose personal incentive for innovation is so high that they develop and deploy their own solutions. Most users fall into the middle of this innovation spectrum, meaning they are not ready to innovate by themselves, but they might be willing to share their experiences and become a part of the innovation process (Iakovleva et al., 2021). The problem is that users often face challenges in sharing their innovative ideas, further developing ideas into solutions, or diffusing the innovation outcome to benefit a larger population (Oliveira et al., 2019).

Releasing the power of users

So users can be involved in healthcare and where they are there seem to be benefits. And innovating organizations could benefit from engaging with this perspective. As von Hippel and colleagues have persuasively shown there is an argument for companies to adopt a new approach based on integrating user insights into their innovation models – the 'free innovation' process (Von Hippel, 2016). But this raises the question which lies at the core of this book – how to hear and amplify user voices to move them along the involvement spectrum, enabling them to play a more active role in the innovation process.

This is not a trivial question. First there is the question of *articulation* – how to help users express insights and ideas? Uncovering and clarifying user needs and aspirations is essential but requires different approaches and tools to simple market surveys and focus groups. Helping them imagine what might be as well as what is wrong with what is currently available is important.

Articulation of ideas is only the start of the innovation process; what follows is a process of learning and developing via a series of steps which bring ideas to life. Central to this is a series of conversations about concepts and how they might be realised – and key to brining in patient user voices to this is the idea of *amplifying*' them so that they can be heard and become part of those conversations.

Prototyping and agile learning is at the heart of agile innovation development process (Ries, 2011). And this raises the third area of need in releasing the power of users – *acting* on their insights and working with them. Once again these are not familiar skills for such users, nor is the approach of co-evolution/co-creation around an emerging 'boundary object' which facilitates a learning and developmental conversation.

This implies the need to help effect a transition from 'voice' to 'action' enabling users to become part of a continuing innovation process.

The role of boundary innovation spaces

Part of this 'conversation around a boundary object' is about bringing together different players with different perspectives, insights and ideas to help co-create an innovation. In the context of our user innovation discussion this is a central activity, but it raises the question of *where* these interactions might take place. Are they one-off exchanges in ad hoc meetings or could they be located in a supportive environment designed to enable open-ended experimental conversations and prototyping activity to take place?

That question underpins the wider experience of a variety of organizations in experimenting with different forms of supportive environment for innovation – something we term 'boundary spaces'. They share the common concern to find places within which such shared conversations can happen, bringing together different stakeholders and perspectives in experimental co-creation. Much has been written about them and there is a long history but the key point is about a physical locus for such co-creative innovation activity (Fritzsche et al., 2020; Grove and Marlow, 2016).

It has long been recognised that Innovation needs space to emerge, somewhere away from the day-to-day pressures and context of delivery and operation. This space is often a physical environment but it has other dimensions – for example time. 3M's innovation success has been partly attributed to their long-standing 15% policy which essentially recognises the need to communicate to employees the availability of uncommitted time during which they can explore ideas (Gundling,2000). Innovation space is also about a climate which is non-judgmental, experimental, explorative and allowing for failure. (The association with the idea of a laboratory as a place where things can be tried and where failure is a part of the process has led to the label being attached to many innovation-linked initiatives of this kind- the innovation lab).

Innovation spaces are also associated with diversity, bringing different knowledge sets to bear and allowing for creative collisions. The Silicon Valley model of rapid innovation owes much to the pattern of cross-fertilising and exchange of ideas which took place in many venues but notable Walker's Wagon Wheel bar where researchers would gather after work for informal exchanges. This continues a long tradition of meeting-places where innovation can emerge, dating back at least to the London coffee shops in the 18th century.

Another element in the space is the potential for creating and realising prototypes. Whilst much can be accomplished in conversation or via simple sketches the possibility of using more advanced techniques to bring prototype ideas and early concepts to life is an important extension of the laboratory idea. Enabling technologies like 3D printing, virtual reality simulations and rapid prototyping tools allow for a much more focused kind of conversation around boundary objects which can quickly be brought to life. Interestingly many successful innovation incubators which host start-ups are now being physically linked with 'makerspaces', allowing shared exploration and elaboration of 'minimum viable products' in physical as well as virtual forms.

One other dimension of such 'boundary spaces' is the range of people who can come together and the ways in which 'creative collisions' can be enabled. Increasingly innovation labs and their derivatives are opening doors to a wide range of people – for example, hackathons aim explicitly to tap into a wide range of people whose interest can be focused on a key challenge. Many companies are locating labs close to university campuses aiming to draw in fresh perspectives from a wide range of fields (and also to identify potential recruits for their future innovation activities). Josephs is an interesting venture developed in Germany by the FAU university and the Fraunhofer Institute; it offers a high street space in the centre of Nuremburg where innovators can share their early-stage prototype thinking and demonstrations with members of the public (Greve and Martinez, 2016).

What makes an effective boundary space?

Different versions of such boundary innovation spaces (BIS) have been around for centuries but in recent years there has been a rapid growth in the field. There is a risk, of course, that much of the proliferation of innovation labs and their derivatives is simply another example of following innovation fashion. But underneath this there has been extensive learning around what makes for an effective BIS as a key resource in the context of an 'open innovation' world where knowledge is widely available but distributed unevenly. Finding effective ways of bringing key people together in a supportive context is a strategic innovation priority.

We know a lot more about the key ingredients of such spaces and the tools and methodologies which enable them to support co-creation. And it's clear this is much more than simply piling bean bags in the corner of a brightly decorated room with some wacky posters and furniture in it. To enhance effectiveness, boundary spaces require structured organization, the right tools, skilled facilitation, and adaptability. They must be meticulously managed, with user relationships nurtured and consistently maintained. These spaces should provide a secure environment where individuals are encouraged to experiment, even fail, and engage in co-creation, fostering a culture of continuous collaboration and innovation.

Above all they need to be able to repeat the innovation trick; successfully co-creating a single innovation might happen as a lucky encounter or a fortunate conjunction. But being able to embed a methodology and process, a systematic way of enabling front end innovation with different stakeholders requires more. Much of the learning around innovation labs has been about this, moving from a focus on 'innovation theatre' with its trappings of creativity to somewhere which can systematically enable a stream of co-created innovation.

Our research has tried to add to this emerging body of knowledge around what works and why and to draw on a wide range of examples from an international context. In reporting it here we can open up some key questions and explore a number of potentially fruitful solutions to the core puzzle of how we release the power of users in healthcare innovation.

Exploring the question – overview of the book

This book compiles a series of case studies from seven countries—Belgium, the Netherlands, Norway, Portugal, the UK, Ukraine, and the USA—that illustrate the challenges of inclusion within the healthcare sector.

We begin this book with a journey through the historical and philosophical landscapes of healthcare transformation, examining the interplay between technological advancements and the ethics of care. The opening **chapter 2**, ***"Reflection on Healthcare's Future through Inclusive Innovation"*** by Elin Oftedal, Tatiana Iakovleva, and Matthias Kaiser, delves into the historical developments in healthcare innovation and the philosophical importance of lead users in this evolution. It discusses the parallel progress of technological innovations and humanistic approaches in healthcare, arguing for a future that harmoniously integrates both to prevent an overreliance on technology. The narrative traces healthcare's evolution from the pre-industrial age through to the digital era, spotlighting significant milestones and ethical dilemmas encountered along the way.

Our book progresses with a collection of chapters detailing user engagement practices in two distinct Living Labs – one situated in Belgium and the other in Norway.

The **chapter 3** titled ***"Sustainable user involvement: building a user community and fostering high-quality research,"*** authored by Nele A.J. De Witte, Annouck De Cat, Hilde Vandenhoudt, Sascha Vermeylen, Vicky Van der Auwera, Leen Broeckx, and Ingrid Adriaensen, unfolds a systematic guide for implementing successful user engagement strategies, drawing from the experiences of LiCalab in Belgium. This detailed strategy ensures that living labs like LiCalab can efficiently integrate stakeholders into the innovation journey, fostering the creation of solutions that are both impactful and in tune with the needs of their target audience.

The next **chapter 4** by Judy Huang, Elin Oftedal and Tatiana Iakovleva ***"The emergence of the boundary innovation space – case of Norwegian Smart Care Lab"***, provides a comprehensive exploration of the Norwegian Smart Care Lab's (NSCL) formation and growth. It chronicles the lab's shift in business model and operational strategy, highlighting its transformation from a solely firm-focused testing hub to an inclusive and cooperative innovation ecosystem. Utilizing interviews with a variety of stakeholders, the chapter furnishes a detailed account of NSCL's evolution over a span of five years. It sheds light on how the lab's initial, somewhat unclear business model evolved into a more structured and impactful framework through continuous stakeholder interaction and strategic redirections. This shift is portrayed as a testament to the critical importance of involving users early in the process—from validating concepts to refining end products—thereby illustrating their significant contribution to the innovation lifecycle and product development.

Following our exploration of Living Labs, our book embarks on a journey into citizen involvement through the lens of the Citizen Lab project in the Netherlands.

Three chapters illuminate the diverse opportunities and challenges that citizen involvement initiatives present, each offering unique perspectives on how such engagements can shape and influence the project's outcomes.

Chapter 5 by Catharina M. van Leersum, Kornelia Konrad and Johan van der Zwart ***"Ageing in your place: Envisioning healthy, happy, and safe ageing in a neighbourhood with citizen science methods"*** explores the challenges and necessities of adapting homes for the growing population of older individuals living independently. It focuses on a study conducted through the TOPFIT Citizenlab in the Netherlands, which employed citizen science to investigate age-friendly living solutions. The research utilized a combination of meetings, photo-voice methods, and scenario-building workshops to gather insights on healthy aging and the integration of personal experiences with statistical health data. The findings emphasize a holistic approach to age-friendly living, highlighting the importance of not just the home environment but also the surrounding community, and the interconnectedness of physical, mental, and social health. Solutions proposed by citizens blend technical, social, and environmental aspects, showcasing the value of involving older individuals and their communities in the planning process.

Next **chapter 6**, written *by* Johan van der Zwart, Catharina M. van Leersum and Kornelia Konrad **"Climbing the Citizen Science ladder: Juxtaposing citizens' levels of participation and influence in research analysis and dissemination"** discusses the intricate roles of citizens in healthcare research, highlighting a model that boosts both the understanding of healthcare issues and citizen empowerment by incorporating their insights into traditionally expert-led research processes. It underlines the importance of involving citizens across various research stages, from data analysis to dissemination, thus democratizing research and ensuring healthcare innovations are user-centered. Moreover, by extending citizens' involvement to encompass not just data collection but also analysis and communication, the chapter argues for a more significant impact of citizen contributions on research outcomes, making findings more accessible and likely to be adopted by the wider community.

Chapter 7 co-authored by Catharina M. van Leersum, Zohrah Malik, Johan van der Zwart and Kornelia Konrad, **"The creation of a community to engage in innovation processes and citizen science"**, delves into how citizen science can enhance health projects by focusing on community engagement, illustrated by the Dutch TOPFIT Citizenlab's work on diabetes, dementia, and other issues. It identifies four crucial processes for community engagement: recognizing capacities, aligning goals, trust-building, and fostering a learning environment, which differ from sporadic traditional user involvement. Highlighting the significance of prolonged collaboration for successful public participation, especially among independently living older adults, the TOPFIT projects showcase strategies for effective community involvement. These include acknowledging individual and collective capabilities, establishing trust, and ensuring goal congruence, underpinned by feedback loops and clear communication of research outcomes. In essence, the chapter underscores the importance of building strong communities in citizen science initiatives for impactful and inclusive health research, offering insights from TOP-

FIT Citizenlab's approach to fostering deepened public engagement and better health outcomes.

The book proceeds into investigation of Living labs in the hospital settings with two chapters from UK. **Chapter 8**, written by Matt Halkes, Nick Peres and John Bessant **"Digital futures – enabling innovation through a boundary space"** explores digital healthcare transformation, spotlighting user engagement's critical role and introducing "boundary innovation spaces" like the Digital Futures Lab (DFL) as key for collaborative digital advancements in healthcare. Authors discuss DFL efforts in developing immersive care technologies, training simulations, and 3D-printed medical apps, while noting the challenges of sustaining innovation. The chapter emphasizes the importance of engaging a broad spectrum of users, including patients and caregivers, in the innovation process to ensure the successful adoption of digital solutions. It presents the DFL as a vital hub within a UK hospital trust for digital experimentation and collaboration, outlining its contributions to healthcare technology and the necessity for strategic support to overcome innovation challenges. The text advocates for continued investment in digital technologies and collaborative spaces like the DFL to enhance healthcare delivery and education.

Next **chapter 9** by Katie Neary, **"Creating an innovation space: Experience with an innovation hub in a UK hospital"**, examines the establishment and operation of a healthcare innovation hub within a UK hospital, detailing the challenges of balancing stakeholder expectations, clinician involvement, and integrating innovation spaces within the hospital's infrastructure. It emphasizes the hub's role in leveraging clinician expertise and emerging technologies like AI and virtual reality to improve patient care, despite facing operational and bureaucratic hurdles. The research reveals a tension between clinicians' altruistic motives and management's demand for quantifiable outcomes, alongside the operational challenges of fostering collaboration and maintaining stakeholder engagement. It suggests that successful management of the hub requires accommodating user needs, strategic communication, and aligning expectations with the hub's goals. The findings underscore the complexity of leading user-driven healthcare innovation and advocate for further research on digital and physical spaces' complementary roles in supporting innovation within hospital environments.

Next, the volume presents two chapters, each focusing on an online platform designed for user empowerment. The first details a special case for patient innovators, while the second describes innovation initiatives that emerged during the recent crisis – the war in Ukraine.

Chapter 10 by Maria João Jacinto, Gemma Tria, Luís Correia, Margarida Oliveira, Joana Afonso, Helena Canhão, Pedro Oliveira entitled **"Patient Innovation as a case-study example of a Multisided Platform for involving patients in the social innovation process"**, describes the Patient Innovation (PI) project in Portugal. This project showcases the untapped innovative potential of patients and informal caregivers, transforming healthcare by harnessing solutions created out of personal necessity. PI stands out as a global platform that rigorously vets and shares healthcare innovations from its community of 300,000 users across over 100 countries, marking it as Europe's most extensive health innovation hub. Beyond connecting patient innovators with the healthcare industry, PI facilitates the commercialization of their solutions, effectively linking user-driven and industry innovations. Highlighting Multisided Platforms (MSPs), the chapter illustrates how PI exemplifies the integration of user and producer innovations, acting as a community organizer, market facilitator, and innovation manager to bring patient-derived solutions to the market

In **chapter 11** by Misha Gipsman; Denis Yagodin, Ilia Rozovskii "**Crisis Entrepreneurship: to be a robust link in the chain**" authors analyse user-led initiatives during the crises like the conflict in Ukraine. Responsible entrepreneurship plays a vital role in meeting social needs when state resources are limited, leading to a rise in social-entrepreneurial initiatives focused on addressing medical and mental health challenges. Despite the ambition to become redundant by solving these issues, some initiatives fall short, highlighting the need for continuous engagement with beneficiaries for impactful support. The crisis has highlighted the importance of innovative tech solutions, like online communication and security tools, to provide essential services efficiently. Successful projects share common principles: specialized assistance ("the link in the chain") and robustness through comprehensive support and stakeholder network integration. These initiatives underscore the significance of community involvement, with successful ones prioritizing direct help and fostering collaborations with stakeholders, including beneficiaries evolving into volunteers, to innovate and adapt in crisis situations.

The following two chapters delve into the challenges of user involvement within firms. In **chapter 12** by Kristian Eiken and Elin Oftedal **"Superpower or Kryptonite? to innovate by involving users"** authors delve into the complex role of user inclusion in health technology innovation in Norwegian companies, highlighting its growing importance in both literature and practical application. It emphasizes the challenges of integrating diverse user needs within the European health sector's unique context, where public entities and end-users often face power imbalances. Acknowledging the difficulties such as cost and representative engagement, it nonetheless posits user involvement as essential for tailoring technology to varied requirements and preferences. This chapter reveals that despite the challenges of bias and managing feedback, companies view user engagement as vital for developing effective products, likening it to navigating with a "bird's-eye view" to address multifaceted user needs. Concluding, authors argues for viewing user involvement as an iterative process crucial in the early stages of innovation, emphasizing continuous adaptation and feedback. It advocates for a strategic and inclusive approach to innovation, ensuring that health technology meets the broad spectrum of user needs, underscoring the benefits and complexities of user inclusion in the innovation cycle.

Chapter 13 by Anna Szopa **"The impact of users on the development of Morphic auto personalization"** outlines the development and impact of Morphic Auto Personalization, an innovative technology designed to dynamically adapt user interfaces to individual preferences, enhancing accessibility, particularly for people with disabilities. The development process of this US-based company, rooted in the principles of responsible innovation, emphasized the integration of ethical, social, and cultural dimensions into technological advancement, with a strong focus on user engagement. Morphic Auto Personalization represents a significant advancement in making digital environments more inclusive, developed through the collaborative efforts at the Trace Research and Development Center. The process involved user feedback, behavioral analysis, and usability testing to refine and optimize the software. Challenges such as ensuring software compatibility and maintaining data privacy were addressed through actions like establishing collaborative networks, focusing on transparent and open-source principles, and introducing innovative features based on user feedback. These included new mouse settings, direct USB access, and Assistive Technology on Demand (AToD), among others. The development of Morphic Auto Personalization illustrates the vital role of users in shaping assistive technology, highlighting a user-centered approach that not only meets technical requirements but also aligns with ethical considerations and societal values, thereby contributing to a more accessible and inclusive digital world.

The last empirical **chapter 14** by Thomas Laudal "***Responsible Innovation in regulated markets: Case: Equipment for the home care sector***" discusses the tension between the need for user feedback in innovation and the public sector's role in subsidizing and distributing innovations to ensure accessibility and affordability It examines the intermediary role of public authorities in four Northern European countries—Norway, Sweden, Denmark, and England—highlighting differences in how these countries manage the purchasing, displaying, and distribution of home care equipment. The chapter discusses the challenges in communication and collaboration between users, innovators, and the public sector in the context of providing subsidized home care equipment. This communication gap can hinder the effective provision of services and the development of innovative solutions tailored to users' needs. Addressing this missing link is crucial for ensuring that public sector initiatives meet the diverse needs of the community, including the elderly and other vulnerable groups requiring home care assistance.

A comprehensive overview of this book is presented in Table 1 below:

In concluding the introductory chapter of "Releasing the Power of the User: Meeting the Inclusion Challenge in Innovation," we underscore the transformative journey from viewing users as mere recipients to recognizing them as central actors in the innovation ecosystem. This book ventures through a rich tapestry of case studies from Belgium, the Netherlands, Norway, Portugal, the UK, Ukraine, and the USA, demonstrating the critical need for user inclusion in the healthcare sector—a domain where technology promises immense potential yet demands a responsible approach that earnestly considers real user needs.

By illustrating the spectrum of user engagement, from passive participants to active innovators, and the predominance of informed and involved users, we delve into

Table 1: Overview of the book.

N	Short name	Themes	Key Insights
1	Introduction	Setting the stage	Introduce the concept of boundary innovation space and provides overview of the volume
2	Healthcare's Evolution	Technological and Ethical Evolution in Healthcare	Importance of balancing technological progress with ethical considerations to maintain humanity in healthcare.
3	LiCalab, Belgium	Stakeholder Involvement in Innovation	LiCalab's success in involving end-users through living labs emphasizes the need for a sustainable user community in healthcare innovation.
4	Norwegian Smart Care Lab (NSCL)	User Involvement and Responsible Innovation	NSCL's transition to a collaborative innovation space highlights the importance of participatory approaches for ethical and socially responsible innovation
5	Age-Friendly Living in Schelhorst, Almelo, the Netherlands	Citizen Science and Age-Friendly Communities	Citizen science approaches reveal a holistic view of age-friendly living, emphasizing green spaces, future-proof homes, and community centers.
6	Citizen Science in Healthcare Research The Netherlands	Participation and Influence in Healthcare Research	Advocates for deeper citizen involvement in research processes to democratize healthcare innovation and leverage situated knowledge
7	TOPFIT Citizenlab Projects The Netherlands	Citizen Science in Health Research	Explores the importance of community-building for successful public participation and innovation in health-related projects through citizen science.
8	Digital Futures Lab (DFL), UK	Digital Transformation and User Engagement	Addresses digital transformation in healthcare, with a focus on the DFL's role in advancing patient care, staff training, and medical technology development.
9	Healthcare Innovation Hub in NHS, UK	User-Led Innovation in Healthcare	Challenges and dynamics of a clinician-led innovation space within the NHS, emphasizing operational hurdles and stakeholder engagement.

Table 1 (continued)

N	Short name	Themes	Key Insights
10	Patient Innovation (PI), Portugal and 100 countries	Leveraging Patient Innovations	PI showcases how patient and caregiver innovations can bridge gaps in healthcare through a community-driven platform.
11	Humanitarian Initiatives in Crisis Ukraine	Social Entrepreneurship in Crisis	Examines the effectiveness of social-entrepreneurial initiatives in addressing urgent needs during crises, emphasizing community involvement and technological solutions such as platforms
12	User Inclusion in Health Technology, Norway	Complexities of User Inclusion	Highlights the importance and challenges of engaging users in health technology innovation in firms, stressing a strategic and inclusive approach.
13	Morphic Auto Personalization, USA	Responsible Innovation in Assistive Technology	Illustrates how user feedback and ethical considerations shape assistive technology development, focusing on inclusivity and accessibility.
14	Publicly Subsidized Services and the PPPI Dilemma, Denmark, England, Sweden and Norway	RRI in Public Sector Innovation	Discusses the challenges of incorporating RRI principles in public sector innovation, particularly in home care services for the elderly.
15	Conclusion	The «apples» we can pick from this project	Summarizes learning from the volume and post future research avenues

the question of how to catalyze their engagement to leverage their invaluable insights. Through the concept of boundary innovation spaces, we explore environments that encourage experimentation, learning from mistakes, and co-creation. These spaces—be they digital, virtual, community-based, or organizational—serve as catalysts for merging user knowledge with innovation processes.

As we navigate the challenges and benefits of user involvement, our aim is to enrich the debate on effective user inclusion, seeking ways to not only listen to but also act on user insights, thereby amplifying their impact on innovation. This book is an invitation to explore how we can co-create with users, tapping into their full potential to drive forward-thinking, inclusive, and sustainable innovation.

Acknowledgments: This book emerged from the research project titled "Releasing the Power of Users: Articulating User Interests to Accelerate New Innovative Pathways in the Digital Health and Welfare Sector," funded by the Research Council of Norway (Project No. 299192/E50). We extend our sincere gratitude for the funding that made this research and the publication of this book possible.

References

Barlow, J. (2017). Managing innovation in healthcare. Singapore: World Scientific.

Bessant, J., & Buckingham, J. (1993). Organisational learning for effective use of CAPM. British Journal of Management, 4(4).

Bessant, J., & Buchanan, D. (1983). Failure, uncertainty and control: The role of operators in a computer integrated production system. Journal of Management Studies, 22(4).

Bessant, J., Iakovleva, T., & Oftedal, E. (2019). The future of responsible innovation. In T. Iakovleva, E. Oftedal, & J. Bessant (Eds.), Responsible Innovation in Digital Health: Empowering the Patient (pp. 232–250). Edward Elgar Publisher.

Bessant, J., & Maher, L. (2009). Developing radical service innovations in healthcare: The role of design methods. International Journal of Innovation Management, 13(4).

Bessant, J., Iakovleva, T., & Oftedal, E. (2019). Responsible innovation in digital health. Cheltenham: Edward Elgar.

Braverman, H. (1998). Labour and monopoly capital. New York: Monthly Review Press.

Cennamo, C., Oliveira, P., & Zejnilovic, L. (2022). Unlocking innovation in healthcare. California Management Review, 64(4), 47–77.

Eason, K. (1988). Information technology and organisational change. London: Taylor and Francis.

Fritzsche, A., Jonas, J., Roth, A., & Moeslein, K. (2020). Innovating in the open lab: The new potential for interactive value creation across organizational boundaries. Oldenbourg: De Gruyter.

Greve, K., Martinez, V., Jonas, J., Neely, A., & Moeslein, K. (2016). Facilitating co-creation in living labs: The JOSEPHS study. Cambridge University Institute for Manufacturing, Cambridge.

Grove, K., & Marlow, O. (2016). Spaces for Innovation: The design and science of inspiring environments. Amsterdam: Frame Publishers.

Gundling, E. (2000). The 3M way to innovation: Balancing people and profit. New York: Kodansha International.

Iakovleva, T., Bessant, J., & Oftedal, E. (2019). Responsible innovation in digital health. Cheltenham: Edward Elgar.

Iakovleva, T., Oftedal, E., & Bessant, J. (2019a). Responsible innovation in digital health. In T. Iakovleva, E. Oftedal, & J. Bessant (Eds.), Responsible Innovation in Digital Health: Empowering the Patient (pp. 1–8). Edward Elgar Publisher.

Iakovleva, T., Oftedal, E., & Bessant, J. (2021). Changing role of users—Innovating responsibly in digital health. Sustainability, 13, 1616. https://doi.org/10.3390/su13041616

Keehan, S. P., Cuckler, G. A., Poisal, J. A., Sisko, A. M., Smith, S. D., Madison, A. J., Rennie, K. E., Fiore, J. A., & Hardesty, J. C. (2019). National health expenditure projections, 2019–28: Expected rebound in prices drives rising spending growth. *Health Affairs*, 38(3), 491–501. https://doi.org/10.1377/hlthaff.2018.05499

Kuenne, C. W., Moeslein, K. M., & Bessant, J. (2013). Towards patients as innovators: Open innovation in health care. In Driving the Economy through Innovation and Entrepreneurship (pp. 315–327). Springer.

Kuhlmann, S., Stegmaier, P., & Konrad, K. (2019). The tentative governance of emerging science and technology—A conceptual introduction. Research Policy, 48, 1091–1097.
Leadbeater, C. (2004). Personalisation through participation. Demos.
Leonard-Barton, D. (1988). Implementation as mutual adaptation of technology and organization. Research Policy, 17, 251–267.
Marmot, M., Allen, J., Bell, R., Bloomer, E., Goldblatt, P., & Consortium for the European Review of Social Determinants of Health and the Health Divide. (2012). WHO European review of social determinants of health and the health divide. *The Lancet, 380*(9856), 1011–1029. https://doi.org/10.1016/S0140-6736(12)61228-8
Mumford, E. (2006b) The story of socio-technical design:reflections on its successes, failures and potential. Information Systems Journal, 16, 317–342.
Oliveira, P., Azevedo, S., & Canhao, H. (2019). Empowering patients to innovate: The case of Patient Innovation. In Responsible innovation in digital health. Cheltenham: Edward Elgar.
Owen, R., Bessant, J., & Heintz, M. (2013). Responsible innovation. Chichester: John Wiley and Sons.
Owen, R., Macnaghten, P., & Stilgoe, J. (2012). Responsible research and innovation: From science in society to science for society, with society. Science and Public Policy, 39, 751–760.
Ries, E. (2011). The lean start-up. New York: Crown.
Rogers, E. (2003). Diffusion of innovations (5th ed.). New York: Free Press.
Stilgoe, J., Owen, R., & Macnaghten, P. (2013). Developing a framework for responsible innovation. Research Policy, 42(9).
Tidd, J., & Bessant, J. (2020). Managing innovation (7th edition). Hoboken, NJ: John Wiley and Sons.
Trist, E., & Bamforth, K. (1951). Some social and psychological consequences of the longwall method of coal-getting. Human Relations, 4(3).
Von Hippel, E. (1988). The sources of innovation. Cambridge, MA: MIT Press.
Von Hippel, E. (2005). The democratization of innovation. Cambridge, MA: MIT Press.
Von Hippel, E. (2016). Free innovation. Cambridge, MA: MIT Press.
Von Schomberg, R. (2013). A vision of responsible research and innovation. In Responsible innovation. Chichester: John Wiley & Sons.
Womack, J. P., & Jones, D. T. (1996). *Lean Thinking: Banish Waste and Create Wealth in Your Corporation*. Simon & Schuster.

Elin M. Oftedal, Matthias Kaiser, Tatiana Iakovleva

Back to the future: Reflection on healthcare's past to understand its future

Abstract: This study delves into the historical evolution of healthcare, emphasizing the critical interplay between technological advancements and ethical principles to inform future healthcare practices. The methodology comprises a comprehensive historical review, tracing healthcare from the pre-industrial era through the digital age, and examines philosophical frameworks like the ethics of care and pragmatism. Findings highlight a dual narrative in healthcare history: significant technological advancements alongside a deepening commitment to humane care. Historical milestones include the formalization of medical training, the establishment of public health systems, and the integration of digital technologies. The study concludes that the future of healthcare should not be driven solely by technology but must incorporate a strong ethical foundation, emphasizing patient-centered and user-inclusive care. The significance of this research lies in its provision of historical insights that underscore the need to balance technological innovation with ethical imperatives, ensuring that healthcare remains a fundamentally humane endeavor. This perspective is crucial for developing policies and technologies that are innovative and ethically sound, promoting an inclusive, patient-focused healthcare system.

Introduction

In a world driven by digital innovation, the healthcare sector is undergoing a transformative journey, shaped profoundly by its historical evolution and current digital revolution. As technology becomes increasingly integral to healthcare, we find ourselves at the crossroads of a critical debate of *technological determinism versus moral agency*. While technology opens new doors and possibilities, it has been argued that we do not become passive observers of its trajectory (Sen, 1999) but realise that incorporating digital advancements into healthcare is a journey that extends beyond mere technical progress. It necessitates a strong ethical foundation rooted in age-old philosophical principles (Nussbaum, 2011)

The paradox of healthcare is, that although it is humane in its essence, historically, it is also deeply intertwined with technological development. As such, one can argue that two threads run through the history of healthcare: On one side, technological development has unwrapped medical problems, and made treatment more achievable for more people. On the other side, pioneers of humanity have increased our understanding of what good healthcare is. The challenge is to let healthcare develop as a deeply humane endeavor, focused on the well-being of its users, so that it does

https://doi.org/10.1515/9783111241036-002

not become a healthcare driven solely by technology and a technological trajectory. In this chapter we first present a historical look into the relationship between technological development and individual agency. Based on this review, we discuss two important philosophical aspects, ethics of care and pragmatism, that might guide the development of future of healthcare.

Historical development: Technological determinism and moral agency

In "The Technological Society" (1954), Ellul argued that technology operates independently, shaping society according to its own principles rather than human intentions. The debate of the role of technology on human progress has been discussed by influential figures ranging from Marx (1867) and Veblen's (1899) analyses of its economic and societal impacts on society, to contemporary thinkers showing optimism about its potential benefits (Kelly, 2010), concerns about its interpersonal effects Turkle's (2011), and critical examination of its broader societal implications Winner's (1986). Each of these angles are important and provides unique insights into how technology shapes and is shaped by human societies. The history of healthcare, as such, reveals an intriguing relationship between human care and technology. Prior to the industrial revolution, healthcare in Europe was limited and large part of the populace had no access to it (Cunningham, 1993; McKeown, 1976). Medical knowledge was rudimentary, often hindering effective treatment and proper care. Hospitals with poor sanitation were contributing to the spread of infectious diseases (Marland, 2000) and was characterized by limited medical knowledge, traditional healing practices, and sparse healthcare facilities (Woods, 2000; French, 1986) and the methods were often harsh (Porter, 1997; Cunningham, 1993). Local practitioners like barber-surgeons provided basic healthcare in rural areas (Starr, 1982; Digby, 1996). High mortality rates, especially among infants, were common due to limited basic medical knowledge (Cunningham, 1993). Likewise, medical education was informal, and there were no standardized medical schools (Starr, 1982). In summary, healthcare before the Industrial Revolution was characterized by significant limitations in medical knowledge and practice, stark disparities in access to care, and a reliance on community and familial support systems for the sick. (Porter, 1997; Harrison, 2000).

During the industrial revolution, significant technological advancements transformed medicine and public health, despite accompanying social challenges. Improvements in water supply and sewage systems played a crucial role in combating rampant diseases in overcrowded cities (Szreter, 1988). The establishment of modern hospitals shifted healthcare from being a privilege for the wealthy to a more inclusive model (Porter, 1997). However, this era also presented substantial challenges and transformations. Medical knowledge remained limited, as evidenced by the delayed acceptance of the germ theory of disease (Porter, 1997). Urbanization meant issues with poor sanitary conditions, leading to frequent disease outbreaks (Hamlin, 1998). Furthermore, new workplace hazards and health problems emerged due to industrial exposures (Wootton, 2006).

This period also witnessed a conflict between practice-oriented midwifery and medically trained surgeons, who predominantly consisted of males. Medical associations and trained doctors sought to monopolize obstetrical care by attempting to ban midwifery. Ignaz Semmelweiss (Loudon, 2000) notably fought against prevailing medical practices, arguing that childbirth procedures endangered patients' lives, contrasting with better survival rates observed in midwife-led units. This conflict persisted into the 20th century, highlighting tensions between practice-oriented knowledge and science-based medical superiority.

Meanwhile, nursing emerged as a formalized profession during the 19th century, with figures like Florence Nightingale advocating for compassionate care practices and emphasizing sanitary conditions and patient welfare (Nightingale, 1859). These advancements marked a step towards more democratic healthcare, making it increasingly accessible and humane.

Significant advances in medical technology and surgery were also made, such as the effective use of anesthesia in the 1840s and the development of the smallpox vaccine by Edward Jenner (Bynum, 2008), the initiation of modern surgery in the 19th century (Ellis, 2001). Further, the development of the germ theory of disease fundamentally altered the understanding of disease causation, leading to antiseptic techniques in surgery pioneered by Joseph Lister (Lister, 1867; Worboys, 2000).

However, medicine as a truly scientific discipline following the critical methods and principles of the Scientific Revolution emerged only at the turn from the 19th to the 20th century. Embracing the ideology of value-free science also implied a dogma of "objectivism" which is also result of the 19th century (Daston & Galison 2010). Herein lies already the root of a conflict with the "subjective" aspects of caregiving as a truly human activity and sphere of knowledge. Human advocacy during the beginning of the 20th century was spearheaded by individuals such as Mother Teresa (Spink, 1997) Cicely Saunders (Clark, 2006); Alexander Fleming (Brown, 2004) and Albert Schweizer (Schweitzer, 1923)

Transitioning into the late 20th to early 21st Century, healthcare became more specialized with the spreading of various medical sub-disciplines (Starr, 1982; Ludmerer, 1999). A growing emphasis on evidence-based medicine emerged, where clinical decision-making is anchored in the latest research findings (Sackett et al., 1996; Guyatt et al., 2002). Also here, there were pioneering individuals that had a large following through popular culture and mass media (i.e. Diana, princess of Wales, Elton John, Kofi Annan). Such pioneering individuals brought something new to the concept and practice of care, whether it was through establishing important healthcare institutions, shaping public health policies, or challenging societal attitudes toward disease and suffering. Ethical considerations, such as patient autonomy and informed consent, became more pronounced (Beauchamp & Childress, 2001; Faden & Beauchamp, 1986) as a direct result of public reaction when learning in the Nuremberg trials about the shocking medical experiments in the concentration camps of Nazi Germany (and Japan), and later about other medical experiments, e.g. in relation to studies of the effects of radioactive exposure during test-explosions of atomic bombs.

The advent of computers and the internet started to significantly impact diagnostics, treatment, and patient care (Haux, 2006; Blumenthal & Tavenner, 2010). Public health initiatives also increasingly focused on disease prevention through lifestyle changes, a response to the rise of chronic non-communicable diseases amidst extended life expectancies (Marmot & Wilkinson, 2005; Rose, 2001). Collectively, their legacies have pivoted the healthcare system and arguably led to a more empathetic, inclusive, and patient-centered healthcare system in many parts of the world.

Amidst this backdrop, digital health has unfolded. Initially centered on the digitization of patient records to alleviate administrative burdens, digital health has since expanded into a vast and intricate landscape including every aspect of health including consumer focused products such as wearable devices to telehealth tools and AI-driven diagnostics focused on the public sphere. Artificial intelligence and machine learning refine diagnostics and treatment planning, blockchain technology fortifies the integrity and privacy of healthcare data sharing (Liao, 2020). Personalized medicine, augmented by genomics and data analytics, is now delivering treatments tailored to individual genetic profiles (Topol, 2015). Augmented Reality (AR) and Virtual Reality (VR), remote patient monitoring, health chatbots, and advances in biotech and nanotechnology are among the other remarkable innovations arguably redefining patient care (Bardram, 2004). These technologies have the potential to make healthcare more accessible and personalized than ever before (World Health Organization, 2015). The World Health Organization pioneering definition of e-health as "the use of information and communication technology (ICT) for health," encapsulating the evolving paradigm of integrating digital solutions into healthcare delivery, improving access, efficiency, and quality of care (World Health Organization, 2015). AI, in particular, is portrayed as holding the promise of enhancing the humanity of healthcare by providing more precise diagnoses, predicting potential health issues, personalizing treatment plans, and allowing healthcare professionals more time for patient care by reducing administrative burdens (Jha & Topol, 2016). Social media influencers have emerged as pivotal figures in healthcare communication, leveraging their platforms to disseminate health information, raise awareness about conditions, advocate for health policies, and shape public perceptions and behaviors related to health and wellness.

Table 1 below outlines key historical milestones and pivotal moments where advancements in technology and human agency have shaped new healthcare paradigms.

Table 1: Main historical developments of technological and human advancements and their pivoting points.

Historical Period	Technological Advances	Human Advancements	Pivoting Points
Industrial Revolution	Invention of stethoscope, initiation of modern surgery, development of germ theory	Florence Nightingale revolution in nursing. Clara Barton's involvement in the Red Cross. Semmelweiss for antiseptic procedures. Albert Schweizer.	Public Health Challenges, Advancement in medical technology and infrastructure
Early 20th Century	Discovery of antibiotics, vaccines, creation of X rays and MRI scans. Advancements in antibiotics, development of new surgical techniques and thebeginning of organ transplant surgery	Mother Teresa's humanitarian work with emphasis on compassion for the destitute. Alexander Fleming for antibiotics, Albert Schweizer for humanitarian work Cicely Saunder pionner for palliative care.	Flexner Report and the move towards universal healthcare Global trend towards establishing national health services (e.g. UK, Norway, US Medicare & Medicaid, Netherlands, Portugal)
Late 20th to Early 21st Century	Specialization of medicine, advent of computers and internet. Evidence – based medicine.	Diana, Princess of Wales work in reducinc stigma, Nelson Mandela anti apartheid work impacting social policies for health, Elton John's HIV / AIDS advocacy, Kofi Annan global health policies	Ethical framework and evidence based medicine
Current Time	Expansion of digital health, AI diagnostics, telehealth platforms, wearable devices.	Myriads of social media profiles (i.e. Dr. Mike, ZDoggMD, and Helsesista) helping transform healthcare.	WHO's definition of e-health. Ethics of care framework, patient autonomy, informed consent, health promotion, health equity, new role of hospital, home hospital.

History suggests that while technology can democratize and humanize healthcare, this transformation is only fully realized when coupled with ethical reflection. While healthcare has long grappled with discrimination and a reliance on generalized medical knowledge that often neglects individual patient needs, technology presents an opportunity to democratize this essential human service. Yet, despite its significant advancements, technology alone cannot be sufficient. This perspective resonates with influential thinkers such as Amartya Sen, who emphasizes freedom and choice in development (Sen, 1999), Martha Nussbaum, who advocates for enhancing individual capabilities in human development (Nussbaum, 2011), and Julian Savulescu, who argues for the ethical deployment of technology to improve human well-being (Savulescu &

Bostrom, 2009). Effective healthcare demands a compassionate care approach that prioritizes moral agency in medical ethics and practice.

This journey through healthcare history underscores a landscape of vast and continuous innovation, where technology intertwines deeply with healthcare's fabric. Recognizing technology's potential to enhance the human aspects of healthcare opens new avenues for creating empathetic, equitable, and effective healthcare systems (Gilligan, 1982; Tronto, 1993; Topol, 2015). At the same time, pioneering individuals remind society that compassion in care remains central, advocating for a patient-centered approach.

In conclusion, this transformative landscape teaches us the importance of balancing innovation's excitement with ethical considerations (Emanuel & Wachter, 2019). Our healthcare innovations must not only be technically robust but also nurture human connections and collective well-being (Post, 2000; Watson, 2008). The ethics of care offers a valuable lens through which to view and shape these technological advancements (Gilligan, 1982; Tronto, 1993).

Enhancing individual moral agency: Ethics of care and capabilities approach

Healthcare's foundational principles, rooted in ancient doctrines such as the Hippocratic Oath, have long grappled with ethical dilemmas. Building on this tradition, Childress and Beauchamp (2001) expanded on the Hippocratic Oath and introduced principle-based medical ethics. Their approach aims to guide modern medical practice by emphasizing four ethical principles drawn from dominant ethical theories: Beneficence, Non-maleficence, Autonomy, and Justice. The overarching goal is to ensure that healthcare innovations and medical interventions prioritize patient benefit and minimize harm. As the technological landscape becomes increasingly complex, rigorous scrutiny of digital tools is crucial to assess potential physical and psychological harms (Childress and Beauchamp, 2001).

While the principled approach of Childress and Beauchamp (2001) as been pivotal in healthcare ethics, it has also faced critique (Holm, 1995; Clouser and Gert, 1990; Sherwin, 1992). In contrast, the Ethics of Care perspective advocated by Gilligan (1982) and Noddings (1984) prioritizes relationships, empathy, and compassion in ethical decision-making. This ethical framework underscores responsiveness to individual needs within caring relationships, emphasizing respect, reciprocity, and the responsibilities borne by both caregivers and those receiving care. The Ethics of Care challenges traditional ethical theories by positing that moral agency is fundamentally relational, shaped by recognition of human vulnerability and interdependence (Gilligan, 1982).

In the realm of digital health technology, another approach to enhancing agency aligns with the Capabilities Approach of Nussbaum (1997) and Sen (1999). This perspective defines moral agency in terms of individuals' freedoms to pursue valuable capabilities, emphasizing autonomy while acknowledging the role of social structures in enabling or constraining these freedoms. By focusing on expanding individual capabilities, this approach seeks to empower individuals within healthcare contexts, fostering greater autonomy and choice in decision-making.

In this landscape, the concept of human dignity, (Nussbaum, 1997), gains importance. This principle asserts every individual's inherent value, transcending their background, circumstances, or characteristics. It insists on recognizing and upholding each person's intrinsic worth in every facet of life, including healthcare. In healthcare, respecting and safeguarding patient data isn't just a regulatory requirement; it's essential to preserving individual dignity in our interconnected, data-driven world. Ensuring equitable healthcare and technological benefits that are accessible to all, irrespective of socio-economic status or other characteristics, is a necessity of human dignity (Daniels, 2008). Safeguarding patient data is crucial in maintaining equity and inclusivity, preventing disparities where certain groups may be unfairly targeted or excluded. Respecting and safeguarding patient data empowers individuals to exercise agency over their health information (Emanuel & Wachter, 2019). It allows for informed consent, ensuring they are active participants in healthcare decisions, not passive data subjects.

Another important aspect of the capabilities approach, which may be central for healthcare is linked with the principle of autonomy—the right of individuals to make informed decisions about their lives, including healthcare (Beauchamp & Childress, 2019). This right is central in the digital age, where patient data is crucial for informed decision-making. Autonomy emphasizes respecting individuals' capacity to make decisions and act based on their values and beliefs. It's critical in healthcare, allowing patients to control their medical treatment and health-related decisions. However, breaches of patient data can undermine this autonomy, shaking individuals' trust in the healthcare system.

Finally, privacy, intertwined with human dignity and autonomy, acknowledges individuals' right to control access to their personal information (Solove, 2008). In the realm of digital health, where personal data is exceptionally sensitive, respecting privacy is a tangible acknowledgment of each patient's dignity. The protection of patient data reflects trust and respect within the healthcare ecosystem (Hall et al., 2019). Patients expect that their dignity will be upheld when they entrust their health information to healthcare systems and digital platforms. Breaches erode the foundation of human dignity in healthcare.

However, a warning might be in place here also and that is the warning of ethical hubris: Ethics may have become a matter of specialized ethical review boards (ERCs), or a rubber-stamping activity of standardized forms. And in the sphere of ethics and basic values of life one needs to recognize diversity of relevant viewpoints and complexity of some of the ethical dilemmas. This is why an ethics of care is much more than the summary of ethical principles. It expresses an active engagement, empathy, and reflection between carer and those cared for. It also is supposed to be sensitive of diversity in views of life and health in general, particularly when dealing with multicultural dilemmas. Ethics of care, however we want to express it, is denying the existence of ethical algorithms, and asking us to develop an attitude of openness and respect to different forms and ways of life. On this basis we need to exercise human judgement. Sometimes principles may be sufficient to encapsule the essential ethical considerations we have to make, but some other times we may have to engage and respect other views of life, health and care. The individual whose autonomy is so dominant in the thinking of the Western, particularly the Anglo-saxon world, may perhaps to step down a bit when communal life and wellbeing is more at the center in some indigenous or Asian cultures.

Consequently, the development of digital healthcare under the guidance of ethics and responsibility is part of an democratic development and integrated in the value-landscapes of our societies (Kaiser, 2022). Post-normal science (Funtowicz & Ravetz 1993) asks for extended peer-reviews as quality checks when issues become complex both regarding the decision stakes and regarding the values involved. We will come back to this aspect of user-involvement below.

Tempering technological determinism through pragmatic responsible innovation

A technological approach that also may include a moral agency perspective is that of Responsible Innovation (Von Schomberg, 2013) Responsible innovation emphasizes the ethical dimensions, social implications, and long-term impacts of technology deployment in healthcare settings. It advocates for the development and use of technologies in a way that is socially desirable, ethically acceptable, and sustainable over time (Pellé, S. (2016, Voegtlin et al 2021). This approach challenges us to look beyond the mere functionality and efficiency of new technologies, to consider how they align with societal values, contribute to equitable health outcomes, and respect patient autonomy and privacy. It prompts a reflective process that includes anticipating potential impacts, engaging in dialogue with stakeholders, and adapting to feedback and societal expectations.

Stilgoe, Owen, and Macnaghten (2013) offer a framework for responsible innovation that includes anticipation, reflexivity, inclusion, and responsiveness, guiding the integration of technology with a focus on ethical and social responsibility. The philosophy of responsible innovation compels us to engage in a continuous dialogue with stakeholders, including patients, healthcare professionals, policymakers, and the public, to co-create technologies that address genuine needs without exacerbating inequalities or compromising ethical standards (Pelleé, 2016). Inclusion means that patients have a say in the tools and platforms affecting their healthcare, fostering trust and improving adherence to health regimens. It's a recognition that not all solutions are universally applicable; understanding diverse cultural backgrounds and socio-economic conditions is essential in developing relevant, accessible solutions (Iakovleva et al 2019, Oftedal et al. 2019). Von Schomberg (2013) discusses the importance of a normative framework to guide such innovation, emphasizing the need for research and innovation to align with societal challenges and ethical considerations. Moreover, responsible innovation calls for a thorough assessment of the long-term implications of technology in healthcare, examining both the potential benefits and the risks or challenges that may arise. This includes evaluating the sustainability of technological solutions and their compatibility with global health goals and ethical principles. Owen, Bessant, and Heintz (2013) explore strategies for embedding responsible innovation within organizational and policy practices, ensuring that technological advancements are developed and implemented in a way that prioritizes societal well-being and ethical integrity.

In this ethical framework, the *'nothing about me, without me'* perspective becomes paramount. This perspective insists on patient inclusion in the development and application of digital healthcare" (Sanders & Stappers, 2008; Clemensen et al., 2007). It's a commitment to involving users directly in creating and refining the technology that will impact their health and well-being. This inclusion is not just about ethical healthcare delivery but also about practical efficacy. When users are actively involved, healthcare solutions are more likely to meet actual needs, be more readily adopted, and lead to better health outcomes (Schuler & Namioka, 1993; Haux, 2006). User-involvement provides for the quality check that is a natural consequence of complex innovations and is the extended peer-review that post-normal science asks for (Funtowicz & Ravetz 1993). This could be very important as guides in the design of future's healthcare and means that even as we use more technology in healthcare, it is important that humans remain in charge of making ethical decisions. We need to ensure that machines and algorithms support healthcare professionals and patients, rather than making critical choices on their own. It's about using technology as a helpful tool for a truly human activity and moral duty, not letting it completely take over the decision-making process that affects people's health and lives. The goal is to enhance healthcare with technology while keeping human values, understanding, and ethics at the center of everything.

All of these perspectives; the ethics of care, capability approach and responsible innovation inherently promote idealistic values, ethical considerations, and long-term societal benefits in healthcare. These frameworks advocate for compassionate relationships, individual freedoms, and the ethical use of technology. However, it is important to note that especially Sen (1999) and Nussbaum (2011) temper their normative and idealistic perspectives with pragmatism, advocating for practical impacts of technology in healthcare. They emphasize solutions that yield tangible benefits amid challenges related to user inclusion, such as the selection, timing, method, location, and frequency of involvement. This pragmatic approach ensures that innovations are not only conceptually robust but also deliver concrete improvements in patient outcomes and healthcare delivery. Addressing these complexities involves evaluating technological impacts on patient outcomes, streamlining healthcare processes, and enhancing overall care quality. Pragmatism (Dewey, 1938) prompts a focus on empirical evidence and real-world data, prioritizing methods that are proven effective.

In summary, as healthcare embraces digital innovations, maintaining a steadfast commitment to ethics, empathy, and inclusivity is crucial. Incorporating a pragmatic approach and ensuring user inclusion allows healthcare to leverage technological advancements while preserving the human-centric principles of care. This commitment to ethical, patient-centered, and pragmatic innovation defines success in the digital health era, ensuring that technologies serve the broader goal of improving healthcare outcomes and patient well-being.

In Figure 1 below, we attempt to summarize this discussion. The figure shows the Ethics of Care as a core in the approach to the new digital era in health care.

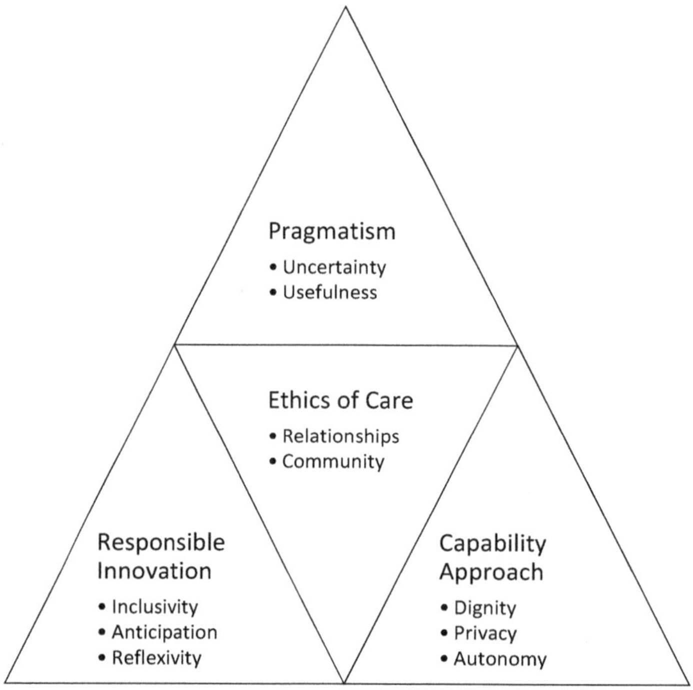

Figure 1: Philosophical Perspective for the Future of Healthcare.

Conclusion: Making thousand user voices into one – aligning progress and ethics in user inclusion

In the digital age, where technological advancements continually reshape the healthcare landscape, understanding and integrating the user's voice is crucial (Sanders & Stappers, 2008). This integration goes beyond viewing individuals as mere consumers of healthcare technology; it involves recognizing and respecting each person's unique healthcare needs, preferences, and challenges (Noddings, 1984). The development of technology, when guided by a profound respect for human dignity, autonomy, and privacy, has the potential to make healthcare more humane, accessible, and effective (Held, 2006).

The evolution of technology in healthcare — from electronic health records and telehealth to AI-driven diagnostics and personalized medicine — presents unparalleled opportunities for improving patient care (Adler-Milstein et al., 2017; Topol, 2015). The true value of these advancements lies not only in their technical capabilities but also in their potential to increase the humanity of healthcare (Emanuel & Wachter, 2019). Technological innovations can amplify the user's voice, respect their autonomy, and protect their dignity and privacy (Liao, 2020). They act as tools that healthcare professionals and patients can use collaboratively to make informed decisions, enhance health outcomes, and preserve the personal touch critical to care (Watson, 2008).

Incorporating the user's voice into the development of healthcare technology requires a comprehensive, pragmatic approach (Clemensen et al., 2007). This includes ongoing dialogue and feedback loops with patients and communities, as well as an appreciation for the practical realities of healthcare delivery (Bardram, 2004). Platforms for user feedback and participation need to be accessible and seamlessly integrated into design and decision-making processes (Schuler & Namioka, 1993). This can take the form of patient advisory councils, user experience research, or community-driven innovation programs, all aimed at ensuring technologies are not only technically robust but also ethically sound and focused on the user (Joan Tronto).

Furthermore, the effort to involve users in the development and refinement of healthcare technology needs to be based on a realistic understanding of diversity and inclusivity (Virginia Held). It is critical to acknowledge the wide range of user diversity and the practical challenges individuals encounter in accessing and utilizing technology (Eubanks, 2018). Efforts to engage underserved or underrepresented populations need to go beyond superficial measures and represent genuine commitments to comprehend and overcome the barriers these groups encounter (Marmot & Wilkinson, 2005). By doing so, healthcare technology can advance towards minimizing health disparities and fostering equity (Daniels, 2008).

As healthcare technology advances, there is an opportunity to integrate technical innovation with ethical considerations, empathy, and inclusivity (Slote, 2007). The aim is that development of technology be a collaborative journey that respects and responds to the human condition, enhancing the ability of healthcare to meet the diverse needs of users (Tronto, 1993). By incorporating pragmatism and humanity into every stage of technological development and implementation, the healthcare sector can ensure that its advancements lead to a more compassionate, equitable, and effective system (Porter, 1997). In this way, technology becomes a means to enhance the human aspects of healthcare, ensuring that as healthcare becomes more digital, it also becomes more human (Winner, 1986).

References

Adler-Milstein, J., Holmgren, A. J., Kralovec, P., Worzala, C., Searcy, T., Patel, V., & Bates, D. W. (2017). Electronic health record adoption in US hospitals: Progress continues, but challenges persist. Health Affairs, 36(8), 1531–1540.

Bardram, J. E. (2004). Applications of context-aware computing in hospital work: examples and design principles. In Proceedings of the 2004 ACM symposium on Applied computing (pp. 1574–1579).

Beauchamp, T. L., & Childress, J. F. (2001). Principles of Biomedical Ethics. Oxford University Press.

Blumenthal, D., & Tavenner, M. (2010). The "Meaningful Use" Regulation for Electronic Health Records. The New England Journal of Medicine, 363(6), 501–504.

Brandt, A. M., & Gardner, M. (2000). Antagonism and accommodation: Interpreting the relationship between public health and medicine in the United States during the 20th century. American Journal of Public Health, 90(5), 707–715.

Brown, K. (2004). *Penicillin man: Alexander Fleming and the antibiotic revolution. Sutton Publishing.*

Bynum, 2008 Bynum W. Oxford University Press; Oxford: 2008. The History of Medicine: a Very Short Introduction. [Google Scholar]

Clark, D. (2006). *Cicely Saunders: Selected writings 1958–2004. Oxford University Press.*

Clemensen, J., Larsen, S. B., Kyng, M., & Kirkevold, M. (2007). Participatory design in health sciences: Using cooperative experimental methods in developing health services and computer technology. Qualitative Health Research, 17(1), 122–130.

Clouser, K. D., & Gert, B. (1990). A critique of principlism. The Journal of Medicine and Philosophy, 15(2), 219–236.

Daniels, N. (2008). Just health: Meeting health needs fairly. Cambridge University Press.

Daston, L. & Galison, P. 2010. Objectivity. Princeton, NJ, Princeton University Press.

Dewey, J. (1938). Logic: The theory of inquiry. Henry Holt and Company.

Digby, A. (1994). Making a medical living: Doctors and patients in the English market for medicine, 1720–1911 (Cambridge Studies in Population, Economy and Society in Past Times). Cambridge University Press.

Ellis, H. (2001). A History of Surgery. Greenwich Medical Media.

Ellul, J. (1954). *The technological society.* Vintage Books (1964 edition).

Emanuel, E. J., & Wachter, R. M. (2019). Artificial Intelligence in Health Care: Will the Value Match the Hype? *JAMA*, *321*(23), 2281–2282. https://doi.org/10.1001/jama.2019.4914

Eubanks, V. (2018). Automating inequality: How high-tech tools profile, police, and punish the poor. St. Martin's Press.

Faden, R. R., & Beauchamp, T. L. (1986). A History and Theory of Informed Consent. Oxford University Press.

Floridi, L. (2013). *The ethics of information.* Oxford University Press.

French, R. (1986). Medicine before Science: The Business of Medicine from the Middle Ages to the Enlightenment. Cambridge University Press.

Funtowicz, S. O. & Ravetz, J. R. (1993), "Science for the Post-Normal Age", Futures 26/6: 568–582.
Gilligan, C. (1982). In a Different Voice: Psychological Theory and Women's Development. Harvard University Press.
Guyatt, G., Rennie, D., Meade, M. O., & Cook, D. J. (2002). Users' Guides to the Medical Literature: A Manual for Evidence-Based Clinical Practice. AMA Press.
Hall, M. A., Dugan, E., Zheng, B., Mishra, A. K., & Trust, J. O. (2019). Trust in physicians and medical institutions: What is it, can it be measured, and does it matter? The Milbank Quarterly, 87(4), 611–639.
Hamlin 1998 Hamlin, C. (1998) Public Health and Social Justice in the Age of Chadwick: Britain 1800-1854. Cambridge University Press, Cambridge, 1–15.
Haux, R. (2006). Health information systems – past, present, future. International Journal of Medical Informatics, 75(3–4), 268–281.
Held, V. (2006). The ethics of care: Personal, political, and global. Oxford University Press.
Holm, S. (1995). Not just autonomy–the principles of American biomedical ethics. Journal of Medical Ethics, 21(6), 332–338.
Iakovleva et al. 2019 Iakovleva, T., Oftedal, E. M., & Bessant, J. (Eds.). (2019). Responsible Innovation in Digital Health: Empowering the Patient (New Horizons in Innovation Management series). Edward Elgar Publishing.
Jha, S., & Topol, E. J. (2016). Adapting to Artificial Intelligence: Radiologists and Pathologists as Information Specialists. JAMA, 316(22), 2353–2354.
Kaiser, 2022: Kaiser, M. (2022). "Taking value-landscapes seriously", in: Transforming food systems: ethics, innovation and responsibility, D. Bruce & A.Bruce (eds.), Wageningen Academic Publishers, Wageningen, pp. 46–51. https://doi.org/10.3920/978-90-8686-939-8_5
Kelly, K. (2010). What Technology Wants pp. 1–17. New York: Penguin Group.
Laennec, R. T. H. (1819). De l'Auscultation Médiate ou Traité du Diagnostic des Maladies des Poumon et du Coeur. Paris: Brosson & Chaudé.
Liao, S. M. (2020). *Ethics of Artificial Intelligence* (1st ed.). Oxford University Press. https://doi.org/10.1093/oso/9780190905064.001.0001 (CHANGE ALSO IN TEXT p. 25 and 32)
Lister, J. (1867). On the Antiseptic Principle in the Practice of Surgery. The British Medical Journal, 2(351), 246–248.
Loudon, I. (2011). Semmelweis. In *The Tragedy of Childbed Fever*. Oxford University Press. https://doi.org/10.1093/acprof:oso/9780198204992.003.0007
Ludmerer, K. M. (1999). Time to Heal: American Medical Education from the Turn of the Century to the Era of Managed Care. Oxford University Press.
Loudon, I. (2000). The Tragedy of Childbed Fever. In *The Tragedy of Childbed Fever* (pp. 88–110). Oxford University Press. (also commented below (n the reference section).
Marmot, M., & Wilkinson, R. G. (Eds.). (2005). Social Determinants of Health. Oxford University Press.
Marland, Hilary (1984). Medicine and Society in Wakefield and Huddersfield 1780–1870. PhD thesis, Cambridge University Press.
Marx, K. (1867). *Capital: A critique of political economy* (Vol. 1). Penguin Classics (1976 edition).
McKeown, T. (1976). The Modern Rise of Population. Academic Press.
Nightinggale 1859 Nightingale, Florence (1859). Notes on Nursing: What it is and What it is Not. London: Harrison. Retrieved 28 November 2018 – via Internet Archive.
Noddings, N. (1984). Caring: A feminine approach to ethics & moral education. University of California Press.
Nussbaum, M. C. (1997). Cultivating humanity: A classical defense of reform in liberal education. Harvard University Press.
Nussbaum, M. C. (2011). *Creating capabilities: The human development approach*. The Belknap Press of Harvard University Press.

Oftedal et al 2019: Oftedal, E. M., Foss, L., & Iakovleva, T. (2019). Sustainability Responsible for Responsibility? A Study of Digital E-health Startups. Sustainability, 11(19), Article 5433. https://doi.org/10.3390/su11195433
Owen, R., Bessant, J. R., & Heintz, M. (Eds.). (2013). Responsible innovation: Managing the responsible emergence of science and innovation in society. Wiley
Pellé, S. (2016). Process, outcomes, virtues: the normative strategies of responsible research and innovation and the challenge of moral pluralism. *Journal of Responsible Innovation, 3(3), 233–254.* https://doi.org/10.1080/23299460.2016.1258945
Porter, R. (1997). The Greatest Benefit to Mankind: A Medical History of Humanity from Antiquity to the Present. HarperCollins.
Rose, G. A. (2008). *Rose's strategy of preventive medicine: The complete original text* (New ed.). Oxford University Press. https://doi.org/10.1093/med/9780191723551.001.0001
Sackett, D. L., Rosenberg, W. M., Gray, J. A., Haynes, R. B., & Richardson, W. S. (1996). Evidence-based medicine: what it is and what it isn't. BMJ, 312(7023), 71–72.
Sanders, E. B. N., & Stappers, P. J. (2008). Co-creation and the new landscapes of design. CoDesign, 4(1), 5–18.
Savulescu, J., & Bostrom, N. (Eds.). (2009). *Human enhancement*. Oxford University Press.
Schuler, D., & Namioka, A. (Eds.). (1993). Participatory design: Principles and practices. CRC Press.
Schweitzer, A. (1923). *The philosophy of civilization. Prometheus Books.*
Sen, A. (1999). *Development as freedom*. Oxford University Press.
Sherwin, S. (1992). No Longer Patient: Feminist Ethics and Health Care. Temple University Press.
Slote, M. (2007). The ethics of care and empathy. Routledge.
Solove, D. J. (2008). Understanding privacy. Harvard University Press.
Spink, K. (1997). *Mother Teresa: An authorized biography. HarperCollins.*
Starr, P. (1982). The Social Transformation of American Medicine. Basic Books.
Stilgoe, J., Owen, R., & Macnaghten, P. (2013). Developing a framework for responsible innovation. Research Policy, 42(9), 1568–1580.
Suchman, L.A. (2002). Located Accountabilities in Technology Production. *Scand. J. Inf. Syst.*, *14*, 7.
Topol, E. J. (2015). The Patient Will See You Now: The Future of Medicine is in Your Hands. Basic Books.
Tronto, J. C. (1993). Moral boundaries: A political argument for an ethic of care. Psychology Press.
Turkle, S. (2011). *Alone together: Why we expect more from technology and less from each other. Basic Books.*
Veblen, T. (1899). *The theory of the leisure class: An economic study of institutions.* Macmillan.
Voegtlin, C., Scherer, A. G., Stahl, G. K., & Hawn, O. (2021). Grand Societal Challenges and Responsible Innovation. *Journal of Management Studies.* https://doi-org.ezproxy.uis.no/10.1111/joms.12785
Von Schomberg, R. (2013). A vision of responsible research and innovation. In R. Owen, M. Heintz, & J. Bessant (Eds.), Responsible innovation: Managing the responsible emergence of science and innovation in society (pp. 51–74). Wiley.
Watson, J. (2008). Nursing: The Philosophy and Science of Caring. University Press of Colorado.
Winner, L. (1986). The whale and the reactor: a search for limits in an age of high technology. Chicago, University of Chicago Press.
Woods, R. (2000). The Demography of Victorian England and Wales. Cambridge Uni
Wootton, R. (2006). Realtime telemedicine. *Journal of Telemedicine and Telecare*, *12*(7), 328–336. https://psycnet.apa.org/doi/10.1258/135763306778682387"https://doi.org/10.1258/135763306778682387
Worboys, M. (2000). Spreading Germs: Disease Theories and Medical Practice in Britain, 1865–1900. Cambridge University Press. Davenport, T., & Kalakota, R. (2019). The potential for artificial intelligence in healthcare. Future Healthcare Journal, 6(2), 94–98.
World Health Organization. (2015). World report on ageing and health. World Health Organizatio

Nele A.J. De Witte, Annouck De Cat, Hilde Vandenhoudt, Sascha Vermeylen, Vicky Van der Auwera, Leen Broeckx, Ingrid Adriaensen

Sustainable user involvement: Building a user community and fostering high-quality research

Abstract: Throughout a design and development phase, stakeholders can help to explore needs and contexts, co-create innovations, test potential solutions, and guide the implementation process. The recruitment of diverse, representative, and motivated users as continuous partners throughout the design and evaluation process will result in innovations, products, and studies that are more likely to meet the true needs of the target group. However, different research questions and study aims for user involvement projects require different participatory approaches and sample sizes. Selecting and recruiting individuals for user communities and research activities can occur in multiple ways. Developing and maintaining a large community of citizens and stakeholders is an intensive yet sustainable way of supporting user involvement. Such a user community forms a large-scale co-creation and test environment of individuals willing to contribute to the development of new concepts, services, or products. The current chapter provides guidelines for building and managing a dedicated user community (on a macro level) and offers practice-oriented insights into the user recruitment for and organization of smaller-scale delineated user activities (on a micro level). Therefore, we firstly discuss seven relevant steps in setting up user communities. Secondly, we provide insight into the prerequisites for high-quality user activities in terms of sample recommendations, recruitment, and data collection (including harmonization across borders and ethical considerations). By setting up a user community and fostering high-quality research, we can facilitate efficient and effective exchange between different stakeholders resulting in better innovations meeting actual needs.

1 Introduction

Good product and service design relies on collecting stakeholder insights. Throughout a design and development phase, we need stakeholders to help us explore needs and contexts, co-create innovations, test potential solutions, and guide the implementation process (De Witte, Broeckx et al., 2021). The way stakeholders are involved, as well as the required sample sizes vary depending on project aims. However, the recruitment of diverse, representative, and motivated users as continuous partners throughout the design and evaluation process will result in innovations, products, and studies

https://doi.org/10.1515/9783111241036-003

that are more likely to meet the true needs of the target group (Jarke, 2021; Suijkerbuijk et al., 2019).

While such user-centred design activities can be performed by academic researchers or product designers, over the past decades such activities have increasingly been performed by living labs. Living labs can be defined as open innovation systems in which stakeholders contribute to the exploration, co-creation, evaluation, and upscaling of solutions to create sustainable impact in real-life circumstances (European Network of Living Labs (ENoLL), 2023). Living labs can operate in different sectors (e.g., smart cities, agriculture, healthcare) and include many different types of stakeholders (e.g., end users, healthcare professionals, governmental partners) in an iterative way. Interative design refers to a fast cyclic process of testing and development, and has been proposed as a good way for rapid product development in a changing market (Maramba et al. 2019). While living labs have been promoted by governmental bodies such as the European Union, over the years, many have also failed at being an enduring cooperative space (Ballon et al. 2018). Therefore, it is relevant to assess how to promote structural and longstanding collaboration between developers and researchers on the one hand and local stakeholders and citizens on the other. To illustrate the factors and processes contributing to the development of a sustainable cooperative space, the current chapter discusses the underpinnings and learnings of LiCalab.

LiCalab is a Belgian living lab that has over 10 years of experience in supporting businesses and organizations by including end users (citizens, care professionals, and other stakeholders) in the development process, from the very beginning of development until market introduction. LiCalab was founded in 2011 as a spin-off of the city council of Turnhout and was incorporated in Thomas More University of Applied Sciences (Centre of Expertise Care and Well-being) in 2019. LiCalab supports human-centred design, predominantly in the areas of medical care, (patient) rehabilitation, care technology, assisted living, active and healthy aging, and mental health. The lab explores and validates new products, services, systems, and business models through services such as co-creation, concept development, market insight, product development, piloting, and validation services (e.g., usability tests, technological test, etc.). To be a sustainable local innovation ecosystem builder, LiCalab has developed a large user community. LiCalab additionally relies on a broad network of local, regional, and EU partners with expertise in healthcare and well-being, including local governments, caregivers, research institutes, small and medium-sized enterprises (SMEs), and multinationals. LiCalab is an accredited member of the European Network of Living Labs (EnoLL) and EIT Health, which is a knowledge and innovation community of the European Institute of Innovation and Technology that focuses on health and aging.

At Licalab, we believe that two important factors contribute to promoting the longevity of user-centred initiatives and joint value creation, that is the quality of research and innovation activities, and the strategy for stakeholder involvement. Building and maintaining a user community, also referred to as a 'user panel', holds many benefits for developers, researchers, local stakeholders, citizens, and living labs themselves. The first section of the current chapter aims to examine the development of a user community as a high-quality cooperative space at the macro level (Figure 1). It concerns how to set up a user community and provides examples from LiCalab. Secondly, we discuss individual user activities at the micro level, introducing important elements in relation to designing specific user-centred activities, including sample recommendations, targeted activity recruitment within or beyond an existing user community, and data collection. We also highlight the importance of not only being embedded in your local community but also collaborating within international partnerships to promote the quality of user activities as well as aid in cross-border research facilitating the upscaling of innovation. This chapter will be illustrated with examples from LiCalab but the insights and recommendations can apply to many organizations in and beyond the Responsible Research and Innovation (RRI) field.

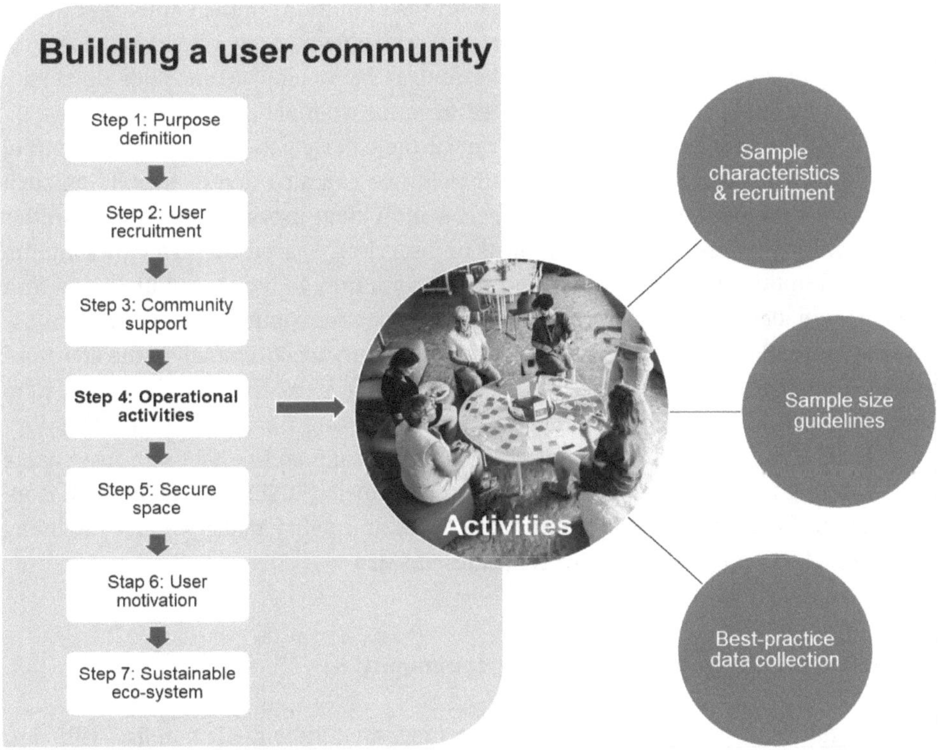

Figure 1: Schematic overview illustrating the steps for building a user community as well as executing specific user research activities.

2 Building a user community

Involving stakeholders can be done in many different ways, from recruiting convenience samples ad hoc, over launching specific recruitment calls, to having a dedicated user community. While the preferred strategy will depend on the goals of the activity, one way to guarantee easy access to your stakeholder group, is to build and maintain a sustainable user community.

2.1 How to build and maintain a user community

Creating a pool or network of people willing to contribute to user research is referred to as building a 'user community' or 'user panel'. While researchers sometimes differentiate between these two terms based on whether they pertain quantitative (panel) or qualitative (community) research, the terms have also been used interchangeably. We will use the term 'community' in line with the definitions of the Cambridge Dictionary: "the people living in one particular area or people who are considered as a unit because of their common interests, social group, or nationality" (Cambridge University Press & Assessment, n.d.). A common interest can for example consist of healthcare innovations; an example of a social group can be the elderly population. A user community can grow organically, but in the RRI field, we can also invest in building such communities. Living labs can actively recruit individual users for new communities that are willing to test innovative products and services. Shared characteristics and interests within this group in combination with community building activities, may lead to a common identity and the establishment of a true user community. We can propose seven steps for developing a sustainable user community for RRI based on the literature and the experience of LiCalab (see also Figure 1). These steps are an update and extension of the previous work on creating a panel-based living lab (Lemey et al., 2015; Vervoort et al., 2013), and incorporate insights from the roadmap to establish a sustainable living lab that LiCalab developed for the ACSELL project (ACSELL, 2023). ACSELL is an Interreg Europe project aimed at informing SMEs and policy makers about the living lab approach to improve innovative capacities of SMEs.

Step 1: Defining the purpose of the user community

A user community consists of interested and motivated individuals that are willing to cooperate in user activities and research projects focused on the specified RRI goals. The community should not be a dormant panel but a community that commits to active participation, preferably in the long term. When a user community is of a substantial size, this can facilitate representativeness, fast and efficient recruitment, and activation of individuals. It can also fulfil the need for scalability that certain projects require and the generation of qualitative, reliable, and correct results. A user community can be seen as a recruitment database, but it can also be the breeding ground from which specific needs, requirements, and trends can be identified in a bottom-up approach. This can serve as a basis for defining new projects and activities.

For LiCalab, the purpose definition is to connect with a large and sustainable user community consisting of adults (healthy citizens, patients, elderly, informal caregivers, care professionals, etc.) interested in contributing to innovations in the field of healthcare and well-being.

Step 2: Recruiting individuals for the user community

Recruitment for a user community should be targeted at obtaining a representative group that captures the diversity within a certain target population. This diversity can present itself in demographic variables, such as age, gender, ethnicity, or socio-economic status, but also in the topic of interest. When research aims and activities branch out, this is ideally reflected in the community as well. For example, the focus of LiCalab was initially on the elderly population and the silver economy but was later diversified to the broad field of health and care. Community members can be end users, but also other stakeholders. User community members can be recruited through various channels such as stakeholder organisations, local authorities, formal caregivers, media, personal contacts, campaigns, and representation at social events and fairs. Early adopters might be more inclined to become members of a user community and, in line with Bessant et al. (2019), it is important to aim to involve individuals from different stages on the spectrum of patient innovation behaviour in the user community. Hereby going beyond "hero innovators" and involved patients to also including informed patients. Innovating patients (hero innovators) are a small patient subgroup who actively use their deep understanding of their healthcare issue to develop and provide (or even prototype or trial) their ideas. The group of involved patients are the ones we probably see most in the RRI field. These are patients willing to test innovations and participate as co-creators in the design process. However, the majority of patients can be categorized as informed patients, individuals who are knowledgeable of their condition and make health decision but might need additional empowerment to become an active partner in RRI (Bessant et al., 2019). Actively reaching out in a personalized way can help to remove barriers and recognise motivators to participate in different end user groups. This also allows to identify and remediate practical barriers (for example high travel costs and lack of time), health-related barriers, and social and cultural issues.

The LiCalab community initially focused on older adults and their informal caregivers, who live in the Flemish region 'Kempen'. However, LiCalab now aims to build a more diverse community i.e., a good distribution in terms of for example age, gender, socioeconomic situation, and health status. The LiCalab user community gradually grew over time (Figure 2). Within this group, we can distinguish between the

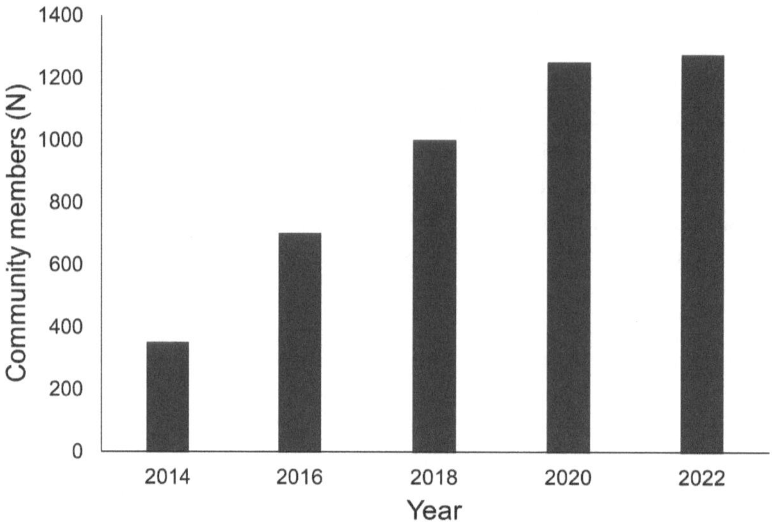

Figure 2: Development of the LiCalab user community over time.

community of practice and the community of interest. The community of practice is a diverse sample of potential end users who regularly take part in activities (approximate N = 300). The community of interest are care professionals, citizens, and other stakeholders from our network who engage on a more sporadic basis. The community is constantly evolving, so the panel managers maintain the community database and update member consent when needed. At present, the community contains slightly more female individuals (approximately 60%) and over a third of the sample is 60 years or older. Mapping the composition of the community is also useful and allows for targeted recruitment to fill potential gaps. Recruitment of members is not done from behind a desk but by actively getting to know possible members and gaining insight into their motivators and barriers. To recruit users and to increase name recognition as a trusted research group, LiCalab repeatedly presents its mission, vision, and concrete activities to patient organisations, local authorities, health care organisations, social organisations, citizen initiatives/representatives (also known as platform panel; ACSELL, 2023) and to international partners (external panel).

Step 3: Supporting the community

To support and to interact with the user community, a known and trusted person is needed as a single point of contact (SPOC) (Lemey et al., 2015). In de living lab sector, this SPOC is commonly referred to as a panel manager. Panel managers are community builders and have an important role in keeping the community alive and supporting members during activities. They are the face of the organisation and therefore in the best position to recruit new community members. To build trust, panel managers are accessible individuals that invest in building personal relations with the community, through both online and face-to-face contact. They can also act as an efficient helpdesk. It can be motivating for the user community to receive updates from the panel managers on the results of projects and on new developments within the healthcare and well-being sector. This can be achieved continuously through for example newsletters but also community building activities, such as network events with inspirational speakers and updates on past activities.

LiCalab started with one panel manager who was the face of the organization for the user community. Due to the expanding user community and number of projects, two additional panel managers were recruited. The panel managers are very approachable, and the community can always address them by mail, phone or in person in case of questions, comments, or concerns. They organize activities and are dedicated to giving members a warm welcome at activities. On top of operational activities, community building activities can consist of small-scale visits to innovative organisations (e.g., a visit to a modular care housing solution to be placed in the garden for informal caregiving) and larger events such as the celebration of LiCalab's 10th anniversary with community members and network partners. Panel managers inform the community about activity reports, calls for future activities, and the results of studies through the monthly newsletter, the website, and posts on social media.

Step 4: Conducting operational activities

The user community is managed in a database from which individuals can be invited for specific activities. Operational activities concern the actual studies and data collection, for example through group discussions, interviews, co-creation, usability research, etc.. The added value of a well-structured database is that it captures central data. This allows for personal follow-up for relevant activities and efficient data collection. How to plan specific user activities is discussed further in section 3.

LiCalab can recruit for operational activities through calls in the monthly newsletter, dedicated e-mails through the community management software, on the website, and on social media. In some specific cases, community members are also contacted directly by the panel managers. Interested individuals can enrol in various ways (depending on study aims), for example through phone or mail contact with the panel manager or by completing an online form. The panel managers are continuously collecting data on the characteristics and personal preferences of the community, allowing for personal and targeted recruitment for operational activities. For these activities, the panel managers aim for a good mix of new members, members of the community of practice and members of the community of interest. Depending on the research question and target group, additional participants can be recruited through e.g., patient organisations or public centres for social welfare (platform panel). For international projects, LiCalab taps into its international network of living labs (external panel). The ability to reach a large group of potential participants is an important skill of a living lab to achieve diversification and to avoid bias in recruitment for research. LiCalab works together with these community members in studies which are part of regional and European projects, as well as private assignments. To give an example, in 2022, LiCalab included 1451 citizens, 272 healthcare actors, and 74 representatives of governmental bodies in a total of 55 activities in both European project and business projects (Figure 3). Other relevant partners are companies (N = 50), students (N = 41), and academics (N = 31). Both the panel managers and the participants evaluate all operational activities like co-creation sessions or real life testings. Based on this feedback, activities are adjusted and needs can be addressed. It is particularly motivating for participants to notice that suggestions were picked up and were put into practice.

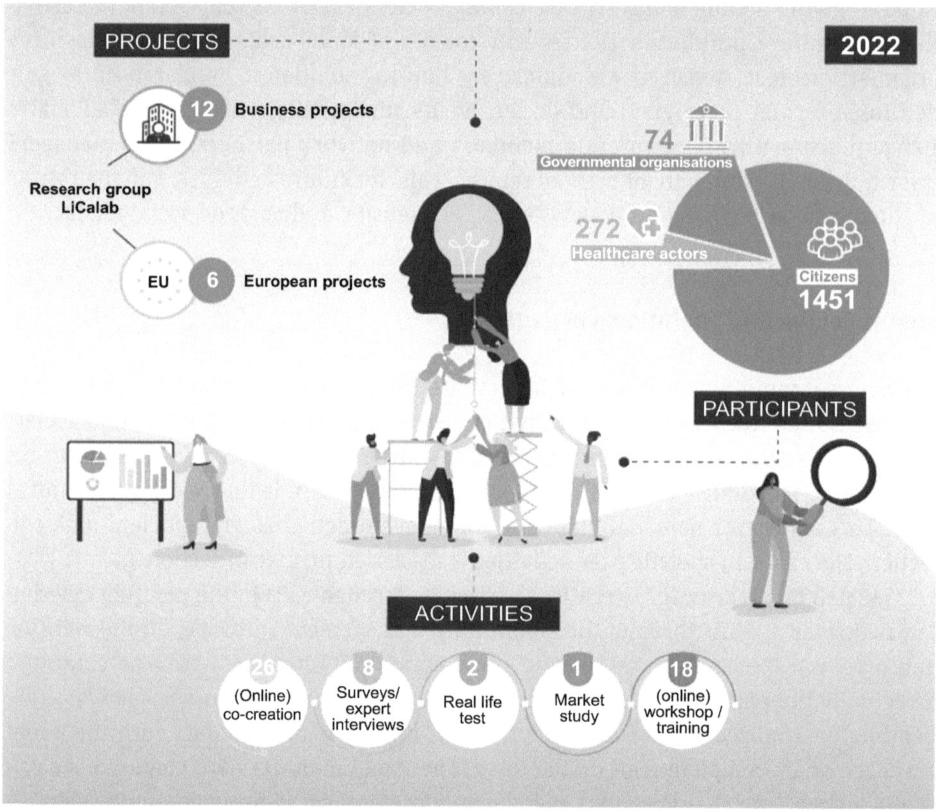

Figure 3: Overview of the activities of LiCalab in 2022.

Step 5: Creating a secure space

When collecting individual data, it is important to create a secure space, both in face-to-face interactions and in online database management. The panel managers are the gatekeepers of the data of the user community. Handling the personal information of participants carefully is the key to building a relationship of trust. Therefore, it is important to offer information about the purpose of data collection, about the people who have access to it, and where the data is stored. An important part of managing a user community is logging the activities, profiling the users and following-up on the status, engagement, and evolution (growth, diversification) of the user community. Therefore, a secure, user-friendly, and efficient software tool can help to monitor the community and to track the community activities. Table 1 lists some relevant features for software selection for which solutions can be evaluated (and regularly reevaluated). The panel manager is the key person to both inform the community and evaluate requests for data acquisition or sharing (with external partners). Community members need to give their consent to be included in a community and allow their information to be used in a confidential way for the purposes that were explained to them. As such, they give their general consent to being contacted in line with European GDPR regulation. To take part in specific activities, additional procedures are in place. These are discussed in section 3.

Table 1: Relevant features of a software tool for managing the community.

Function	Description
Database overview	Community member lists with personal data allowing to segment and filter.
Project overview	An overview of participants per project or activity.
Survey tool	A survey tool that can be connected to the community members (unique survey links and integration of results into personal details).
Communication tool	A communication tool to send out invitations, surveys, etc. to a selected group of (potential) participants.

LiCalab uses GDPR-approved panel management software supporting all Table 1 functionalities to securely store the data of the user community. The data is managed by the three panel managers, who do not share this information with other researchers inside or outside the LiCalab research group. For specific data collection activities, an additional informed consent is always requested from the participants and approval by an ethical committee is obtained when needed. In the face-to-face activities, panel managers spend a lot of attention to introductions, warming up exercises, and creating a feeling of relatedness between participants to create a safe and open environment for discussion.

Step 6: Analysing user motivation

Previous work has provided insight into motivations to participate in a user community. Lemey et al. (2015) point to the importance of intrinsic motivation (loyalty, civic duty, the wish for improvement, responsibility), trust in co-creation initiatives, and belief in one's abilities. Ståhlbröst et al. (2013) and Antikainen (2011) also show that motivating factors can relate to learning, curiosity, entertainment, a sense of community, a sense of efficacy, experiencing the ability to influence something that is meaningful and can have an impact on one's personal life. Recognition, fun, and feedback are more important than presents or payments according to Logghe et al. (2014). Therefore, acting on intrinsic motivators can be a powerful strategy for creating a user community but also for maintaining and expanding this user base. For specific user activities, intrinsic motivation can additionally contribute to the quality of the data. Nevertheless, external rewards can also be important to provide additional motivation for groups that are harder to reach or studies that require substantial participant effort. Whether incentives are needed can also depend on the local culture (see also section 3.3.3. on harmonisation and international collaboration). While the use of incentives is generally accepted, Grant & Sugerman (2004) do identify cases where offering financial compensation has ethical implications and can become problematic: a dependency relationship between participant and researcher, a high-risk research activity, and when a participant complies due to the large incentive but has a strong (principled) aversion towards the study. When it comes to the field of RRI, we believe that altruism or an interest in the topic might be a more important motivator than in traditional (e.g., medical) research. Carrera et al. (2017) has identified that altruistic motivations for research participation can consist of a connection to common humanity, a connection to science, and a connection to community organizations. In this respect, presenting project results to the community can also add to the motivation.

Group sessions with LiCalab community members have provided insight into their motivation for participation (unpublished data). Personal motivations that were mentioned consisted of the interest in learning new things and getting to know technologies that could improve their own daily life or that of their loved ones at present or in the future. Besides the interest in innovation in the health and well-being sector, social interaction was another reason to join a session. Participants loved to get inspired by the opinions of others and to gain insight into the thoughts of people with a different background and varying care needs. It was perceived as very pleasant that people listen to each other's opinions without judgement. A final big reason to participate in a session was the desire to contribute to society and to collectively think about how to improve care. The participants felt the need to defend the interests of the target group they belonged to. Community members also enjoyed coming to the sessions, stating things like "It is something positive in my life. I have good feelings about it." and "When I come to LiCalab activities, I always feel at home.". The LiCalab user community clearly shows a high intrinsic and altruistic motivation. However, after each activity, participants also always receive an appreciative mail and regularly a small incentive (e.g., a LiCalab umbrella, a book voucher, or a voucher for local shops).

Step 7: Building and maintaining a sustainable eco-system

Building and maintaining a user community is an intensive and continuous process. To ensure long-term involvement over different activities and projects, a clear brand for the living lab can enable group identification leading to commitment and norms of reciprocity (Lemey et al., 2015). A logo and corporate identity increase the recognizability of the living lab and can be used in communication with the stakeholders. In line with the quadruple helix model, four major actors are required in the innovation system to create impact and promote sustainability: science, policy, industry, and society. Irrespective of how often members participate in living lab activities, it is important to let members feel like they are part of the living lab community by keeping them informed and activated. However, increasing sustainability does not necessarily mean to maintain all community members but to let the community evolve, grow, and blossom. To let the community grow over time, Lemey et al. (2015) recommend creating an environment where it is easy for current members to suggest new members, to pamper community ambassadors, provide people with a central place where information about several projects can be shared (e.g., a website, a newsletter, . . .). When individuals decide to leave the user community, it is also important to understand why they do not wish to participate further since this information can be used to inform on the management of the panel.

The experience of LiCalab confirms that the longevity of a living lab with a user community is supported by an elaborate and active network with core actors in the field, including public, social and societal actors (e.g., public authorities, healthcare providers), economic actors (e.g., companies), and knowledge institutions and research centres. Additionally, LiCalab is a member of the ENoLL community and participates in large European projects. Such a network can support the acquisition of new projects and collaborations and also facilitate transferring new innovations and research findings into practice. We also performed a survey among participants who decided to leave the community to gain insight into factors that might influence community longevity. Reasons for community drop out consisted of diminished health and mobility, lack of time, and lack of interest. To maintain the ecosystem, LiCalab also attends national and international events on care and well-being and provides presentations of the organization and scientific papers on performed activities, organises workshops, and networks with the partners of the quadruple helix model.

3 Recruitment and data collection for user activities

Having a user community sets the stage for the organization of and recruitment for activities with stakeholders. Nevertheless, it is not enough, nor will it always contain the individuals needed for each specific project or activity. In this section we will describe the recruitment study flow, focusing on sample characteristics and recruitment, sample size recommendations, and best-practice data collection, including harmonization across borders as well as ethical considerations. We will end with a brief practice example.

3.1 Sample characteristics and recruitment

When setting up an operational activity, performing stakeholder mapping allows you to identify the relevant actors in your application field. However, identifying and classifying stakeholders can be a challenging endeavour. To give an example, Nilsen et al. (2020) developed a complex model containing twelve different internal and external stakeholders with interesting yet varying interrelations in the field of eHealth implementation in community healthcare. Their study illustrated that it can be relevant to recruit beyond traditional stakeholder groups (end users and professionals) in the context of eHealth since many others within the end user's network will provide a context that can promote or deter the use of such an application, e.g., next of kin, municipal administration, IT-departments.

Including a good representation of potential stakeholders helps to guarantee that the research and innovation meets the needs of all end users. Research shows that user experience can be influenced by individual differences (e.g., Magsamen-Conrad et al., 2015; Rodger et al., 2004). To cater to all, it is recommended to recruit and assess as broadly as we can. Therefore, including a diverse sample in terms of age, gender, ethnicity, socioeconomic status, and other relevant factors is generally advised. When designing products to be used in a relatively high-risk context, such as the healthcare context (e.g., innovative medication dispensers to prevent errors in medication use), it can be relevant to not merely test products in a sample of high-functioning and skilled individuals. To promote safety and usability, innovations can also be tested with your most vulnerable users (for example, those with low digital or health literacy (De Witte, Broeckx et al., 2021)).

Several recruitment channels can be used to spread flyers and invitations for participation. The use of a user community has been discussed above. However, recruitment efforts beyond this community might be needed depending on the size and diversity of your community and the research topics at hand. A common and effective recruitment strategy consists of using intermediary organizations to recruit specific populations, for example working with a local elderly council, a professional association, or a patient organization. Such intermediary partners can not only be relevant due to their existing relationship with the target group, but also because these are often representational bodies that have a lot of knowledge on the target group. Working with such organizations is used effectively in different countries and contexts (De Witte, Adriaensen et al., 2021). Convenience sampling, referring to a form of non-probability sampling mostly focusing on recruitment of easily accessible individuals (e.g., recruiting in the personal environment of the living lab), is also commonly used by living labs and is deemed fairly effective (De Witte, Adriaensen et al., 2021). Other recruitment channels, which are used less frequently or deemed less effective, consist of mailing lists, website advertisement, printed advertisement, face-to-face contact and word of mouth, or going through recruitment or marketing agencies. Different recruitment channels can be combined in a flexible way, depending on the context. When working with target groups with limited availability or lower motivation, it is important to lower thresholds for participation by for example organizing recruitment and activities in their specific context (e.g., a hospital or community spaces such as libraries, community kitchens or community restaurants).

3.2 Sample size guidelines

The required sample size of a user group to obtain reliable input depends on study design, data collection methods, and sample characteristics. Including too little users will preclude generalization of findings and obtaining high-quality data, but including too many can lead to redundancy, prevent in-depth analyses, and induce undue burden on the user group (Sandelowski et al., 1995). For the purpose of this section, recommendations will be formulated based on the selected data collection strategy, differing between qualitative, experimental, and usability research. The guidelines do not take into account expected attrition rates which can be around 15% (De Witte, Adriaensen et al., 2021).

Qualitative research aims to explore opinions and impressions in depth and therefore often uses purposive sampling, which means selecting 'information-rich cases' with the goal of promoting efficiency and data quality (Visileiou et al., 2018). Since the quality of research can be hampered by having an overly small or overly large sample, studies aim to achieve a level of 'saturation'. This refers to a sample size in which all relevant information has been collected and where recruiting new participants no longer provides new information. Based on previous empirical research on the point of saturation, sample size suggestions can be determined. For focus groups (and in line with that, co-creation sessions or other group sessions for qualitative data collection), it is advised to aim for three sessions of about eight participants (Guest et al., 2017; Carlsen et al., 2011). The authors suggest having a minimum of around four to six participants and a maximum of around twelve participants per session. Interpersonal dynamics influence the point of saturation and Guest et al. (2017) suggest that two focus groups with four individuals can generate more insightful data than one focus group with eight individuals. In case of individual interviews, the findings from Morse (2000) and Guest et al. (2017) suggest aiming for a sample size of 15 to 30 participants, and to not go above 40 to 50 interviews or lower than 10 to 12.

Based on the work of Morse (2000), Guest et al. (2017), and Visileiou et al. (2018), there are four relevant study criteria to determine sample size within the ranges mentioned above. These are the scope of the study, the subject or topic, data quality, and pragmatic criteria (Table 2). Additionally, it is important to mention that cross-cultural research requires a higher sample size to identify meta-themes across multiple contexts (Hagaman & Wutich, 2017).

Table 2: Criteria for sample size selection for qualitative research, based on an integration of the guidelines based on Morse (2000), Guest et al. (2017), and Visileiou et al. (2018).

Criterion	Arguments for a smaller sample size	Arguments for a larger sample size
Scope	Focused research, a structured approach and a homogeneous sample	Wider scope of the research
Subject	Clear and straightforward research topic	Vague or sensitive topic
Data quality	Rich dataset full of experience and reflection (e.g., through open questions)	Less rich or in-depth data collection
Pragmatic criteria	Limitations in access to the population or time	

Experimental research requires a larger sample size for statistical analysis and often uses convenience sampling or probability sampling, consisting of randomly selecting a sample from a population. Sample sizes for traditional quantitative scientific research (using questionnaires or pre-post designs for example) can often be calculated effectively with formulas and (online) tools (e.g., Gpower software) based on the expected significance level, power and effect size. The outcome of these tools might, however, need to be increased in uncontrolled conditions and when drop-out is expected to be high.

Usability research focuses on investigating user behaviour and identifying usability problems of an innovation. The review of Carayon et al. (2015) shows that such research generally uses a mixed methods approach with a combination of qualitative and quantitative data collection as well as varying sample sizes. Cazañas et al. (2017) indicate that 10 to 20 participants appear to be enough to detect the major usability problems, which is in line with other recommendations such as those of the American Food and Drug Administration (FDA) (Food and Drug administration, 2016). When using an iterative design with multiple cycles of user involvement, a lower sample size per iteration can be applied. For Human Factors studies and Think Aloud paradigms, a sample size of about 8 users per condition is generally included (De Witte et al., 2021; Maramba et al. 2019). Human factors studies (sometimes also termed usability studies) consist of having users interact with an innovation in simulated real-life circumstances with the goal of improving safety, performance, and user acceptability (Bergman, 2012; Weir et al., 2020). In Think Aloud Protocols, users are asked to share their actual thoughts during an activity or task in order to gain insight into the problem-solving process (Wolcott & Lobczowski, 2021).

3.3 Best-practice data collection

3.3.1 High-quality protocol design

Over the past decade, the number of studies using living lab, usability and user experience, and participatory design methodologies has shown a sharp increase. However, there is great variability in the data collection methods that are employed. For example, In the field of usability of eHealth and mHealth tools, 70% to 80% of studies implement questionnaires, however, all other methodologies were used in less than 50% of publications (Maramba et al., 2019; Wang et al., 2022). These other methods consisted for example of Think Aloud paradigms, interviews, performance metrics, focus groups, and also screen recordings or eye-tracking in rare cases. About one in three studies used an iterative design. Clearly, and in contrast with for example effectiveness research, the current field is characterised by a large variability in implemented methodology. The evaluation method should be determined for each study depending on study aims, topic or innovation of interest, and the target population. Nevertheless, it is relevant to apply existing paradigms and validated questionnaires since they can promote research quality and facilitate research communication and comparison across studies and borders. Going into specific research paradigms would take us too far, but we would like to touch upon two important common factors in protocol design, i.e., research ethics and harmonization in data collection.

3.3.2 Ethical guidelines

When conducting research on humans, it is important to design a study in a way that minimizes individual risks and guarantees high ethical standards. International guidelines exist to promote ethical and scientific quality in research, such as the declaration of Helsinki of the World Medical Association (WMA) and the Good Clinical Practice guidelines from the European Medicines Agency (EMA). These guidelines can be very technical and are not always suitable for the field of living labs and RRI. However, it remains important to identify potential ethical challenges before starting a specific study or activity.

Legislation for research varies between countries. However, reflecting on the ethical implications of the research and the need for ethical approval is warranted especially in some conditions, for instance when working with patient populations or children, when healthcare professionals participate with the aim to develop their knowledge and practices or to change their way of working, or when performing research with medical devices (in line with the European Medical Device Regulation (MDR) 2017/745). Ethical committees can help to reflect on the potential dangers of a study and to implement high-quality study procedures in terms of e.g., recruitment, obtaining informed consent and sharing data. Even if a study does not require ethical approval, it is required and/or good practice to provide an informed consent document detailing which data is collected and how they will be managed in line with local and international regulations.

3.3.3 Harmonization of data collection

The fields of RRI, living lab research, Human Factors research, and user-centred design have been rapidly growing over the past decades. While they all assign the user a central role in innovation, design, and research, they sometimes appear to speak a different language and use a different terminology. This can prevent smooth cooperation between these related fields. Vervoort et al. (2022) have indicated that the foundation of a strong and sustainable living lab community consists of a harmonized evaluation framework for living labs and living lab projects. In 2021, a large Horizon 2020 project Virtual Health and Wellbeing Living Lab Infrastructure (VITALISE) with partners from 11 countries (including LiCalab) was set up with the goal of harmonizing living lab procedures and open infrastructures to facilitate international collaboration (Bernaerts et al., 2022). Such structural international partnerships are needed to support the development of a common language, benchmarking, standardization, and setting up quality standards.

Technological advancements can contribute to the management of global challenges in areas such as health, aging, and climate. However, this requires an understanding of the factors that contribute to the success of innovations in different social, environmental, and cultural contexts (Mulder & Stappers, 2009). User experience is influenced by cultural differences, for example relating to uncertainty avoidance, individualism-collectivism, or a focus on task-related functions and/or emotional experience (Choi et al., 2006; Hwang, 2005; Santoso & Schrepp, 2019). Therefore, successful international upscaling of innovation relies on effective local research activities that inform on preferences and customs across borders.

While some extent of harmonization and use of standardized cross-border protocols are key to obtaining data that can be compared between or generalized beyond contexts, we also shouldn't neglect cross-cultural differences that influence data collection. Standardized protocols for recruitment and study execution will probably need to be tailored to the local context to provide a representative and rich dataset. A survey in 36 living labs from 20 countries (in Europe, Asia, the Americas, and Oceania) shows many shared practices but also key differences between user experience studies across borders (De Witte, Adriaensen, et al., 2021). For example, intrinsic motivation for gaining appreciation or knowledge appears to be an important driver for participation in Europe and Australia while external (monetary) reward appears required in Central America and Eastern Asia. It is unclear whether this is caused by cultural differences or economic conditions. Social norms and status of group members can also influence how open individuals are to sharing their opinions, which has implications for organizing group sessions with individuals that differ in gender, age, ethnicity, and professional status (e.g., healthcare professionals vs. patients) (De Witte, Adriaensen, et al., 2021). Scholl et al. (2018) for example indicate that ideas of individuals with more social status can get endorsement from other participants, even though they don't always benefit all.

With regard to the specific execution of cross-border research activities, several recommendations can be made to promote the collection of high-quality data, based on Liamputtong (2011) and De Witte, Adriaensen et al. (2021). It is recommended for study protocols containing cross-border data collection to maintain high methodological standards and allow comparisons (through standardisation) but also be sufficiently flexible to allow for harmonization for local needs and preferences with the goal of obtaining good representation from the target population and high-quality data collection. Creating a non-threatening and non-judgmental environment in group sessions can help to promote an open discussion of ideas and opinions. In this respect, it is important to engage a highly skilled panel manager and moderator, who knows the local context and communication preferences and who can find the right balance between a facilitating and directive stance. In such sessions, equal representation could be promoted by directly addressing specific individuals and using multimodal data collection (based on e.g., verbal communication, written communication, creative interactions). Groups can be (temporarily) split up into smaller or more homogeneous groups when the topic or context calls for this.

4 Case example

To illustrate how a user community and the processes mentioned above can be implemented in practice, we will describe a case study that started with a healthcare challenge definition and resulted in the development of two innovations and the establishment of a not-for-profit organization. The project was funded by CrossCare, an Interreg Flanders-Netherlands project (coordinated by LiCalab) that aimed to contribute to the development and implementation of healthcare innovations (product, service, or concept) by accelerating innovation projects with R&D funding and living lab support. The different activities that were carried out throughout the case study were based on the SHINE methodology (Weemaes, & Bruneel, 2017). The SHINE methodology consists of tools for value-based innovation in healthcare and aims to support the development of an integrated business model with partners, in this case healthcare professionals and companies, and stakeholders. The four phases of this framework are discussed in brief in Table 3.

Table 3: Overview of the SHINE methodology.

Phase	Tasks
Phase 1: value definition	Defining shared values and goals. Conducting a stakeholder and market analysis. Defining end users and their challenges (personas).
Phase 2: value creation	Defining the unique selling points (USP). Developing a theory of change intervention logic.
Phase 3: value capture	Defining the partnership and roles. Developing the business model.
Phase 4: value delivery	Setting up a sustainable partnership. Developing a governance model.

Phase 1 of the multi-year project started with a call to local care professionals, specifically the steering group of the prevention centre in Turnhout, a centre that operates under the association of general practitioners (GP) and focuses on supporting GPs to integrate preventative activities into their daily practice. The steering group consisted of representatives of local GP groups, the regional hospital, a representative of the local pharmacists, the locoregional health council and organisation (Logo Kempen) and Thomas More University of Applied Sciences (represented by a member of LiCalab). The steering group proposed sleeping disorders as an important regional healthcare challenge, since it was a health problem affecting one in three Belgians and for which GPs and pharmacists had no good non-pharmaceutical solutions. Four members of the steering group (3 GPs and 1 pharmacist) were personally interested to address the challenge and established a consortium. Their proposal was positively evaluated by the CrossCare steering committee. The next step was to launch a call for Flemish organisations who had innovative yet feasible ideas to help address this challenge. The healthcare actors selected two partners that most closely matched their vision. The first was a newly founded company with an innovative idea, i.e., to design a tactile breath pacer which could support slow breathing exercises promoting sleep quality (now known as Moonbird). The second partner was a group practice of psychologists named Faresa with an online platform for self-care psycho-education. Further round table discussions with the consortium and companies resulted in shared values and goals regarding the need for an integrated and blended care approach for sleep disorders and the initiation of the Flemish multi-actor project 'Welgerust' (which translates as well-rested). As a next step, personas were co-created based on adults with chronic insomnia as end users and a stakeholder and market analysis were conducted.

The first step in the value creation phase (phase 2) took place in 2020 and consisted of a combination of live and online co-creation (online due to the COVID pandemic and the excess burden on the healthcare system). Seven participants with chronic sleeping problems, recruited through the LiCalab user community, assessed a first prototype of the tactile pacer and its app regarding look and feel, ergonomics, user-friendliness and functionality. To assess the online platform and the sleep checklist of Faresa, an online survey was launched. Thirty-four LiCalab community members enrolled and tested the platform, 25 of those completed the online survey. After the co-creation, life testing of the tactile breath pacer and the online platform took place from August to November. Participants with chronic sleeping disorders were recruited by 2 GPs and 1 pharmacist. After an introductory session, testing took place at home during a four-week period and in batches of 10 people (because of the limited number of prototypes). Validated questionnaires on sleep quality (Pittsburgh Sleep Quality Index (PSQI); Buysse et al., 1989) and technology acceptance (Flemish questionnaire on the Unified Theory of Acceptance and Use of Technology; De Witte & Van Daele, 2017) were administered pre and post-test. Since the protocol involved a novel methodology (the breath pacer) in a sample with sleeping problems, the researchers sought approval from the Ethical Committee of Antwerp University Hospital (in line with Belgian law). Twenty-eight adults participated, with a drop-out of 7 at the post-survey. One month later, an online feedback session was set up to give general feedback and to get further specific insights into experiences and opinions regarding the look and feel of the screens of the app (Moonbird) and the web platform (Faresa). Participants' feedback steered the innovation cycle and improved the prototype development. The input of participants was used to refine the USP and to develop a Theory of Change intervention logic. At the end of phase 2, both Moonbird (Figure 4) and Faresa had working prototype of their respective product and platform.

In phase 3 of the SHINE methodology (value capture), the Innovatrix-framework was used to help develop the business model (Schuurman, Herregodts, Georges, & Rits, 2019). Innovatrix is an innovation management framework tailored to the living lab context. It must be noted that going through the entire cycle of business model innovation and collaboration proved not to be feasible within this 1-year project, but important foundations for effective future collaboration between living labs, healthcare actors and companies were laid.

To assess if care professionals were interested in integrating the project results into their daily practice, a short online survey was sent out to local GPs and pharmacists. A total of 35 GP and 34 pharmacists showed great interest in getting started with a care pathway for sleep disorders together with the sleep labs, to strengthen the collaboration between pharmacists and GPs regarding sleep disorders, and to have solid alternatives to refer people with sleep problems to. Both care professions could see

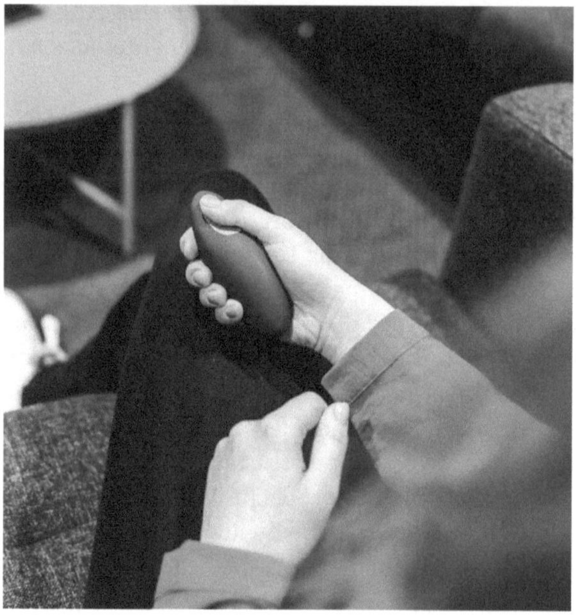

Figure 4: The Moonbird breath pacer.

themselves actively participating in this (66% of GPs wanted to help test the care pathway, and 70% of pharmacists). The survey also indicated that there was a need for improved knowledge on sleep disorders in general and benzodiazepine withdrawal in particular. Eight GPs and six pharmacists expressed a concrete interest in actively participating in a working group.

In terms of value delivery (phase 4), the current approach, starting from a need from healthcare actors and subsequently attracting companies to take part in living lab research involving all stakeholders, proved valuable. The project involved healthcare actors, scientists, citizens, and companies. Both selected companies developed their innovations together with the stakeholders, with the Moonbird tactile breath pacer even moving from TRL 4 to TRL 7. A second live test was set up to investigate the acceptability and usability of the Moonbird tactile breathing device and to provide preliminary evidence regarding its impact on subjective sleep quality in people with sleep problems. The protocol included both qualitative and quantitative data collection in a pre-post design with 40 potential end users, of which one participant dropped out. This sample size was large enough to allow for statistical testing but not too large as to hinder the qualitative analysis. Due to limited availability of prototypes, the data collection needed to be conducted in two successive groups of 20 participants. Individuals with self-reported sleep problems were invited to participate by a general e-mail to the LiCalab community complemented with additional recruitment via newsletters to the personnel of Thomas More of Applied Sciences and social media posts addressed to the general

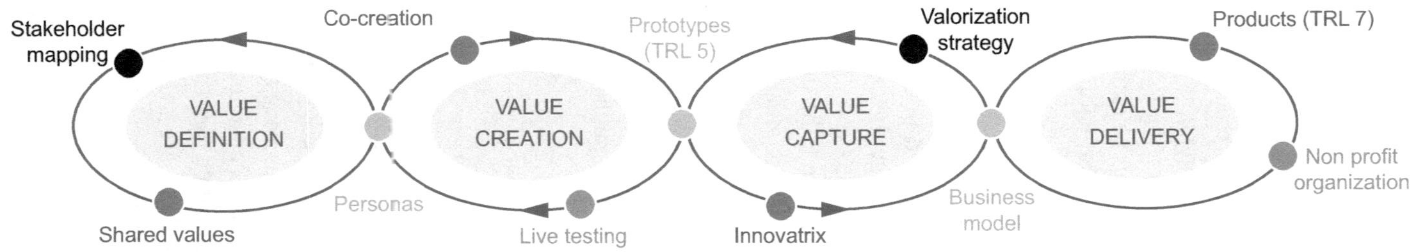

Figure 5: Schematic representation of the 'Welgerust' (well-rested) trajectory according to the four phases of the SHINE methodology.

public in order to achieve the target sample size of individuals with sleeping problems. The details and results of this live test were published in Vermeylen et al. (2022). About half of participants observed a reduction in sleep problems and many would recommend the device to friends and family. By virtue of the extended iterative living lab approach, this breath pacer has achieved a successful launch and implementation. After completion of this 1-year collaboration, the healthcare actors additionally established a not-for-profit organisation that is working on the assessment and approval of an integrated care pathway for sleep disorders. Incorporating products in a defined care pathway creates added value for all partners as these products can be embedded in regular healthcare services. Therefore, the not-for-profit organisation will involve companies again when needs are detected. A schematic representation of the different elements and activities of the current project are presented in Figure 5.

After the initial project, the Moonbird company continued to collaborate with LiCalab and apply the living lab approach to explore other target populations, for instance children and professional athletes. Each collaboration resulted in a newly designed research activity, ethics evaluation, and recruitment strategy (beyond the existing user community due to the specific target profiles).

The current case suggests that partnerships between developers and the field (in this case, regional healthcare stakeholders) benefit from starting with stakeholder needs to utilize the full potential of the living lab approach. Recruitment of the relevant individuals from the quadruple helix is greatly facilitated if a user community has already been established. Such a sustainable collaboration with multiple iterative living lab activities (adhering to ethical and research standards) can result in products and care pathways that align with practice needs. Findings can also be published for the benefit of the wider scientific community.

5 Conclusion

Technological advances can significantly impact how we live, work, age, and stay healthy. However, in order to obtain innovations that meet an existing need and that can easily be adopted in today's global fast-track world, understanding stakeholders' needs is essential. Building a sustainable user community can seem intensive at first. However, it can greatly facilitate user involvement and stakeholder consultation in the long run. The current chapter presented seven steps for setting up a user community and applied them to the context of LiCalab, a Belgian health & care living lab. Although these steps (and their order) may not be universal, they can provide directions for (new) organizations and initiatives to develop and manage a sustainable community in their field of interest. Having a user community in place offers the opportunity to easily involve participants in user activities, such as co-creation, concept development, market insight, product development, piloting, and validation services.

Nevertheless, it is also strongly advised to adhere to quality standards for scientific research in order to obtain rich insights that reflect the diversity of the target group for specific user activities.

Different research methods can be applied in the field of user involvement. Qualitative and quantitative research requires different sample sizes and sampling methods to obtain high-quality data. On the one hand, small sample sizes preclude generalization. On the other hand, overly large sample sizes can be challenging in terms of qualitative analyses or big data management and analyses. While the size of the sample is important, the profile of the participants is paramount. Traditionally, we merely involve end users (patients) and professionals in the field of healthcare, but many other individuals or organisations in their network also influence the potential impact and implementation of innovations. Therefore, as illustrated in the case example, involving different stakeholders in a large variety of activities (from problem definition to product development and implementation) will set the stage for scalable innovations and long-lasting partnerships.

References

ACSELL (2023). *Establishing a sustainable living lab*. https://projects2014-2020.interregeurope.eu/acsell/library/

Antikainen, M. (2011). *Facilitating customer involvement in collaborative online innovation communities: Dissertation*. [Dissertation, Tampere University of Technology (TUT)]. VTT Technical Research Centre of Finland. https://publications.vtt.fi/pdf/publications/2011/P760.pdf.

Ballon, P., Van Hoed, M., & Schuurman, D. (2018) The effectiveness of involving users in digital innovation: measuring the impact of living labs. *Telematics and Informatics*, 35, 1201–1214. https://doi.org/10.1016/j.tele.2018.02.003

Bergman, E. (2012). Introduction to Human Factors. *Journal of Diabetes Science and Technology*, 6(2), 229–230. https://doi.org/10.1177/193229681200600202

Bessant, J., Iakovleva, T., & Oftedal, E. M. (2019). The future or responsible innovation. In T. Iakovleva, E. M. Oftedal, & J Bessant (Eds.), *Responsible innovation in digital health*. (pp.232–250). Edward Elgar Publishing. https://doi.org/10.4337/9781788975063

Bernaerts, S., De Witte, N. A. J., Van der Auwera, V., Bonroy, B., Muraru, L., Bamidis, P., Frantzidis, C., Kourtidou-Papadeli, C., Azevedo, N., Garatea, J., Muñoz, I., Almeida, R., Losada, R., Fung, J., Kehayia, E., Lamontagne, A., de Guise, E., Duclos, C., Higgins, J., . . . Konstantinidis, E. (2022). Rehabilitation Supported by Technology: Protocol for an International Cocreation and User Experience Study. *JMIR Research Protocols*, *11*(3), e3453. http://dx.doi.org/10.2196/34537

Buysse, D. J., Reynolds III, C. F., Monk, T. H., Berman, S.R., & Kupfer, D.J. (1989). The Pittsburgh Sleep Quality Index: a new instrument for psychiatric practice and research. *Psychiatry Research*, *28*(2), 193–213. https://doi.org/10.1016/0165-1781(89)90047-4

Cambridge University Press & assessment. (n.d.). Community. In *Cambridge dictionary*. Retrieved Novembre 6, 2023 from https://dictionary.cambridge.org/dictionary/english/community

Carlsen, B., & Glenton, C. (2011) What about N? A methodological study of sample-size reporting in focus group studies. *BMC Medical Research Methodology*, *11*, 26. https://doi.org/10.1186/1471-2288-11-26

Carayon, P., Kianfar, S., Li, Y., Xie, A., Alyousef, B., Wooldridge, A. (2015). A systematic review of mixed methods research on human factors and ergonomics in health care. *Applied Ergonomics*, 51, 291–321, https://doi.org/10.1016/j.apergo.2015.06.001

Carrera, J. S., Brown, P., Brody, J. G., et al. (2017). Research altruism as motivation for participation in community centered environmental health research. *Social Science & Medicine*, 196, 175–181.

Cazañas, A., de San Miguel, A., & Parra, E. (2017). Estimating Sample Size for Usability Testing. *Enfoque UTE*, *8*(1), 172–185. https://doi.org/10.29019/enfoqueute.v8n1.126

Choi, B., Lee, I., & Kim, J. (2006). Culturability in mobile data services: a qualitative study of the relationship between cultural characteristics and user-experience attributes. *International Journal on Human-computer Interaction*, 20(3), 171–203.

De Witte, N. A. J., Adriaensen, I., Broeckx, L., Van Der Auwera, V., & Van Daele T. (2021). Cross-cultural differences in user-centred research: an international living lab survey. *Health Informatics Journal*, *27*, 1–16. https://doi.org/10.1177/14604582211038268

De Witte, N. A. J., Broeckx, L., Vermeylen, S., Van Der Auwera, V., & Van Daele, T. (2021). Human Factors in Living Lab Research. *Technology Innovation Management Review*, 11 (9/10), 21–29. https://doi.org/10.22215/timreview/1462

De Witte, N. A. J., & Van Daele, T. (2017). *Vlaamse UTAUT-Vragenlijsten [Flemish UTAUT-Questionnaires].* Antwerp: Applied Psychology, Thomas More University of Applied Sciences.

The European Network of Living Labs (ENoLL) (2023, September 5). *About us.* https://enoll.org/about-us/

Food and Drug administration (2016). *Applying Human Factors and Usability Engineering to Medical Devices. Guidance for Industry and Food and Drug Administration Staff.* US Food and drug administration. https://www.fda.gov/regulatory-information/search-fda-guidance-documents/applying-human-factors-and-usability-engineering-medical-devices

Grant, R. W., & Sugarman, J. (2004). Ethics in human subjects research: do incentives matter? *The Journal of Medicine and Philosophy*, 29(6), 717–738.

Guest, G., Namey, E., & McKenna, K. (2017). How Many Focus Groups Are Enough? Building an Evidence Base for Nonprobability Sample Sizes. *Field Methods*, 29(1), 3–22. http://doi.org/10.1177/1525822X16639015

Hagaman, A. K., & Wutich, A. (2017). How Many Interviews Are Enough to Identify Metathemes in Multisited and Cross-cultural Research? Another Perspective on Guest, Bunce, and Johnson's (2006) Landmark Study. *Field Methods*, *29*(1), 23–41. https://doi.org/10.1177/1525822X16640447

Hwang, Y. (2005) Investigating enterprise systems adoption: uncertainty avoidance, intrinsic motivation, and the technology acceptance model. *European Journal of Information Systems*, 14, 150–161.

Jarke, J. (2021). *Public Administration and Information Technology: Co-creating Digital Public Services for an Ageing Society. Evidence for User-centric Design.* Springer Cham. https://doi.org/10.1007/978-3-030-52873-7

Lemey, J. (2015). Towards a sustainable panel-based living lab approach in older adult care innovation. *In OpenLivingLab Days Istanbul, Turkey* (blz. 180–194). European Network of Living Labs. http://www.scribd.com/doc/276089123/ENoLL-Research-Day-Conference-Proceedings-2015.

Liamputtong P. (2011). *Focus group methodology: principle and practice.* London: SAGE Publications,

Logghe, S. (2014). *Uit passie of voor de poen? Een exploratie van gebruikersmotivaties voor deelname aan innovatie onderzoek in Living Labs.* Paper presented at Etmaal van de Communicatiewetenschappen 2014, Wageningen, The Netherlands.

Magsamen-Conrad, K., Upadhyaya, S., Joa, C. Y., & Dowd, J. (2015) Bridging the divide: using UTAUT to predict multigenerational tablet adoption practices. *Computers in Human Behavior*, 50, 186–196. https://doi.org/10.1016/j.chb.2015.03.032

Maramba, I., Chatterjee, A. Newman, C. (2019). Methods of usability testing in the development of eHealth applications: a scoping review. *International Journal of Medical Informatics* 2019, 95–104. https://doi.org/10.1016/j.ijmedinf.2019.03.018

Morse, J. M. (2000) Determining Sample Size. *Qualitative Health Research*, 10(1), 3–5. http://doi.org/10.1177/104973200129118183

Mulder, I., & Stappers, P. J. (2009). Co-creating in Practice: Results and Challenges. In: *Proceedings of the 15th international conference of concurrent enterprising: ICE 2009*, Leiden, The Netherlands

Nilsen, E.R., Stendal, K. & Gullslett, M.K. (2020). Implementation of eHealth Technology in Community Health Care: the complexity of stakeholder involvement. *BMC Health Services Research*, *20*, 395. https://doi.org/10.1186/s12913-020-05287-2

Rodger, J. A., & Pendharkar, P.C. (2004). A field study of the impact of gender and User's technical experience on the performance of voice-activated medical tracking application. *International Journal of Human-Computer Studies*, 60(5–6), 529–544.

Sandelowski, M. (1995). Sample size in qualitative research. *Research in Nursing & Health*, *18*(2). 179–83

Santoso, H. B., & Schrepp, M. (2019). The impact of culture and product on the subjective importance of userexperience aspects. *Heliyon*, 5(9), e02434.

Scholl, A., Sassenberg, K., Ellemers, N., et al. (2018). Highly identified power-holders feel responsible: the interplay between social identification and social power within groups. *British Journal of Social Psychology*, 57, 112–129.

Schuurman, D., Herregodts, A.- L., Georges, A., & Rits, O. (2019). Innovation Management in Living Lab Projects: The Innovatrix Framework. *Technology Innovation Management Review*, *9*(3), 63–73. http://doi.org/10.22215/timreview/1225

Ståhlbröst et al. (2013). *Social media for user innovation in Living Labs: a framework to support user recruitment and commitment*. This paper was presented at The XXIV ISPIM Conference – Innovating in Global Markets: Challenges for Sustainable Growth in Helsinki, Finland on 16–19 June 2013.

Suijkerbuijk, S., Nap, H. H., Cornelisse, L., Ijsselsteijn, W. A., de Kort, Y. A. W., & Minkman, M. M. N. (2019). Active Involvement of People with Dementia: A Systematic Review of Studies Developing Supportive Technologies. *Journal of Alzheimer's Disease*, 69, 1041 –1065.

Vasileiou, K., Barnett, J., Thorpe, S., & Young, T. (2018) Characterising and justifying sample size sufficiency in interview-based studies: systematic analysis of qualitative health research over a 15-year period. *BMC Medical Research Methodology*, 18, 148. https://doi.org/10.1186/s12874-018-0594-7

Vermeylen, S., Honinx, E., Broes, S, & De Witte, N. A. J. (2022). Evaluation of a tactile breath pacer for sleep problems: a mixed method pilot study. *Frontiers in Digital Health*, *4*, 908159. https://doi.org/10.3389/fdgth.2022.908159

Vervoort, K., (2013). *Working with users: Living labs bottom up*. WS 7; 4th ENOLL Living Lab Summer School, Manchester, Consulted at 7 May at https://vimeo.com/channels/4thenollsummerschool/80471087

Vervoort, K., Konstantinidis, E., Santonen, T., Petsani, D., Servais, D., De Boer, D., Spagnoli, F., Onur, O., Bertolin, J., Trousse, B., Desole, M., & Bamidis, P. (2022). Harmonizing the evaluation of living labs: a standardized evaluation framework. *XXXIII ISPIM Innovation Conference "Innovating in a Digital World"*. https://doi.org/10.5281/zenodo.7434406

Wang, Q., Liu, J., Zhou, L., Tian, J., Chen, X, Zhang, W., Wang, H., Zhou, W., and Gao Y. (2022) Usability evaluation of mHealth apps for elderly individuals: a scoping review. *BMC Medical Informatics and Decision Making*, 22, 317. https://doi.org/10.1186/s12911-022-02064-5

Weemaes, S., Bruneel, J. (2017). *Retrospective case STudy – Project Report, outcome of the North Sae Region SHINE project*, http://www.northsearegion.eu/shine

Weir, N.M., Newham, R., & Bennie, M. (2020). A Literature Review Of Human Factors and Ergonomics within the Pharmacy Dispensing Process. *Research in Social and Administrative Pharmacy*, 16(5), 637–645. https://doi.org/10.1016/j.sapharm.2019.08.029

Wolcott, M. D., & Lobczowski, N. G. (2021). Using cognitive interviews and think-aloud protocols to understand thought processes. *Currents in pharmacy teaching & learning*, *13*(2), 181–188. https://doi.org/10.1016/j.cptl.2020.09.005

Judy Hong Huang, Elin M. Oftedal, Tatiana Iakovleva

The emergence of a boundary innovation space – the case of Norwegian Smart Care Lab

Abstract: This chapter explores the transformation of the Norwegian Smart Care Lab (NSCL) from a vague idea to a firm-centric testing center to a collaborative innovation hub, emphasizing the critical role of user involvement in the innovation process. Research highlights that early user engagement enhances solution quality and accelerates adoption by aligning innovations with real-world needs. NSCL adapted to the Norwegian Coordination Reform, which encouraged integration between public healthcare services and the private sector, fostering a space for diverse stakeholder collaboration. Through 30 interviews with 27 stakeholders between 2021 and 2023, this study illustrates how NSCL incorporated responsible innovation practices, emphasizing continuous user engagement to manage the societal impacts of new technologies effectively.

The chapter also discusses NSCL's advocacy for innovative procurement practices in response to municipal challenges with digitalization, which influence institutional policy and enhance the healthcare landscape. In conclusion, NSCL's journey showcases the profound impact of user-centric innovation in healthcare, demonstrating significant institutional changes and setting a benchmark for the sector. The insights gained highlight the importance of user involvement and responsible innovation in successfully navigating the intricate dynamics between technology development and institutional adaptation.

Introduction

At the heart of contemporary innovation and design lies the concept of user involvement. User involvement is fundamental to contemporary innovation and design, shaping the entire innovation journey. Extensive research has shown that involving users early enhances solution variety and depth by integrating their knowledge, experience, and insights, thereby expanding the design team's capabilities, and sometimes introducing valuable tacit knowledge (Von Hippel, 2005). This involvement ensure that innovations align with their intended environments, increasing the likelihood of quicker, broader adoption (Rogers, 2003). Additionally, including users legitimizes solutions and promotes public acceptance (Stilgoe, Owen, and Macnaghten, 2013). Responsible Innovation involves users and anticipates societal impacts, facilitating technology development to meet societal needs, as outlined by multiple policy and research frameworks (Iakovleva et al., 2021; European Commission, 2007; 2021; OECD, 2014; ENTELIS+ Consortium,

https://doi.org/10.1515/9783111241036-004

2020; United Nations Development Programme, 2020; World Economic Forum, 2022). This approach uses participatory techniques to include public dialogue with NGOs and stakeholders typically excluded from science and innovation, aiming to open up the innovation process.

One limitation in the domain of Responsible Innovation (RI) within firms is implementing practices of actual user inclusion, which can be time-consuming and sometimes conflict with business interests. In response, "boundary innovation spaces" facilitate stakeholder inclusion, providing a safe environment for diverse stakeholders to co-create innovations through discussions, prototyping, and experimental conversations. These spaces require more than just well-equipped rooms; they need structured organization, appropriate tools, skilled facilitation, adaptability, and effective management. They also must foster a secure environment for experimentation and potential failure, promoting a culture of continuous engagement, collaboration, and innovation.

This chapter examines the development and transformation of NSCL, a Norwegian test center and living lab for welfare technology, illustrating its shift from a firm-centric testing center to a collaborative innovation space, and addresses the complexities and challenges of user engagement in the innovation process, asking the question:

How do user inclusion and responsible innovation practices influence the evolution and operational strategies of NSCL in developing digital healthcare solutions?

Through 30 interviews with 27 stakeholders, including NSCL's founders, managers, clients, and users, we offer a comprehensive portrait of NSCL's evolution over five years (2019–2023). This study reveals how NSCL's initial business model, though initially vague, matured through ongoing stakeholder interactions and strategic pivots, highlighting the essential role of diverse stakeholder perspectives, especially users, in the innovation ecosystem.

Moreover, this chapter examines NSCL's contribution to advancing responsible innovation, detailing its user engagement methods and tools. We spotlight pivotal moments in NSCL's history where the innovation concept adapted to new insights, often stemming from broader stakeholder involvement—a key principle of responsible innovation.

In tracking NSCL's development within the health and welfare service sector, we aim to provide insights into the factors that influenced its transformation and the challenges and opportunities of fostering a user-inclusive, responsible innovation environment. Our study proposes viewing NSCL's journey from an evolutionary perspective, acknowledging the internal and external catalysts of change and the essential role of user inclusion in responsible innovation.

Literature: Responsible innovation and boundary spaces

Responsible innovation (RI) and user involvement

Responsible Innovation (RI) emphasizes ethical considerations, societal impacts, and environmental sustainability in the development of new technologies, gaining traction across science, engineering, and business. This approach demands transparency and accountability from innovators, urging them to disclose their processes and anticipate societal needs proactively (Von Schomberg, 2019). Ethical responsibility is central to RI, assessing innovations not for profit only, but also for their potential societal impacts, such as job displacement or inequality, aiming to align with sustainable development principles and tackle global challenges like climate change (Owen et al., 2013; Von Schomberg, 2013). Especially, it promotes inclusivity and stakeholder engagement, involving end-users, community members, and experts to ensure ethically sound and socially accepted outcomes. User-driven innovation, supported by Von Hippel (2005), significantly enhances product acceptance and user satisfaction, while its absence can lead to misalignments with user needs, increased costs, and potential failures (Kujala, 2003). Sanders and Stappers (2008) advance the shift from traditional participatory design to co-creation in co-design landscapes, where users transition from passive participants to active co-designers, deeply involved as "experts of their experiences." This transformation is essential in Responsible Innovation (RI), which not only addresses functional design but also integrates societal and ethical considerations, emphasizing the crucial role of user inclusion for ethical and socially responsible outcomes as outlined by Stilgoe, Owen, and Macnaghten (2013).

Furthermore, ethical aspects of user involvement, such as data privacy and equity, are vital for fostering sustainable and responsible innovation (Van den Hoven, 2014).

These principles are foundational in creating resonant and accountable solutions, highlighting the importance of user involvement in both the design process and broader RI objectives. User engagement not only anticipates and meets user needs but also ensures that innovations are ethically sound and aligned with societal values, making it crucial for the success and sustainability of innovations.

However, while user inclusion is key to innovation, it is also difficult to implement (*cross reference to Eiken and Oftedal . . .*). As we look to the future, prioritizing user involvement will be key to achieving outcomes that are both successful and beneficial to society. Bounded innovation spaces may allow for a greater focus on user innovation, as they are places where different stakeholders may interact.

Boundary innovation spaces for user involvement: Living lab

Within the innovation literature, there is a growing interest in seeking avenues that engage multiple actors and cultivate relationships with users (Caccamo, 2020). Initially centred within companies (Moultrie et al., 2007), the exploration has expanded to encompass diverse forms of innovation spaces like innovation labs, open labs, fab labs, and living labs (Fritzsche, 2018). Discussions on the design facets of these spaces span multiple disciplines, delving into processes, environmental elements, and strategies for effective collaborations (Capdevila, 2019; Cohendet et al., 2014).

Among these innovation spaces, the living lab has emerged as a notable phenomenon gaining prominence in recent years. Following the establishment of the European Network of Living Labs (ENoLL) in 2006 (Leminen & Westerlund, 2019), European funding has propelled national and regional living lab initiatives aimed at addressing societal and technological challenges in various sector such as health and wellbeing, urbanization, and social development (ENoLL, 2023). Amid its swift expansion across various domains, the term "living lab" has acquired multiple meanings. However, a prevailing perspective among scholars frames it as both an innovation space and a user-centric approach for co-creation, involving stakeholders, particularly users, in real-life settings (Bergvall-Kareborn & Stahlbrost, 2009; Huang & Thomas, 2021). The notion of living lab emphasizes an open space across organizational boundaries for exploring and experimenting with innovation through knowledge co-creation among stakeholders especially users, thus user involvement is a focus here (Leminen, 2013). Jakobsen et al. (2019) posit the living lab concept as a practical perspective for RI to operate within innovation dynamics and respond to specific societal and technological needs. As the discourse on user involvement unfolds, the multifaceted nature of living labs and their emphasis on user inclusion remains integral to effective design and responsible innovation, offering a conduit for understanding and anticipating user needs while fostering collaborative and ethical solutions that align with societal values. Navigating the future of innovation will invariably hinge on prioritizing user involvement ensuring successful, responsible, and beneficial outcome for society.

Method and data collection

We employ a narrative methodology to analyze NSCL as a noteworthy example of RI (Riessman, 2008; Polkinghorne, 1988)) approach allows for a thorough examination of the organisation development and the identification of pivotal factors guiding its progress. In constructing the narrative of NSCL from its inception to the present, we aim to elucidate both the drivers of its growth and the obstacles it encounters. This method sheds light on the contextual backdrop—historical, cultural, and social—in which the case is situated, facilitating an accurate interpretation the nuanced understanding of intricate processes and organizational dynamics inherent in NSCL. Narratives, in this context, not only humanize data but also resonate with readers, rendering the case study accessible and relatable.

Contextual background plays a crucial role in narrative construction (Riessman, 2008; Andrews et al., 2013). The study encompasses a four-year longitudinal investigation of a welfare services lab in Norway. This research methodology has allowed researchers to observe activities spanning an extended period, gather comprehensive data for "thick description," and unfold the dimension of temporality for analysis (Langley & Abdallah, 2015). Researchers have been closely monitoring events from its inception in 2019 as a firm-oriented testing center to its transformation in 2022 into a boundary innovation space with a focus on involving users from the early stages of innovation. Over time, the roles of researchers in these events have gradually shifted from being mere "outsiders" to a blend of co-designers and observers of the unfolding events. This participatory approach (Bergold & Thomas, 2012) has fostered relationship-building and facilitated the collection of deeper insights. Simultaneously, it has imposed higher standards on researchers to ensure the rigor of the study. We employed various data collection methods to gather information from diverse sources and collaborate over clearly defined tasks. From March 2021 to August 2023, four researchers conducted 30 interviews with 27 informants, including living lab staff, users, representatives of public organizations, and private companies (NSCL clients). The narrative analysis involves a detailed examination of interview data, where respondents' perspectives on historical developments, growth stimulants, and barriers are critically analyzed. To ensure the integrity of our narrative, we adhere to rigorous research ethics, prioritizing truthfulness, and the welfare of society. All participants provided informed consent, and their confidentiality was strictly maintained. The quotations included in our publication are verbatim, reflecting the genuine voices of the participants and preserving the authenticity of their contributions to our narrative.

Table 1 shows a summary of the number of interviews conducted. Interviews took place after each NSCL event (Table 2 in the later section elaborates on the events), asking participants about their experiences during the events. Follow-up interviews were conducted with living lab managers to track its development; therefore, some informants were interviewed multiple times to capture evolving perspectives. All interviews were recorded, transcribed. and anonymized. Additional data were collected through observation and archival sources, ensuring the validity and quality through triangulation (Yin, 2003). Researchers discussed and agreed on the protocols and schemes for analysis. Further interview details are available in the appendix.

Table 1: Summary of interviews.

Role of informant	Count of interviews
Living lab staff	8
Companies & organizations	8
Users	14
Total	**30**

Context

The story of NSCL traces back to The Norwegian Smart Care Cluster (NSCC), which was established in 2013 under the national cluster program. NSCC's primary goal is to develop smart care digital solutions by integrating user-patients with municipal hospitals (NSCC, 2023). Originating in Stavanger, NSCC expanded to include Bergen and Grimstad, now encompassing 280 members, including companies, municipalities, and public institutions across Norway and internationally (NSCC, 2023).

NSCC's expansion was significantly supported by the Norwegian Coordination Reform, introduced by the Norwegian Ministry of Health and Care Services in 2011, which fostered collaboration between public healthcare services and private enterprises. This reform coincided with the establishment of the Norwegian Directorate of e-Health in 2019 and the launch of the national e-health strategy for 2017–2022, creating a supportive environment for NSCC's development. Despite these advancements, municipalities encountered challenges in adapting to digitalization, with existing procurement procedures restricting market access for new innovations (Oftedal and Foss, 2019). NSCC was instrumental in transforming institutional assets and championed 'innovative procurement' practices, notably adopted by Stavanger Municipality in 2019 (Innovative anskaffelser, n.d.).

In 2017, NSCC established NSCL to assist companies in testing and verifying projects, focusing on compliance with legal and industry standards. The COVID-19 pandemic in 2020 further amplified the demand for digital health solutions, leading NSCC to conduct various webinars addressing new digital healthcare methods.

Key regional actors, including The Innovation Park Stavanger and incubator iPark, were instrumental in NSCC's formation and the creation of NSCL. NSCC's membership, dominated by small entrepreneurial firms, benefits from the proactive leadership of the cluster administration, facilitating competence building and realization of economic and societal value from innovations (Rypestøl et al., European Planning Studies, 2020). Figure 1 illustrates the timeline of NSCC's development.

NSCC has significantly impacted the regional economic restructuring of the Stavanger region, aiding diversification into the health and digitalization sector. Initiatives like 'Pumps and Pipes' demonstrate the successful recombination of resources

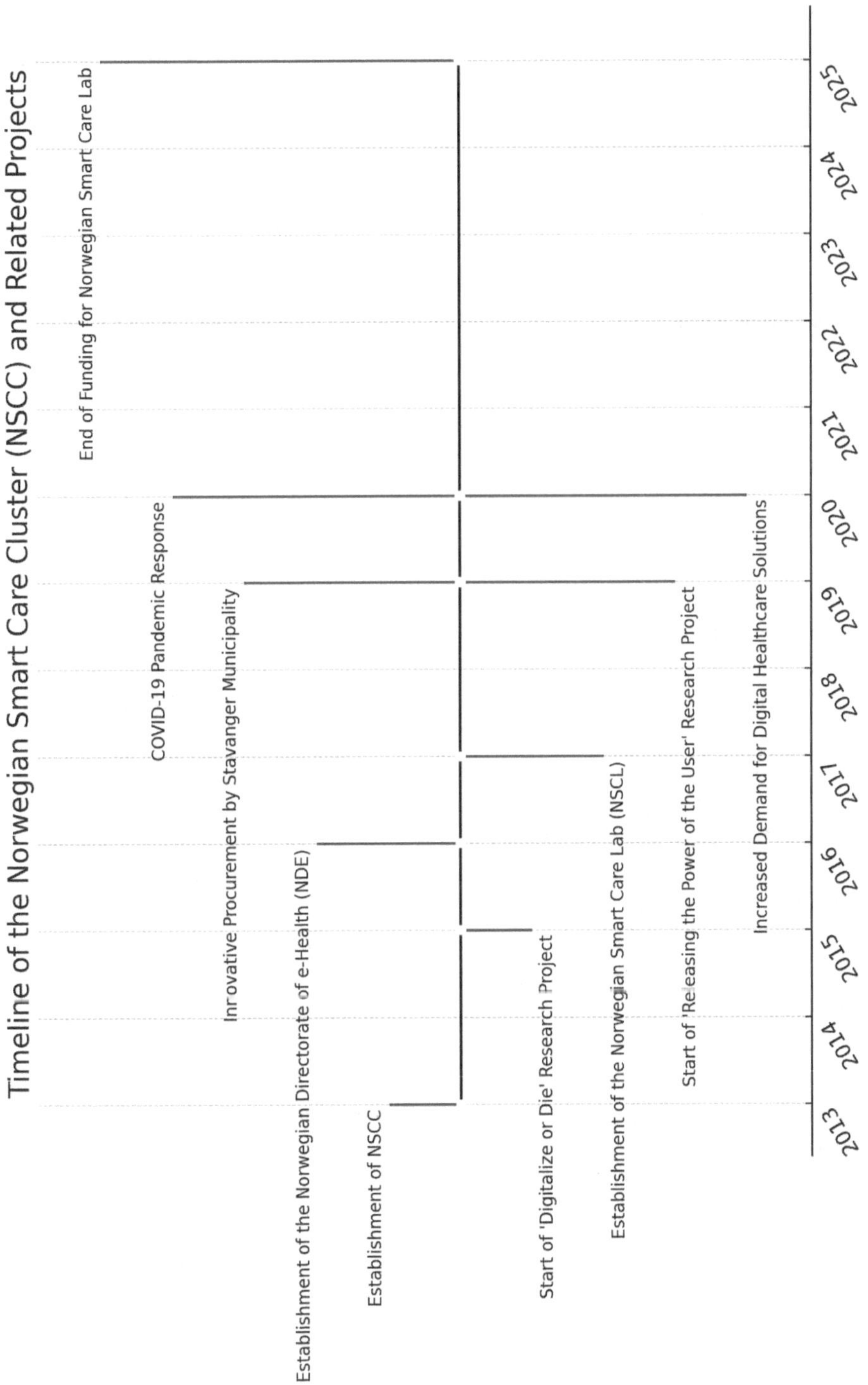

Figure 1: Timeline of NSCC development.

across industries (Lyng & Brun, 2020). Despite the limited economic contribution of NSCC's member companies compared to the dominant oil and gas sector, the cluster's efforts in diversification and path creation are strategically important for the region's future development.

NSCC has actively partnered with UiS in two consecutive research projects since 2016

The first research project, titled "Digitalize or Die: Dynamic Drivers of RRI in Health and Welfare Services" (2016–2019), commonly known as the "Digitalize or Die" project, concentrated on exploring the practical application and interpretation of the RI concept within the healthcare and welfare sector. Led by Professor Tatiana Iakovleva at the University of Stavanger (UiS) Business School, the international project involved NSCC as a key partner over several activities. Researchers at UiS have studied the concept of Responsible Innovation in managing the Lab, focusing on the execution of inclusion, anticipation, and reflection among firms interacting with the Lab. Gradually, the importance of early and continuous stakeholder involvement became a core tenet of the Lab's own approach. Subsequently, the project, "Releasing the Power of Users – Articulating User Interests to Accelerate New Innovative Pathways in the Digital Health and Welfare Sector," known as the Releasing project (2019–2024), came as an extension of the "Digitalize or Die" project. It is also an international research project run by UiS and Western Norway University of Applied Sciences (HVL). Its primary objective was to facilitate broader implementation of inclusive and responsible innovation in welfare technologies. The project application included the establishment of a boundary innovation space/living lab – originally conceptualized as the Shared Innovation Futures Lab and was realized with the work of NSCL. The HelseCampus Stavanger, opened in 2019 in the Innovation Park as hub for research-based health cluster, has since served as the central environment for NSCC and NSCL's user engagement activities with the research team.

The collaboration with academia, mainly through the research team, has been pivotal for NSCL, shaping their understanding and approach to user involvement and responsible innovation. Jointly organizing events like user cafés further underscores the importance of such collaborations in driving innovation and fostering meaningful engagement with users and stakeholders.

> *We have been working with the team since the Digitalized or Die project. Definitely, it has shaped the team's work on the user side. We have learned a lot from being a part of these two projects about users and responsible innovation. Very good project. I think you have done a very good job. We have collaborated well with the team. (R38, NSCL)*

The early development of NSCL

In this section, we delve into the early phase of NSCL's development, covering its establishment, positioning, and several milestone activities for user inclusion with the research team.

From a project to a Lab

In the initial two years following NSCC's establishment, the team dedicated efforts to shaping the concept of NSCL and securing funding from various sources, including the Stavanger municipality and Innovation Norway, a stated-owned body that funds innovation and development programs. By 2017, NSCC finalized the business plan for NSCL and successfully acquired sufficient funding to launch it as a three-year project. NSCL officially opened at the end of 2017 as a test centre for digital healthcare technologies. R38, from NSCL recounted the story of this journey.

> *We were established in 2014 as the Norwegian Smart Care Cluster. We applied for various small amounts of money from Rogaland County. In 2015–2016, we developed the Norwegian Smart Care Lab concept. With that, we interacted with our members. We had, for instance, the Stavanger Municipality and smaller municipalities. We had various sizes of companies and users. We tried to build the concept, especially with the view of companies – what you need to develop faster and better solutions that fit users' needs and the needs of municipalities and hospitals. We did various studies. In 2017, we had a fully formed business plan for the Norwegian Smart Care Lab but did not have the money. That was not built overnight. Then, we were lucky that Stavanger municipality and Innovation Norway had some extra funds. Between those two and some money from the County, we managed to secure the funds for a three-year project. We started formally at the end of 2017 and at the beginning of 2018.*

NSCC appointed their manager, transitioning from concept to action. Initially virtual, NSCL tested e-health solutions at facilities like hospitals and nursing homes. Over two years, NSCL developed work packages aiding solution development, spanning idea verification to implementation. In 2020, NSCL became a commercial identity, managing sites in Stavanger, Bergen, and Agder along the west coast of Norway. NSCL is situated within the same Innovation Park as HelseCampus Stavanger. The proximity has offered opportunities for collaboration and enhancement. Additionally, NSCL has gained broader access through partnerships with Oslo Cancer Cluster and Norway Health Tech, two large networks for healthcare innovation in Norway. NSCL also secured funding from the Releasing project.

NSCL as a living lab

Observing the widespread emergence of living lab or living lab-like initiatives across various countries, particularly in Europe, NSCL formulated a conceptual idea of the living lab during its initial setup stage. NSCL conceptualized the idea of the living lab and included it as part of the broader vision outlined in their application. However, this phase was marked with challenges and uncertainties, including a shortage of both understanding and funding.

> *In the Norwegian Smart Care Cluster application, there was a reference to establishing a living lab. So, when I started to build the cluster, I had to understand "what is a living lab" and "what does it mean?". So basically, we had no funding for this at that time. It was just a line in the application and not really thought through. (R38, NSCL)*

The Releasing project introduced a work package titled "Creating Boundary Innovation Space," aiming to establish a collaborative workspace for stakeholders and potential users to co-create innovative solutions. NSCL played a central role in this initiative. Through collaboration, NSCL further integrated this concept into its operational, emphasizing user input and fostering an open, flexible environment for collaboration.

The research project also introduced NSCL to ENoLL, an international association with over 150 active members in the field of living labs. NSCL managers participated in training with ENoLL, focusing on living lab setup, methodologies, user, and stakeholder involvement. Subsequently, NSCL integrated the acquired knowledge in their daily operation especially when it comes to user inclusion. Furthermore, through the Releasing team, NSCL was introduced to ENoLL members and experts, such as the LiCalab, a well-established living lab from Belgium in the health and care sector, fostering collaboration through physical and virtual activities.

Attempts at user inclusion in collaboration with the research team

The development of user inclusion started with small initiatives and then developed into larger and more strategic efforts. Here we explain three major initiatives done in the period. As detailed in this section, that the living lab concept was actualized through a series of activities co-organized with the research team.

1. Small-scale user café

NSCL has engaged in a collaborative effort with the Releasing project, organizing a series of events aimed at incorporating users, public and private firms, organizations, and various stakeholders into the innovation process. Together, they developed one user involvement method called the User Café. User Café represents an interactive and conversation-driven workshop specifically designed to involve older adults in the early phase of the innovation process. Each session of the User Café revolves around a specific theme, and its format is flexible and customizable. A noteworthy component of the User Café includes small group discussions, contributing to its dynamic and adaptable nature.

NSCL and the Releasing project members co-organized three User Cafés. sessions spanning from December 2020 to October 2021. The initial two sessions were conducted online due to the COVID-19 restrictions, while the final session took place in person in Stavanger. All user participants in these sessions were retirees aged 65 and above. Table 2 presents a summary of the User Café sessions.

Table 2: User Cafés with NSCL.

Theme	Fire Safety at Home	Early signs of dementia	Using digital services
Client	Rogaland Fire Department	Sensio (a Norwegian welfare technology company)	Kakadu (a Norwegian creative technology company)
Date	7 & 14 December 2020	7 April 2021	11 October 2021
No. of sessions	2	1	1
Length	2–2.5 hours each	4 hours	2.5 hours
No. of user participants	13	9	13
Other participants	The Fire Department representatives, NSCL, UiS	Company representatives, NSCL, UiS	Company representatives, municipality representatives, NSCL, UiS
No. of groups for discussion	3	4	3

The first virtual User Café, "Fire Safety at Home", featured a collaboration with the Rogaland Fire Department. Two sessions were held involving older adults to explore their needs, experiences, and suggestions for enhancing the Fire Department's services. The facilitators involved participants through interactive small group discussions and assigned home assignments. A representative from the Fire Department shared insights into their participation in the user café and its outcomes:

> *We haven't had the same process involving the participants or older people in the innovation. So, that was new to us, or for me [. . .]. It was beneficial to get new insights to reach the population with fire safety information. Also, users had a good experience learning something new and getting*

tips about their safety. Both of us facilitating and the people participating had a good learning from the Café. (R2, Representative from The Fire Department)

Kakadu, a Norwegian start-up, had a physical User Café with NSCL to gather insights into older adults' opinions on digital services and assess the potential of a portal designed to teach them using digital services. Kakadu found it to be a valuable learning experience:

We have been talking to people since we started. But we have never done this scale by gathering people like the User Café did. [. . .] That is also the value we see of doing this on a greater scale and with a structure. (R21, Company representative from Kakadu)

Participants in the session provided positive feedback, expressing interest in the topic, and noting that they gained new insights from the events and from their interactions with fellow participants. They believed that their contribution could help them and those who need better solutions. One common thread in their feedback was the value the appreciation for the small-group discussion format. Additionally, some pointed out that this method fostered a relaxed atmosphere and promoted equal participation among all attendees.

The group worked fine. We were happy to be a few. It was good to get ideas from others. It went smoothly, and it seemed like most people had been involved in something like this before. People were open and confident in themselves during debates and things like that. (R5, User participant 1 from the Fire Department session)

I am always willing to learn and curious . . . Everyone was equally active. (R25, User participant 3 from the Kakadu session)

Although NSCL initially envisioned the User Café as a separate paid service for their members, they encountered difficulties selling it. Despite willingness from companies to participate, they are hesitant to invest in activities like the User Café primarily due to cost considerations. There is a notable discrepancy in how companies perceive the value of early-stage user involvement, with some prioritizing tangible outcomes over such initiatives. Therefore, companies may be more inclined to engage in similar activities if they are offered for free or if they address specific new areas of interest. Instead, this user Café model might be better suited for municipal approaches.

We can do it if the company is willing to pay for it but it's hard. They were unwilling to pay for that kind of approach, even though they ran a company with a lot of money. They do not want to have a User Café. They don't see the need for that kind of service or at least to pay for it. They could be part of it for free. Maybe, it's more like if they're planning to do a new area, for instance, then they set up a focus group and have the questions for that specific idea and then take the inputs to the developing process. Maybe the User Café is better for the municipal approach because they need to sort out different problems or topics. (R4, NSCL)

2. Scaling it up: Living the whole life at home "Bolig for livet"

On 24th May 2022, a modestly sized exhibition themed "Housing for life" ("Bolig for livet" in Norwegian) was held at HelseCampus Stavanger, co-organized by UiS, NSCL, and Nordic Edge Innoasis. The aim was to create inclusivity among stakeholders like innovators, architects, public sectors, users, and researchers, focusing on addressing health challenges and envisioning future living spaces. The event, open to the public, allowed companies, public sectors, and universities to showcase their projects. Attendees participated in idea exchange through presentations and discussions. UiS student volunteers manned company stands, collecting information from visitors testing technologies. Nine companies consented to the data collection. NSCC member companies did not pay for the stand. While they appreciated the event's organization, they desired business-related outcomes and events with immediate values.

> *If we had to travel to an event like this, we would have to be engaged for more than one hour. There would have to be some if there could be more business-related outcomes, more near term. That would likely motivate us to go there. There could be potential customers from the municipalities or hospitals that we could meet and talk to. That would be interesting. (R35, Company representative)*

NSCL reflected on this event by comparing the cost and outcome, expressing uncertainty about running the initiative in its current form, and the hesitation to take the lead in a national-scale implementation.

> *We need to measure everything, including the cost and value of things. I am not sure if we can run it like this. We are meeting a company that wants to do it nationally. I don't think we will be the one putting "Bolig for Livet" in Norway. But maybe we can play in and recruit, but I don't think we will take the lead. (R38, NSCL)*

While engaging users appears to be a relatively uncomplicated task for NSCL, the sustainable execution of activities presents a significant challenge. This challenge is particularly evident in the reluctance of companies, especially startups, to participate in or fund activities such as the User Café during the early stages of innovation. Their hesitancy often stems from a preference for direct outcomes, such as product testing and sales volume, significantly influencing their willingness to participate and invest in such initiatives.

3. A strategic approach to user involvement: User panel

The third initiative between NSCL and the Releasing project is the establishment of a user panel. There was a shift from the initial company-driven approach towards incorporating user perspectives into the innovation process. As a commitment to a sustained and growing user engagement strategy, NSCL started to build its user panel in 2021.

> *In the earlier phase, we focused on the companies getting our services up. We recruited users more on that, but now we are continuously building the user panel in the Lab. We have students on that . . . That is why we also engage users more closely in this. So, it is driven from companies to users, but it is all on the same matter – we want to create better solutions that fit the users. The users can be end users, but also municipalities and hospitals. Many companies don't have the technologies yet but plans and the vision. We guide them with user involvement in the right development direction, from idea to prototyping to testing the finished products. (R38, NSCL)*

An ongoing effort exists to build and expand the user panel. However, the sustainability of such a panel can be challenging due to associated costs and the need to engage and recruit participants continually. Maintaining this user panel incurs significant costs, requiring resources for running various activities, and identifying suitable users is a persistent challenge.

> *We have a small group in the user panel, mainly elderly around 80. We have some experience running this group now. It is also a discussion on how to build up a sustainable panel. For those who are part of the panel, we have an idea of meeting with them and having them as part of the processes. But we need to recruit others. If you see the focus areas for health, they are not only about older adults but could be all kinds of users. In each case, we need to work with the municipality and the hospital. So, we have a connection with the hospital . . . But it's also up to each company if they need a particular group of patients or users. And it's very costly to have all the users in a panel, so we do recruitment for the companies in each case. We set up a User Cafe or a stakeholder panel. We see that it's challenging. (R4, NSCL)*

The initiatives reflect a shift towards inclusivity with users and challenges in convincing companies of its value. The user panel is a pivotal element in NSCL's innovation process, although challenges persist in financial sustainability for NSCL. To ensure the panel's viability, NSCL must explore strategies for its continuity. A potential solution involves leveraging digital tools such as surveys and social media platforms to broaden outreach to users at a more cost-effective rate.

Strategic moves into the future

NSCC has gone through a rapid development and several strategic decisions has been made along the way. Here we are showcasing some major steps in the development and points to a possible future. An alternative approach involves leveraging strategic alliance networks, such as the Oslo Cancer Cluster, to secure access to a more extensive user base. NSCL also collaborates with SESAM, a research group founded in 2010 and under the ownership of the Western Norway Regional Health Authority. Within SESAM, there is a user group known as WiseAge, comprising citizens aged 65 and above. WiseAge actively promotes and facilitates collaborative activities involving users, healthcare professionals, social actors, and researchers in the research and development of solutions for the aging society. NSCL aims to leverage the user access provided by this collaboration.

A new business model

As the base funding is running out in two and half years, NSCL has worked out a strategic plan for its financial sustainability, including a shift towards revenue generation through service sales, setting turnover goals for growth, and exploration of alternative financing models to ensure continued operation. NSCL partners with the Technology Communication Foundation (Stiftelsen Teknologiformidling in Norwegian), a nonprofit foundation that supports small and medium businesses.

> *We get base funding from the cluster project. But we need to build a business model where we sell services like other companies. The cluster funding will disappear. We know that. In two years, there will be zero. We need to have a model that can sustain itself. We are on the right path to achieving that. We need to have some alternative financing model to continue doing this . . . I am looking at new sources of income, and the Lab is a very important one that we want to keep running. (R38, NSCL)*

National partners and HealthCatalyst

In an interview in August 2023, the NSCL manager unveiled their strategic vision: transforming into a comprehensive testing hub. The aim is to become a one-stop shop by establishing collaborations with various testing entities in Norway and offering a multitude of services to members through these partnerships. The strategy emphasizes the importance of leveraging external competencies, such as partnering with companies and organizations possessing diverse competencies to offer a wide range of services in the development of digital health technologies.

> *We do not have all the competencies, so we need to connect with partners with special competencies. It could be for now. Many companies have unique competencies needed for doing some tests. We will revitalize this kind of collaboration because we need that kind of competence to grow and serve companies with different test opportunities. [. . .] We are a one-stop shop. Together with partners, we can deliver all kinds of testing for the companies that they need for taking the product from idea to implementation. (R4, NSCL)*

In 2022, Oslo Cancer Cluster, Norwegian Health Tech, and NSCC jointly established HealthCatalyst to build a national testing infrastructure and improve the healthcare value chain. NSCL outlined its strategy, including consolidated testing activities, a specialized web platform, team collaboration, expert partnerships, and engagement in government. Figure 2 shows the evolution and strategic positioning of NSCL.

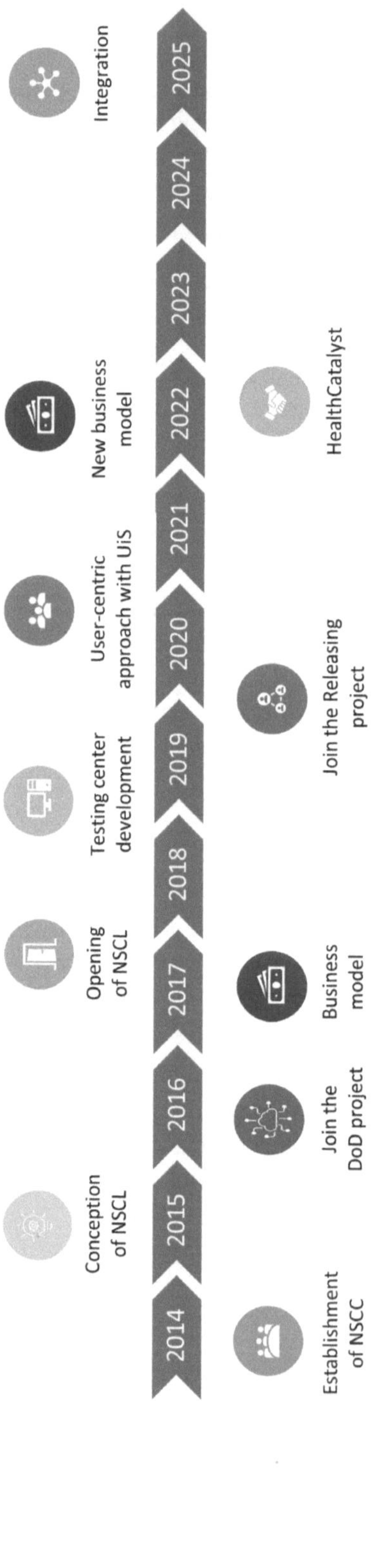

Figure 2: Evolution and strategic positioning of NSCL.

We will merge everything we do on tests into HealthCatalyst. We're trying to find a working method among the teams. We have now developed a new web page for the HealthCatalyst. For companies, they can ask for testing through this website. We have meetings every second week among the teams . . . We need to connect to one of the technical partners that we already mentioned. In that case, we will offer a combined test for the companies. Afterward, we need to report a document, and there is also discussion on whether HealthCatalyst also be responsible for some verifications on behalf of the government to align with the national requirements. (R4, NSCL)

Discussion and conclusion

This chapter shows the rapid development of a government-funded cluster organisation that aims to create an ecosystem among companies and organizations. The cluster's growth underscores the necessity of its efforts. We followed NSCL's shift from a company-centric to a more inclusive and collaborative model, actively engaging users, including citizens, municipalities, and hospitals. NSCL's commitment to guiding companies while emphasizing user involvement throughout the innovation journey is evident.

This analysis delves into a few areas during the dynamic evolution in the NSCL's approach. The evolution signifies a significant institutional change, addressing challenges municipalities face in adapting to digitalization. NSCL/NSCC played a pivotal role in modifying institutional assets and advocating for innovative procurement practices, leading to its establishment. The focus on competence building contributed to the realization of economic and societal value from innovations. Collaboration between public healthcare services and private companies, driven by the Norwegian Coordination Reform, has been instrumental in integrating the healthcare sector, highlighting the significance of collaboration in driving innovation.

In addition to the inclusion activities, NSCL and researchers acknowledge the importance of reflexivity in nurturing inclusive and ethical innovation practices. They engage in reflexive practices after each event, critically assessing and refining the process based on valuable insights gathered. NSCL emphasizes user involvement, fostering user-centric solutions. Despite positive feedback, challenges remain, including financial considerations and stakeholder perceptions. Initiatives like the User Café and Bolig for Livet offer an interactive platform for involving older adults in innovation, fostering the development of user-centric solutions. User participants gave positive feedback. However, it is essential to navigate the complexities of user involvement, including financial considerations and stakeholder perceptions. These initiatives, supported by research projects or government funding, face challenges as funding runs out, such as sustaining user panels and securing ongoing support. Difficulties also come from companies' hesitancy, especially startups, to participate in or fund initiatives. Should the municipality or other organizations be responsible for funding the events instead? NSCL is exploring alternative methods such as digital tools and partnerships, to overcome these challenges.

NSCL faces the need to establish a sustainable business model beyond cluster funding, involving selling services to member companies and seeking alternative funding avenues. Strategic partnerships with other testing bodies aim to diversify service portfolios. Initiatives like HealthCatalyst stress the significance of such partnerships in fostering innovation and expanding the healthcare value chain. However, there is a concern about potentially losing touch with users as direct interaction decreases and ensuring the continued ability to adequately articulate user needs.

The evolution of NSCL underscores its crucial role in driving innovation and societal progress. Key areas of focus include effecting institutional change, promoting collaboration between public healthcare services and private companies, and fostering academic partnerships to shape user involvement and responsible innovation. Despite challenges, NSCL remains committed to catalyzing positive change in the healthcare sector and beyond.

Appendix. Overview of the data collection

S/N	Informant Code	Informant's affiliation	Date	Type of data collection	Duration	Event/theme
1	R1	Public organization	17-Mar-21	Video interview	30mins	User Cafe – fire safety
2	R2	Public organization	17-Mar-21	Video interview	30mins	User Cafe – fire safety
3	R3	Public organization	02-Apr-21	Video interview	30mins	User Cafe – fire safety
4	R4	Living lab	25-Mar-21	Video interview	30mins	User Cafe – fire safety
5	R5	Living lab	21-Mar-21	Video interview	30mins	User Cafe – fire safety
6	R6	User	21-Mar-21	Phone interview	30mins	User Cafe – fire safety
7	R7	User	21-Mar-21	Phone interview	30mins	User Cafe – fire safety
8	R8	User	21-Mar-21	Phone interview	30mins	User Cafe – fire safety
9	R9	User	21-Mar-21	Phone interview	30mins	User Cafe – fire safety

(continued)

S/N	Informant Code	Informant's affiliation	Date	Type of data collection	Duration	Event/theme
10	R10	User	21-Mar-21	Phone interview	30mins	User Cafe – fire safety
11	R11	User	21-Mar-21	Phone interview	30mins	User Cafe – fire safety
12	R12	User	21-Mar-21	Phone interview	30mins	User Cafe – fire safety
13	R13	User	21-Mar-21	Phone interview	30mins	User Cafe – fire safety
14	R14	User	21-Mar-21	Phone interview	30mins	User Cafe – fire safety
15	R15	User	21-Mar-21	Phone interview	30mins	User Cafe – fire safety
16	R16	User	21-Mar-21	Phone interview	30mins	User Cafe – fire safety
17	R17	User	21-Mar-21	Phone interview	30mins	User Cafe – fire safety
18	R18	User	21-Mar-21	Phone interview	30mins	User Cafe – fire safety
19	R19	Private company	25-Aug-21	Phone interview	30mins	User Cafe – early signs of dementia
20	R5	Living lab	24-Aug-21	Video interview	30mins	User Cafe – early signs of dementia
21	R21	Private company	10-Nov-21	Video interview	30mins	User Cafe – digital service for elders
22	R4	Living lab	28-Oct-21	Video interview	30mins	User Cafe – digital service for elders
23	R23	Living lab	28-Oct-21	Video interview	30mins	User Cafe – digital service for elders
24	R24	Living lab	05-Nov-21	Video interview	30mins	User Cafe – digital service for elders
25	R25	User	05-Nov-21	Phone interview	30mins	User Cafe – digital service for elders
26	R35	Private company	20-Jun-22	Video interview	30mins	Bolig for livet

(continued)

S/N	Informant Code	Informant's affiliation	Date	Type of data collection	Duration	Event/theme
27	R36	Private company	29-Aug-22	Video interview	30mins	Bolig for livet
28	R37	Private company	31-Aug-22	Video interview	30mins	Bolig for livet
29	R38	Living lab	12-Jul-22	Face-to-Face interview	60mins	Follow-up interview: NSCL development
30	R4	Living lab	25-Aug-23	Video interview	60mins	Follow-up interview: NSCL development

References

Andrews, M., Squire, C., & Tamboukou, M. (2013). Doing narrative research. Sage.

Bergold, J., & Thomas, S. (2012). Participatory research methods: A methodological approach in motion. Historical Social Research/Historische Sozialforschung, 191–222.

Bergvall-Kareborn, B., & Stahlbrost, A. (2009). Living Lab: an open and citizen-centric approach for innovation. International Journal of Innovation and Regional Development, 1(4), 356–370. https://doi.org/http://doi.org/10.1504/IJIRD.2009.022727

Caccamo, M. (2020). Leveraging innovation spaces to foster collaborative innovation. Creativity and Innovation Management, 29(1), 178–191.

Capdevila, I. (2019). Motivating participation in collaborative spaces. Journal of Business Strategy, 40(2), 14–21.

Cohendet, P., Grandadam, D., Simon, L., & Capdevila, I. (2014). Epistemic communities, localization and the dynamics of knowledge creation. Journal of economic geography, 14(5), 929–954.

Direktoratet for e-helse. 2019. Årsrapport 2019: Direktoratet for e-helse. https://ehelse.no/om-oss/om-direktoratet-for-e-helse

ENoLL. (2023). The European Network of Living Labs (ENoLL). https://enoll.org

ENTELIS+ Consortium. (2020). Digital inclusion: A white paper. Retrieved from https://www.entelis.net/wp-content/uploads/2020/12/publications_digital_inclusion-a_white_paper_final-1.pdf

European Commission. (2007). Together for health: A strategic approach for the EU 2008–2013. Retrieved from https://ec.europa.eu/health/ph_overview/Documents/strategy_wp_en.pdf

European Commission. (2021). Measuring access to healthcare in the EU. Retrieved from https://health.ec.europa.eu/system/files/2021-10/measuring_access-to-healthcare_en_0.pdf

European Commission, Directorate-General for Research and Innovation. (2011). Towards responsible research and innovation in the information and communication technologies and security technologies fields (R. Schomberg, Ed.). Publications Office. https://data.europa.eu/doi/10.2777/58723

Fritzsche, A. (2018). Corporate foresight in open laboratories – a translational approach. Technology Analysis and Strategic Management, 30, 1–12. https://doi.org/10.1080/09537325.2017.1380180

Huang, J. H., & Thomas, E. (2021). A Review of Living Lab Research and Methods for User Involvement. Technology Innovation Management Review, 11(9/10). timreview.ca/article/1467

Iakovleva, T., Oftedal, E., & Bessant, J. (2021). Changing role of users—Innovating responsibly in digital health. Sustainability, 13(4), 1616. https://doi.org/10.3390/su13041616
Innovative anskaffelser. n.d. Aktivisering og egenmestring. Retrieved from https://innovativeanskaffelser.no/nye-losninger-i-heldognsomsorgen/
Jakobsen, S.-E., Fløysand, A., & Overton, J. (2019). Expanding the field of Responsible Research and Innovation (RRI) – from responsible research to responsible innovation. European Planning Studies, 27(12), 2329–2343. https://doi.org/10.1080/09654313.2019.1667617
Journal of Responsible Innovation. (2021). Taylor & Francis.
Kujala, S. (2003). User involvement: a review of the benefits and challenges. Behaviour & information technology, 22(1), 1–16.
Langley, A., & Abdallah, C. (2015). Templates and turns in qualitative studies of strategy and management. In Research methods for strategic management (pp. 155–184). Routledge.
Leminen, S. (2013). Coordination and Participation in Living Lab Networks. Technology Innovation Management Review, 3(11). https://doi.org/http://doi.org/10.22215/timreview/740
Leminen, S., & Westerlund, M. (2019). Living labs: From scattered initiatives to a global movement. Creativity and Innovation Management, 28(9). https://doi.org/http://doi.org/10.1111/caim.12310
Lyng, H. B., & Brun, E. C. (2020). Making your knowledge mine: the integration of external knowledge in cross-industry innovation. International Journal of Innovation Management, 24(05), 2050050.
Ministry of Health and Care Services. 2011. Innovation into the Care Services. NOU 2011:11,Chapters 1, 2, and 3. Retrieved from https://www.regjeringen.no/contentassets/5fd24706b4474177be c0938582e3964a/en-gb/pdfs/nou201120110011000en_pdfs.pdf
Moultrie, J., Nilsson, M., Dissel, M., Haner, U.-E., Janssen, S., & van der Lugt, R. (2007). Innovation Spaces: Towards a Framework for Understanding the Role of the Physical Environment in Innovation. Creativity and Innovation Management, 16, 53–65. https://doi.org/10.1111/j.1467-8691.2007.00419.x
Norman, D. A. (2013). The design of everyday things: Revised and expanded edition. Basic Books.
NSCC. (2023). Who is the Norwegian Smart Care Cluster? Retrieved 15 July 2020 from https://www.smartcarecluster.no/om-nscc
OECD. (2014). All on board: Making inclusive growth happen. Retrieved from https://www.oecd.org/inclusive-growth/All-on-Board-Making-Inclusive-Growth-Happen.pdf
Oftedal, E. M., Iakovleva, T., & Bessant, J. (2019). Challenges in healthcare – the changing role of patients. In T. Iakovleva, E. Oftedal, & J. Bessant (Eds.), Responsible Innovation in Digital Health: Empowering the Patient (pp. 23–41). Edward Elgar Publishing Limited.
Owen, R., Heintz, M., & Bessant, J. R. (2013). Responsible Innovation: Managing the Responsible Emergence of Science and Innovation in Society. John Wiley & Sons, Incorporated. http://ebookcentral.proquest.com/lib/uisbib/detail.action?docID=1166329
Polkinghorne, D. E. (1988). Narrative knowing and the human sciences. Suny Press.
Riessman, C. K. (2008). Narrative methods for the human sciences. Sage.
Rogers, E. (2003). Diffusion of innovations (5th ed.). New York: Free Press.
Rypestøl, J. O., Isaksen, A., Eriksen, E. L., Iakovleva, T., Sjøtun, S. G., & Njøs, R. (2021). Cluster development and regional industrial restructuring: agency and asset modification. European Planning Studies, 29(12), 2320–2339.
Sanders, E. B.-N., & Stappers, P. J. (2008). Co-creation and the new landscapes of design. Co-design, 4(1), 5–18. https://doi.org/https://doi.org/10.1080/15710880701875068
Scholten, V. E., & Blok, V. (2015). Foreword: Responsible innovation in the private sector. Journal on Chain and Network Science, 15(2), 101–105. https://doi.org/10.3920/JCNS2015.x006
Stilgoe, J., Owen, R., & Macnaghten, P. (2013). Developing a framework for responsible innovation. Research Policy, 42(9), 1568–1580. https://doi.org/https://doi.org/10.1016/j.respol.2013.05.008
United Nations Development Programme. (2020). Strategies for supporting inclusive innovation. [URL not available]

Van den Hoven, J. (2014). Responsible innovation: A new look at technology and ethics. In Responsible innovation 1: innovative solutions for global issues (pp. 3–13). Springer.

van Huijstee, M., & Glasbergen, P. (2010). NGOs moving business: An analysis of contrasting strategies. Business & Society, 49, 591–618. https://doi.org/10.1177/0007650310365516

Van Tatenhove, J. P., & Goverde, H. J. (2002). Strategies in environmental policy: A Historical institutional perspective. In Greening Society: The Paradigm Shift in Dutch Environmental Politics (pp. 47–63). Springer.

Von Hippel, E. (2005). The democratization of innovation. Cambridge, MA: MIT Press.

Von Schomberg, R. (2013). A vision of responsible research and innovation. Responsible innovation: managing the responsible emergence of science and innovation in society, 51–74.

Von Schomberg, R. (2019). Why responsible innovation. International handbook on responsible innovation: a global resource, 12–32.

World Economic Forum. (2022, June 29). A blueprint for equity and inclusion in artificial intelligence. [Publisher not specified]

World Economic Forum & McKinsey & Company. (2022). Resilience for sustainable inclusive growth. [Publisher not specified]

Yin, R. K. (2003). *Case Study Research: Design and Methods* (3rd ed., Vol. 5). SAGE.

Catharina M. van Leersum, Zohrah Malik, Johan van der Zwart, Kornelia Konrad

The creation of a community to engage in innovation processes and citizen science

Abstract: The use of scientific principles and methods by non-professional scientists, commonly referred to as citizen science, may be a promising way to improve public participation in research as well as public health. In contrast to forms of user involvement that are concentrated at particular moments of time, citizen science often requires a collaboration between a group of citizens and professional researchers over an extended period of time, and accordingly, the formation of a community. In a set of citizen science projects on different health-related topics (diabetes, dementia, living independently in older age, loneliness) that were conducted as part of the Dutch TOPFIT Citizenlab we found that this process of community-building required a set of recurring elements: 1) recognizing and acknowledging each other's capacities, 2) acknowledging different goals, 3) building a relationship of trust, and 4) creating a learning environment. This chapter explores how these four processes played out throughout the different cases, and how they were perceived by the co-researchers.

Background

The number of older adults living independently at home is expanding. One way to facilitate this is to provide more or new forms of technological assistance. Thus, lots of research into the design, development, implementation, and evaluation of new ambient assisted living technologies to improve the living circumstances of the ageing

Acknowledgements: The authors would like to thank all co-researchers for collaborating with us in every research step, and providing valuable insight. The authors also thank all colleagues of TOPFIT Citizenlab for their regular support and collaboration. This study was powered by the Twente Regional Deal and received financial support from the Central Government's Regional Budget, the Province of Overijssel, the Region of Twente, and the Twente Board. The funders had no role in study design, data collection and analysis, the decision to publish, or preparation of the manuscript.

Catharina M. van Leersum, Department of Technology, Policy, and Society, Faculty of Behavioural, Management, and Social Sciences, University of Twente, Enschede, the Netherlands; Faculty of Humanities, Open Universiteit, Heerlen, the Netherlands
Zohrah Malik, Technology, Health, and Care Research Group, Saxion University of Applied Science, Enschede, the Netherlands
Johan van der Zwart, Kornelia Konrad, Department of Technology, Policy, and Society, Faculty of Behavioural, Management, and Social Sciences, University of Twente, Enschede, the Netherlands

https://doi.org/10.1515/9783111241036-005

population has been conducted. Most technologies are developed to provide health, care or well-being solutions, but as Krick et al. [2019] show, implementation of these technologies remains a challenge due to a lack of knowledge among researchers and developers about the care environment or users. Citizen science could contribute to overcome this challenge.

Citizen science, or the use of scientific principles and methods by non-professional scientists, comprises a range of participatory approaches, and might be a powerful method to improve public participation [Wiggins and Wilbanks 2019]. In contrast to forms of user involvement that are concentrated at particular moments of time, citizen science often requires a collaboration between a group of citizens and professional researchers over an extended period of time. Citizen science is a flexible concept that could be defined in different ways and applied in diverse disciplines [Robinson et al. 2018; Eitzel et al. 2017]. A common aspect in citizen science is the active involvement and collaboration between researchers and citizens in the production of knowledge [Remmers et al. 2023]. However, this is not the only aspect in citizen science. Robinson et al. [2018] have described ten principles of citizen science (Table 1).

Table 1: Ten principles of citizen science [Robinson et al. 2018].

Principles of citizen science [Robinson et al. 2018]
1. Citizen science projects actively involve citizens in scientific endeavour that generates new knowledge or understanding. Citizens may act as contributors, collaborators or as project leaders and have a meaningful role in the project.
2. Citizen science projects have a genuine science outcome.
3. Both the professional scientists and the co-researchers benefit from taking part.
4. Co-researchers may, if they wish, participate in multiple stages of the scientific process. This may include developing the research question, designing the method, gathering and analysing data, and communicating the results.
5. Co-researchers receive feedback from the project.
6. Citizen science is considered a research approach like any other, with limitations and biases that should be considered and controlled for.
7. Citizen science project data and metadata are made publicly available and where possible, results are published in an open-access format.
8. Co-researchers are acknowledged in project results and publications.
9. Citizen science programmes are evaluated for their scientific output, data quality, participant experience and wider societal or policy impact.
10. The leaders of citizen science projects take into consideration legal and ethical issues surrounding copyright, intellectual property, data-sharing agreements, confidentiality, attribution and the environmental impact of any activities.

The use of citizen science principles is promising to improve implementation of technologies in health, care or well-being as a way to collaborate with the actual users as experts on their own needs and life conditions. Although citizen science in the healthcare domain is a relatively new and rare phenomenon, it is already an established approach in research fields such as ecology, conservation, and biology [Den Broeder et al. 2018; Kullenberg and Kasperowski 2016]. The inclusion of citizens appears particularly valuable when the expertise of a specific population of citizens is needed to understand a problem and design adequate solutions [Danielsen et al. 2018]. However, citizen science projects also deal with challenges with regard to the selection of participating citizens, the needed and available competences of citizens, the credibility of knowledge gathered by or with citizens, and the collaboration practices in a community of citizens and researchers [Den Broeder et al. 2018; Wright et al. 2005].

The collaboration between researchers and non-professional scientists, also called co-researchers, is crucial in citizen science. In order to start a collaboration, interested persons or organizations will have to be reached and willing to participate in a project and become part of a research community. In healthcare settings, interested groups could include citizens, such as residents of a neighbourhood, patients, and healthcare professionals, such as doctors, nurses or community workers. The relationship between all the different stakeholders is central in the collaboration. Therefore, we aim to understand how to create a community and an environment in which researchers and co-researchers can actively engage and collaborate as part of citizen science research projects.

The communities as part of citizen science can be compared to communities of practice. Communities of practice can refer to practices in which people work alongside each other, share a common interest, and have a common task [Barab and Duffy 2012]. As Wenger [2011] described them: "Communities of practice are groups of people who share a concern or a passion for something they do and learn how to do it better as they interact regularly." People could live in a particular area, neighbourhood, or share a common interest due to deteriorating health or the need for a particular type of care. These practices in which they meet could take a form of research and in that direction relate to citizen science. Within communities of practice, the co-researchers engage in joint activities and discussions, help each other, and share information [Wenger 2011]. However, how to create and sustain such communities of practice is not evident and most research includes one-time participatory activities, and citizens are not involved for a longer period or become part of a research community. In this chapter, we therefore ask what is needed to create these communities, appeal to someone's motivation, and ensure long-term commitment?

TOPFIT Citizenlab is a research and innovation programme in the Netherlands that ran from 2020–2022 with the core goal to increase citizen involvement in researching, testing, modifying, and implementing technological innovations for health. By drawing on the experience gained in different research projects that were performed as part of Citizenlab, we show and reflect on a multiplicity of community building activities, their common aspects, and the lessons we have learned. In particular, four recurring aspects stood out that were needed in all community building activities to be successful: 1) recognizing and acknowledging each other's capacities, 2) acknowledging different goals, 3) building a relationship of trust, and 4) creating a learning environment. In the remainder of the chapter, we start with a description of TOPFIT Citizenlab, followed by a discussion of each of the four common aspects, illustrated with examples of the Citizenlab research activities.

TOPFIT Citizenlab

The research and innovation programme TOPFIT Citizenlab has been enabled by a governmental regional support programme and focused on the Twente region, located in the East of the Netherlands. Citizenlab started from the widely shared assumption that the availability and affordability of healthcare will become increasingly challenging in the future and, thus, new ways to prevent, replace, and relocate healthcare are needed. Furthermore, citizens are likely to play an increasing role in the process of improving local and personal health, in line with current trends of self-management and self-reliance. The programme aimed to join forces with citizens, healthcare professionals, and companies to develop and implement technological innovations for health and welfare [https://www.topfitcitizenlab.nl/]. Citizen science was chosen as an overarching approach for increasing citizen involvement in research and innovation processes.

In order to work on citizen science methodologies and develop solutions for and by citizens, 12 researchers affiliated to a university and a university of applied sciences formed the core team of TOPFIT Citizenlab. Besides the universities, many partners from the healthcare sector, industry, technology development, and municipalities were part of the project consortium. These researchers and partners collaborated with citizens who represented a specific social group, such as people with diabetes mellitus type 2, people with rheumatoid arthritis, informal caregivers, older adults with a migration background, or older adults living in a specific neighbourhood. Overall 12 studies were conducted, which took the situation of a particular social group as a starting point, for example considering a particular health issue, working environment, neighbourhood, or users of a particular health application.

Researchers, partners and citizens collaborated in various ways in the programme. We used different qualitative research methods, such as interviews and focus groups, but also organised digital and physical workshops, seminars, discussion platforms, and co-creation sessions. Besides these activities, citizens were asked to test and use technologies, collect and analyse data, lead focus groups, present their experiences and the findings, and write reports or summaries of findings. In the following section we discuss different cases from the Citizenlab research activities and how aspects of community building featured in those activities.

Common aspects of community building

Throughout the projects we encountered four recurring and interrelated aspects that proofed crucial for enabling and sustaining community-building among citizens, professional researchers and further partners: the recognition of each other's capabilities, the need to acknowledge different goals, a relationship of trust, and the creation of a learning environment. These four common aspects resonate strongly with the concept of communities of practice when we consider the practice of citizen science. Communities of practice recognise the importance of mutual interactions between novices and experts and focus on learning as a social system [Wenger 1998; Wenger 2011]. The four common aspects can assist in improving the interaction as well as assisting co-researchers in the creation of their professional identity within the community [Li et al. 2009]. Especially the aspect of creating an informal and mutual learning environment as part of communities of practice has received attention in healthcare [Li et al. 2009; Wenger 2011]. In healthcare, the communities of practice can guide developments and emphasize the need to have mentoring and experiential learning as part of a health or illness process [Cruess et al. 2018]. However, there is a lack of structure and operational definitions of community of practice to use in research which could support learning, sharing knowledge or building a relationship. The descriptions of the four common aspects in the following part of this section as well as the observations and cases of TOPFIT Citizenlab can provide a starting point to develop such a structure and increase effectiveness of communities of practice.

Textbox 1: Recognize each other's capabilities

Case: What are your strengths and preferences as co-researcher?

To investigate the perceptions of patients with type 2 diabetes before and after the use of mobile health apps for diabetes control and self-management, we performed a citizen science project in collaboration with this group of patients. Twenty-five patients were recruited to start using mobile health apps, and they all became our co-researchers. At the start of the project, all co-researchers performed a short exercise called flower association [Higgins and Reeves 2006]. They received a picture of a flower with empty leaves (Figure 1). They were asked to share their motivations to participate in the study regarding their role as co-researchers, and write them down on the leaves of the flower [Bults et al. 2023]. After this exercise the flower associations were discussed. In these discussions the co-researchers got the opportunity to share their preference whether they wanted to contribute as a co-researcher and if so, how they envisioned their contribution. The researchers had the opportunity to explore on the strengths of the co-researchers and afterwards determine together the most suitable ways of collaborating in the project.

Figure 1: An empty flower as part of the flower association exercise. The co-researchers were asked to think about their role within a project.

Because of the history and current forms of research, interested co-researchers often assume that the professional researcher is in charge. However, the professional researchers in the Citizenlab projects wanted to fully collaborate with co-researchers without taking the lead, or give the co-researchers a leading role. This was sometimes difficult for the co-researchers, who expected a structured situation. *"In the beginning I felt lost, we talked a lot about possible directions for research. I assumed that she [referring to the researcher] had decided this beforehand, but now we discussed about it and came up with research ideas together."* This kind of research structure was new for all involved and asked for consideration of each other's capabilities.

Both professional researchers and co-researchers have relevant knowledge and capabilities with regard to research, technology, and health. Often, the co- researchers are experts by experience. They have knowledge and experience of the context in which the research takes place, for example because of living with a chronic condition or living in a certain environment. Professional researchers have knowledge and capabilities that are important for executing the research, and in addition they have theoretical knowledge about technology and health. For the co-researchers in Citizenlab, it was motivating to experience that someone takes their experiences seriously. One patient reflected on this aspect: *"After the meeting we got a summary and I noticed that my concern about the insurance was included. During the follow-up meeting we continued and thought about research aims to tackle the problems."* With the different projects in Citizenlab, we always tried to follow up on expressed concerns or problems, for example, including these in possible research questions. The goal of follow-up meetings was to jointly determine the most appropriate research aims and methods.

Professional researchers in general have certain expected research skills and capabilities. However, the capabilities of co-researchers are less known and will differ a lot from person to person. In research collaboration these could be, for example, problem analysis, recruitment of participants, collecting or interpreting data, observing or writing. In several Citizenlab projects we asked the co-researchers about their preferred role and how they imagined they could contribute. Co-researchers did not want to contribute in activities in which they did not have experience or feel comfortable. For each research activity, it needed to be established who has the relevant capabilities, professional researcher or co-researcher, and how to collaborate. In one project an older adult was asked to collaborate with the interpretation of data and he emphasized the importance of that. *"You [referring to the researchers] already defined very important topics, but I can point you towards more interesting directions. I make the topics more specific and because I am part of the research population, I know how we think."*

In addition to recognizing and appreciating mutual knowledge and capabilities, the possibilities that someone has to take certain actions also plays an important role when we look at motivation and long-term collaboration. It is important to support and strengthen each other, as one of the co-researchers said during a co-creation session when the researchers asked to choose a research method: *"I want to propose something else. I have a certain view on the situation, but I think you have more experience in choosing the most suitable research method."* This co-researcher was always very proactive in dividing tasks to those who were most competent for the task. As researchers we appreciated his position in the group and learned from the need for knowing who is able to take certain actions.

Textbox 2: Acknowledging different goals

Case: Research goals versus community goals

One project took the neighbourhood of Schelfhorst as a starting point. The overall aim of this project was to gain insight into safe, happy and healthy independent living at home. Citizen science methodologies were applied to make the voices of older people heard. A group of older residents of the neighbourhood became the co-researchers in this project. Together with the co-researchers, the researchers explored which knowledge and experience they all had to share as well as which goals and stakes each person had in the realization of the project. The research goals were among others to gain insight in the process of citizen science, to discover new directions for future research, and to create a community of organizations and co-researchers that could continue to work by themselves after the project. The community goals of the residents were diverse and ranged from getting heard by the municipality to get involved in the community, and from having a social space to increase the use of technologies at home. During the first meetings of this project these different goals were explored, discussed, and acknowledged by each other. The goals were documented in infographics and all involved recognized that despite the diversity, these goals could be aligned in execution of the project.

All co-researchers involved in a citizen science project will have a goal, which might differ between the co-researchers. The goals do not necessarily strive for generalizable knowledge, but will also recognize the value of an individual's knowledge. In order to acknowledge all different goals, this includes knowledge on an individual level and on a collective level. At the start of a project, the professional researchers may initially only aim to provide relevant knowledge on a scientific level or value for a large group of citizens. However, co-researchers often have the goal towards insight on a more individual or local level. Gaining this insight for the individual can motivate co-researchers to be and remain involved.

Quite often the desired goals or values for the individual co-researchers fitted with the current trend around personal care and attention. For many interested parties of Citizenlab, personal value is the most important motivation to be part of a project [van Leersum et al. 2021]. As part of acknowledging different goals, it is important that professional researchers recognize and appreciate the value of knowledge at the individual level and that co-researchers recognize the value of generalizable knowledge and strive for it. To reach towards mutual acknowledgement, the Citizenlab project organized meetings to discuss the purpose of a research and collaboration for each co-researcher. Several question which were discussed included: What is the purpose and for whom will it provide value? Does this value mainly serve the general interest or does it serve an individual or community? These goal orientation meetings were planned at the start of a project, thus at a moment the different co-researchers were getting to know each other.

It was interesting to observe that most co-researchers had a more political goal, for example, having the municipality involved or reach out to the minister to raise awareness on a topic. *"I would like to have as much media attention with this project as possible. The municipality has to see how important it is to us and maybe they understand that it is needed to take action."* Although professional researchers acknowledge this goal, they often had a separate goal to investigate citizen science research methods. The co-researchers did not see any difficulty here: *"You [referring to the researcher] can use the most suitable research methods and obtain scientific knowledge, but we can use the same findings to reach out to the minister."* It was beneficial to share the different goals and know different purposes of collaboration.

However, the different goals sometimes caused struggles when discussing research questions and research methods in a team of co-researchers. As already mentioned, not all co-researchers wanted to be involved or felt capable to define research questions and methods, but with some Citizenlab projects there were meetings to define these. During the meetings it seemed that all agreed with the outcome, but became a bit irritated at later stages. *"It took very long to get started. At a moment I wanted to stop due to lack of progress. However, now I know why this took so long and I am glad I stayed involved until the end."* The co-researchers had no experience and did not understand that starting and performing a research project would take so much time. Thus, although they acknowledged that there were different goals (scientific, personal and political), they experienced a slow reach of the goals which were most interesting for themselves.

A possibility to overcome this issue is by not only acknowledging the different goals, but also keep everyone informed about each step taken. For instance, in one project the group of co-researchers received updates before, after, and in-between different meetings and activities. Furthermore, different infographics were shared among each other of each meeting and activity, based on written notes that were attached as well. All co-researchers were in the loop and got the opportunity to react and change the notes. *"The communication is very good. Most of the time everything we discussed is in the picture, just sometimes I would like to specify some elements. This is taken seriously and a new infographic is made together"* The infographics were appreciated and used by the co-researchers. For example, on the basis of the first meeting a infographic was made with all different goals and interesting topics brought up by the co-researchers. During a follow-up meeting, it was discussed how to group these different goals and topics. All co-researchers draw connection on the infographics and as a result there was a list of individual and collective goals, and who will be served. Reflecting on the infographics a co-researcher said that *"it is nice to see how all the goals complement each other and how we are able to discuss every important topic."* Sharing of goals was beneficial, because everyone knew which goals were present, and could anticipate on or understand certain actions as part of the project. Furthermore, to keep someone motivated, the individual and collective goals had to be approached or achieved.

Textbox 3: Relationship of trust

Case: Combating loneliness

The municipality of Nijverdal aimed to lower the number of older adults suffering from loneliness. The first Corona wave in April 2020 caused many older adults to end up in isolation. Together with the municipality, flyers were made to reach lonely older adults. In the spring of 2020, 2,000 flyers were distributed in Nijverdal, a website was developed and a video with the counsellor was recorded and posted online. The aim of this campaign was to reach lonely older adults and recruit volunteers to support these older adults. However, there was only one response from an older adult and mainly volunteers signed up to provide support. One possible explanation for the low response could be the lack of trust in the campaign and unfamiliarity with the organisation behind it. To reach older adults it seems important to ensure a relationship of trust.

When citizens are approached to participate in a project, in particular aimed at starting an extended collaboration, establishing a relationship is important, preferably a relationship of trust. A relationship of trust means that professional and co-researchers recognize and respect each other's role in the project. In that case, it does not matter whether a project is initiated by a professional or a co-researcher. It is crucial that professional researchers collaborate with the co-researchers not as an object of study, but a subject with whom they enter into a relationship. Conversely, the same applies to those who are collaborating with the professional researchers, all should be treated with respect. In almost all projects of Citizenlab, a great effort has been made to attract different possible co-researchers. Most do not simply respond to an advertisement, thus different communication channels had to be used. However, once co-researchers were involved in a project, they often wanted to remain involved for a longer period of time. To reach this long-term involvement, it was important that everyone starts to see and treat each other as partners and support each other. Having regular meetings and keep in touch with everyone was time consuming, but created a personal relationship.

At the start of a new project, the collaboration process and needs were discussed with the co-researchers in order to establish a relationship between them. An often mentioned important part of the relationship of trust is ensuring transparency and showing appreciation for each other. It was acknowledged that this could be reached by raising awareness of the relationship at the start of a collaboration, and discuss the role that everyone has or can and wants to fulfil as part of a community. How to name the professional researchers and co-researchers, for example, played an important role for framing the relationship. In this respect you could think of scientists and citizens, researcher and patient, or researchers and co-researcher. In a Citizenlab project with elderly with a migration background, we stated in the beginning that: *"you will become our co-researchers"*. The status of co-researcher gave them a feeling of pride and being part of the development process. It also raised awareness of the fact that they were part of a developmental phase and all knew the technology which they tested was still under development and did not expect that everything was working optimal. As one of the co-researchers mentioned about his role: *"Some things are not working properly, but that is why I am involved. I will test the technology at home to face all ailments and provide important feedback to adjust where needed. Everyone is free to share personal needs and everything can be brought onto the table. Where one of us would like to have a different interface for the medication, someone else needs an alarm button."*

Another important element in a relationship of trust is communication. Crucial for some co-researchers was the manner in which the communication was organized. This could be anonymous by e-mail/letter or through phone or live contact. All professional researchers and co-researchers agreed that having a name and a face strengthens the relationship. It is important to know with whom you communicate. Furthermore, communication could be a one-way channel or a multiple-way channel. In one Citizenlab project the communication started one-way from a researcher towards the co-researchers The communication was experienced crucial to get the project started and create a community, as one co-researcher argued *"without the intensive communication and keeping me in the loop, I am not sure if I wanted to continue"*. Although communication was initially one-way, after a while personal details were shared, with consent of the community members, and the co-researchers started to communicate among each other. This was similar in a study by Dewa et al. [2020], they created a safe place for communication among young adults with mental health issues. A WhatsApp group was created and became the place for discussion between co-researchers. With communication, the aim is to create a relationship of ease in which everyone feels they can contribute, respond, and dare to tell what is on their mind. Often there is a sense of power imbalance between the professional researchers and co-researchers; it is important that with a citizen science project this is eventually overcome.

In another Citizenlab project with elderly suffering from loneliness, a very broad network was built with different partners and a variety of collaborations. However, connecting with people who are lonely was a big challenge. Through counsellors it was made easier to reach volunteers and elderly from the local community. Here, it came afore that the project should not only involve the lonely elderly, because in order to combat loneliness all different stakeholders should create this relationship of trust and actually make contact with each other as part of the community. When lonely elderly become co-researchers, were present at research activities, and experienced a trustful relationship in the community, they started talking about their life and became more open about their loneliness. One woman told the group she had not been outside for two years. *"I would have turned around, but you [she pointed to the researcher] were there to pick me up at the entrance."* After the first meeting this woman took part in all activities and got in touch with the other co-researchers. The connection within the community could be just the final touch they needed to step outside.

Other researchers, such as Kanstrup et al. [2016] already pointed towards the influence of choices, such as location to organise meetings, on the relationship of trust. Kanstrup et al. [2016] initially planned research activities in a classroom setting, but the participants expressed a dislike of classrooms and preferred activities in the gym. Therefore, the research activities were integrated with the physical activities in the gym. It is important that a researcher who is doing citizen science has an open attitude, flexibility, and context sensitivity to make changes towards needs and preferences of the co-researchers [van Leersum et al. 2022]. As part of Citizenlab projects, most started with a small group of co-researchers. In consultation between the co-researchers and the researchers, plans were made and the next steps of citizen science research were determined. Before each step, extensive collaboration took place and it was discussed how to proceed. On the basis of these conversations, both the professional researchers and the co-researchers determine whether and how they want to participate. This created a dynamic group that slowly grew. During the projects, it was noticed that everyone came up with more and more ideas during follow-up meetings. They started arguing with each other and sometimes reacted on something discussed in an earlier meeting. For example, in one project a co-researcher came up with examples from other neighbourhoods to share with each other and the professional researchers. She explained: *"I read this in the newspaper and had to think about what we discussed last time. Maybe this could also be a solution in our neighbourhood?"* They started to see the group as a whole with which they could do research and take action. In addition, the co-researchers did not experience power imbalance between the various stakeholders such as employees from the municipality, medical professionals, researchers, and themselves.

Overall, in the Citizenlab projects, there was often a personal approach from professional researchers. This was experienced as valuable to start a community and with long-term collaboration having a relationship of trust among all involved stakeholders.

However, this active involvement of a professional researcher sometimes had the disadvantage that when the researchers left at the end of the research activities, the co-researchers missed contact with this corresponding person. It was not easy to have the same relationship and contact with another person taking over in follow-up actions. Besides giving a feeling that a project or group is accessible to everyone, all changes in involved stakeholders need to be introduced clearly and gradually.

Textbox 4: Learning environment

Case: Creating informed consent for people with a migration background
Most of TOPFIT Citizenlab's projects are about improving health and the motivation that comes with it. Most people who responded to participate were partly already motivated to take care of their health or use technology, but the researchers also collaborated with target groups that were less able or interested to do so, for example, a group of older adults with starting dementia and a migration background [van Leersum et al. 2023]. Creating a learning environment in which it was accepted that the new technology is not easily understood and mistakes can be made was important. In the beginning, a session was organized to discuss the informed consent. This was done in a playful way where the older adults could throw a ball and where the researchers and caregivers played-out a story in which the informed consent was explained. After this session, the researchers and caregivers created a short video in Turkish language about the project, in order to better inform the older adults about the technology and the research. Besides the video, get-togethers in which the older adults could learn from each other about the use of technology were organized by caregivers.

The last common aspect considers creating a learning environment for all. When looking at collaboration in citizen science projects, it is an added value to assist both professional researchers and co-researchers to know their learning needs. The professional researchers often want to learn about the lives of the co-researchers, but they have different learning needs. *"I can tell about my experiences with my diabetes and the technology, but if you want me to conduct an interview I need some assistance."* Besides asking all co-researchers about their preferences considering collaboration and tasks, it was also discussed what they would like to learn or what they need to perform an action and remain involved. By responding to the learning needs of all co-researchers, a foundation is laid, which is connected to the relationship of trust within the project.

Understanding the learning needs of co-researchers was part of the Citizenlab projects. Retrieving the learning needs starts with listening carefully to what someone is saying, what questions are asked, and what prior knowledge someone has. The learning needs were formulated during discussions and a learning path was conceived. *"I wanted to lead the focus group discussion, but had no idea how to start. The researcher planned separate meetings to explain common procedures and discuss what would suit me. Of course I was still nervous, but it was very helpful and in the end the focus group discussion went very well."* The Citizenlab project experimented with several options to achieve the learning needs, such as face-to-face explanation given by project supervisors, a webinar with companies or a supporting video. When designing the suitable learning path, it was important to take the target group into account. For example, with the older adults with early dementia and a migration background a more personal approach was chosen in combination with a supporting video, to recall important topics at a later stage [van Leersum et al. 2023]. The personal approach was especially appreciated, *"we knew the faces of the researchers and when they visited us at a later moment at home this felt familiar."* Also most of them felt not comfortable in using video-calling devices.

Besides choosing an appropriate learning path, the general learning needs within citizen science projects can be divided into citizen science general, procedure, and involvement. The learning needs within citizen science begin with the explanation of what citizen science is and what definition is used. Also the acknowledgement of different goals is connected to this learning need. Increased understanding of the project was obtained when citizen science, as a research method, was explained and discussed with the co-researchers. Some older adults got a feeling of pride based on their role of co-researcher. *"I am a real co-researcher and the project needs me to know what matters to me and how to adjust this device."* The learning needs considering procedure include for example obtaining informed consent or the test of a new technology. All co-researchers should understand the procedure as written in the informed consent. If this appears to be a challenge, a personal approach or supportive tools could be used to provide explanations. Related to the test of a new technology, for some co-researchers, it was shown beneficial to provide instructions on how to handle and use the relevant technology. Finally, the learning needs related to involvement include, for example, the method of communication and feedback on results. Something mentioned by almost all co-researchers: *"Will you share the findings with me?"* Communication about the project is appreciated at all stages of a project and will keep co-researchers motivated to stay involved. However, not only findings as obtained by the professional researchers are appreciated, also the individual experiences of others are valued. *"I really enjoyed testing this app and sharing my experience. But on top of that, I especially enjoyed hearing all experiences of others."* This shows the mutual learning environment, not only between professional researchers and co-researchers, but actually between all stakeholders.

Challenges in community building

Citizen science is a flexible concept that The TOPFIT Citizenlab programme investigated and aimed at increasing citizen involvement in researching, testing, modifying, and implementing technological innovations for health. Their aim was in line with the ten principles of citizen science [Robinson et al. 2018]. However, did the different projects that were part of the programme adhere to these principles, and what were the reasons to deviate? We used the concept communities of practice as environments in which co-researchers and researchers could collaborate and share a concern or passion for something [Wenger 2011]. In all projects we, as researchers, had regular interactions with different groups of co-researchers. The concept of communities of practice connects the four common aspects, and the common aspects can provide a starting point for a structure in communities of practice.

In several projects we tried to build communities of practice in order to actively engage with different groups of co-researchers, create a welcoming environment, create mutual learning possibilities [Cruess et al. 2018], and at the same time design research and develop or improve technologies. In creating the communities, there was the common practice of doing research. However, within the groups of co-researchers there were different practices as having diabetes, rheumatoid arthritis or living in the same neighbourhood. There was a mix of a shared interest in doing research and a common concern such as coping with an illness, which is important in communities of practice. In the Citizenlab project, there were just some projects in which the communities collaborated for a year or longer. Therefore, we cannot qualify all co-researcher groups as communities of practice. In view of the groups which collaborated for a longer period of time, the four common aspects can relate to the core of communities of practice. By recognizing each other's capabilities and knowing the goals of all involved, it is possible to find the common interest. By understanding and building on these common interests, the researchers and co-researchers can build a relationship of trust. Furthermore, knowing each other also leads into knowing how to create a welcoming space for mutual learning.

Reflecting on all projects which were part of the Citizenlab programme, they all managed to adhere to some of the citizen science principles (Table 2). However, adherence to all principles was only reached by a small number of the projects. For example, the principle of contribution and taking part in multiple stages of the project was not possible in all projects. It was, for example, a challenge to have a group of co-researchers who desired to stay active for a longer period of time. The four common aspects could assist in reaching this principle. Although it would be beneficial to work with the same group for a longer term, it should as well be in line with desires of the co-researchers [van Leersum et al. 2021] and it should be beneficial for both the professional researchers and co-researchers to contribute.

This last aspect was often a challenge and point of discussion. The professional researchers involved in a project are paid a salary, but the co-researchers are contributing on a voluntary basis and do not receive an hourly wage. It was a challenge to find a suiting way of compensating their contribution. This topic was discussed with people with diabetes type 2 [van Leersum et al. 2021]. In this study, most desired by the co-researchers was receiving products or technology for free, and second an expenses allowance. In all the different TOPFIT Citizenlab projects we discussed the preferences for compensation at the start, because it remains challenging to determine general guidance regarding compensation. Overall, the most important is having a topic to which they can connect or a technology they can actually test, and acknowledging the co-researchers for their expertise. Reflecting on the communities of practice, having a common concern or passion strengthens the connection between professional researchers and co-researchers and is the core of a community [Wenger 2011].

A main aspect we have achieved in almost all projects in different formats, was adhering to the principle of "co-researchers receive feedback from the project" [Robinson et al. 2018]. This was as well a crucial element in the communities of practice in order to enhance mutual learning [Wenger 2011]. We used diverse methods of feedback provision, for example, we shared summaries of findings, infographics with the main findings, visualized summaries of meetings to have conversation support during a follow-up meeting, oral presentations, and anonymized transcripts of interviews. The aim of sharing these diverse documents was to get feedback from the co-researchers. Can they find themselves in these presentation of the findings? Which elements are translated rightly or wrongly into the findings and what elements of the research are missing in their view? All these methods to provide feedback to the co-researchers about the projects were useful, but the different documents using a form of visualization seemed to empower the co-researchers more. With these documents there was a larger contribution of the co-researchers to the professional researchers.

Table 2: Ten principles of citizen science [Robinson et al. 2018] and links between these and the four common aspects (recognizing and acknowledging each other's capacities, acknowledging different goals, building a relationship of trust, or creating a learning environment).

Principles of citizen science [Robinson et al. 2018]	Common aspect
1. Citizen science projects actively involve citizens in scientific endeavour that generates new knowledge or understanding. Citizens may act as contributors, collaborators or as project leaders and have a meaningful role in the project.	Recognizing and acknowledging each other's capacities Acknowledging different goals Building a relationship of trust Creating a learning environment
2. Citizen science projects have a genuine science outcome.	Acknowledging different goals
3. Both the professional scientists and the co-researchers benefit from taking part	Acknowledging different goals Creating a learning environment
4. Co-researchers may, if they wish, participate in multiple stages of the scientific process. This may include developing the research question, designing the method, gathering and analysing data, and communicating the results.	Recognizing and acknowledging each other's capacities Acknowledging different goals
5. Co-researchers receive feedback from the project.	Building a relationship of trust Creating a learning environment
6. Citizen science is considered a research approach like any other, with limitations and biases that should be considered and controlled for.	–

Table 2 (continued)

Principles of citizen science [Robinson et al. 2018]	Common aspect
7. Citizen science project data and metadata are made publicly available and where possible, results are published in an open-access format.	Creating a learning environment
8. Co-researchers are acknowledged in project results and publications.	Recognizing and acknowledging each other's capacities Building a relationship of trust
9. Citizen science programmes are evaluated for their scientific output, data quality, participant experience and wider societal or policy impact.	Creating a learning environment
10. The leaders of citizen science projects take into consideration legal and ethical issues surrounding copyright, intellectual property, data-sharing agreements, confidentiality, attribution and the environmental impact of any activities.	–

References

Barab, S. A., & Duffy, T. (2012). From practice fields to communities of practice. In *Theoretical foundations of learning environments* (pp. 29–65). Routledge.

Bults, M., van Leersum, C. M., Olthuis, T. J. J., Bekhuis, R. E. M., & den Ouden, M. E. M. (2023). Mobile Health Apps for the Control and Self-management of Type 2 Diabetes Mellitus: Qualitative Study on Users' Acceptability and Acceptance. *JMIR diabetes*, *8*, e41076.

Cruess, R. L., Cruess, S. R., & Steinert, Y. (2018). Medicine as a community of practice: implications for medical education. *Academic Medicine*, *93*(2), 185–191.

Danielsen F, Burgess ND, Coronado I, Enghoff M, Holt S, Jensen PM, et al. The value of indigenous and local knowledge as citizen science. In: Hecker S, Haklay M, Bowser A, Makuch Z, Vogel J, editors. Citizen Science: Innovation in Open Science, Society and Policy. London: UCL Press; 2018. p. 110–23.

Den Broeder L, Devilee J, Van Oers H, Schuit AJ, Wagemakers A. Citizen Science for public health. Health Promot Int. 2018;33(3):505–14. Epub 2016/12/25. doi: 10.1093/heapro/daw086. PubMed PMID: 28011657; PubMed Central PMCID: PMCPMC6005099.

Dewa LH, Lawrence-Jones A, Crandell C, Jaques J, Pickles K, Lavelle M, et al. Reflections, impact and recommendations of a co-produced qualitative study with young people who have experience of mental health difficulties. Health Expect. 2021;24 Suppl 1:134–46. Epub 2020/06/10. doi: 10.1111/hex.13088. PubMed PMID: 32515538; PubMed Central PMCID: PMCPMC8137486

Eitzel, M., Cappadonna, J., Santos-Lang, C., Duerr, R., West, S. E., Virapongse, A., . . . & Jiang, Q. (2017). Citizen science terminology matters: Exploring key terms. *Citizen science: Theory and practice*, 1–20.

Higgins, M., & Reeves, D. (2006). Creative thinking in planning: How do we climb outside the box?. *The Town Planning Review*, 221–244.

Kanstrup, A. M., & Bertelsen, P. (2016). Bringing New Voices to Design of Exercise Technology: participatory design with vulnerable young adults. In *Proceedings of the 14th Participatory Design Conference: Full papers-Volume 1* (pp. 121–130).

Krick T, Huter K, Domhoff D, Schmidt A, Rothgang H, Wolf-Ostermann K. Digital technology and nursing care: a scoping review on acceptance, effectiveness and efficiency studies of informal and formal care technologies. BMC Health Serv Res. 2019;19(1):400. Epub 2019/06/22. doi: 10.1186/s12913-019-4238-3. PubMed PMID: 31221133; PubMed Central PMCID: PMCPMC6585079.

Kullenberg C, Kasperowski D. What Is Citizen Science?–A Scientometric Meta-Analysis. PLoS One. 2016;11(1):e0147152. Epub 2016/01/15. doi: 10.1371/journal.pone.0147152. PubMed PMID: 26766577; PubMed Central PMCID: PMCPMC4713078.

Li, L. C., Grimshaw, J. M., Nielsen, C., Judd, M., Coyte, P. C., & Graham, I. D. (2009). Evolution of Wenger's concept of community of practice. *Implementation science*, *4*, 1–8.

Remmers, G., Hermann, J., Siebrand, E., & Van Leersum, C. M. (2023). Mind the Relationship: A Multi-Layered Ethical Framework for Citizen Science in Health. *Etica & Politica*, *25*(2), 171–196.

Robinson, L. D., Cawthray, J. L., West, S. E., Bonn, A., & Ansine, J. (2018). Ten principles of citizen science. In *Citizen science: Innovation in open science, society and policy* (pp. 27–40). UCL Press.

van Leersum, C. M., Bults, M., Sloof, M., Pouwe, F., van Manen, J. G., & Konijnendijk, A. A. (2021). Patiëntparticipatie bij de ontwikkeling en toepassing van e-health: Bereidheid en voorkeuren van mensen met diabetes mellitus type 2. *Tsg*, *99*(3), 110.

van Leersum, C. M., Jaschinski, C., Bults, M., & van der Zwart, J. (2022). Citizen involvement in research on technological innovations for health, care or well-being: a scoping review. *medRxiv*, 2022–11.

van Leersum, C. M., Konrad, K. E., Siebrand, E., Malik, Z. B., den Ouden, M. E., & Bults, M. (2023). Engaging older adults with a migration background to explore the usage of digital technologies in coping with dementia. *Frontiers in Public Health*, *11*, 1125834.

Wenger, E. (1998). Communities of practice: Learning as a social system. *Systems thinker*, *9*(5), 2–3.

Wenger, E. (2011). Communities of practice: A brief introduction *University of Oregon Libraries*.

Wiggins A, Wilbanks J. The Rise of Citizen Science in Health and Biomedical Research. Am J Bioeth. 2019;19(8):3–14. Epub 2019/07/25. doi: 10.1080/15265161.2019.1619859. PubMed PMID: 31339831.

Wright J, Parry J, Mathers J. Participation in health impact assessment: objectives, methods and core values. Bull World Health Organ. 2005;83(1):58–63. Epub 2005/02/01. doi:/S0042-96862005000100015. PubMed PMID: 15682250; PubMed Central PMCID: PMCPMC2623465.

Catharina M. van Leersum, Kornelia Konrad, Johan van der Zwart

Ageing in your place: Envisioning healthy, happy, and safe ageing in a neighbourhood with citizen science methods

Abstract: The number of older people living independently at home is expanding. This brings often the need for more assistance or adjusting the environment, in particular the home itself. There is no shortage of more or less futuristic visions and concepts for adjusting homes to older age. However, futuring old age is largely done by others – developers of welfare technologies, public sector actors, or by family members and older people's personal networks. In a project of TOPFIT Citizenlab, a Dutch regional initiative to experiment with forms of citizen science for health and wellbeing, we explored needs and priorities for age-friendly living in a neighbourhood, building on three diverse methods. We started with three meetings and a photo-voice method to explore research goals and methods. Then scenario-building workshops served to explore visions for healthy ageing and living in the neighbourhood, and finally, personal experiences and perspectives were discussed in relation to statistical health data of the neighbourhood, in order to explore how the structural data relates to the lived experience of the inhabitants. Each method had a different contribution regarding the effectiveness of the process, the findings, and the engagement of all stakeholders. Our findings show that citizens took a holistic approach as to what matters for age-friendly living: not only the inside, but also the surroundings of homes, physical, mental and social health are seen as interrelated, and possible solutions include and often merge technical, social and 'green' elements.

Acknowledgements: The authors would like to thank the company LangZultUWonen, and all partners and citizens of Schelfhorst for collaborating with us in every research step, and providing valuable insights. The authors also thank all colleagues of TOPFIT Citizenlab for their regular support and collaboration. This study was powered by the Twente Regional Deal and received financial support from the Central Government's Regional Budget, the Province of Overijssel, the Region of Twente, and the Twente Board. The funders had no role in study design, data collection and analysis, the decision to publish, or preparation of the manuscript.

Catharina M. van Leersum, Department of Technology, Policy, and Society, Faculty of Behavioural, Management, and Social Sciences, University of Twente, Enschede, the Netherlands; Faculty of Humanities, Open Universiteit, Heerlen, the Netherlands
Kornelia Konrad, Johan van der Zwart, Department of Technology, Policy, and Society, Faculty of Behavioural, Management, and Social Sciences, University of Twente, Enschede, the Netherlands

https://doi.org/10.1515/9783111241036-006

Introduction

In the Netherlands, the number of older people living independently at home is expanding, a development that is supported by policy [Black and Oh 2022]. This policy is in line with the phenomenon ageing in place, which refers to the fact that most older adults prefer to stay in their own home and neighbourhood [Vanleerberghe et al. 2017]. Important aspects to make ageing in place and independent living possible, are housing, public spaces, transportation, and social engagement [Aung et al. 2022]. In view of healthy, happy, and safe ageing, Bosch-Farré et al. [2020] discussed that ageing is experienced different among older adults. Furthermore, health status is influential in relation to social participation and attitude towards their lives. Ageing in place in a favourable way for the older adults is dependent on their connection to the community, experience of autonomy and well-being, and availability of services and products [Bosch-Farré et al. 2020] Having age-friendly features in the homes and vicinity eases independent living. This often brings the need for assistance or making changes in the neighbourhood.

The most common forms of enabling assistance to older adults include assistive services and technologies, and a lot of innovations are envisaged and developed in the field of ambient assisted living technologies [Vercelli et al. 2017]. However, both the development of technologies and futuring old age in the digital age is largely done by others – developers of welfare technologies, public sector actors, or by family members and older people's personal networks. Ageing futures that are envisaged from 'outside' tend to be rather stereotyped, have blind spots, for instance with regard to diversity in gender, ethnicity or culture, and in their generality can hardly cater for the personal and local circumstances and needs of individual persons or local communities [Cozza et al. 2019]. There is no shortage of more or less futuristic visions and concepts for adjusting homes to older age, but these visions are quite often not developed according to expressed needs and priorities by the older adults living in the futured homes and neighbourhoods [Cozza et al. 2019]. For example, Wright et al. [2014] describe a utopia for older adults of 75 years and older based on a workshop with care professionals, yet older adults were not involved.

Against this backdrop, we aimed to explore the needs and priorities for age-friendly living in a neighbourhood together with the citizens of a Dutch neighbourhood. To reach this aim, we made use of three different citizen science methods. 1) Diverse meetings and the use of a photo-voice method to explore research goals and applicable research methods. 2) Scenario-building workshops to explore visions for healthy ageing and living in the neighbourhood. 3) Personal experiences and perspectives interpreting statistical health data of the neighbourhood.

Citizen science could be understood as a collection of diverse epistemic practices in which knowledge is produced and the world is explored and understood [Strasser et al. 2019]. At the same time, hierarchical classifications are avoided and citizens can collaborate at different levels of participation. A common aspect in citizen science is the active involvement and collaboration between researchers and citizens in the production of knowledge [Remmers et al. 2023]. Citizen science is a flexible concept that could be defined in different ways and applied in diverse disciplines (for more information on citizen science, reference to chapter on community) [Robinson et al. 2018; Eitzel et al. 2017].

Needs and priorities are not simply ready to be voiced or acted upon, but rather need to be formed, clarified, and explicated. In this chapter we used citizen science methods to discuss needs and priorities for healthy, happy, and safe ageing. These methods were applied in one neighbourhood. We discuss and reflect on the findings as well as on the methods. Although each method took a different angle and had a different process, there are differences as well as similarities in the effectiveness of the process, the findings, and the engagement of all stakeholders.

Schelfhorst as context for citizen science

What do you need as a neighbourhood resident to grow old in a healthy, happy and safe environment? That was the central question raised by a resident of the neighbourhood Schelfhorst in Almelo, the Netherlands. To address this question, we chose a design in which we do not conduct research *about* the older adults living in this neighbourhood, but enter into a dialogue *with* them, and in this way clarify their perspective and shape the research in collaboration with them. Citizen science methods can help to give a voice to the older adults instead of making decisions for and about them. The study was set up in the community centre of the neighbourhood, and this also became the central location where discussions and research activities took place.

The Schelfhorst project was part of the TOPFIT Citizenlab programme. The research and innovation programme TOPFIT Citizenlab was situated in the Twente region, in the East of the Netherlands. The aim of the programme was to keep Dutch citizens longer healthy by joining forces with citizens, healthcare professionals, and companies to develop and implement technological innovations for health and welfare [http://www.topfitcitizenlab.nl]. [for more information: reference to chapter on community building].

As a starting point, citizens were recruited through partners within the project. Here a number of contacts were made within already existing networks. In addition, an advertisement was placed on social media channels and in local newspapers of the municipality of Almelo, and flyers were hung or placed in the community centre and other central locations in the neighbourhood. For all follow-up research steps, the citizens from the previous part were approached with an invitation. In addition, they were asked to approach other interested parties, and further advertisements were set out.

For the first step of exploring research goals and methods a total of 18 citizens were recruited. Eight residents from the neighbourhood and ten experts. We considered as experts people who fulfilled a specific role in the neighbourhood, such as being involved in the church, active in a council, director of a residential centre or community support worker. Three of the experts were themselves residents of Schelfhorst. For the scenario-building workshop, 22 citizens had applied, but due to illness or other reasons, some opted out and 14 citizens participated. For the personal experiences and perspectives on quantitative health data, 13 citizens signed up for the meeting and 12 citizens were present.

In total, 39 citizens (Table 1) became part of this project and collaborated in one or more of the different research steps. Of these citizens, 67% were female, and 33% were male. While this implies that women were overrepresented, we assume that the group was still sufficiently diverse to cover well viewpoints of both men and women. Age groups were rather well distributed. A smaller group was aged between 50 and 59

Table 1: Socio-demographic information of the 39 citizens involved in the project.

	Percentage (N=39)
Gender	
Male	33%
Female	67%
Other	0%
Age	
50–60	18%
60–70	33%
70–80	36%
80+	13%
Educational level	
No or low education	13%
Middle education	38%
High education	49%
Nationality	
Dutch	95%
Other	5%
Housing	
Owner	92%
Tenants	8%
Marital status	
Married	41%
Living together	31%
Single/widow(er)	28%

years (18%) and 80 years or older (13%), and a larger group was between 60 and 69 years (33%) or 70 and 79 years (36%). Most participants had received a higher educational degree (49%), 38% had a middle educational degree, and 13% had no or a low educational degree. There were two participants with a non-Dutch nationality and a minority (8%) was tenants. Compared with the numbers of 2022 (CBS 2023), 38% of the housing stock consists of rental properties, and 25% had a non-Dutch migration background. To recruit tenants we organised one separate meeting specifically for them. It was difficult to reach this population and one of the involved tenants mentioned that she was there as a spokesperson for other tenants. With regard to education, almost half of Schelfhorst citizens has a middle educational degree (CBS 2023), 19% a higher, and 33% a lower educational degree. However, this larger proportion of participants with a higher education degree is expected in citizen science research. Compared to other citizen science projects in which 60% or more has a higher educational degree (Hackley 2018), our population was more diverse. A clear bias is the very low number of non-Dutch citizens. However, for these groups specific recruitment efforts may be needed; an approach we followed in another project dedicated to older adults with a migration background (van Leersum et al. 2023).

Applied citizen science methods

Framing of research

We organized meetings to discuss the neighbourhood. Three meetings were held with residents from the neighbourhood, they formed the 'residents panel', and the same three meetings were held with experts involved and/or living in Schelfhorst, they formed the 'expert panel'. The aim of these meetings was to set up and define the goals of a joint study on the theme of healthy, happy, and safe ageing.

1. A photo-voice method was applied during the first meeting [Lal et al. 2012; Mysyuk and Huisman 2020]. As a way to ease talking about life in Schelfhorst, the citizens were asked to take four photos. All citizen could decide for themselves what kind of picture to take and bring to the meeting, for example, a place they like or something they want to change. The pictures were taken as a starting point for the meeting. This meeting was organized to get to know each other and share first ideas: Citizens were asked to share their stories about Schelfhorst. What is going well, what is less pleasant, and how can the neighbourhood be improved? It was also discussed what a future implies in which more and more older adults live in the neighbourhood. What does that mean for you, housing, care, transport, and social contacts in the neighbourhood? After the first meeting, the researchers made a visualization of the initial findings. This visualization was shared with the citizens to ask for their feedback.

2. In the second meeting the main goals of the research were determined. The meeting started with a short reflective part by briefly looking back at the previous meeting. Then the citizens jointly decided which aspects they considered as most important and which topics they would like to take as a starting point. Based on the visualization, all previous discussed topics were reviewed and the most important ones distilled.
3. The third meeting served to plan the research and follow-up. This third meeting started again with a reflective part based on the visualizations of the previous meeting, followed by decisions on how the most important aspects should and can be tackled. The main research objectives were formulated, suitable research questions discussed, as well as possible actions and methods.

Each meeting was organized in the community centre 'Schelf' and lasted 90 minutes. During the meeting, observations and notes were made by one researcher and two students. These notes were processed into a visualization, shared with the citizens and their feedback incorporated. In addition, all data was analysed and the findings were divided in different categories. The analysis was performed by two researchers. Interim findings were discussed with each other and the (sub)categories were jointly determined and defined. The findings are presented in textbox 1.

Textbox 1: Exploration of research goals and methods

What is going well in Schelfhorst, what is pleasant, what is less pleasant, and how can this be improved? Although everyone recognized that Schelfhorst is a very pleasant neighbourhood to live in, complaints were made about the fences, and lack of plants in the streets. *"It doesn't look good, I'm ashamed of the street when my family comes to visit."* It would be ideal if neighbours were mobilized to take action, take out a paving stone and put in a plant. The park is a very nice place to walk in with lots of greenery, but it is becoming less safe over time, especially in the evenings. Other themes of discussion were loneliness and housing. It was suggested that loneliness could be lowered with *'the launderette against loneliness'*. Due to the housing shortage, participants saw not many alternatives for the ageing residents of Schelfhorst to move. During the second and third meeting, themes were selected for future research. Living was discussed as a very important theme, but it was also immediately said *"living is more than just being in the house, it is also about activities and how people get out of the house."* Three main themes emerged on which the older adults in Schelfhorst would like to work: 1) an inviting community centre, 2) greenery in the streets, and 3) creating future-proof homes.

1. An inviting community centre: There is a lot to do in the neighbourhood and especially in the community centre. However, the citizens do not know about it and the community centre does not seem accessible from the outside. *"It's not alive and you don't get the village feeling here."* In order to conduct further research, the citizens developed the research question *"What would residents of Schelfhorst want to do in the community centre and how do we improve the information about the community centre?"* The citizens had ideas ranging from organizing a market in collaboration with the associations that are already in the community centre, to flower pots in front of the door to make the community centre inviting.
2. Greenery in the streets: When entering the neighbourhood, it seems neglected, lots of grey, stones, walls, and fences. The main research question by the citizens was *"How do we get more greenery in the neighbourhood?"* This seemed an impossible task according to the residents of

Schelfhorst. Assistance from the municipality could possibly help, such as having subsidies or starting greening in one street and using this street as an example. To take action, research was not seen as the next step. A suitable action seemed raising awareness on this issue with the municipality.

3. Creating future-proof homes: *"All seniors should and can continue to live in their homes."* The research question that emerged was *"How can we make the homes in Schelfhorst future-proof and how can people take action themselves to reach this goal?"* On the one hand, the homes have to be examined and home scans can be made to provide advice. This theme included ideas such as establishing a housing coach, multiple information markets or even an information desk in the community centre where people can learn about and test products.

Scenario-building workshop

The second citizen science research method was a scenario-building workshop of two days. In the scenario-building workshop, we looked ahead to the year 2030. How will Schelfhorst look like in the future? What does the future look like when it comes to new technology for housing, care, and well-being? How would you consider your own role and responsibilities in these developments? On the basis of three group works and two individual assignments, a future scenario was jointly devised, described, and discussed. The workshop was held twice, one with older adults who own a property and one with tenants. Each workshop was spread over two days, the meetings on both days lasted two hours.

Day 1 consisted of an individual assignment, followed by two group works. Each citizen participated in all assignments in the same order.

1. Individual assignment 1 – Reflection on your own wishes and life
   The first step was to fill in the tool 'What matters to me'. This was handed out on paper to the co-researchers and assisted them with a short individual reflection [van Leersum et al. 2020].
2. Group work 1 – Hope
   The second step was to discuss personal hopes and dreams for the future of Schelfhorst. The citizens were asked to write down all their hopes and dreams on sticky notes. What do the citizens hope the future will look like in terms of housing, care, and well-being in Schelfhorst? What kind of images do they have about the future? How will or should the neighbourhood change? All sticky notes were discussed and linked to each other. The hopes and dreams were divided into four groups: 1) health, 2) neighbourhood and home, 3) products and services, and 4) social contacts.
3. Group work 2 – Current situation
   In the last step on the first day, we discussed when the hopes and dreams could be realized in the future. How far in the future will a possible new situation arise? Using a timeline, the sticky notes from the previous group work were redis-

tributed. For each hope or dream, it was discussed how realistic it is and when it could become reality in the neighbourhood. Is this a near future and are all the necessities to fulfil the dream already present or is it more futuristic and does it require a lot of (technological) development?

The findings of the first day are shown in textbox 2.

Textbox 2: Envisioning the future Schelfhorst

The first day started with dreaming. What are the dreams of the citizens and what do they hope the future of the neighbourhood will look like? All dreams and hopes were discussed and divided into four categories: home and neighbourhood, social contacts, health, and services and products. One idea discussed by the citizens considered energy transmission. It would be great if there was a network with power stations specifically for the neighbourhood. Also, they dreamed of a car-free neighbourhood and the possibility to arrange special transport for everyone or shared mobility options. However, not all agreed with this idea and *"would rather have a car nearby, especially for older adults it is convenient to have a car instead of waiting for someone or something to pick you up."* More greenery in the neighbourhood is the dream of the citizens. More trees and wild flowers as well as hanging and picking gardens. *"If it all works out, we can become self-sufficient in food."* Regarding healthcare, there is hope for a movement towards more personalized care, which can all be made easier when different care providers collaborate and use one digital platform on which all are connected.

The citizens initially thought that almost all ideas can be achieved in the near future. *"You just have to take action. All technology is already there, but it is also quite difficult to imagine what kind of technologies could yet come in the future."* Who would be responsible was an important topic of discussion. Some said that *"these are tasks for the municipality and the government. I wouldn't know how to do it differently and who should do it differently."* However, not all citizens agreed, for example suggesting that the idea of picking gardens could very well be initiated and organized by the residents themselves.

Based on the dreams and their vision on the future, a scenario of Schelfhorst 2030 was developed by the researchers (Textbox 3). At the beginning of the second day, a researcher read the scenario aloud. After the scenario was read, everyone was given a copy and asked to write on sticky notes what they would like to continue, what they would like to avoid, and what they would like to add to the scenario.

Textbox 3: Scenario Schelfhorst 2030

Transition to a life-long and sustainable neighbourhood
What is needed to live healthier, safer, happier, and independently at home in Schelfhorst? Residents of Schelfhorst have made plans for this in 2022. Investigating possibilities for communication, social contacts, activities, and adapting homes so that everyone can live and grow old healthy, safely, and happily in their sustainable and green neighbourhood.

It is now 2030 . . .

A number of retired residents in Schelfhorst have the role of housing coach. They have been trained by professional housing coaches. Together, some of the homes in the neighbourhood have been adapted with smart technological tools, and the houses have been made sustainable. Residents of other homes do not like this, do not have the resources or still have to take care of this themselves. The housing coaches and companies have created online model homes where residents can find information about smart tools, and making their home more sustainable. Healthcare is often arranged through community care. Communication and, in part, coordination surrounding an individual's care is arranged via an online platform. Family members or informal caregivers can view this platform and communicate with each other.

The community centre is the central location in the district. The building has been renovated and it looks cozy with flower pots. A canopy has also been created to the shopping centre. There is free entry for activities every day, and a market once a week. There are walk-in consultation hours in the community centre where residents can ask questions or borrow and test new products. For example, a remote control to close curtains, products for more security at home or a doorbell with camera. Services can be provided upon online request. Robot-controlled cars come by to pick up laundry, and groceries are delivered free of charge by drones from the shopping centre. Everything about the neighbourhood, such as activities and new services, is communicated via an online platform where residents can share information. Through this platform, everyone can indicate preferences and receive personal messages.

Some streets are very grey, but part of the neighbourhood is becoming greener. Some residents have jointly become green coaches, and grow wild flowers on the roadsides. There are several large and small residential complexes where older and young people live together and help each other. The older adults look after the children and the youth helps with chores and digital matters. These complexes are maintained by the municipality and require a significant additional contribution from the residents, in other places neighbours have organized this in groups themselves.

Throughout the neighbourhood there are gardens and roofs full of solar panels. The energy generated in the houses is stored in small power stations nearby. Everything is organized with a cooperative of residents, and only available for the people who participate in this shared energy supply.

The park is equipped with lights and cameras, more opportunities for exercise for the older and young people, and a coffee cart every Friday afternoon. Residents go to the park to walk around, drink an occasional cup of coffee, receive guidance on exercise, and have a chat. The park is also visited for gardening together. A garden has been created together with a cooperative of local residents, and everything for gardening together is arranged. Residents can garden themselves or together, and the products are sold in the park during the weekly market at the shopping centre.

Day 2 consisted of one group work and one individual assignment. Each citizen participated in both parts in the same order.

1. Group work 3 – Scenario
   Based on the conversations of day 1, a scenario was made by the researchers. It was presented at the start of day 2. In this scenario, the hopes, dreams, and expectations are confronted with possible positive and negative effects in the future of their neighbourhood. We started talking to each other based on this scenario. How do the citizens perceive this future? Do they envision this scenario as a possible future? What should we do to solve possible unwanted situations? The citizens got three questions: 1) what should we continue 2) what should we avoid, and 3) what do we need to add to the scenario? They were asked to write down their thoughts on sticky notes. All of these were discussed with each other and grouped on the basis of the three questions.

2. Individual assignment 2 – Reflection on personal role and responsibility
   As a last step, each citizen was asked to complete a short questionnaire. This questionnaire focussed on the envisioned role and responsibilities for the citizens regarding the follow-up research and the future in their neighbourhood.

The findings of the second day are presented in textbox 4.

Textbox 4: Desirable changes and continuations of the scenario

What should we continue?
The citizens definitely wanted to continue the idea of gardens in the park, preferably by creating a food forest with a herb and vegetable garden. The park should be used for multiple purposes and seen as *"the outdoor centre of the neighbourhood"*. The roof between the community centre and the shopping centre would certainly have added value for the neighbourhood. The residential complexes for young and old together were expected to strengthen social contacts, thus the citizens would like to continue them. In a similar vein, the cooperation within healthcare institutions was considered an important aspect to provide more personal care and to pay more attention to issues such as loneliness. The online platform described in the scenario was seen as very valuable. All care should be bundled in this, and possibly also the housing coaches. The energy proposal was approved as well, but the solar panels should be placed on the roofs and not in gardens.

What should we avoid?
With the presented scenario, some citizens got the impression that a gap could be forming between the residents in the neighbourhood. Such a gap should definitely be prevented, for example, the part on online health can become *"something far away"* for some and there is a concern of increased loneliness. Regarding the power stations, this must certainly be available to all residents. As for adjusting homes, it seemed necessary to reach everyone in the neighbourhood, but this may not be realistic within 4 years. Volunteers or coaches were seen as specifically important for people with low health and digital literacy or people with a migration background. Furthermore, the participants saw privacy as an important point of attention for the integrated platforms.

What do we need to add?
The participants suggested to bring together all current plans, in order to create one vision and policy. They would also like to see more opportunities for sports and exercise, which could be done in the park, but would depend also on appropriate infrastructure: *"if you want to get more people moving, you have to start by getting the sidewalks and cycle paths properly arranged."* Furthermore, it was discussed that 'face-to-face' should remain important next to all online opportunities. In addition, participants felt that loneliness is not reflected sufficiently in the scenario, while they saw a high risk of loneliness with several of the described scenario elements.

Roles and responsibilities
The citizens envisioned several roles and responsibilities for themselves. The most prominent was being a volunteer, but the concrete tasks and responsibilities mentioned varied a lot among the participants. For example, one citizen wanted to engage in active communication with the adolescents in the neighbourhood, while another suggested to organise more passive forms of communication via the internet or a newsletter. The overall aim was to have a neighbourhood focused approach and a variety of communication approaches that will reach different populations: *"we need to ensure that a broad selection of residents is brought together."* Also with regard to technological options, citizens considered

different needs and roles for themselves. Some wanted to serve as volunteers in testing phases, others need more information, and yet another group would like to provide an exemplary role. This exemplary role could entail having the responsibility to promote among others and spread knowledge. *"I come from the educational sector and will be able to explain in an understandable way."*

Investigating perspectives on statistical health data of the neighbourhood

The third research method was used to investigate the personal stories and views of the citizens on quantitative health data, three different themes were discussed in groups: 1) lifestyle, 2) living and environment, and 3) well-being and social participation. A factsheet (Figure 1) was made for each of these themes based on the results of the most recent municipal health service monitor for older adults [Boom et al., 2021]. The purpose of the meetings was to get an impression of the lived and situated experiences, and personal stories that citizens relate to the health statistics of their neighbourhood. Where do they recognize themselves in the numbers, where do they want to add something to the quantitative data, and what do they think is remarkable?

During the meeting, the citizens were divided into three groups, for each theme there was one table with a moderator and an observer who took notes. After three rounds of approximately 45 minutes each, everyone had discussed each theme with the group. A discussion guide was developed for each of the factsheets. Each guide consisted of an icebreaker and follow-up questions to support the discussions. Considering for example the theme lifestyle, the icebreaker question was about participants' favourite dish. After discussing the icebreaker, all citizens received a printed version of the corresponding factsheet, read it and identified points that caught their attention. Striking matters were shared in the group and where relevant, possible causes and solutions for the neighbourhood were discussed (Textbox 5 shows the findings). At the end of each round, advice for the municipality was collected.

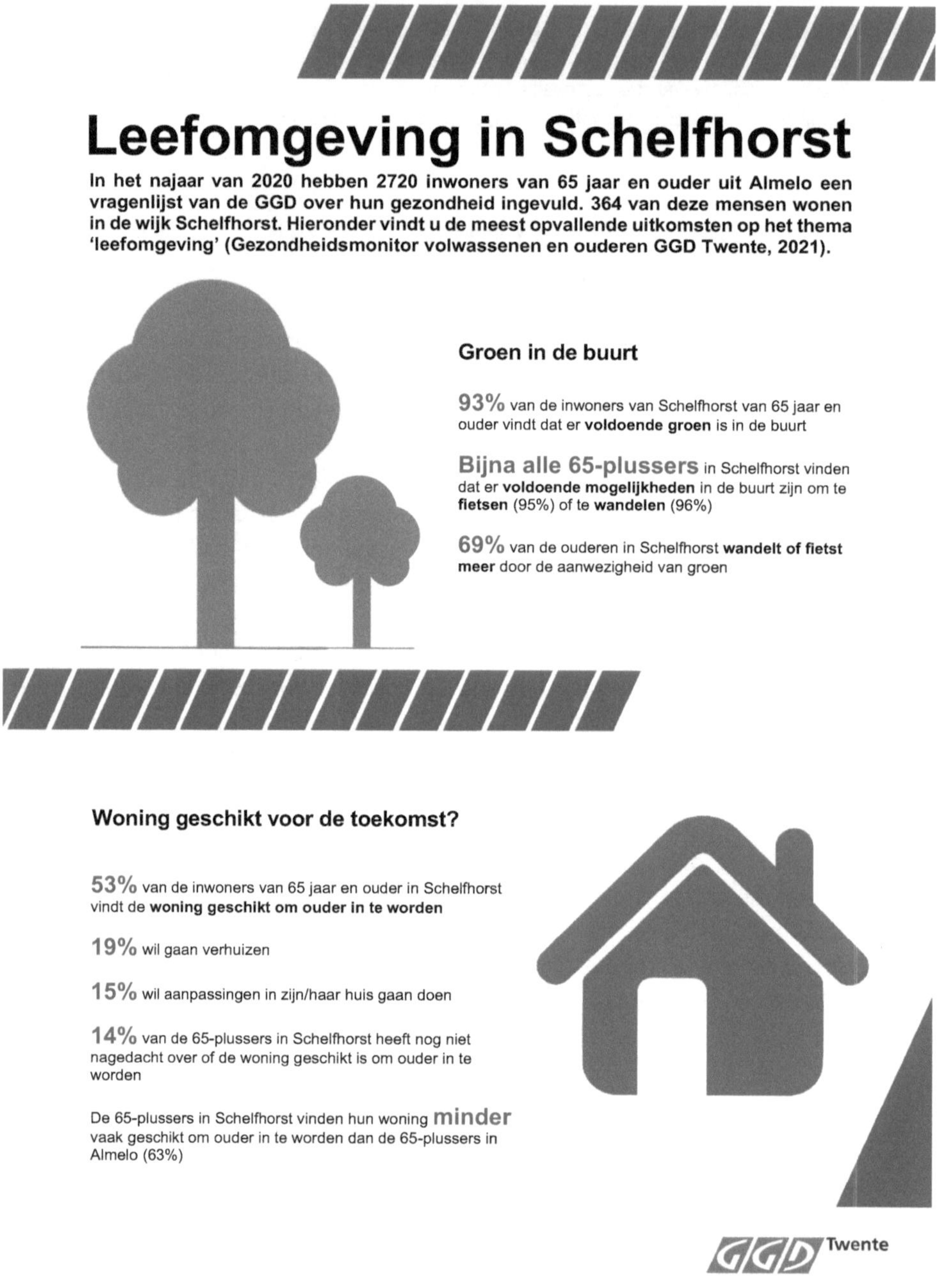

Leefomgeving in Schelfhorst

In het najaar van 2020 hebben 2720 inwoners van 65 jaar en ouder uit Almelo een vragenlijst van de GGD over hun gezondheid ingevuld. 364 van deze mensen wonen in de wijk Schelfhorst. Hieronder vindt u de meest opvallende uitkomsten op het thema 'leefomgeving' (Gezondheidsmonitor volwassenen en ouderen GGD Twente, 2021).

Groen in de buurt

93% van de inwoners van Schelfhorst van 65 jaar en ouder vindt dat er **voldoende groen** is in de buurt

Bijna alle 65-plussers in Schelfhorst vinden dat er **voldoende mogelijkheden** in de buurt zijn om te **fietsen** (95%) of te **wandelen** (96%)

69% van de ouderen in Schelfhorst **wandelt of fietst meer** door de aanwezigheid van groen

Woning geschikt voor de toekomst?

53% van de inwoners van 65 jaar en ouder in Schelfhorst vindt de **woning geschikt om ouder in te worden**

19% wil gaan verhuizen

15% wil aanpassingen in zijn/haar huis gaan doen

14% van de 65-plussers in Schelfhorst heeft nog niet nagedacht over of de woning geschikt is om ouder in te worden

De 65-plussers in Schelfhorst vinden hun woning minder vaak geschikt om ouder in te worden dan de 65-plussers in Almelo (63%)

GGD Twente

Figure 1: First page of the living and environment factsheet that was shared with the citizens to discuss the statistical health data of their neighbourhood.

Textbox 5: Investigating personal stories and contextualising health data

Lifestyle
Citizens believe that things are actually going quite well in terms of lifestyle among the older adults in their neighbourhood. The factsheet showed a high number of people with overweight. The citizens agreed and considered this the largest problem in terms of lifestyle. A possible cause of overweight according to the citizens was that the meal is the highlight of the day for many older adults. The citizens disagreed with the low number of older adults who want to exercise more. They acknowledge that they often have fewer opportunities or physical limitations to exercise. Having the possibility to have a cup of coffee somewhere might motivate people to take a walk, for example through the park. Also exercise in groups was considered a real boost. Someone of the neighbourhood should take the lead and organize activities, a neighbourhood sports coach or street coach. Furthermore, the use of apps was also considered a good motivation to exercise, for example a fit app or walk app. In view of the numbers of smokers and alcohol consumption, the low number of older adults who smoke seems correct, but the citizens think the number of excessive drinking is higher. Meaning that more citizens drink one or two glasses a day than represented in the current data.

Living and environment
Most citizens were satisfied with the park, but less satisfied with the greenery in the middle of the neighbourhood. This was strongly conflicting with the numbers represented by the data in the factsheet. Large trees were cut down and green areas around the houses have disappeared. The citizens like to see people in the neighbourhood green their gardens themselves. Furthermore, there was low maintenance and quality of the cycling and walking paths. Citizens indicate that they experience problems with loose paving stones, crooked fences, overhanging greenery, and poorly maintained cycle paths. This causes problems for people to walk, especially with a stroller, walker or wheelchair. This experience was not represented in the data. On the topic of future-proof living, the citizens preferred to continue living in their current home, if necessary with technological adjustments. *"I would rather make arrangements than have to go somewhere else."* In addition, the presence of adapted homes in the neighbourhood is considered important, because people like to continue living in the area. They agreed with the data on suitable housing, but the data shows that 14% of 65 years and older people did not consider future living. The citizens think this is a much larger portion of the older adults in their neighbourhood. The citizens understand that people want to stay in Schelfhorst, because all services are available. *"Everything is here and within walking distance."* Although the citizens acknowledge the usefulness of the shopping centre, the meeting function of the community centre could be improved in order to have a space where people are more likely to sit, drink coffee or read the newspaper. This aspect of services, important according to the citizens, was not mentioned in the data.

Well-being and social participation
What makes someone get out of bed? A large number of citizens indicate that they have busy daytime schedules. This was in agreement with the data on the factsheet. The factsheet presented data on healthy and meaningful living. In view of this, the citizens made a distinction between mental, physical, and social health. *"Social health is the most important thing for many people. If you feel socially healthy, your body is less important. Because if you have pain, you can think 'Hatsjikiedee' I'll continue. I am currently going through a difficult period myself, and getting out of bed is always a struggle. It is precisely that social aspect that gives meaning to your day. Sometimes hard to find . . . but extremely important."* Almost all citizens recognize loneliness in their neighbourhood, for example the neighbour, which agrees with the data of the factsheet. These neighbours have visits from family and friends, but still experience loneliness. It is suggested that this is mainly due to the feeling of exclusion or the loss of a partner, *"coming home alone, eating alone, going to bed alone"*. Several citizens indicate that it is a big step to

take action against loneliness, and to seek help someone often needs another person to take the first step. An important aspect is self-reliance and *"living the way you want"*. Some citizens indicate that you should not pamper older adults too much because you take away someone's own control. Currently, the numbers show that 19% of older adults experience low self-control. Furthermore, the citizens see a discrepancy between loneliness and societal participation.

Citizen participation in formulating and presenting results

At the end of the project, an extensive report was prepared by the core team and a summary of this report was written together with the citizens. Citizens indicated which parts of the report they considered most important, either via a phone call, by highlighting paragraphs of by writing a summary of keywords. A researcher started working with this input, a first version was shared and discussed with the citizens and a final version was written by the citizens.

To finalize the project, a project presentation was organized in the community centre of the neighbourhood and planned together with the citizens. On the basis of the summary, all citizens were asked to rank their top five wishes, actions, and recommendations. Citizens participated in the presentation of these main recommendations. This took the form of a dialogue between researchers and citizens who explained why a particular point was important. This interaction between researchers and citizens also created interaction and dialogue with the broader audience. Furthermore, the summary with rankings and the extensive report were given to a representative of the municipality.

A holistic view of age-friendly living

Needs and priorities are not simply ready to be voiced or acted upon, but rather need to be formed, clarified, and explicated. The three citizen science methods were chosen to empower older adults in Schelfhorst to explicate their needs and priorities. This section highlights the main findings across all steps.

Our findings show that citizens took a holistic approach as to what matters for age-friendly living. Initially, the project aimed to focus on the homes of older adults, which is a more narrow approach. A holistic approach considers the inside of homes as well as the surroundings, it is about the physical, mental and social health of older adults, and it is about services or technologies and the social environment in the neighbourhood. The citizens all agreed on the broad approach to living, including the world beyond the 'doorstep'. It is not only about the inside, but also the surroundings of homes; physical, mental and social health are seen as interrelated, and possible solutions include and often merge technical, social and 'green' elements. This holistic approach of what matters for healthy, happy, and safe ageing and living is in line with a holistic view on health [Huber 2016]. According to such a holistic view, health is not only about physical health, but mental and social health are evenly important. This was also explicitly discussed by the citizens in several parts of our project. Thus, for healthy ageing and independent living not only homes, services and technologies matter, but also the wider social and material environment in the neighbourhood (Figure 2).

Figure 2: Holistic approach towards age-friendly living.

During all research steps, different sorts of coaches were mentioned. In literature on ageing in place, coaches for people aged 60 years and over have been mentioned as well. However, in these studies, health coaches are supposed to provide specific support to manage chronic conditions or change health behaviours [Tiedemann et al. 2016; Haynes et al. 2020; Haynes et al. 2021; Markert 2021]. The co researches in our study saw the need for integrated healthcare, but also in the coaching perspective they took a more holistic approach. They mentioned that living or greening coaches were beneficial for the neighbourhood. They envisioned living coaches as people who visited the homes of older adults regularly and arranged possible changes to a home in a person-centred manner. In this vision, the coaches were older adults themselves living in the neighbourhood. This could support social connections and create a mutual learning environment. The same holds for the greening coaches. These older adults are supportive in making the neighbourhood 'green'. As the citizens mentioned 'tile out, plant in'. The greening coaches can provide examples to make streets greener. Furthermore, they can search for funding opportunities, for example via the municipality.

Connected with these coaching aspects was the possibility to test assistive technologies at home or the community centre. The coaches can share knowledge about available technologies and the community centre would be seen as a place to borrow it for a short time and try-out what would fit best into someone's life and living environment. We noted a similar desire in a study on the use of self-management technologies [van Leersum et al.; Bults et al. 2023]. It is often experienced as a threshold to buy something with which people are unfamiliar. The opportunity to test can lower the threshold by providing an option to test and to show or advice others to test something as well.

Reflecting three methods of citizen science

Considering the engagement, the project reached 39 citizens in the neighbourhood. Some of the citizens participated in all methods of the project and some only in one. A similarity with all methods was the level of involvement. The citizens got a role as a partner and were the experts regarding all topics [Arnstein 1969]. The researchers were present to support the conversations. The differences were in specific aspects of the methods, the first method started with two panels, an expert and residents panel. The idea was to have a safe space for all to share their opinion. This method worked out well, but at the end participants desired to learn about the findings of the other panel. The second method used a variety of creative assignments during which individual consideration and group discussions were combined. Although one citizen troubled at first in getting his own thoughts on sticky notes, once the discussion started he also started to write on the sticky notes. This combination of individual and group thinking was not only beneficial to get all involved, but as well to make sure all were able to express their thoughts. Even though during the third method some citizens had met at meetings of previous methods, there were some new citizens. In order to create an equal relationship and break the ice, questions such as 'what is your favourite dish', were used as conversation starters, and a pleasant dynamic was created in which all felt invited to participate. Collaboration with stakeholders in multiple occasions is often experienced as a challenge. In this project, most citizens were not present at all meetings, but it was visible and noted that they connected over time and appreciated talking to each other. Another challenge with engagement is reaching a diverse population. At first, we had only residents who were home owners and therefore we had to use different recruitment methods to involve also residents who rent a home in the neighbourhood.

The overarching findings of the different methods are pointing in similar directions. During the first step, both panels ultimately arrived at similar themes for future research in the neighbourhood. And although participants voiced very different stories from the neighbourhood in the beginning, during the conversations all citizen were able to connect and recognize the stories. During all steps, the citizens responded well to each other and generated lively ideas. With the future scenario workshop, one citizen went a little further in dreaming than others, but they complemented each other well. In all methods it seemed the 'easiest' to discuss on products and services, and the topic of social contacts was the most difficult. Placing actions on a timeline was also challenging for the citizens, mainly because technologies of the future are unknown. During the discussions of all methods, the citizens wanted to pass on a number of recurring advices and solutions to the municipality. To ensure passing on of findings, the findings from the method where we enriched the statistical health data with perspectives of the citizens, were translated into a list of recommendations for the municipality. Furthermore, at the end of the project we organized a public meeting and handed the report as well as the summary made by the citizens to a representative of the municipality.

In view of the effectiveness of the process, all methods were intended to empower the citizens. The first method was most suitable to determine valuable research questions and initial plans to conduct research. Based on the findings a group of residents can gather and take further steps. In order to move forward, it seems necessary to involve and reach a larger group of residents, but also cooperation with other professional parties and the municipality. As mentioned before, at first it was difficult to discuss the topic of social contacts. With the use of the scenario, on the second day of the workshop, there was a lot of attention to social contacts and loneliness. While this was an underexposed topic during the first day, social and also physical contact became important. The scenario triggered discussions about forming a community, solidarity, and reducing loneliness. In addition, the scenario made the citizens more aware of the underlying feeling that they want to become more self-sufficient, more independent, and individual. The researchers deliberately wrote some parts of the scenario to provoke responses. These were picked up by the citizens who suggested aspects to add to the scenario, such as the creation of a gap between different groups of residents if they cannot contribute to the shared energy supply system. With the third method fact sheets were used. The fact sheets displayed various figures from the health monitor [Boom et al. 2021]. The citizens found it interesting to see these fact sheets and it helped them to discuss different topics. However, some figures raised questions and the citizens tried to add up the data, which was not always possible.

Overall, all methods were intended to empower the citizens. While a number of joint concerns and desires were recurring in the different steps, the combination of methods allowed to successively enrich the emerging vision of how the neighbourhood can become a place for safe, healthy and happy ageing.

References

Arnstein SR. Ladder of Citizen Participation. J Am I Planners. 1969;35(4):216–24. doi: Doi 10.1080/01944366908977225. PubMed PMID: WOS:A1969Y429300002.

Aung, M. N., Koyanagi, Y., Ueno, S., Tiraphat, S., & Yuasa, M. (2022). Age-friendly environment and community-based social innovation in Japan: A mixed-method study. *The Gerontologist*, *62*(1), 89–99.

Black, K., & Oh, P. (2022). Assessing age-friendly community progress: What have we learned?. *The Gerontologist*, *62*(1), 6–17.

Boom, C., Hieltjes, I., Huisjes, T., Nies, J., van Stenus, C., Tijhuis, K., & Waanders, W. (2021). Gezondheidsmonitor – Volwassenen en Ouderen 2020 Twentse rapportage. *GGD Twente, versie 1.0*, https://www.twentsegezondheidsverkenning.nl/report/style_%5CGezondheidsmonitor%20Volwassenen%20en%20Ouderen%202020%20-%20Twentse%20rapportage.pdf?rnd=1624949492588.

Bosch-Farré, C., Malagón-Aguilera, M. C., Ballester-Ferrando, D., Bertran-Noguer, C., Bonmatí-Tomàs, A., Gelabert-Vilella, S., & Juvinyà-Canal, D. (2020). Healthy ageing in place: enablers and barriers from the perspective of the elderly. A qualitative study. *International journal of environmental research and public health*, *17*(18), 6451.

Cozza, M., Crevani, L., Hallin, A., & Schaeffer, J. (2019). Future ageing: Welfare technology practices for our future older selves. *Futures*, *109*, 117–129.

CBS (2023). Cijfers op de kaart. *Central Bureau voor de Statistiek*, https://www.cbs.nl/nl-nl/visualisaties/cijfers-op-de-kaart

Eitzel, M., Cappadonna, J., Santos-Lang, C., Duerr, R., West, S. E., Virapongse, A., . . . & Jiang, Q. (2017). Citizen science terminology matters: Exploring key terms. *Citizen science: Theory and practice*, 1–20.

Haklay, M. (2018). Participatory citizen science. *Citizen science: Innovation in open science, society and policy*, 52–62.

Haynes, A., Sherrington, C., Wallbank, G., Lester, D., Tong, A., Merom, D., . . . & Tiedemann, A. (2020). "Someone's got my back": Older people's experience of the Coaching for Healthy Ageing program for promoting physical activity and preventing falls. *Journal of Ageing and Physical Activity*, *29*(2), 296–307.

Haynes, A., Sherrington, C., Wallbank, G., Wickham, J., Tong, A., Kirkham, C., . . . & Tiedemann, A. (2021). Using self-determination theory to understand and improve recruitment for the Coaching for Healthy Ageing (CHAnGE) trial. *PLoS One*, *16*(11), e0259873.

Huber, M., van Vliet, M., & Boer, I. (2016). Heroverweeg uw opvatting van het begrip'gezondheid'. *Nederlands tijdschrift voor geneeskunde*, *160*, A7720.

Lal S, Jarus T, Suto MJ. A scoping review of the photovoice method: Implications for occupational therapy research. Canadian Journal of Occupational Therapy. 2012;79(3):181–90.

Markert, C., Sasangohar, F., Mortazavi, B. J., & Fields, S. (2021). The use of telehealth technology to support health coaching for older adults: literature review. *JMIR Human Factors*, *8*(1), e23796.

Mysyuk Y, Huisman M. Photovoice method with older persons: A review. Ageing & society. 2020;40(8):1759–87.

Remmers, G., Hermann, J., Siebrand, E., & Van Leersum, C. M. (2023). Mind the Relationship: A Multi-Layered Ethical Framework for Citizen Science in Health. *Etica & Politica*, *25*(2), 171–196.

Robinson, L. D., Cawthray, J. L., West, S. E., Bonn, A., & Ansine, J. (2018). Ten principles of citizen science. In *Citizen science: Innovation in open science, society and policy* (pp. 27–40). UCL Press.

Strasser, B., Baudry, J., Mahr, D., Sanchez, G., & Tancoigne, E. (2019). " Citizen science"? Rethinking science and public participation. Science & Technology Studies, 32(ARTICLE), 52–76.

Tiedemann, A., Rissel, C., Howard, K., Tong, A., Merom, D., Smith, S., . . . & Sherrington, C. (2016). Health coaching and pedometers to enhance physical activity and prevent falls in community-dwelling people aged 60 years and over: study protocol for the Coaching for Healthy AGEing (CHAnGE) cluster randomised controlled trial. *BMJ open*, *6*(5), e012277.

van Leersum, C. M., Konrad, K. E., Siebrand, E., Malik, Z. B., den Ouden, M. E., & Bults, M. (2023). Engaging older adults with a migration background to explore the usage of digital technologies in coping with dementia. *Frontiers in Public Health*, *11*, 1125834.

Vanleerberghe, P., De Witte, N., Claes, C., Schalock, R. L., & Verté, D. (2017). The quality of life of older people ageing in place: a literature review. *Quality of Life Research*, *26*, 2899–2907.
Vercelli A, Rainero I, Ciferri L, Boido M, Pirri F. Robots in elderly care. *DigiCult Sci. J. Digit. Cult.* (2017) 2:37–50.
Wright, D., Buys, L., Vine, D., Xia, B., Skitmore, M., Drogemuller, R., . . . & Li, M. (2014). EUTOPIA 75+: Exploratory futures scenarios for baby boomers' preferred living spaces. *Journal of Futures Studies*, *19*(2), 41–60.

Johan van der Zwart, Catharina M. van Leersum, Kornelia Konrad

Climbing the citizen science ladder: Juxtaposing citizens' levels of participation and influence in research analysis and dissemination

Abstract: This study explores the evolving role of citizens in scientific research through citizen science initiatives, particularly emphasizing their involvement beyond data collection to include analysis and dissemination phases. Focusing on the healthcare context, the research aims to enhance the democratic engagement of citizens in the scientific process, potentially transforming traditional research dynamics.

The methodology incorporates a framework connecting levels of citizen participation to their influence on research outcomes. The study examines citizen involvement across various stages of the research process in several projects within a Dutch Citizen Science program. Key aspects analyzed include framing research questions, analyzing data, writing reports, and presenting findings.

Results indicate that citizens' deeper engagement in these activities can shift the balance of power, enhancing their influence on research outcomes. This participation not only enriches the research with diverse perspectives but also leads to more democratized processes. Citizens involved in research activities demonstrated increased capability in shaping research agendas and influencing outcomes directly related to their community's needs. The study concludes that involving citizens more comprehensively in research processes does not merely augment research but transforms it, fostering a more collaborative and inclusive environment.

Introduction

Active involvement of citizens in multiple stages of research and innovation processes is the core of citizen science, an emerging approach for user inclusion. In the context of healthcare, the inclusion of the patient is of particular relevance for empowering end-users with the aim to shape and direct new technologies that matter to them (Iakovleva, Oftedal & Bessant., 2019). Citizen science has the potential to contribute to

Acknowledgements: The authors would like to thank all co-researchers for collaborating with us in every research step, and providing valuable insights. The authors also thank all colleagues and partners of TOPFIT Citizenlab for their regular support and collaboration. TOPFIT citizenlab was financialy supported by Regio Deal Twente, a regional support programme enabled by the Dutch Government.

https://doi.org/10.1515/9783111241036-007

Responsible Research and Innovation (Wickson & Carew, 2014), and it is presumed to lead to improved understanding, uptake and implementation of transparent and responsive research in society (Kieslinger et al, 2017).

One of the premises of citizen science is that it strengthens research and innovation through a better understanding of the context due to better access to citizens' situated knowledge, and simultaneously fosters citizens' empowerment. In order to strengthen the position of citizens in research, scientists sometimes have to take a more facilitating role, supporting the citizens in the research process, rather than doing the research for them, or 'in name of' the citizens. What is more, citizens are likely to gain a more substantial and influential role in the research, if they are not only involved in data collection, but also in the analysis of data, the writing process and the presentation of research results, which is traditionally the scope where scientists can distinguish themselves within their own research field. In this chapter, we examine whether including citizens as co-researchers in these research steps could contribute to a more equal collaboration between scientists and co-researchers, as well as democratisation of the research process itself. For this, we examine the role of citizens across a set of projects that were conducted as part of a Dutch Citizen Science programme, in the domain of technology for health and wellbeing. In several projects, citizens were involved in developing research questions, gathering data, framing and analysing research results, writing research reports and articles, and communicating research results to a broader audience (read more on TOPFIT Citizenlab in chapter 5 community).

Building upon Citizenlab's experiences with the involvement of citizens in science, this chapter attempts to provide more insight in how the participation of citizens in different research activities contributes to a democratization of science and an empowerment of citizens. For this, we first develop a framework that builds on multiple categorizations of citizen science and connects the level of participation of citizens in research activities to the level of influence on the actual research results. Then we examine the role of citizens in various instances of framing research questions, analysis, writing and presenting of research results in the Citizenlab projects. In a further step, we take an overarching perspective considering the findings as a whole and ask whether we observe patterns in how the participation in research activities relates to empowerment of citizens, in particular whether the level of participation shifted the balance of power towards citizens. As a result, we suggest that the diverse ways of involving citizens in advanced research activities as analysing and disseminating research results can indeed be clustered into different steps on a 'Citizen Science ladder'. Climbing this ladder implies step by step expanding the participation of citizens in research activities and increasing the influence on research outcomes.

What is citizen science?

Citizen science is a flexible concept that has been defined in different ways and applied in diverse disciplines (Robinson et al. 2018; Eitzel et al. 2017). Still, a common aspect across all variations is citizens' active involvement and collaboration with scientists in the production of knowledge (Remmers et al., 2023). The heterogeneity of citizen science is visible in the many different perspectives that have been described in the literature so far. In the following, we draw on several typologies, categorizations and classifications, in order to provide a better understanding of the diversity of citizen science projects. Cooper and Lewenstein (2016) distinguish two main trends in citizen science: a '*democratic*' perspective that emphasises the responsibility of science to society, against a '*participatory citizen science*' as a practice in which people contribute to scientific enterprise. Furthermore, citizen science can also be regarded from a *political perspective*, as a social movement that tries to gain legal or political influence on specific topics (Kasperowski et al, 2017).

Democratic perspective

The democratic perspective puts emphasis on the societal responsibility of science, in which involvement of citizens in science is necessary for science to be relevant to society. For example, Wiggings and Crowston (2010) distinguish citizen science projects according to the goals and purposes. Goals can be to improve a specific situation, to be able to carry out certain tasks, generating knowledge or educate citizens about science. A more recent view on citizen science as a democratic perspective on research looks to the kind of knowledge that is sought: knowledge that can be generalized or knowledge that is of value only to the individual. From a traditional scientific perspective, knowledge is only socially useful knowledge if it refers to a generally valid pattern. From the perspective of citizens however, knowledge is already socially useful if it is 'true' or useful for the individual. Within the domain of health, Wolf and De Groot (2020) call this 'Personal Science'. Further development of this form of citizen science is particularly relevant within health research because many patients have the impression that their own insight and observations are ignored within regular medical science. This makes Personal Science, although it does not directly provide knowledge that can be generalized, a breeding ground for more formal medical scientific research and therefore intrinsically an important part of the scientific community (Remmers et al., 2023).

Participatory perspective

A more pragmatic view on citizen science is visible in approaches that distinguish forms of participation with a focus on the actual scientific research tasks that citizens participate in. Projects are analysed and described based on the practical tasks performed by the involved citizens along the different steps of research. These tasks can range from contributing data, helping researchers to collect data, up to being a co-researcher in an equal partnership, or even becoming a citizen initiator of new research projects.

Haklay (2018) defined four levels of participation in citizen science research activities: level 1) crowdsourcing, in which participation is limited to the provision of resources and the cognitive engagement is minimal; level 2) distributed intelligence, where citizens participate in research by applying their cognitive ability, for example in collecting data and/or carry out simple interpretation activities after some basic training; level 3) participatory science, citizens are participating in setting the problem definition and/or in consultation with scientists, the data collection method is devised, the citizens are involved in data collection, but need the expert assistance in analysing and interpreting results; and level 4) collaborative science (also called extreme citizen science by Haklay), in which non-professional co-researchers are involved in all steps of the research process.

Political perspective

According to Haklay (2018), many categorisations and typologies of participation to date try to bridge the democratic and participatory perspective on citizen science. However, these two perspectives do not address fully the political aspects of citizen science, as one could also argue that citizen participation in research is part of a process of empowerment. In this political perspective on citizen science, reference is often made to the ladder of Arnstein (1969), in which citizen participation is viewed in the context of urban planning. Arnstein's ladder of citizen participation consists of eight steps and is divided into three parts: manipulation and therapy are forms of non-participation; informing, consultation and advisor are forms of tokenism; partnership, delegated power and citizen control are forms of citizen empowerment.

This ladder of Arnstein is now also used in other domains than urban planning and helps to assess power and influence in the contacts between citizens and societal agencies. Applied to citizen science, citizens can gain more control over the outcomes and increase their 'level of citizen influence' by participating in research, for example by collecting research data and further developing knowledge about a theme that is important to them. In this perspective on citizen science, the higher parts of the ladder can be seen as empowering citizens by conducting research activities in which the power dynamics increasingly shift from scientists to citizens. Power in this context is defined as the degree of influence that citizens have on the final results, with different forms of citizen participation confirming or changing the common division of work and decision-making between researchers and citizens.

Conceptual frame to describe and analyse citizen science projects

The three perspectives on citizen science provide a useful conceptual frame to describe and analyse citizen science projects, which will be used in the following section to analyse the role of citizens in the different research activities of five projects within TOPFIT Citizenlab.

Table 1: Three perspectives on citizen science as analytical frame.

Democratic perspective	Participatory perspective	Political perspective
Goal	Roles	Citizen <-> Society
Purpose	Research tasks	Citizen <-> Scientists
Gained knowledge	Level of participation (Haklay)	Degree of power (Arnstein)

First, we exemplify how citizen science distinguishes from more traditional citizen participation in research that is normally conducted in the healthcare sector. For this, we describe the goals and purposes of different citizen science projects within TOPFIT, the gained knowledge and how citizens were involved in framing the research. Then, we elaborate on the different roles and tasks of the citizens as co-researchers with a focus on how co-researchers contributed to analysing data and understanding the outcomes, but also how they were involved in writing about the research results and presenting the outcomes in society. Further on, we analyse how the participation in research activities relates to empowerment of citizens and whether the level of participation shifted the balance of power towards citizens.

Citizen science in practice – TOPFIT Citizenlab

In this section we provide a short description of five Citizenlab projects that we analyse and use to further develop the conceptual framework.

Textbox 1: Short description of five Citizenlab projects

People with rheumatoid arthritis (Grünloh et al., 2023)
People with rheumatoid arthritis often have questions about the status of their physical condition and the best way to manage it. Therefore, scientists, medical experts, organizations and citizens as co-researchers collaborated to design and conduct a study of fatigue among patients. The aim of the project was twofold: to gather scientific knowledge about rheumatoid arthritis and to give people with rheumatoid arthritis insight into their own condition. To this end, a secure digital environment was created in which co-researchers can collect and view research data themselves. Citizens were involved

in framing the research, determining the research question, and helped to analyse and interpret the data on personal and group levels.

Informal caregivers (Driesche & Kerklaan, 2022)
This project focused on care professionals who act in parallel as informal caregivers and inquired into the perceived burden experienced by these care professionals in relation to their double roles. Besides informal caregivers as co-researchers, this research also involved Human Resource Management (HRM)-advisors as co-researchers. The goal of the project was thus to gain knowledge on the perceived burden of informal caregivers in balancing between work and informal care tasks. The informal caregivers and HRM-advisors contributed ideas about the design of the study, in particular in the implementation of follow-up steps. The co-researchers were involved in re-framing the research, determining the research focus, and analysing and interpreting the data. (Van der Zwart, 2023)

Older adults with dementia and a migration background (Van Leersum et al., 2023)
During the corona pandemic, scientists worked together with a local organisation that offers daytime activities for older adults with a migration background and dementia in their search for digital resources to continue the provision of good care. This project concerned the use of the digital tool Anne4-Care among Turkish older adults with (mild) dementia. Making this virtual assistant suitable for people who have another native language, required involvement of older adults with a migration background. To gain knowledge on the background, wishes and needs of this specific group, they were involved as co-researchers in preparing the interview guide, code tree, coding of one interview and reviewing the final report.

People with type 2 diabetes (Bults et al., 2023)
There is a wide range of digital tools and platforms available for people with type 2 diabetes mellitus (T2DM). Each app has different functionalities and many of these products can support a healthy lifestyle. This project inquired into the added value of these digital products and services and the circumstances under which they support the lives of people with T2DM. Additional objectives of this project were to gain insight into the influence of digital tools on the daily lives of people with T2DM, and the influence of these tools on the relationship between caregivers and patients. Co-researchers were involved in preparing and moderating group sessions, testing applications, feedback on the research report, and writing a policy letter with recommendations.

Happy, healthy, and safe living in a neighbourhood (Van Leersum, 2023)
The aim of this project was to gain insight into happy, healthy, and safe independent living at home in a neighbourhood in a medium sized city. Doing citizen science was regarded as a way to make the voices of older adults heard. Citizens and scientists explored how the neighbourhood could be improved to enable living healthy, safe and happy in older age. Co-researchers were involved in framing the research, analysing and interpreting outcomes, and writing and presenting the results. (Read more about this project in chapter 6).

In these projects, scientists have experimented with various methodological steps to include citizens as co-researchers in framing the research, analysing the research data, contextualising results and communicating the outcomes through writing and presenting. Table 2 summarises the different methods that were used in the different projects.

Table 2: Applied methods to include citizens in research activities.

	Rheumatism (r.)	Informal care (i.)	Dementia (d.)	Type 2 diabetes (t.)	Neighbourhood (n.)
Framing (.f)	Feedback defining research questions and methods	Reframing research question / focus	Preparing interview guide	Prepare and moderate group session	Feedback on storyboards
Analysing (.a)	Personal data on fatigue	Categorising quotes	Preparing code tree	Testing applications	Input and feedback on future scenario
Contextualising (.c)	Results group data analysis	Labelling quotes	Joint coding interview	Co-researchers were involved in analysing data	Feedback on factsheets MHO's health monitor
Writing (.w)	Feedback on research poster		Reviewing report	Feedback on report	Summary of report
Presenting (.p)	Presentation of research poster			Writing policy letter	Public presentation

Citizens' contribution in framing the research

How were citizens involved in framing the research and supported this involvement a democratisation of science?
Citizens participated in the framing of the research by providing their own perspectives in discussions and meetings leading up to the definition of the research focus and by giving reactions on reports, short videos, infographics, and storyboards that summarised and condensed the content of meetings or preliminary research findings. These summaries were prepared by the scientists, and helped to bring in the findings of previous steps into the next. The feedback on these summaries served as a first check on the correct interpretation of what has been discussed in previous conversations. Although the citizens were given the opportunity to respond in writing or orally, most of the times they confirmed the supplied summaries without further changes or additions. The organised group meetings, interviews and surveys contributed to (re)framing the research questions (informal care project and neighbourhood project), determining the specific focus and research design (rheumatism project), the content of the interview guide (dementia project and diabetes project), and topics of the group discussions (diabetes project).

Textbox 2: Knowledge and insight into fatigue by people with rheumatoid arthritis

At the start of this project, the perspectives of citizens were collected by way of questionnaires, interviews and group discussions. The results were analysed by the scientists and fed back to the participants after each step in the project. For this purpose, short summaries of 3–4 pages were made and, in some cases, supplemented with a YouTube video. Participants could indicate if information was missing in the summary or whether they disagreed with parts of the summaries. In practice this did not happen, as there were only positive reactions to the summaries of the conversations and choices. The input of the participants ultimately contributed to determining fatigue as the most important topic that participants wanted to work on. Specifically, the study design focussed on the capriciousness and unpredictability of fatigue. (Grünloh et al. 2023)

In most projects, citizens together with scientists made choices and decisions about several steps in the research. By involving citizens, a broader and more varied knowledge base was included in the research, in which both parties complemented each other and recognized each other's strengths, specifically in framing the research, adjusting research methods and determining approaches to the data analysis. When considering the appropriate research methods for the specific context, scientists brought in their experiences about research methods, whereas citizens built upon their personal experiences. In three projects, citizens had a more active role as co-researcher in how to apply the chosen research methods in this specific context. By providing input in the interviews' topic list (dementia project), by preparing and moderating a group discussion (diabetes project), and by discussing suitable research methods to answer a research question (neighbourhood project), citizens were brought into the research process as active co-researchers. Through their active involvement in framing the research, these co-researchers have left their mark on the studies. For example, interview topics were suggested that were not previously listed. A possible disadvantage of this kind of strong involvement of co-researchers could be that a citizen is less able to take a distance to the material and subject, and might therefore be less objective. This requires that both the scientists and co-researchers stay aware of possible biases during the research process.

Active involvement of citizens in finding out how to apply existing research methods required that the scientists explained these methods to the co-researchers. This resulted in a more equal collaboration between the scientists and citizens and contributed not only to the quality of the research itself, but also led to a democratisation of scientific research methods. Citizens know what kind of answers they are looking for, what questions they want answered and whether the results match their personal experience. Scientists know more about possible analysis methods and their respective advantages and disadvantages. In the diabetes project for example, an imbalance that surfaced at the beginning of the project between knowledge from co-researchers, who base their input knowledge on their own experiences, and knowledge of the scientists who tried to place the topics in a larger context, was dealt with by jointly going through the interview guide to decide together how to apply the interview strategies. On a number of occasions, the scientists' preliminary ideas were carried out unchanged. Sometimes however, input form the citizens changed the research question. Occasionally, the scientists' ideas were regarded as too complex by the citizens and therefore not implemented.

Citizens' participation in analysing and interpreting the research results

What were the roles of the citizens in research activities and how did citizens participate in analysing data and contextualising results?
Citizens engaged in the analysis and interpretation of the research data through contextualising the outcomes, as co-researcher actively taking part in the analysis of qualitative data or in the form of exercising personal science in finding patterns in individually collected data. The inclusion of citizens in analysing data and interpreting research results are forms of participatory science (Haklay, 2018). In participatory research, analysis of data by co-researchers can for example consist of trying to find patterns in your own recorded personal data, such as the daily measurement of glucose levels or blood pressure, before the data is aggregated and analysed on group levels. For citizens, this form of personal science (De Groot, 2020) could already provide useful knowledge on individual level.

Citizens could analyse data on the level of personal science in two of the projects. In the Rheumatism project, co-researchers were able to discover patterns in their own collected data on fatigue. For this purpose, the digital environment that was used to collect data during a period of three weeks provided graphs on personal level to the co-researchers. In the diabetes project, while testing, collecting use-data and giving feedback on different applications, co-researchers had the opportunity to get better insight in their glucose levels, potentially finding patterns related to their daily activities.

In most projects, the interpretation and contextualisation of the analysis results was done together with co-researchers, who thus got a clear influence on the interpretation of the research results. Although the scientists were responsible for the basic data analyses in most projects, by including citizens in the interpretation of the analysis results, they contributed their lived experience to make the research results more accessible and contribute to a better understanding of the knowledge gained. In the rheumatism project, for example, the aggregated group data was analysed by the scientists in collaboration with a rheumatologist. After these quantitative analyses, the interpretation of the results was done together with the co-researchers during a group discussion. As another example, in the neighbourhood project, citizens discussed the Municipality Health Organisation (MHO) Health monitor, providing contextual qualitative interpretations relating to their lived experience on the quantitative data form the MHO (reference chapter 6 Schelfhorst).

Especially for qualitative research methods, the inclusion of co-researchers in analysing and interpreting the data proved to be very helpful. For example, the involvement in the design of a code tree for the interview analysis (dementia project) provided important topics for analysis that otherwise would have been missed. This project also included a co-researcher in interpreting qualitative data by coding one interview together with a scientist. Based on the topics that were stipulated as important by the co-researcher, the other interviews were coded accordingly by the research team. During the coding and analysis, aspects have also been included in the report that might not have been included without this involvement.

Textbox 3: Coding of qualitative data by older adults with dementia and a migration background

One of the older adults with a background as a researcher was interested in participating as a more active co-researcher. This person had user experience with the digital tool and knew the other older adults. It was examined how the knowledge and expertise of this specific co-researcher could contribute to the research. In coordination with the care organisation, it was decided that this co-researcher could provide input in the interviews' topic list. He also contributed to the design of a coding tree, which is a collection of labels that help structure the results of interviews. By making the coding tree together, the co-researcher was able to pinpoint important topics for the analysis of the interviews. Furthermore, he also assisted in coding one of the interviews. The interview in question was conducted with another participant and then transcribed, shortened, and anonymized. In addition, this co-researcher was involved in reviewing the final report and making recommendations, for which he is acknowledged in the final report. (Van Leersum et al., 2023; Siebrand, 2023)

The dementia project made clear that greater participation and more influence requires a greater investment of time and attention, which can result in overburdening the involved co-researchers. When collaborating with vulnerable citizens, an external caregiver was constantly present during the research activities to monitor the extent to which the co-researcher was involved and to stop the activities if this deemed to be necessary (Siebrand, 2023).

In another project, citizens discussed the future of their neighbourhood. On this basis, the scientists analysed the input and condensed it in a scenario of a possible future. The co-researchers responded along three themes to this scenario, adding a deeper understanding, contextualisation, and more integration of the separate topics. Although most of the time the scientists took the initiative presenting a number of options to the co-researchers, the added value of the scientific knowledge was mainly in the research methods and process management. On the subject matter however, the citizens were in the lead.

Also in the informal care project, citizens were involved in analysing data and contextualising results. The inclusion of co-researchers in categorising and labelling interview quotes, resulted in a much richer interpretation of the data, providing context in wording and themes that expressed deeper experiences and emotions (Van der Zwart, 2023). This project made specific use of citizens' insight in their own contextual situation, their priorities, compared to those of the scientists or, in this specific context, the employers of the informal caregivers.

Textbox 4: Categorization and labelling of qualitative data by informal caregivers

In the first phase of this project, five informal caregivers working in healthcare were interviewed about the balance between work-life and informal care. In the next phase of the research, informal caregivers were involved as co-researchers to categorise and label the interview quotes. For this purpose, the interviews were fully transcribed and the two scientists independently selected typical statements and quotes. After mutual coordination, a large number of quotes were selected and presented for categorisation in separate online sessions to the participants. Participants included four informal caregivers, four HRM-advisors and three scientists from TOPFIT Citizenlab. Participants were asked to group the quotes into themes, to divide those themes into categories and to assign labels to them based on common characteristics. It was striking that the HRM-advisors arrived at far fewer categories than the other two groups and that the wording of the themes by the informal caregivers expressed more subjective experiences and emotions. More specifically, the different viewpoints of the informal caregivers and HRM-advisors seemed to complement each other. (Driesche & Kerklaan, 2022; Van der Zwart, 2023)

Citizen collaboration in dissemination

How has participation in writing about, and presentation of, research outcomes empowered citizens in their position towards scientists, society and policy?
Citizens contributed in different forms to the writing of research outcomes, such as reviewing an article or research reports, as critical readers during the writing process of an article, or they made their own summaries of the report as input to the final conclusions.

For example, at the end of the neighbourhood project, a summary of the extensive report was written together with the citizens. Co-researchers willing to participate in this co-writing activity indicated the most important parts in the extensive report. The scientist started working on the summary, then this first version was discussed with the co-researchers and a final version was written jointly with three co-researchers (Van Leersum, 2023).

The contribution of the co-researchers in providing recommendations, reviewing reports and writing of summaries changed the division of work and the possibilities of taking influence on the research outcomes between the scientists and the co-researchers. Although the scientists were in most projects still in the lead in the writing process, the inclusion of the co-researchers implied that the scientists had to give up some of their control on this part of the research process. In the diabetes project for example, the scientists made a first draft of a summary of all findings, which was shared with all co-researchers who were the first to read the drafts, give their feedback, and write additions. Also, during the process of writing a scientific article, the co-researchers were the first to provide feedback on the draft versions.

Almost all writing activities in the projects were initiated by the scientists, except from a policy letter in the diabetes project. The co-researchers wrote this recommendation letter to the government to plea for a change in the rules for reimbursement of a certain technology, based on the research they did themselves within the TOPFIT Citizenlab.

Textbox 5: Writing a policy recommendation letter by people with T2DM

The co-researchers initiated and prepared in collaboration with the scientists a letter to the Dutch minister of health in which they presented the findings of the study. The letter concerned the reimbursement of glucose meters. Whereas the same technology is reimbursed by health insurances for people with type 1 diabetes, patients with type 2 diabetes need to pay for it themselves. During several co-creation sessions, a sense of injustice surfaced among the co-researchers about how the focus of policies for type 2 diabetes is mainly on treating the disease and that prevention supported by these technologies played a limited role. With regard to the content of the letter, the co-researchers made many decisions themselves, in consultation with the scientists. The scientists provided support where necessary, which mainly concerned communication with TOPFIT Citizenlab and the Dutch Diabetes Association. (Bults et al., 2023; Van der Zwart, 2023)

Another example of citizen empowerment occurred in the neighbourhood project, where the citizens presented the research results to the municipality and discussed the results in a plenary session moderated by the scientist. Furthermore, the programme was structured largely according to the suggestions of the citizens and citizens participated in the presentation and explanation of the project results. This session gave a voice to the citizens to present the research and their recommendations about their future neighbourhood in a political context (cross link to chapter 6 Schelfhorst).

Level of participation and influence on research outcomes

In the previous section, we examined how citizens participated as co-researchers in specific research activities and, in so doing, how they influenced the end results. In the following, we take an overarching perspective considering the findings on different research steps and projects as a whole and ask whether we observe patterns in how the participation in research activities relates to empowerment of citizens, in particular whether the level of participation shifted the balance of power towards citizens. Therefore, we simultaneously position the research activities alongside Haklay's levels of participation (2018) and the Participation Ladder of Arnstein (1969). While Arnstein's ladder is helpful to capture the influence citizens can exert as a form of citizen empowerment, Haklay's levels of participation focus on the type of research activities in which citizens participate. Co-researchers' influence and level of participation in the research activities in the different projects are summarised in Table 3 and Figure 1 visualizes the different routes that the projects followed from one research activity to another.

Table 3: Summary of level of participation and influence on results per research activities in the projects. Legenda level of participation: d.i.=distributed intelligence, p.sc.=participatory science, co.sc.=collaborative science.

framing		**analysing**		**contextualisation**		**Writing**		**Presenting**	
level	influence	level	influence	level	influence	level	influence	level	Influence
				Rheumatism					
d.i.	partner	p.sc.	delegate	d.i.	advisor	d.i.	advisor	co.sc	Delegate
Decisions on research focus, questions and methods made by citizens together with scientists (r.f).		Analysing individually collected data on fatigue as form of personal science (r.a).		Scientists in the lead of the analysis, asking the co-researcher for their perspectives on the results (r.c).		Citizens gave feedback on research poster made by scientists (r.w).		Public presentation of research poster on an international conference together with scientists (r.p).	
				Informal caregivers					
p.sc.	advisor	p.sc.	partner	co.sc.	partner				
The co-researchers initiated a re-framing of the research topic to their needs together with the scientists (i.f).		Grouping and categorising quotes that scientists selected out of the interviews (i.a).		Labelling the categorised quotes and describing potential scenarios that fits the citizens' needs (i.c)					
				Dementia					
d.i.	advisor	p.sc.	partner	d.i	partner	d.i.	advisor		
Brining in interview topics, but citizens conformed to the pre-determined framing of the research (d.f).		While preparing the code tree, the co-researcher brought in topics for further analysis (d.a).		During the joint coding of an interview, knowledge and experiences of the co-researcher contributed to the interpretation (d.c).		As first reviewer giving feedback on the outcomes, for which the co-researcher was acknowledged in the final report (d.w).			

Table 3 (continued)

framing		analysing		contextualisation		Writing		Presenting	
level	influence	level	influence	level	influence	level	influence	level	Influence
				Type 2 diabetes					
d.i.	partner	p.sc.	delegate	p.sc.	partner	d.i.	advisor	co.sc.	Control
Moderating a group session based on a topic list that was prepared together with a scientist (t.f).		Testing applications, collecting use-data and giving feedback on the technologies (t.a).		Analysing collected data together with scientists (t.c).		First reviewers of summary of findings and critical first readers of article drafts made by scientists (t.w).		citizens initiated writing a policy recommendation letter, facilitated by scientists (t.p).	
				Neighbourhood					
d.i.	partner	p.sc.	Partner	d.i.	consult	p.sc.	partner	co.sc.	delegate
Feedback on story boards prepared by scientists to decide on research topic, questions and methods (n.f).		Citizens had an active role in interpreting the collected data by responding on future scenarios prepared by scientists (n.a).		Giving feedback on factsheets of the MHO's health monitor in round table discussions (n.c).		Citizens indicated the most important parts in the extensive report and were co-writers of the final summary (n.w).		Co-researchers presented their own view on the content matter on stage, facilitated by the scientist (n.p).	

Cross-project analysis of research activities

Building on the visualization of Figure 1, the analytical diagram in Figure 2 highlights that across different projects similar research activities use similar levels of participation in research, resulting in similar levels of influence.

Scientist initiated framing research with co-researchers

Three projects started the framing of the research in the form of a partnership on the level of distributed intelligence (r.f; t.f; n.f). These three projects had a relatively large group of citizens involved in different roles, as respondents, interviewees and co-researchers. In addition to the citizens and scientists, there were many other organisations involved in these projects, like patient organisations, companies and governmental agencies. Content wise, the framing of the research was mainly in the hands of the scientists, as mediator between the citizens and other involved partners in the project.

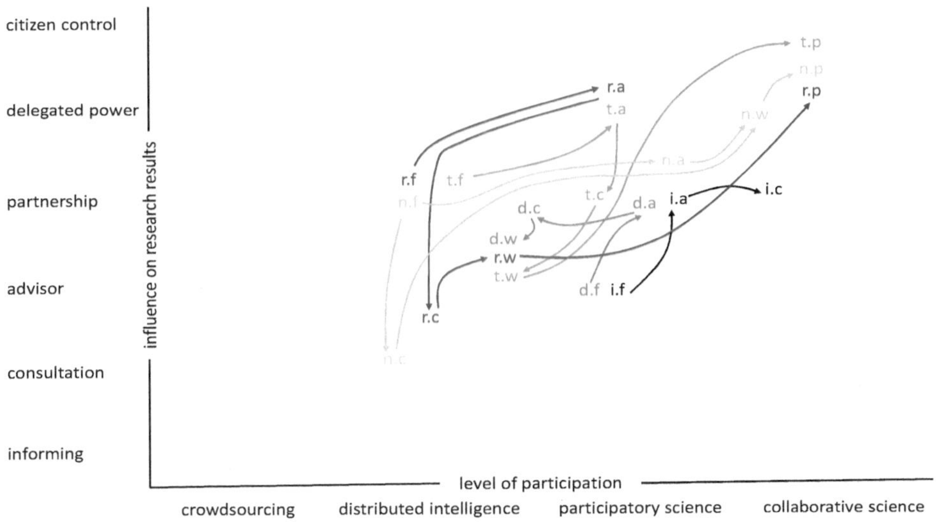

Figure 1: Level of participation in research activities and citizens' influence on results. Legenda projects: r.=rheumatism, i.=informal caregivers, d.=dementia, t.= type 2 diabetes, n.=neighbourhood. Legenda research activities: .f=framing research, .a=analysing data, .c=contextualising results, .w=writing, .p=presenting outcomes.

Co-researcher initiated re-framing research with scientists

At the beginning of two projects (d.f; i.f), the framing of research resulted in co-researcher-initiated re-framing of the original research objectives. In these two projects, the involvement of the co-researchers led to a change of the research questions (i.f) or additional interview questions (d.f), based on the co-researchers' experiences and purposes for the research. These two projects worked with a relatively small group of co-researchers within their daily context of work and care. Another similarity is that beyond the context of the employer (i.f) and care organisation (d.f), there were no other external partners involved. The research collaboration was more participatory, while the influence had a more advisory nature.

Analysing personal data

Both projects that involved patient organisations as external partners (Rheumatism and Type 2 Diabetes) created the possibility for analysing personal data by co-researchers. Citizen involvement in developing and testing a new application (r.a) or testing existing applications (t.a) delegated power from the scientists to the co-researchers in a participatory approach to science. However, in the following research activities of contextualising the results on group levels (r.c) or writing about the results (t.w), this high level of influence on research activities moved towards a more advisory role for the co-researchers.

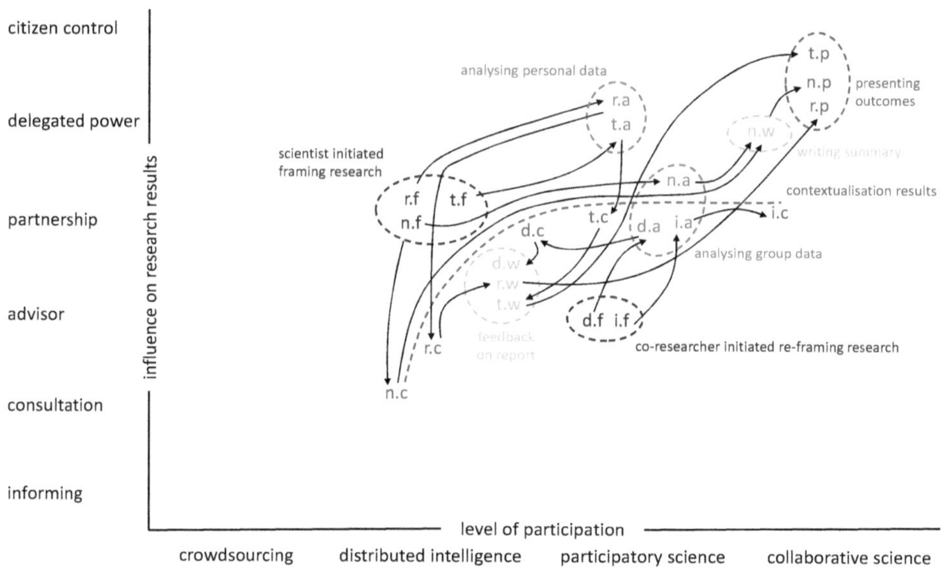

Figure 2: Cross-project analysis of research activities and citizens' influence on results. Legenda projects: r.=rheumatism, i.=informal caregivers, d.=dementia, t.=type 2 diabetes, n.=neighbourhood. Legenda research activities: .f=framing research, .a=analysing data, .c=contextualising results, .w=writing, .p=presenting outcomes.

Analysing group data

In three projects, co-researchers were involved in analysing data on group level (n.a; i.a; d.a). In analysing the data together, scientists and co-researchers found each other in a partnership on the level of participatory science. Although in these projects the scientists prepared the analyses by anonymizing the data (d.a), selecting quotes from the interviews (i.a) or preparing a scenario based on the citizens' input (n.a), the citizens were the ones who applied these analytical methods to the content. Then scientists brought in knowledge about analyses, the co-researchers build upon their experiential knowledge on the topic. These partnerships resulted in a deeper and more contextualised analysis of the data.

Contextualising analysis results

Maybe the most interesting research activity that is visible in Figure 2, is the contextualisation of analysis results, which manifests itself not as a cluster in the diagram, but a line that goes from distributed intelligence with consultation of the citizens (n.c) in the direction of an advisory role (r.c) towards partnership (d.c; t.c; i.c) in a more participatory science approach. Both in the neighbourhood project (n.c) and rheumatism project, the contextualisation was based on a quantitative data analysis, prepared by the scientists in collaboration with external partners, in which the co-researchers provided qualitative interpretation of the results. The other three projects (d.c; t.c; i.c), in which the contextualisation of data was carried out in partnership between scientists and co-researchers, built upon qualitative data, with the co-researchers providing context to the results, while they were also part of the analysis. Especially the informal care project, in which the co-researchers translated the results of the analysis into possible solution-oriented scenarios that would fit their context of work and care, is an example where the contextualisation of the research results was not possible without the involvement of the co-researchers.

Feedback of co-researcher in writing reports and articles

In three projects (r.w; d.w; t.w), the co-researchers gave feedback on the posters, reports and articles that were written by the scientists. In these projects, the co-researchers were involved in testing digital applications and contextualising the results of the analysis. However, when becoming involved in the writing process, the scientists mostly took the lead, and the role of the co-researchers changed from partnership towards advisor to the scientists. Nevertheless, the input given by the co-researchers contributed to the quality of the reports, as it allowed to highlight topics that were particularly important to the citizens.

Co-writing summaries and conclusions

In the neighbourhood project, the co-researchers were involved in writing the final summary and conclusions of the research report (n.w). This research activity delegated some influence on the final results from the scientist towards the citizens. Although the scientists were in the lead of the writing process, the co-researchers were leading on the content matter.

Dissemination of research

The policy recommendation letter (t.p), presentation of a poster at an international conference (r.p) and the public presentation of the research results in the neighbourhood project (n.p) are research activities that empowered the co-researchers' position in society. Facilitated by the scientists, citizens were in the lead and they controlled largely the final outcomes. Both projects exemplify how citizens can gain more control over project outcomes and increase their 'level of citizen influence' through active participation in science and by further developing knowledge about a theme that is important to them.

The citizen science ladder

In traditional research, analysing, writing, and presenting research results is the core of research work and the scope where scientists can distinguish themselves within their research field. Starting from their discipline and related epistemological world views and research paradigms, the collected data is described, interpreted, and disseminated. Including users and citizens as co-researchers in this part of the research process democratizes to a certain extent the research process and requires that scientists take a more facilitating role, supporting the citizens in the research process. To enable a more citizen inclusive research process, this facilitating role requires at the same time a pro-active role of the scientists and new or sometimes adjusted uses and implementation of existing research methods. With this chapter, we aimed to provide insights on how citizens can be involved in research activities, and how they can have influence on the research results. Figure 3 summarises our own reflections on how the involvement in various research activities in the different projects contributes to citizen science. Additionally in Figure 4, we reflect on how citizens' involvement in science together with insight in the steps between different levels of participation and influence could be perceived as a 'ladder' that step by step leads to more ambitious forms of citizen science projects.

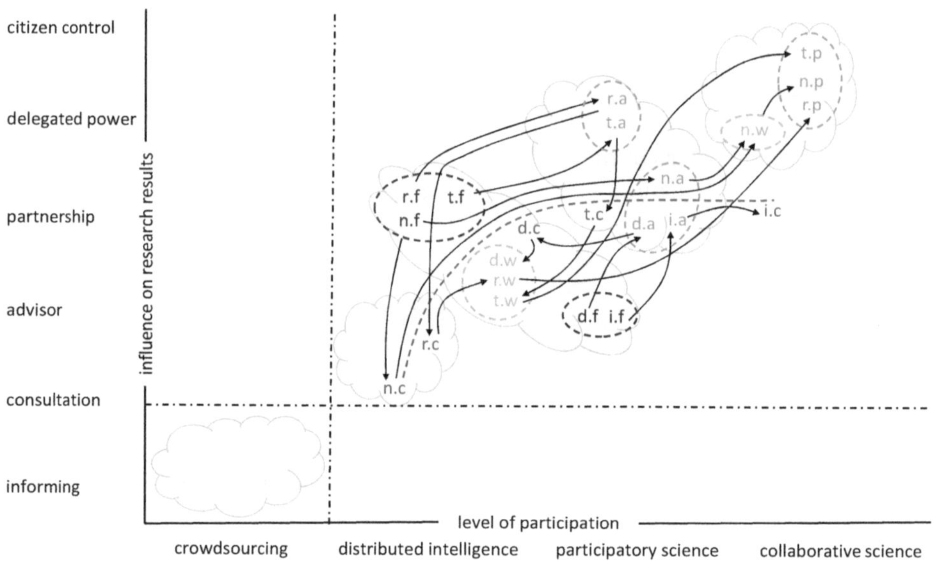

Figure 3: Juxtaposing levels of participation and influence in research. Legenda projects: r.=rheumatism, i.=informal caregivers, d.=dementia, t.=type 2 diabetes, n.=neighbourhood. Legenda research activities: .f=framing research, .a=analysing data, .c=contextualising results, .w=writing, .p=presenting outcomes.

As citizens' participation in a scientific study without playing an active part in the study itself is not citizen science (Haklay, 2018), the cloud at the left-bottom represents non-participation in citizen science activities. Activities mainly aim at obtaining data for research, but the participants do not have an active role in addition to providing data. Within TOPFIT Citizenlab for example, both the rheumatism and diabetes projects started with questionnaires send out by the scientists in collaboration with patient representative organisations. The activities in this cloud are beyond the scope of this chapter, as we focussed on participation of citizens in research activities beyond providing data.

The next cloud can be labelled as advisory-participation. In these activities, participants were actively approached and continuous interaction allowed to transfer insights both ways between the citizens and the scientists. However, this still happened on the scientists' initiative and the citizens' opinions were mainly taken into account in decisions made by the scientists.

The third cloud captures a form of advisory-collaboration. In the research activities that took place here, citizens did not only give their advice, but in most cases also entered into a collaborative conversation with the researchers to discuss and explain the advice in more detail. Nevertheless, in the end, the scientists took in most projects the final responsibility for the choices made.

The fourth cloud could be called partner-participation. The activities positioned here were done in active collaboration between citizens as co-researchers and scientists. In addition, the co-researchers, together with the scientists, had a role in making decisions about the analytical research methods and in some projects were also involved in the implementation of these methods.

Finally, the fifth cloud could be labelled as partner-collaboration, with the differentiating feature being who it is that takes the final decisions in the research process. While the final say is still a balance between co-researchers and scientists within partner-participation, within partner-collaboration the final say is given to co-researchers, and scientists have merely a facilitating role.

Zooming in on the differences between the clouds of research activities, each step adds another perspective on citizen science. The first step focusses on the activation of citizens in science, by inviting citizens to participate beyond passively contributing data. The second step focusses on the goals, purposes and gained knowledge for citizens and adds the democratic perspective on citizen science. The third step adds the participatory perspective in citizen science, in which citizens as co-researchers have defined roles and research tasks in the project. Finally, the fourth step adds the political perspective on citizen science, in which citizens apply the gained knowledge for their own purposes and goals. Although the empowerment of citizens through involvement in science is eminent in all these steps, it is in this final step that this empowerment becomes visible to the broader society.

The described projects show that there is not necessarily one way of citizens' inclusion in research, but rather a plurality to research activities that activates and enables

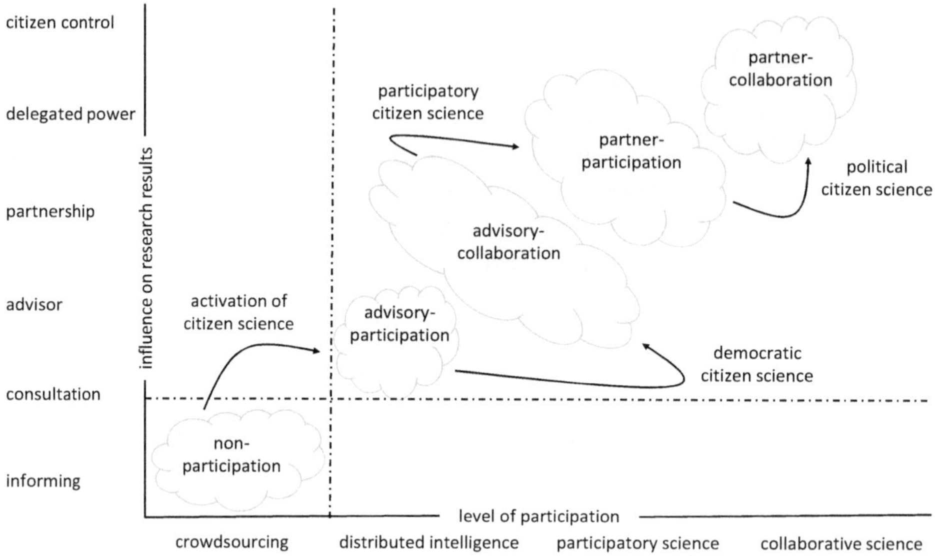

Figure 4: Citizen science ladder.

Table 4: Three perspectives on citizen science as analytical frame.

Democratic perspective	Participatory perspective	Political perspective
Goal	Roles	Citizen <-> Society
Purpose	Research tasks	Citizen <-> Scientists
Gained knowledge	Level of participation (Haklay)	Degree of power (Arnstein)

citizens in science. The conceptual model on democratic, participatory and political perspectives on citizen science and the simultaneously juxtaposing of research activities in levels of participation and citizens' influence on the final results may be useful as a guide to support designers of future collaborative research projects.

References

Arnstein, S. R. (1969). A ladder of citizen participation. *Journal of the American Institute of planners*, *35*(4), 216–224.

Bults, M., van Leersum, C. M., Olthuis, T. J. J., Bekhuis, R. E. M., & den Ouden, M. E. M. (2023). Mobile Health Apps for the Control and Self-management of Type 2 Diabetes Mellitus: Qualitative Study on Users' Acceptability and Acceptance. *JMIR diabetes*, *8*, e41076.

Cooper, C.B. and Lewenstein, B.V. (2016). Two meanings of citizen science. *The rightful place of science: Citizen science*, 51–61.

Den Broeder, L., Lemmens, L., Uysal, S., Kauw, K., Weekenborg, J., Schönenberger, M., . . . & Wagemakers, A. (2017). Public health citizen science: perceived impacts on citizen scientists: a case study in a low-income neighbourhood in the Netherlands. *Citizen Science: Theory and Practice*, *2*(1), 1–17.

Driesche, C. van den & Kerklaan, S. (2022) The value of visual co-analysis models for an inclusive citizen science approach. Fteval Journal for Research and Technology Policy Evaluation. Special Issue: Participatory Evaluation and Impact Assessment in Citizen Science.

Eitzel, M., Cappadonna, J., Santos-Lang, C., Duerr, R., West, S. E., Virapongse, A., . . . & Jiang, Q. (2017). Citizen science terminology matters: Exploring key terms. *Citizen science: Theory and practice*, 1–20.

GROZ (2019) Transitieteam GROZ: Onderzoek voor en door patiënten: een kennisagenda voor hogere kwaliteit van leven en meer maatschappelijke participatie door patiënt-gedreven onderzoek in gezondheid.

Grünloh, C., Kip M., Koffijberg, E., Tabak, M. Heesink, L. & Wolkorte, (2023) R. Naar een onderzoeksprotocol en portal voor burgerwetenschap. In *VELDBOEK BURGERWETENSCHAP VOOR GEZONDHEID: PRAKTIJKERVARINGEN IN REGIO TWENTE* (pp. 64–73). TOPFIT Citizenlab.

Haklay, M. (2018). Participatory citizen science. *Citizen science: Innovation in open science, society and policy*, 52–62.

Iakovleva, T., Oftedal, E. M., & Bessant, J. (2019). Responsible innovation in digital health. *Responsible Innovation in Digital Health: Empowering the Patient; Iakovleva, T., Oftedal, EM, Bessant, J., Eds*, 1–8.

Kasperowski, D., Kullenberg, C., & Mäkitalo, Å. (2017). Embedding Citizen Science in Research: Forms of engagement, scientific output and values for science, policy and society.

Kieslinger, B., Schäfer, T., Heigl, F., Dörler, D., Richter, A., & Bonn, A. (2017). The challenge of evaluation: An open framework for evaluating citizen science activities.

Remmers, G., Hermann, J., Siebrand, E., & Van Leersum, C. M. (2023). Mind the Relationship: A Multi-Layered Ethical Framework for Citizen Science in Health. *Etica & Politica*, *25*(2), 171–196.

Robinson, L. D., Cawthray, J. L., West, S. E., Bonn, A., & Ansine, J. (2018). Ten principles of citizen science. In *Citizen science: Innovation in open science, society and policy* (pp. 27–40). UCL Press.

Siebrand, E. (2023). De burger als co-onderzoeker. In *VELDBOEK BURGERWETENSCHAP VOOR GEZONDHEID: PRAKTIJKERVARINGEN IN REGIO TWENTE* (pp. 90–93). TOPFIT Citizenlab.

Van der Zwart, J. (2023). Samen begrijpen, beschrijven en uitdragen van onderzoeksresultaten. In *VELDBOEK BURGERWETENSCHAP VOOR GEZONDHEID: PRAKTIJKERVARINGEN IN REGIO TWENTE* (pp. 141–155). TOPFIT Citizenlab.

Van Leersum, C. M., Konrad, K. E., Siebrand, E., Malik, Z. B., den Ouden, M. E., & Bults, M. (2023). Engaging older adults with a migration background to explore the usage of digital technologies in coping with dementia. *Frontiers in Public Health*, *11*, 1125834.

Van Leersum, C. M. (2023). Met burgerwetenschap de wijk in. In *VELDBOEK BURGERWETENSCHAP VOOR GEZONDHEID: PRAKTIJKERVARINGEN IN REGIO TWENTE* (pp. 82–89). TOPFIT Citizenlab.

Wickson, F., & Carew, A. L. (2014). Quality criteria and indicators for responsible research and innovation: Learning from transdisciplinarity. *Journal of Responsible Innovation*, *1*(3), 254–273.

Wiggins, A., & Crowston, K. (2010). Developing a conceptual model of virtual organisations for citizen science. *International Journal of Organisational Design and Engineering*, *1*(1–2), 148–162.

Wolf, G. I., & De Groot, M. (2020). A conceptual framework for personal science. *Frontiers in Computer Science*, *2*, 21.

Katherine Neary

Creating new paths: Collaborative challenges in establishing an innovation hub

Abstract: This chapter shares key lessons learnt from studying an NHS hospital-based innovation hub which was undergoing a period of reflective learning, following a successful start-up phase. The complexity of operating a collaborative innovation hub led by clinical users is explored through sharing insights from data collection and research findings. The aim of the chapter is to enable the reader to understand the experience of setting up a Hub and the key lessons learnt. Through recounting the story of the Hub to date, the chapter explains the importance of key operational aspects necessary for sustained success. Key research outcomes are structured to share practical suggestions for readers interested in understanding hospital-based healthcare innovation hubs from a research and practitioner perspective. The importance of Hub space and location are explored in conjunction with stakeholder contribution, expectation and disparate priorities. In response to the challenges of sustaining collaborator participation the evolution of Hub staff roles and responsibilities are discussed. The emergence of the importance of adequate project management resource enables user time and knowledge to be focused effectively. This in turn aids pace and progress of concept development as conflicts emerge between users' primary healthcare delivery role and innovation activity.

The experience of trying to set up a Hub – lessons learnt

A healthcare innovation hub (Hub) located within a hospital campus is a rarity in the UK. Thus, stakeholders are often divided in their expectations and priorities as there are few points of comparison (Savory, 2009, Thune and Mina, 2016). The location of a hospital-based hub has the potential to involve users much more effectively than an offsite hub, due to the proximity to their primary reason for being in the hospital (Samet, 2016).

This chapter will explore lessons learnt from primary research conducted at a public hospital in the UK which is part of the National Health Service (Neary, 2022). The chapter is structured into sub-sections to illustrate key findings which share the author's critical reflections on experiences witnessed and shared by key stakeholders.

Katherine Neary, Liverpool John Moores University, UK.

https://doi.org/10.1515/9783111241036-008

The Hub space

The content of this chapter is drawn from a hospital-based Hub which had operationally reached a point in development where the initial excitement and anticipation during start-up had passed. Key stakeholder groups were seeking clarification as to the purpose and potential impact of the space and resource. Within this, the purpose of users and their contributory role was considered an essential factor.

The Hub was clinician-led, meaning the group of users actively participating in the innovation process within the Hub included Advanced Nurse Practitioners, Junior Doctors, Surgeons and Consultants (Lüthje and Herstatt, 2004, Svensson and Hartmann, 2018).

Within this chapter the terms 'Users' and 'Clinicians' collectively refer to these contributors. The inclusion of clinicians as the user group was a consequence of the complexities of collaborating with patients and families due to their areas of vulnerability whilst in the treatment process (Geiger and Hirschl, 2015). There were plans to broader user involvement at a later stage of Hub development. Yet the involvement of clinical users was not without its complexity.

Understanding the context of the study

The Hub described in this chapter is a 1000 square metre single level space, located within a UK hospital which is part of the public healthcare system in the UK, the NHS. At the time data collection commenced the Hub had existed for just over a year. Data was collected for a period of 12 months during which time core Hospital stakeholders were reviewing and reflecting on the Hub and its current and future effectiveness. The Hub team had evolved to have a core non-clinical team of 12 staff and 3 clinical staff who hot desked within the space on a semi-regular basis subject to the changeable demands of their primary healthcare delivery role. The Hub had established some significant collaborative partnerships to aid the development of innovation concepts. The objectives of innovation projects commonly revolved around improving patient experience in terms of their quality of medical and emotional care. Products which were launched were anticipated to be both sold commercially and implemented within the NHS, locally within the hospital environment and latterly across healthcare settings nationwide. Project teams comprising of hospital clinicians and a local partner were at varied stages of producing new products. The focus was on using emerging technologies including artificial intelligence, gamification and virtual reality to deliver an improved patient experience or clinical outcomes. Although there was not yet any tangible evidence of impact, significant collaborations with external partners were underway and informing the development of user-led ideas. Local Universities, national and international commercial organisations and local SMEs were actively contributing to active Hub projects.

'This is not about great ideas' – Understanding the disparity of stakeholder priorities

The novelty of a physical, dedicated innovation space within a hospital campus carried initial clinical stakeholder emotions of anticipation, excitement and possibility (Magadley and Birdi 2009). Users were skilled, knowledgeable and trained to adhere to embedded structures, designed to uphold healthcare safety, pace and quality standards. Clinical users described the scope of their role as predictable, with known boundaries. At the outset, the Hub was actually the opposite, it was a blank windowless space which became available due to changes in space allocation plans. Yet for the clinical users, this physical space was important as it represented a place to seek to overcome current clinical barriers in practice. Clinicians shared their personal stories of frustration and emotional pain when current approved clinical pathways were not sufficient to help every patient. Access to Hub space provided an opportunity to work on solutions to current challenges they came across when caring for patients.

The depth of their clinical skills combined with their understanding of the healthcare system and tacit knowledge led those interested in the power of innovation to the Hub space (Von Hippel, 1994). A commonality amongst clinicians was a desire to improve current processes, 'to do good.' This required the design of bespoke processes and operating principles to reflect Hub goals. Implementing existing norms from the main hospital did not align to the innovation environment, culture or objectives, despite causing anxiety amongst some staff. Initially structure and process were not a core priority. A key lesson is appreciating how to develop Hub processes which acknowledge that for Clinicians, working in the Hub requires a shift in mindset, approach and the mental and physical space to do so (Peschl and Fundneider, 2012). Working collaboratively is supported when outlined processes aid stakeholder interaction and achievement of Hub objectives. Complexity arises from understanding, defining and agreeing what these are. This issue was being explored at the time of data collection. Users were engaged in Hub projects in one of three main ways. Users who were most involved, and largely held either a surgical or advanced nurse practitioner role worked to lead the direction of collaborators who were developing a product concept. The idea for the product concept was based on a challenge the User had identified when working in the hospital. Some also Users worked to contribute specific clinical knowledge as part of a project team. There was a wider pool of Users who were less directly involved in Hub activities but had shown an interest in health innovation. They had a less well-defined idea and were enrolled onto a development programme to help them clarify and explore potential innovation options. This programme was overseen by an external collaborative partner and there was no in person participation needed in the Hub space whilst completing the programme.

Clinicians valued the opportunity to seek to overcome current barriers to their practice. Space and resource to work on the 'if only we could do things differently ideas' which came to them as proficient problem-solvers in a clinical context (Saidi et al 2017). From their perspective, achieving 'something good' was a primary motivation for becoming involved in health innovation. This intention could be seen through existing Hub projects which explored the role of emerging technologies and their place in clinical treatment and improving patient experience.

The importance Users attributed to creative ideas to address healthcare challenges they experienced when undertaking their clinical role illustrated a key difference between stakeholders' priorities (Herrera, 2016, Secundo et al 2019). After the initial set-up phase of the Hub, excitement amongst Hub staff, Board members and external collaborators waned as practical considerations necessitated equal consideration.

Hospital management, who were in full support of the notion of the Hub began to ask questions. Their concern related to an expectation that the Hub would produce preliminary tangible indications of progress. This expectation reflected their normal hospital-based work environment where time, linear process and evidence-based reporting were essential aspects of operational systems. Thus, they found the fluidity in the Hub space was challenging and somewhat concerning. Progress was happening but it was difficult to demonstrate, and specifically quantify. This prompted a 'so what' response when clinicians continued to share visionary ideas, emerging from their practice which had the potential to modernise patient care, increase capacity and increase safety by utilising advances in technology (Herstatt, Schweisfurth and Raasch, 2016).

Over time processes were implemented into the Hub as a way to establish Hub regularity in terms of how innovative ideas were appraised, and latterly how projects were managed through standardised working patterns. Stakeholders broadly concurred that it was not sufficient for the Hub to be about great ideas, although creativity had an initial role aligning with findings from existing research (Hattori and Wycoff 2002). The need to protect conceptual ideas and their potential commercial value emerged as a significant area of importance. This was complex due to the topical technological focus of ideas and a lack of existing policy within healthcare. Collaboration with commercial organisations was also a complicating factor. Clinical staff shared a distain for the connection between innovations which could benefit healthcare provision and the revenue this could generate. Thus, designing appropriate processes to operate and manage a multi-stakeholder collaborative environment emerged as a key strategic area of importance.

The Hub was part of the hospital campus, it was connected in terms of aligned patient care goals. But importantly it was different in terms of environment, process, culture and working patterns. Recognising, understanding and protecting these differences were necessary to enable the Hub space to thrive (Hansen and Jakobsen, 2006). This required Hub staff to educate stakeholders as to why an innovation space needed to operate differently to a hospital-based healthcare setting. Specifically, what was an appropriate pace, level of risk and set of processes for a Hub, and why these looked different to the main hospital and indeed the commercial norm. These skills were beyond the expertise of Users and required a broader Hub staff team to be established (Guinan at al, 2019).

Managing users in a collaborative Hub environment

For external collaborators the ongoing participation from clinicians was a competitive and differential aspect to the Hub compared to commercially run Hubs which operated without the involvement of clinician staff. Protecting and benefitting from this value with the Hub environment was an evolving area of complexity. Involvement in healthcare innovation has highlighted an aspect of clinician's skill sets which were not previously recognised as valuable within their role as healthcare providers. As additional clinicians became involved in healthcare innovation, understanding and managing this issue continued to grow.

Initially, founding Hub staff members included clinicians who had innovation activity as an acknowledged as part of their role and workload. This was made possible following recognition of innovation as a strategic hospital objective. This had in turn mobilised resource to support, identify and recruit clinicians into a hospital staff medical position, with time ringfenced for innovation activity. However, for these select staff, the practical divisions between their practice and the innovation work needed to be flexible as the former understandably took priority. Practically, this created last minute changes to availability for clinicians' availability to attend project meetings and the anticipated days where innovation activity would be the focus. This in turn impacted Hub project pace and Users ability to respond to communications in a timely manner.

Acknowledging the impact of Clinicians existing hospital role proved an ongoing area of complexity. This impacted the management of external stakeholder expectations and the challenge of addressing hospital capacity pressures to facilitate User Hub involvement. During the start-up phase, events in the Hub space supported by Hospital Board enabled some staff to access the Hub and latterly share initial innovative ideas. This provided an initial pipeline of potential innovation projects. However, aspirations to construct a standardised pathway to support Users to practically pursue innovation within their workload was recognised as important by the Board, but was not yet addressed.

User willingness to contribute within this Hub setting demonstrated their concerns and reluctance to work with external commercially focused alternatives were addressed by an onsite collaborative innovation space (Tietze et al, 2020). However, for the Hub to access the breadth of necessary resources, there was a need to work in collaboration with carefully selected Universities and businesses. The rarity of direct access to skilled clinicians was a motivating factor in Externals willingness to collaborate as the Hub was recognised as a valuable space for collaborative co-creation (Björklund et al 2019). Yet the practicalities of this involvement challenged external stakeholder's expectations of access to clinicians in terms of frequency, regularity and levels of disclosure. This prompted recognition of the importance of a Hub staff team who could oversee stakeholder management and project process (Howells, 2006, Long et al, 2013). To function, the Hub required staff with transferable commercial project management and business development experience.

Structuring the Hub for sustained success

The Hub functioned using a collaborative approach, collaborating with clinicians as key Users, in partnership with external organisations supported by Hub staff who administered and managed the projects. University involvement was important for research input and a commercial organisation for their industry expertise and practical connections. Both partnerships organisations were able to provide finance and resource depending on the project in focus and alignment with their existing objectives. However, the processes followed at the time of data collection differed from those described in the literature (Caccamo, 2020).

Over the first 3 years the Hub staff team grew in number and areas of specialisation (Neary,2022:106). The initial driving forces behind the establishment of this Hub were clinicians, who had entrepreneurial and creative personalities. Thus, a key lesson learnt was that the importance of the skills base needed to operationally run the Hub. Over time the staffing structure reflected a sub-division and clarification of roles to enable the complexity of the hub environment to be more effectively managed. This aspect of what was needed to run and sustain an Innovation Hub had initially been underappreciated by the founding staff member who prioritised knowledge and forming external collaborative working opportunities. This in-part also reflected a lack of budget for administrative and project management staff during the set-up phase of the Hub. However, as the constraints on clinician's time and areas of competence in the Hub became clear so did the need for additional staff appointments.

This Hub was a new type of activity for the Hospital and so a process of learning and reflection was underway at the time data was collected. Overtime the founding Hub staff and connected Hospital Board members had begun to appreciate that collaborative innovation was a more complex and slower process than anticipated. Founding Hub clinicians were beginning to identify areas of workflow which needed additional resourcing to operate effectively. These insights highlighted where skills gaps and competencies existed in the team, and how these were contributing to weaknesses in the collaborative innovation process. This reflective learning enabled specific additional job role profiles to be identified and written for external advertisement. Their anticipated contribution helped focus and clarify Hub staff roles and the functionality of a wider team structure. Thus, Hub staff were able to better articulate to the Hospital Board how the appointment of additional organisationally focused staff would positively contribute to the existing team of clinicians. Overtime, hiring staff with existing expertise in areas of administration, project management and business development enabled user time to become better focused and aligned to their skillset (Howells, 2006, Lauritzen, 2017). Users were freed from attempts to be successful in areas like administration and commercial negotiation which were outside their area of competency and interest.

This improvement to process maximised a productive return from Users as Hub staff realised that Users functioned best when directed towards giving formative developmental feedback to aid the development of innovations. Their ability to share critical contributions which combined their clinical knowledge and working understanding of the healthcare setting was irreplaceable in the project team. Whereas other tasks could be done effectively by others. Growth in the Hub team showed a respectful recognition of a team structure which functions due to a co-dependency of staff who hold roles of equal value. The skill of clinical and project focused staff equally drew on prior experience needed to make effective contributions. This development took time and a willingness amongst the original Hub team to release responsibilities to others in the Hub staff team. This display of trust showed recognition that a division of responsibilities would help sustain Hub activities. Originally Users wanted to personally lead and control all tasks, but this did not prove operationally effective.

Responding to areas of arising tension within the Hub and hospital became essential contributory elements of success. A further key lesson can be learnt by appreciating the importance of reflecting on the complexity of a collaborative team structure originally explored by seminal work by Van der Ven (1986). Managing stakeholders' skills to achieve a complementary balance is necessary. This is difficult when the team works often concurrently but remotely.

Effective communication to aid stakeholder cohesion

Overtime it became increasingly evident that innovation in a healthcare context meant very different things for each stakeholder group. Thus, part of understanding how to function as a complex team required an appreciation of the importance of effective communication for Hub success and preservation. This recognition arose due to a concern which existed amongst some staff working in the main the hospital. A problematic lack of understanding emerged amongst the broader hospital staff regarding the distinction between innovation, improvement and change agendas. Furthermore, the incorrect conjecture around how and why the Hub was able to obtain expensive technology, whilst the NHS itself was under such financial pressure illustrated an ignorance about Hub structure and collaborative partnerships. There was an incorrect assumption that the Hub had received an injection of capital to enable expensive and technologically advanced experimentation, giving rise to disparaging comments from some hospital staff who referred to the Hub innovation activity as 'the boys with their toys'. This comment reflected the technology which was showcased for visitors to the Hub, but this was part of a longer-term strategy to share aspirations for the Hub's contribution to the future of healthcare. These aspirations were starkly different to the day-to-day operational reality of the Hub environment.

Far from being a wash with money, Hub equipment was often loaned from commercial partners to facilitate early-stage innovation activity on site. Initially Hub staff repurposed donated office furniture and computers using their personal connections within and outside the hospital campus. The stark and rather barren industrial interior of the Hub space was known affectionally by Hub staff as 'the bat cave'.

Hub budgets were tight, but this was not the perception amongst hospital staff. Hub staff became frustrated about the lack of understanding of their objectives, activities and operational limitations within the hospital. Yet attempts clarify and improve communication were challenging despite the close proximity of the Hub and main hospital concurring with findings in existing research (Lawton Smith, 2019). Staff shift patterns, transient working locations, a lack of shared staff recreational space and difficulty accessing and leaving the wards were barriers to communication.

The complexity of inter-staff communication – Hub actions to address misinformation

Users working in the Hub were effective peer communicators. Their position in the hospital often inspired respect and encouraged collegial involvement. Initially this was a positive factor, but demand for Hub resources quickly surpassed available resources. There was a perception that finance was available and waiting to be allocated which was not the case. Enthused hospital staff submitted ideas which they anticipated would receive a rapid, actioned Hub response. There was not sufficient staff capacity or resource for this.

This misunderstanding prompted a prioritisation of in-situ peer education using staff break rooms, to communicate about the Hub personally and directly. Hub administrative staff were despatched to circulate within the hospital, spreading key messages amongst staff. This outreach was necessary as Hub staff recognised that although some senior clinicians had flexibility in their movements between the hospital and the hub sites most staff were not able to leave the ward when on shift. This meant break rooms provided a rare place to connect within the constraints of the operational environment. Taking active steps to articulate and clearly communicate the purpose, function, scale, scope and objectives of the Hub was important to manage the expectations of all stakeholder groups linked to the Hub. Without this direct intervention stakeholders were free to envision what working with the Hub would facilitate, often unrealistically.

Overtime this began to result in feelings of resentment and disappointment which required the experienced mediation of Hub staff. The personal investment hospital staff made creating an initial solution to a challenge they had experienced or witnessed cannot be diminished. To them, their idea was revolutionary, and the lack of immediate interest seemed personal, without considering existing Hub work and areas of focus. During the outreach Hub staff were able to contextualise, depersonalise and validate choices of which ideas had been actioned in connection to Hub strategic priorities.

When working with collaborators Hub staff were able to appreciate the spoken and underlying frustrations arising from the differences between standardised working relationships. The reality of the complexities arising from involvement with the healthcare sector were significant. These include added bureaucracy, a sectoral risk avoidance, a complex operational environment and a lack of existing process to structure technology driven healthcare innovations. Hub staff could communicate delays within the context of connected health sector legalities, operational constraints and best practice. This facilitated a consistency of communication and emerging documented processes expected by external collaborators.

Not as expected; using the Hub space to support collaboration

A further area of misconception was the organisation and environment of a Hub space and how this best aligned with the goal of creating impactful technology driven healthcare innovations (Svensson and Hartmann, 2018). To a visitor, the Hub space may only partially meet expectations of a collaborative working innovation space. There were the expected examples of intriguing pieces of technology and the outputs of their use, accompanied by banners explaining ongoing project work and overall aims. Yet the space was almost silent. Indications that this space was for collaborative working were evident from comfortable furniture in zoned areas. But this was secondary to the extensive amount of office desks. Some used consistently by one staff member and others available for hot desking. When looking past the exhibition space at the entrance the Hub largely resembled an office space. This raises an important lesson about how the space functioned to support innovation, particularly the involvement of users (Saidi et al, 2017).

At the time of data collection, the Hub space comprised of a large main space with four smaller rooms leading off this, each with a designated purpose. A Virtual Reality suite signalling partnership with named involvement of a local University, complete with equipment. A commercially funded room to test products in a simulated at home environment. A room set up as a boardroom for meetings and a designated casual meeting room with sofas and IT connectivity. These spaces had an anticipated purpose, but practically they served to help visitors envision the breadth of activities undertaken within the Hub rather than be actively contributing on a regular basis. Often all separated spaces served as places for meetings as the Hub main space consistently served as a space for quiet office-based work.

When Users were present within the Hub, they were either meeting with existing or potential collaborators, or more commonly also seeking a quiet desk-based environment. Challenges for Users predicting their availability to physically attend meetings resulted in an expectation that emails could serve as a secondary method of retrieving input, responses and suggestions in-between in-person meetings. In this Hub, the digital focus extended beyond being an intrinsic part of the products in development. Reflecting advances in societal communication patterns, digitalised communication was important function element within collaborative innovation teams supporting existing work in this area (Crupi et al, 2020). Attempts had also been made to mobilise and track project progress through digital systems where named individuals were allocated tasks. This sought to overcome the tension between being physically present in the Hub space and managing demands of collaborators main role, be that within the hospital or in their main work-based setting. This was a work in progress, as regular engagement was needed for it to be effective which proved challenging for clinicians.

The clinician's hospital role was most often mobile, moving between areas to perform an aspect of their patient focused role. The desk space in the Hub was important to enable them to engage with innovation work and have the space and quiet to do so. This forms part of a key lesson around the functionality of space in a hospital-based innovation hub, and how this is different due to the requirements of the healthcare sector (Sharma and Meyer, 2019).

Practicalities of a hospital hub location

Locating the Hub within the hospital campus, but not within the main hospital building was important in terms of branding and strategic positioning. External collaborators were able to connect in meetings based at the hospital address, thus they had succeeded in overcoming the hurdle of working with or visiting clinicians. This direct access was hugely valued due to its rarity and the significance of the learned inputs. Due to the risk of infection and patient safety, the location of the Hub was appropriate as it was separate from the medical areas.

Visitors required admittance as the Hub main door was part of the hospital door swipe system, without a reception point and was an external point of access to interconnected hospital buildings. This necessary barrier positively protected the hospital environment, but in doing so impeded the free-flowing nature of people accessing the space. Thus, a key lesson that emerged concerns how to meet the necessary security requirements of the hospital whilst considering the place of spontaneous and emergent stakeholder interactions with the collaborative Hub space. Hub meetings had to be planned, and therefore attendees were known prior. In cases of open events, attendees usually registered online and then were welcomed into the Hub space and managed by Hub staff. During events, the main Hub floor space functioned as a hosting space, displacing office-based activity. Thus, the frequency and timing of these events needing prior planning and consultation within the wider team. Within examples of collaborative innovation spaces in other sectors there are often expectation that innovations result from unplanned coincidental meetings (Jiménez, 2019).

For this Hub, to observe important sectoral considerations this proved less probable. Practically, as mentioned, the opportunities for Hospital staff to access the Hub space and benefit from the distinct differences of environment, pace and process were limited. This obstacle prevented staff from accessing these potential benefits due to role working constrains as discussed. Latterly, further process-based obstacles emerged. Hub access via the outdoor swipe point was not automatically enabled on staff access cards and siloed innovation activity taking place within main hospital teams which were not becoming associated with Hub activities.

During data collection, questions as to the lack of appetite to centralise innovation activities revealed areas of concern. Practically it proved difficult to schedule time for hospital stakeholders to meet to discuss opportunities to unite activities despite the shared aim of improved patient experience. Concerns were disclosed that ownership and credit from existing successful established projects may be lost if alliances were made under the broader umbrella of the somewhat, undefined Hub activities. These concerns led to contacts and skills being protected as part of siloed activity. Thus, ultimately opportunities to sustain Hub activities were impacted as Hospital Board members and potential collaborators were prevented from accessing examples of tangible outcomes of innovation activity they sought. This complicated decision making and confidence levels regarding the type, level and duration of commitment made to Hub activities. Understandably, the lack of tangible outputs from the investment of time and money in the Hub space were a barrier to achieving this, when outputs from business as usual in the main hospital were evident and well-documented. This raises a key lesson around realistic expectation from innovation activity amongst stakeholders unfamiliar with the innovation process.

In summary, when establishing an innovation space, like a Hub it is important to consider existing areas of innovation activity within the Hospital and if it is appropriate and practical to attempt to centralise these. If the Hub is established without inclusion of existing activity, it can introduce added complexity in terms of justifying the alignment between Hub space and hospital strategic aims of how innovation seeks to improve care quality. Yet it is understandable that individuals will want to preserve their autonomy and visibility, especially if they have existing connected funding pathways and distinct objectives. The apprehension regarding a diluted presence within a broader Hub agenda is valid and requires consideration. This was evident in the case of existing innovative work regarding the use of art and music to support paediatric healthcare experiences which was funded in part by external grants.

When selecting a Hub location it is significant to consider accessibility. This will impact internal and external user participation in the Hub space. If access to Hub space requires entry through an external unstaffed door it is likely that it will be controlled by security procedures like swipe access. It is important that access is managed so it is functional for all types of users and visitor. Separate processes will be appropriate to maintain fluent lines of connectivity for internal and external stakeholders.

Although there are strong advantages to locating an innovation Hub on a Hospital campus it is important to consider both the point of access and then the physical journey to the Hub space. As explored within this chapter, a degree of physical separation from the main healthcare environment is a positive aspect when considering a suitable Hub location. Thus, it is important to be mindful of balancing accessibility, visibility and infection control. If access to the Hub is disrupted, so too are the lines of communication and participation. It is therefore vital to consider appropriate ease of access to maintain stakeholder support and engagement through stages of the complex and changeable innovation process. Oversights in this practical area can lead to Hub activity becoming siloed. There are connected concerns regarding disrupted access and a spread of misinformation amongst Hospital staff about the process and purpose of innovation activity, especially when working in collaboration with private sector organisations.

Defending the voice of users within healthcare Hubs

Working with Users adds complexity and requires skilled staff to manage a series of accommodations to facilitate their involvement adding the novelty, impact and specificity that is possible. The research supported existing research findings which emphasised the importance of the involvement of healthcare lead users when helping address growing challenges in a range of medical, experiential and operational areas (Luthje & Herstatt, 2004, Schweisfurth & Raasch, 2015). Thus, sustaining the involvement of users is a meaningful challenge.

When establishing a Healthcare Hub, the range and severity of challenges facing the hospital environment are illustrated through the scope of innovation projects suggested by Users. Ensuring that all hospital users share their tacit knowledge and potential solutions is important to create innovations which understand existing processes and structures. Currently encouraging engagement from staff working in all roles, and at all levels is important. Thus, appreciating the fear held by some staff who connected hospital innovation to job losses was valid. In part, this can be attributed to apprehension about potential use of technology reducing a need for human staff to undertake manual roles. This emerged as a misguided reason for withholding suggestions to improve locating available equipment like wheelchairs within wards in an attempt to protect current staffed positions.

Conversely, Hub objectives to address staffing levels is concerned with a desire to extend benefits to patient experience amid capacity restrictions. Digital Innovation was being used as a way to extend patient access to resources to support their patient experience. The hospital itself was an innovative space and had received funding to integrate digitalisation into patient care pathways as part of a national NHS scheme. In the Hub, the objective of utilising digital innovation sought enable scalable universal access that would benefit patients accessing the resource. For example, a project was underway to extend aspects of play therapy which traditionally were provided by a hospital play therapist. Developing a digital resource which used gamification to integrate similar types of support for Users was seen as beneficial as it was scalable without incurring additional costs per patient user. The holistic care needs are particularly important for paediatric patients (Lacy et al, 2016, Wolf, 2019). Play therapy is a way to engage, distract and calm patients whilst in hospital with the aim of reducing stress and improving their patient experience. The introduction of a gamified resource aimed to provide some support to all patients through an online app. One anticipated intention of this innovation was to reduces access limitations in place when support was limited due to the current staff to patient ratio. Reducing pressure on in-person staff and enabling patients with less severe but equally valid needs to receive some support.

Providing a patient experience which acknowledges holistic patient care needs, beyond the medical intervention was recognised as important by clinicians (Bauer et al, 2019). They felt that the appropriateness of paper based information, especially for paediatric digital natives has passed. Paediatric patients seek digital sources to provide answers to their questions, and when these are not available or accurate issues can arise. Additionally, there is a current lack of material designed and written specifically for paediatric patients. Thus, in the Hub space, the collaborative innovation process enables experiential insights of clinicians to inform the design and content of digital resources. This valuable connection enables development of medically informed content for interactive digital resources which can support patient experience. The design is informed by users' tacit knowledge from practice and the industry knowledge of commercial partners. It is this fusion of skill that provides developmental insights which will help create a product which is medically informed and aligns jointly with hospital process-based needs and user expectation. User recommendation indicated that improved provision of emotional support will help to address capacity concerns in the NHS. Some clinicians suggested they expected increased levels of patient confidence from accessing on-demand digital support could correlates to fewer cancelled appointments and procedures. Although this was not yet evidenced by Hub innovation activity it does align with existing research into the role of patients as users, and their increased participation and expectations of healthcare (Oftedal et al, 2019). This expectation highlights an important point regarding the quality of patient experience and how integrating additional layers, in addition to the medical procedures received will bring added stability to their experience of being in hospital. This aligns with existing research regarding the increasing interest from patients to be both informed and engaged with this healthcare, rather than solely being a recipient of treatment (Schiavone, 2020).

Developing technologically enabled innovations informed by User knowledge and insight can provide patients with reassurance (Tettegah and Garcia, 2016). Digital delivery of medically endorsed answers on-demand using AI, was being explored within the Hub. The broad aim was to extend the period patients can receive answers to generic hospital-based questions. Clinicians also anticipated this will aid a medical focus within appointments rather than including time to address broader concerns about aspects of hospital admission, visiting times, parking and food provision. In wider daily life using digital technology is a primary method to retrieve on demand information. There is an expectation identified by clinicians that patients expect such resources when accessing hospital services. For paediatric patients, this provides opportunity to use gamification to support the reassurance, praise and distraction of patients who are often experiencing a hospital environment for the first time. Without the user voice, and the location of the Hub this type of innovation would be much more complex.

A key lesson can be recalled by considering an analogy shared by a User. He suggested using an analogy of a theme park to explain how clinicians seek to support patient experience through healthcare innovation by contextualising the hospital experience as one which has a range of emotions. He drew parallels between what we expect when we are at the venue and our overall holistic experience, which we later reflect upon and importantly informs our feelings about a potential future visit. Thus, for patients visiting a hospital it is important to acknowledge the associated anxieties and provide authoritative yet generic information on what to expect and how the process works. This enables the experience, here in a hospital context, for patients, to prepare and build resilience. When going to a theme park, we expect to experience a range of emotions as we have an initial understanding about what will happen, and the overall aim that the experience seeks to bring benefits. In a hospital context, especially for patient groups with specific needs, like children. Communication methods need specific and careful design and accessibility.

In this Hub, work was underway to provide paediatric patients with digital resources to support their need for information during different phases of their patient experience. Integration of this nature of communication adds patient preparedness and seeks to ensure some aspects of the experience are positive. In the case of paediatric patients using gamified technologies is perhaps even enjoyable (Dimitri, 2019). Thus, in line with the theme park analogy, the hospital experience is intense, but not so much so that you never want to return.

Users provide a valuable holistic perspective within collaborative teams. This is broader than other stakeholders, extending beyond a core focus on potential revenue, intellectual property, meeting project objectives or supporting hospital reputation to attract and retain staff within a competitive marketplace. Users are neither task nor time focused. They are people focused, and ultimately healthcare is about people. This is often lost due to the job focused roles from which other stakeholders approach the Hub and its potential contributions to their existing problems. The User voice is an impactful one. Users have a level of tacit knowledge and lived experience which is a fundamental part of designing innovations which are differentiated from those developed externally, without access to such insights.

Clinician's opinions carry impact which are attributed to their position, learnt and experienced skill and tacit knowledge. This is recognised as hugely valuable, but there is a limit to its effectiveness. A key lesson learnt is that clinicians as a representative user-voice, cannot fully represent the needs of other hospital users like patients and their families (Demonaco, Oliveira and Von Hippel, 2020, Oftedal, Iakovleva and Bessant, 2019, Pereno, 2020). Therefore, as the Hub becomes more established, working with the wider hospital to integrate patient and families support groups as Hub users is necessary. This will bridge the gap between needs and requirements of different users by providing a safe and appropriate method of participation (Schiavone,2020). This level of organising and planning is feasible once the Hub has become established and somewhat focused in its initial objectives (Hattori and Wycoff,2002). Involvement of knowledgeable staff who appreciate the complexities involved in working with different healthcare users is necessary within this process to observe safety, welfare and legal considerations.

Additionally, when seeking to test innovations within the hospital it is important to mobilize clinical users as part of attempts to inform and prepare colleagues. An example was recounted regarding the disappointment a parent and child faced when excitingly downloading a beta version of an innovation in development ahead of a hospital visit. Despite best attempts of Hub staff, the patient was cared for by staff who were unaware of the ability to provide digital scanned rewards as part of a gamified patient praise process. The difficulties associated with preparing staff when solely relying on the small Hub staff team are unrealistic. Therefore, the breadth of impact of the user voice is important in disseminating key messages at a departmental level, especially as verbal communication amongst peers is often faster than anticipating staff will read innovation related emails. Clinical users are a crucial point of connectedness between patients and the Hub, and support endeavours to gain feedback on beta versions of products whilst meeting expectations of patients eager to interact with the technologies during their visit.

The user voice provides a core point of differentiation for hospital-based healthcare hubs. This is useful to counter the added complexities and frustrations collaborators experience which arise from this interaction. It can be argued that the user insight, tacit knowledge and critical feedback accessible through the development process is strategically and commercially greater than the slowed pace, complexity of communication and associated organisational bureaucracy. The UK public health system is arguably not yet able to recognise and benefit from this value in a uniform manner, and a standardised approach is unlikely to be effective given the influence of individuals. But, due to the increasingly devolved power structure, regional Hospital Trusts have opportunities to shape the contribution of innovation spaces within their immediate environment.

Users have a key role within a wider team of collaborators who each have distinct areas of expertise (McNichol, 2012). An innovation space, like a Hub, requires appropriate levels of experienced staff to facilitate the collaborative process. They are central to providing and communicating a structured approach, process and scope for levels of experimentation. They have the oversight of stakeholder expectations, priorities and competencies. This therefore enables them to direct the involvement of collaborators to orchestrate pace, progress and impactful experimentation.

Conclusion

In conclusion this chapter summarises key findings from an extensive research study on the role of innovation hubs in supporting collaborative user-led innovation (Neary, 2022). The research contributes to existing studies regarding the importance of user participation in healthcare innovation (Schiavone 2020, Wrigley, 2020). In summarising lessons learnt from the wider study this chapter includes some key research findings from the broader study which make a contribution to the academic literature. First, the chapter draws on a case study which provides additional understanding about the role and development of a hospital-based Innovation Hub and associated challenges, contributing to existing research by exploring the varied priorities of key stakeholders within a UK NHS paediatric hospital (Djellal and Gallouj 2007, Savory, 2009, Miller and French, 2016). The case study makes a valuable contribution to a small number of existing case studies, exploring some similar themes to that of work on innovation space in Groote Hospital in South Africa within work by Saidi (2017). The research findings highlight the significance of adequately managing Hub space to provide an environment which meets the expectations of multiple users. The challenge of delivering a quiet workspace and an aspirational display of potential innovation impact using digital technology are discussed. Second, the case study provides an in-depth analysis of a specific paediatric hub to illustrate challenges and priorities around meeting the needs of a particular demographic of patients adding to work by Dimitri (2019) which focuses on the role of digital technology in paediatric care. Third, the findings of this research critically analyse the emerging disparate needs of stakeholders within the Hub environment and how this influenced the Hub staff team structure. This adds to valuable work on the role of Hub staff and responds to calls for additional studies (Howells, 2016, Guinan et al, 2019). Fourth, the broader research explores a valuable phase of Hub development which is initially shared in this chapter through discussions regarding the complexity of the concept development amid conflicting and diverse stakeholder priorities, extending existing research in this area (Barlow, 2017, Sharma and Meyer, 2019). This research documents and explains how process supports and responds to stakeholders' individual expectations to sustain Hub activity. To date, there is little research on this aspect of hub development. Although there is a developed literature on the longitudinal process of innovation, a focus on the specific process in a healthcare context hub is still scarce. This research contributes by emphasizing the importance of relationship between and the role of Hub staff and stakeholders.

The study from which this chapter has drawn content was subject to limitations which link to the generalisability of findings. These could be addressed in future studies which included a broader sample of clinical users and a number of comparable hospital-based hubs. There is scope for additional research which considers the role of clinical users as boundary spanners (Herstatt et al, 2016, Long et al, 2013). Additionally, to extend research on the role of space to support hospital-based hubs, there is a need to explore the role of digital space in addition to add to the existing research on physical and digital hub spaces (Crupi, 2020, Peschl and Fundneider 2012).

References

Barlow, J. (2017) *Managing Innovation in Healthcare*, World Scientific Publishing Com

Bauer, G., Roy, M., Bakibinga, P., Contu, P., Downe, S., Eriksson, M., Espnes, G., Jensen, B., Canal, D. J. & Lindström, B. (2019) 'Future directions for the concept of salutogenesis: a position article.' Health Promotion International, 35, (2) 187–195.

Björklund, T. A., Keipi, T., Celik, S. & Ekman, K. (2019) 'Learning across silos: Design Factories as hubs for co-creation', European Journal of Education, Research, Development and Policy, 54, (4) 552–565.

Caccamo, M. (2020) 'Leveraging innovation spaces to foster collaborative innovation', Creativity and Innovation Management, 29, (1) 178–191.

Crupi, A., Del Sarto, N., Di Minin, A., Gregori, G. L., Lepore, D., Marinelli, L. & Spigarelli, F. (2020) 'The digital transformation of SMEs – a new knowledge broker called the digital innovation hub', Journal of Knowledge Management, 24, (6) 1263–1288.

Demonaco, H., Oliveira, P., Torrance, A., Von Hippel, C. & Von Hippel, E. (2020) 'When patients become innovators' MIT Sloan Management Review, 60(3), 81–88.

Djellal, F. (2007) 'Innovation in hospitals: a survey of the literature', *The European Journal of Health Economics*, 8, (3) 181–193.

Dimitri, P. (2019) 'Child health technology: shaping the future of paediatrics and child health and improving NHS productivity', Archives of Disease in Childhood, 104(2), 184–188.

Geiger, J. D. & Hirschl, R. B. (2015) 'Innovation in surgical technology and techniques: Challenges and ethical issues', Seminars in Pediatric Surgery, 24(3), 115–121.

Guinan, P. J., Parise, S. & Langowitz, N. (2019) 'Creating an innovative digital project team: Levers to enable digital transformation.' Business Horizons, 62(6), 717–727.

Hansen, S. & Jakobsen, H. (2006) 'Idea development as a creative platform' in: Gersten, F. Kyvsgard, P.H, & Boer, H. (eds.) Innovationsledelse. Aalborg, Denmark: Aalborg University, Denmark.

Hattori, R. & Wycoff, J. (2002) 'Innovation DNA: A good idea is not enough. It has to create value', Training and Development, 56(2), 25–39.

Herrera, M. (2016) 'Innovation for impact: Business innovation for inclusive growth', Journal of Business Research, 69(5), 1725–1730.

Herstatt, C., Schweisfurth, T. & Raasch, C. (2016) 'When Passion Meets Profession: How Embedded Lead Users Contribute to Corporate Innovation', in: Harhoff, D. & Lakhani, K.R. (eds.) Revolutionizing

Innovation: Users, Communities, and Open Innovation. Cambridge, Massachusetts: MIT Press, pp 397–419.
Howells, J. (2006) 'Intermediation and the role of intermediaries in innovation', Research Policy, 35(5), 715–728.
Jiménez, A. (2019) 'Inclusive innovation from the lenses of situated agency: insights from innovation hubs in the UK and Zambia', Innovation and Development, 9(1), 41–64.
Lacy, A. (2016) 'Patient Emotions and Patient Education Technology' in: Tettegah, S., & Garcia, Y., (eds.) *Emotions, Technology and Health*. Elservier: London, 23–38.
Lauritzen, G.D. (2017) 'The Role of Innovation Intermediaries in Firm-Innovation Community Collaboration: Navigating the Membership Paradox.' Journal of Product Innovation Management, 34(3), 289–314.
Lawton Smith, H., Bagchi-Sen, S. & Edmunds, L. (2019) 'Handbook of Universities and Regional Development. Universities, the bioscience sector and local economic development in Oxfordshire: challenges and opportunities. Edward Elgar Publishing: Cheltenham, UK, 230–250.
Long, J.C., Cunningham, F.C. and Braithwaite, J., (2013) 'Bridges, brokers and boundary spanners in collaborative networks: a systematic review', BMC Health Services Research Journal, 13(1), 1–13.
Lüthje, C. & Herstatt, C. (2004) 'The Lead User method: an outline of empirical findings and issues for future research', R&D Management, 34(5), 553–568.
Magadley, W. & Birdi, K. (2009) 'Innovation labs: an examination into the use of physical spaces to enhance organisational creativity', Creativity and innovation management, 18(1), 315–325.
McNichol, E. (2012) 'Patient-led innovation in healthcare: The value of the 'user' perspective', International Journal of Healthcare Management, 5(4), 216–222.
Miller, F. A. & French, M. (2016) 'Organizing the entrepreneurial hospital: Hybridizing the logics of healthcare and innovation', *Research Policy*, 45(8), 1534–1544.
Neary, K., 2022. The Role of Innovation Hubs in Supporting Collaborative Innovation: A Case Study of User-Led Healthcare Innovation. The University of Liverpool (United Kingdom).
Oftedal, E., Iakovleva, T. & Bessant, J. 2019. Challenges in healthcare – the changing role of patients. in: Iakoleva, T., Oftedal, E., & Bessant, J. (eds.) Responsible Innovation in Digital Health. Cheltenham, UK.: Edward Elgar, pp 21–41.
Pereno, A. & Eriksson, D. (2020) 'A Multi-Stakeholder Perspective on Sustainable Healthcare: From 2030 Onwards', Futures, 122, 1–21.
Peschl, M.F. & Fundneider, T. (2012) 'Spaces enabling game-changing and sustaining innovations: Why space matters for knowledge creation and innovation', Journal of Organisational Transformation and Social Change, 9(1), 41–61.
Saidi, T., De Villiers, K. & Douglas, T. S. (2017) 'The sociology of space as a catalyst for innovation in the health sector', Social Science Medicine, 180(1), 36–44.
Samet, K. A., Fache, and Smith, M.S. (2016) 'Thinking Differently: Catalyzing Innovation in Healthcare and Beyond', Frontiers of Health Services Management, 33(2), 3–15.
Schweisfurth, T. & Raasch, C. (2015) 'Embedded lead users—The benefits of employing users for corporate innovation', *Research Policy*, 44(1), 168–180.
Schiavone, F. (2020) '*User innovation in healthcare: How patients and caregivers react creatively to illness*', Hiedelberg: Springer: Germany.
Secundo, G., Del Vecchio, P., Simeone, L. & Schiuma, G. (2019) 'Creativity and stakeholders' engagement in open innovation: Design for knowledge translation in technology intensive enterprises', Journal of Business Research, 119(1), 272–282.
Sharma, S. K. & Meyer, K. E. (2019) 'Industrializing Innovation: The Next Revolution', Cambridge: UK, Springer International Publishing.
Svensson, P. & Hartmann, R. (2018) 'Policies to promote user innovation: Makerspaces and clinician innovation in Swedish hospitals', Research Policy, 47(1), 277–288.
Tettegah, S. Y. & Garcia, Y. E. (2016) Emotions, Technology, and Health, Elsevier Academic Press: London.

Thune, T. & Mina, A. (2016) 'Hospitals as innovators in the health-care system: A literature review and research agenda', Research Policy, 45(8), 1545–1557.

Tietze, F., Pieper, T. & Schultz, C. (2020) 'To share or not to share – Exploring how sharing behaviour impacts user innovation', in: Tiwari, R. & Buse, S. (eds.) Managing Innovation in a Global and Digital World: Meeting Societal Challenges and Enhancing Competitiveness. Wiesbaden: Springer Fachmedien Wiesbaden, 159–182.

Savory, C. (2009) 'User-led Innovation in the UK National Health Service' PhD thesis, Faculty of Mathematics, Computing and Technology, The Open University.

Samuelson, P. (2016) 'Freedom to Tinker', in: Harhoff, D. & Lakhani, K.R. (eds.) Revolutionizing Innovation: Users, Communities, and Open Innovation. Cambridge, Massachusetts: MIT Press, pp 217–234.

Schiavone, F. (2020) 'User innovation in healthcare: How patients and caregivers react creatively to illness', Hiedelberg: Springer: Germany.

Sharma, S. K. & Meyer, K. E. (2019) 'Industrializing Innovation: The Next Revolution', Cambridge: UK, Springer International Publishing

Van Der Ven, A. H. (1986) 'Central Problems in the Management of Innovation', Management Science, 32(5), 590–607.

Svensson, P. & Hartmann, R. (2018) 'Policies to promote user innovation: Makerspaces and clinician innovation in Swedish hospitals', Research Policy, 47(1), 277–288.

Van Der Ven, A. H. (1986) 'Central Problems in the Management of Innovation', Management Science, 32(5), 590–607.

Von Hippel, E. (1994) '"Sticky information" and the locus of problem solving: implications for innovation.' Management Science, 40(4), 429–548.

Wrigley, C., Nusem, E. & Straker, K. (2020) 'Implementing Design Thinking: Understanding Organizational Conditions', *California Management Review*, 62(2), 125–143.

Wolf, J. A. (2019) 'Reframing innovation and technology for healthcare: A commitment to the human experience', *Patient Experience Journal*, 6(2), 1–4.

Matt Halkes, Nick Peres, John Bessant

Digital futures – enabling innovation through a boundary space

Abstract: This chapter explores the challenge of digital transformation and user engagement. It introduces the concept of "boundary innovation spaces" as platforms where diverse stakeholders can collaborate to enhance healthcare services through digital innovation. Highlighting the historical context and evolving role of user involvement, the text underscores the importance of creating spaces like the Digital Futures Lab (DFL) within healthcare settings. The DFL serves as a hub for exploring, sharing, and understanding the potential of digital technologies to improve healthcare delivery, patient and staff experiences, and education. It details the lab's initiatives, including immersive technologies for patient care, staff training simulations, and the development of medical applications through 3D printing and modelling. The chapter reflects on the challenges of sustaining innovation within the healthcare system, advocating for strategic support and resource allocation to realize the potential of digital technologies.

Introduction

As the introductory chapters in this book have highlighted innovation has become a central and strategic concern in healthcare management. But whilst the word is on everyone's lips there is a real risk that much of this rhetoric is 'innovation theatre' using slogans to substitute for focused and sustainable action. Amongst the many themes which also find their way into the ongoing narrative are those of 'digital transformation' and 'user engagement'. The former refers to the considerable potential which a wide range of digital solutions (now including AI) have to offer in terms of both improving efficiencies and also extending the range of treatments and services which could be offered. And the latter, explored extensively elsewhere in this book, refers to the potential for improved design and accelerated adoption of innovation which involves users.

Both of these themes are, of course, significant but both need to unpacked and their innovation potential mobilised. In the case of digital transformation there is a need to understand the wide range of capabilities offered by a whole suite of technologies in applications ranging from robotic surgery through patient data management, optimisation of provision through simulation and modelling, automation of key service processes, embedding of intelligent sensors in medical equipment right through to providing significant extensions to self-care via apps, smart homes and wearable technologies.

https://doi.org/10.1515/9783111241036-009

On the user side the case for user involvement has been well made elsewhere; users can and do make a difference. However, the question of *which* users is often overlooked with the bulk of medical user innovations involving clinical users – doctors, nurses, allied health professionals, technicians, admin staff, etc. The role of patients and care-givers has not always been recognised or mobilised.

The emergence of 'boundary innovation spaces'

The history of user involvement in innovation goes back to early studies, for example by von Hippel and others. Importantly although there is extensive literature about user input in product design there is also a less well documented counterpart around process innovation, often appearing in accounts of change management. In trying to secure acceptance for major technological changes in organizations – for example the introduction of computerisation – there is considerable evidence that involving users helps enable not only the implementation process but also secures its downstream continued acceptance and further development (Mumford, 1979; Eason, 1988; Burne, 1992)

In the case of healthcare and medical innovations there is widespread acceptance of the important role which users can play but the majority of these studies concern clinicians and other medical professional as the 'users' in question (Von Hippel, 1988). A much smaller group of studies focus on the 'end user' – the patient or those responsible for their care (Iakovleva, Bessant and Oftedal (2019). This pattern has shifted in recent years with the growing recognition that listening to patient voices enhances both 'front end' ideation but also 'back end 'adoption, diffusion and re-innovation.

Examples include the active involvement of stoma patients in the design and testing of new products within Coloplast, the participation of out-patients in cancer clinics to improve service design and the many cases of 'hero' patients and their carers who develop their own solutions to enable them to live with disease and disability (Tidd and Bessant, 2020)(Bessant and Maher 2009)

The role of space as an enabler of user engagement

This raises the question of where and how users of different kinds might engage early enough with the innovation process to help explore, contribute insights, test prototypes, etc. Such spaces – often called 'Innovation Labs' reflect a wider concern with bringing diverse perspectives in early on in the innovation process (Fritzsche et al. 2020).

In the healthcare space the twin pressures of growing rhetoric around the need for patient involvement and the recognition of the potential value of user input has led to considerable experimentation with version of such 'labs' and in this book there are many examples. – for example Living Labs and the Smart Care Cluster activities.

This chapter looks at the experience of a continuing effort within a major UK hospital trust to build such a capability around digital innovation and to maintain and evolve it as a boundary space for different stakeholders. It highlights both the potential for doing so and the difficulties involved in interposing such an approach and establishing its presence as a long-term resource for innovation.

The Digital Futures Lab

In its current form the Digital Futures Lab (DFL) is located within the Horizon Centre and provides a focus for conversations around digital innovation with a wide variety of stakeholders in the Torbay area of south Devon in the UK. *'I see it as our role . . . .to help inform the conversation around the value of this technology both with staff and patients . . . . And we do this through co-design, collaboration and partnerships . . .'*

As Nick Peres, Head of Digital Technologies explains *'. . . our Digital Futures Lab . . . is an innovation space . . . .that enables us to explore, share and understand the potential that digital technologies can bring to healthcare settings. Staff can directly experience and learn about a range of technologies, including augmented and virtual reality, and creatively explore how they can be used to support healthcare delivery, enhance patient and staff experience and deliver education and training . . . .*

Programmes include:

- Technology research and application support around immersive technologies (VR, AR, etc.) using digital technology and virtual reality-driven solutions to help improve patient care and complement staff training. Patients who are seriously ill, undergoing treatment or are end of life, have been offered immersive experiences for therapeutic support and it has also helped train staff in real life scenarios. (Some specific examples can be found here)
- Simulation to help enhance the training and skills of staff. '*. . . the lab offers us a platform and space to co-design some use cases and custom experiences – for example we've been creating virtual community and home based settings where those environments place such a big factor in understanding the patient's back story . . .'*
- Education and training services including patient information and support for clinical staff
- 3D modelling and printing for medical applications and engaging with multiple users to co-create such 3D models to order
- 3D visualistaion for immersive reality – the team now have the capacity to scan and create credible environments (like operating theatres, clinical wards, etc) in less than an hour
- Horizon scanning around future key technologies such as AI
- Acting as national centre of expertise in areas like VR/AR and immersive technologies

History

The origins of the Digital Futures Lab (DFL) lie in efforts to create focused innovation capacity within the Torbay and South Devon healthcare Trust. (In the UK National Health service care is organized on a regional basis around community trusts, each of which carries responsibility for acute care (hospitals) but also for primary care and other services in the surrounding community). In 2008 funding was secured to build a centre of excellence for training in elective care – the Horizon centre – which was conceived as a facility which would provide a physical focus for education, research and innovation. The timing was fortuitous; a new Medical School had just been established in the region and so the Horizon Centre could offer opportunities for training and exposure to new ways of thinking about the future for healthcare to a new generation of staff.

Like much investment in the NHS this was an opportunistic development and the staffing model reflected this, involving a combination of dedicated new posts, secondment of existing staff and a wider network of interested volunteers and supporters.

Its early work pioneered a variety of novel approaches, especially around the use of simulation for training, and it also offered a physical focus for conversations and other activities around promoting innovation across the Trust. This included participating in a variety of external networks and shared research projects in the field of innovation management. An Innovation Lead was appointed to co-ordinate activities which also included taking responsibility for the innovation pathway for ideas and inventions from Trust employees which could be scaled and commercialised. (An example of this is the Health TV application discussed in an earlier book (Iakovleva, Bessant and Oftedal (2019)).

It offered several opportunities to bring innovation into the mainstream work of the Trust; for example one of the education programmes involved training for junior doctors to carry out live innovation projects based on process improvements. A number of national programmes were also being rolled out – for example the Productive Ward and Lean Six Sigma initiatives which were aimed at engaging nurses and other staff in quality and process improvement innovation work. Again these were supported and guided by the small innovation team based at the Horizon Centre.

However its existence as a focused innovation hub was precarious, depending on goodwill, sponsorship from senior management and considerable part-time effort on the part of a handful of people interested in innovation. Whilst there was interest space never got formally allocated so there was just an office; '*the innovation element was a very small one within the Horizon Centre building*', where most activity was around education and training.

Whilst there was enthusiasm there was little sense of a widespread innovation culture across the Trust; this was reflected in differences in understanding and the language used to describe 'innovation'. The term was recognised as being of importance but it was something of an umbrella term to cover a wide range of activity, from operational improvement programmes through to the pathway for developing and commercialising new ideas emerging from employees. There was no formal innovation strategy and the result was that the focus was often driven by external national initiatives (such as the Productive Ward quality programme or the product innovation pathway being promoted by the regional Academic Health Sciences Network (AHSN).

As the level and range of digital technology used in the Centre increased it became necessary to appoint someone with responsibility for supporting it and helping staff work with it. The current director of DFL, Nick Peres, joined in 2015 to play this role on a full-time basis (having previously worked for a contractor company providing this service) and he quickly became involved in informal conversations with others around a shared vision for a more focused approach to innovation.

The next iteration at a strategic level was the setting up of the 'Horizon Institute', an initiative inspired by the model of Jonkoping in Sweden which offered inspiration for an integrated new approach to healthcare delivery through high levels of engagement with the wider community. Several exploratory visits took place and the Jonkoping team made presentations in Torbay; the idea was to create a similar centre, based around the physical Horizon Centre. But whilst there was enthusiastic support the initiative failed to get off the ground. The general feeling was that it tried to do too much too quickly; part of the problem was that whilst the Swedish centre was an inspiration there was no clear method or blueprint for how Torbay would emulate it.

The unfortunate consequence of this was that the pendulum which been swinging in support of innovation moved in the opposite direction. The residual impact was a suspicion or unease about innovation. Fortunately for the core team an opportunity arose (2016) to participate in an Erasmus + project exploring new ways of teaching and learning about innovation. It enabled them to widen their horizons and experience both geographically and through engagement with a variety of other international companies partnering in the project including BMW, Lego, Generali Insurance, Nokia, Lufthansa as well as several universities. That mixture of education around concepts and the exposure to a wider network proved valuable; in particular it demonstrated the way in which innovation and its management could move from a somewhat vague aspiration to something extensively practiced and strategically deployed. One component of this, visible in all the participating organizations, was the importance of a dedicated space, an innovation laboratory where experiments and conversations around innovation could take place.

Back in Torbay development were somewhat asymmetric. On the one hand there was growing interest and involvement in a variety of innovation activities,drawing different teams together and developing an identity for the Horizon Centre as an innovation focus. This included a growing number of digitally-driven projects such as e-learning, a health information service (HealthTV) and various projects around simulation, 3D printing, etc. The need for 'digital advisors' became clear and funding was assembled from a variety of sources and projects to help develop this role. An opportunity also arose to use a building on the edge of the hospital campus which had become vacant as a place to locate the nascent 'digital horizons' team.

In principle this was an important development, giving the digital innovation team space and a physical identity, the foundations for what could become an innovation hub for the Trust. However in practice it proved difficult to get staff to move or to visit the centre, especially since engagement with mainstream hospital staff had to squeezed in during short breaks in their clinical duties. It highlighted the psychological distance between innovation as a desirable but peripheral activity and the 'core' business of healthcare delivery and the difficulty in bridging between these two worlds.

In practical terms the momentum behind an innovation centre slipped and instead of developing the centre time was lost to a protracted round of further discussions and planning revisions. Pressures on space across the wider Trust led to a reallocation of the site and further reorganization meant that the core innovation team were moved under the 'education' umbrella. The disadvantage of this was that the growing identity for innovation was subsumed into a wider organization but on the plus side it meant that the team were relocated physically back in the Horizon Centre.

The 'Digital Horizons name had been adopted by the production side of the e-learning projects within the Trust and so the digital innovation team's focus moved from being futures/innovation oriented to occupying an organizational niche within a business unit focused on delivery. In effect '. . . .*'Digital horizons stopped looking at the horizon and became an in-house production facility!'*

However on the plus side it placed the digital team within a collaborative working space interacting with different stakeholders inside and outside the Trust – with the big theme of getting staff in to experience first hand the technology. The group adopted the label Digital Futures Lab (DFL) to reflect this.

Then the COVID-19 pandemic hit and changed the game; a key consequence was that much physical activity stopped, the building emptied and there was both space available and a renewed interest in thinking about digital innovation and the role it could play in a radically changed delivery environment. This enabled the DFL to become established in its current location. Some of the difficulties involved in trying to build something abstract like an innovation culture and out enabling mechanisms and structures in place suddenly found a new focus. In particular the Digital Lab's work on immersive technologies managed to attract attention and involvement of previously disinterested parties.

Its current position remains physically in the Horizon Centre but its reach extends across the Trust and into the surrounding community. The team has grown but still faces limits on what it can achieve due to capacity constraints. In 2015 it was a single person with some part-time support from the innovation team; the DFL now has a core staff of 6 and an extended network of 10 people. Key core roles include:

- a Digital Innovation facilitator, whose role is to look after the Lab – '. . . *he's the jack of all trades, reception, first point of contact and facilities management, plus he now runs the education outreach programme around the technologies. He also has content development skills which we use from time to time . . .'*
- a junior version of that role, with an emphasis on content develop to pilot/proof of context level
- a 'digital apprentice' who is responsible for much of the coding work. The role is currently filled by a young man with extensive experience in the different world of video game engineering
- an allocation of time within the Director of Medical Education role with the responsibility for developing both programmes and links to clinical teams, translating between digital and clinical language
- a digital education liaison role, filtering educational needs and product development to support these – for example with digital skills passports, online and video support materials etc.
- a second part-time developer
- a dedicated post-doctoral researcher specialising in the evaluation of digital technologies in the healthcare space, helping write up projects for publication, and contributing to new funding applications
- in addition there are multiple student interns from universities around the country seconded to the team to work on key projects such as applications of immersive technology in dentistry and paediatric care

It's an eclectic mix of developers and educators and there is extensive crossover in the project work. The operation of the DFL is not confined to the physical base; the underlying model is very much that of a hub and network. '*..we don't want it all to happen in the lab . . . we have to bring innovation to their settings, don't want the Lab to be the only place to go for innovation..'* For example one of the team spends a lot of time working on digital technologies in paediatrics and so needs to understand their context, their language and their constraints; since the staff are under operational pressures they don't have time to visit the Lab so she takes it out to them.

Discussion

Innovation as a slogan has been widely used across the National Health Service for decades but the practical enactment of it has varied widely. In the context of the Trust the experience might be described as 'punctuated strategic equilibrium' in which there are occasional; flashes of commitment and specific initiatives followed by a reversion to focus on other priorities with innovation operating in the background. *'We've had support during that journey but its not been strategically led as a key organizational priority . . . it's been acknowledged and supported in steps . . .'*

Within that context much has happened below the radar screen and there is an extensive network of innovation-interested players across the Trust. Having a physical focus, an innovation hub, becomes an important element in maintaining that interest and activity – a boundary space within which conversations and experiments can take place. In its current form the DFL is playing a key role as such a boundary space, acting not only as an important focus for digital; innovation but also providing a hub for other innovation activity.

There is growing acknowledgement of its importance, especially in the digital space but *'. . . there's almost an attitude of 'they're doing good stuff, let them get on with it'. But we're getting to the point where we need more – it's no longer OK to work under the radar, we're now ready to go beyond that and become an integral part of what the Trust wants to achieve . . . .'*

> *Within DFL there has always been the vision of becoming a centre of around digital innovation built around particular digital technology strands . . . .the difference now is that there's actually funding becoming available for such centres of excellence*

This growing profile is reflected in the national level input which DFL is now making, for example in helping formulate policy around AR/VR technologies.

The DFL team see the future building on the experience with Digital Horizons and there is now convergence with other key themes like ensuring digital literacy across 6500 staff so that they are ready and digitally competent for the future. In this sense the location of the DFL in the education centre which the Horizon Centre has become is relevant since the innovation future will depend on skills and capabilities. The vision for the near term would see an established educational programme where all staff are involved in upskilling and with key staff acquiring and passing on new skills. For example a nurse and a midwife might be doing some research around a technology and then becoming the innovators. *'. . . the only way we're going to get people using these technologies is if we have a champions network, people who know their need and can team up with digital specialists . . .'*

In addition there would be networks of *'. . . .digital volunteers, people walking around – training staff and patients to be able to think about digital pathways, use the technology . . .'*

Beyond the educational role comes the exploration, development and testing of digital technologies in the context of their application, prototyping and co-designing with staff and patients.

> *'Put all that together and digital becomes centre stage, rather than a specialist function, it's what everyone does, how the word 'digital ' becomes reframed and is simply part and parcel of the service*

Realising the vision raises some big challenges linked to the context in which innovation is taking place. Unlike a large corporation there is no core focus on innovation, or innovation strategy and resource allocation is spasmodic rather than continued. Most innovation-related finding comes from external programmes and sources. The situation is similar across the country and is not helped by a continued series of nationally-driven initiatives which change the strategic focus for Trusts on a frequent basis.

Building capability in this context becomes difficult; whilst it requires long-term programmed development funding the resources available are often limited both in size and duration. '. . . . you're often fighting the system – *'a lot of my time as an innovator has been spent on finding ways round an unsupportive system . . .'*

The lack of a clear innovation strategy is also reflected in the shifting emphasis; not only is there a crisis focus on operational delivery in a system under severe pressure but also there is a lack of clarity about where innovation sits in the strategic picture. It oscillates between being a sub-set of the major educational transformation going on and having a separate future-oriented focus.

Against this backdrop the role of evidence becomes key, being able to demonstrate that investment in innovation does pay off in terms of impact on qualitative and quantitative performance indicators. There is some evidence that this is happening; for example the early innovation work pioneered around health information videos has now become a significant success at scale with the Connect Plus app, leading to time and cost savings.

Outreach remains a key priority for DFL; although physically located on the hospital campus extensive efforts are made to spread its footprint across the whole region covered by the Trust. This has led to setting up various mobile activities taking the message (and the enabling technologies) out into the field. For example a specially equipped van can be taken to any location and used to demonstrate VR/AR and other technologies and to engage with a wide variety of users in developing applications based on this technology.

Work is also going on with a local college to explore potential digital apps, working with students to co-create and test relevant innovations. And there is even a 'digital tea trolley' taking the message around the hospital, built on the (old) experience of the tea trolley going around the wards which provided a locus for conversations and idea exchanges. This provides an opportunity to demonstrate new digital possibilities but also to engage with a wide range of users, staff and patients, and draw them into early stage product development.

Concluding thoughts

The potential for innovation to improve healthcare is significant and the need urgent. In particular digital technologies hold out great promise but their effective design and implementation will depend on users being involved throughout the innovation process. The role which a boundary space can play in enabling this conversation and co-design approach is clear; '. . . *we all have a story to tell and the most important thing is that we make sure those stories are heard and the technology, well it's just another way to enable that sharing collaboration . . . .human focused, human centred design is always going to be key..*'

The case demonstrates the potential for such spaces but also highlights the difficulties of implementing them in a system where the 'innovation weather' constantly changes. Without consistent support and strategic guidance there is a risk that bottom-up initiatives like DFL will fail to gain significant traction.

References

Burne (1992). Burnes, B. (1992). Managing change. London: Pitman.

Bessant, J., & Maher, L. (2009). Developing radical service innovations in healthcare: The role of design methods. International Journal of Innovation Management, 13(4), Art. no. 4.

Eason, K. (1988). Information technology and organisational change. London: Taylor and Francis.

Fritzsche, A., Jonas, J., Roth, A., & Moeslein, K. (2020). Innovating in the open lab: The new potential for interactive value creation across organizational boundaries. Oldenbourg: De Gruyter.

Habicht, H., Oliveira, P., & Scherbatuik, V. (2012). User Innovators: When Patients Set Out to Help Themselves and End Up Helping Many. Die Unternehmung – Swiss Journal of Management Research, 66(3), Art. no. 3.

(Iakovleva, Bessant and Oftedal (2019) Iakovleva, T., Bessant, J., & Oftedal, E. (2019). Responsible innovation in digital health. Cheltenham: Edward Elgar.

Mumford, E. (1979). Designing human systems. Manchester: Manchester Business School Press.

Pickles, J., Hide, E., & Maher, L. (2008). Experience Based Design: A practical method of working with patients to redesign services, 13, 51–58.

Tidd, J., & Bessant, J. (2020). Managing innovation (7th edition). Hoboken, H.J.: John Wiley and Sons.

Von Hippel, E. (1988). The sources of innovation. Cambridge, MA: MIT Press.

Maria João Jacinto, Gemma Tria, Luís Correia, Margarida Oliveira, Joana Afonso, Helena Canhão, Pedro Oliveira

Patient innovation as a case-study example of a multisided platform for involving patients in the social innovation process

Abstract: The chapter examines the role of the "Patient Innovation" project as a multisided platform (MSP) in healthcare, aiming to transform how healthcare solutions are conceived, developed, and disseminated by directly involving patients in the innovation process. Using a case-study approach, it investigates how the platform functions as a community organizer, market matchmaker, and innovation manager. The study draws data from platform metrics, user testimonials, and interviews with innovators and healthcare professionals, alongside the analysis of the regulatory and safety review processes that innovations undergo before being shared.

The findings indicate that the "Patient Innovation" platform has successfully engaged over 300,000 users from more than 100 countries, with thousands of solutions shared and validated, ranging from simple home adaptations to complex medical devices requiring regulatory approval. The platform has facilitated numerous connections between patient innovators and industry partners, leading to the commercialization of several patient-developed innovations.

The "Patient Innovation" project effectively demonstrates how MSPs can leverage patient-led innovations to enhance healthcare outcomes. By providing a structured environment for sharing and developing innovations, the platform ensures that these solutions are safe, effective, and aligned with market needs, underscoring the potential of user-driven innovation in healthcare and its capacity to complement traditional R&D approaches.

The significance of this study lies in its demonstration of the potential for MSPs to revolutionize healthcare innovation by involving patients and caregivers. This approach not only accelerates the adoption of innovative solutions tailored to real-world needs but also fosters a more inclusive and responsive healthcare system. The findings advocate for broader adoption of similar platforms across other sectors, suggesting a shift towards more user-centered innovation frameworks in healthcare and beyond.

Introduction

As it is increasingly urgent to address challenges populations face, such as aging population and the availability of quality healthcare, the future must go through a broader stakeholder inclusion into the decision-making process, anticipation of societal needs,

https://doi.org/10.1515/9783111241036-010

and reflection of concerns, which calls for new innovation policies. The inclusion of patients and caregivers, not only as end-users but as a valuable source of knowledge for effective solutions will thus be key for successful achievements. Recognizing patients and informal caregivers not just as passive participants but as the drivers of development can help reshaping the landscape of healthcare innovation. The intimate familiarity of these stakeholders with their needs and challenges, positions their contributions as incredibly efficient and pertinent. This profound understanding ensures that the innovation they pioneer is not only tailored but also exceptionally effective.

This chapter examines user healthcare innovation, emphasizing patient-driven solutions and the 'Patient Innovation' project. It explores this initiative as a multisided platform linking producer and user innovation networks. Through an analysis of its roles — community organizer, market matchmaker, and innovation manager — it showcases its influence on transforming healthcare innovation. This exploration aims to highlight the key role of patients and informal caregivers and the impact of multisided platforms on shaping the future of healthcare innovation.

Patients as a great source of valuable innovation

Until recent years, the innovative power of patients wasn't acknowledged by healthcare stakeholders and was not considered part of any established innovation value network. Patients who develop innovative solutions exist at the margins of the healthcare industry in local community networks, as patient associations. These innovative patients were thus faced as rare and uncommon innovators, instead of valuable sources of innovation worth of developing mechanisms to bring these novel solutions to the healthcare innovation value network.

Oliveira *et al.* (2015) have thus defined 'patient innovators' as patients and informal caregivers, creators of novel solutions for their own personal needs related to the medical condition they face. The novel solutions range from very simple approaches, like a mom who used colorful helium balloons to stimulate her disabled son to do his walking exercises, to complex technological and medical devices – some of them requiring regulatory approval to be used, such as an exoskeleton or a cardiac support device (de Jong *et al.*, 2015). Patient innovation is thus a segment of a broader effect of user innovation, which reveals itself as a framework that faces users as a source of relevant knowledge about real-life needs and problems, and innovations they developed for their own use and consequent benefit (von Hippel, 1988).

During the design process of these personal solutions, patients don't spend too much time and effort trying to fit a general market need or developing a detailed cost-benefit analysis for profit maximization. Patients create solutions to solve their own pressing problems, which will probably be relevant to others with similar needs but not framed to products and services available in the market. The innovations created by patients might thus be framed outside established market and innovation frameworks, which makes the healthcare industry unaware of such needs, or consider them as less relevant (DeMonaco *et al.*, 2019).

A study regarding user innovation in different countries showed that up to 0.5% of adult citizens innovate in healthcare (von Hippel *et al.* 2012; Kim, 2015). Oliveira *et al.* (2015) interviewed 500 patients and informal caregivers and found that over 30% of them claimed to innovate, and 8% create solutions new to the world; on the other hand, only 5% of them shared their solutions with the medical community, but 89% shared it locally with other patients.

Patient Innovation – a project to revolutionize healthcare through user innovation

From this background, the Patient Innovation (PI) project was born as a global open online platform that eases the sharing and dissemination of solutions developed by patients and informal caregivers who face any disease and have developed novel products to solve their own needs.

The Patient Innovation platform started as a global concentrated venue for patients to share their innovative solutions, receive feedback from other platform users, and increase the promotion of their solutions. This solution sharing aims to increase ideation by other users and validation of the shared solutions.

In order to assure the safety and quality of the solution sharing, each post submitted by a platform user follows a designed process. First, the Patient Innovation staff checks if the post content is in conformity with the terms of service and intellectual property protection. The posts that are approved in this first filter, are then reviewed by the Patient Innovation medical team, which checks the solutions' safety, rejecting those that pose intrinsic dangers, lack proper regulatory validation, or involve consumables such as food/drink or drugs (e.g., non-scientifically tested teas or topical solutions). In case the Patient Innovation medical team is not sure about the solution under analysis, e.g., it is out of the medical doctor's area of expertise, specialized medical experts are consulted, including some of the advisory board members, and/or it is requested more information from the innovator. Once the posts get this final validation, they will then be published and available online for the platform user community. Around 50% of the submitted solutions don't follow the referred quality parameters and are thus rejected in the review process. Approved solutions might range from simple adaptations for daily life activities (e.g., an adapted cup for cerebral palsy patients created by a caregiver) to class III medical devices (e.g., a heart adaptor created by a patient); the distribution range is negatively related with the increased solution complexity.

Each post consists of a text description regarding the novel solution and the creator profile, complemented with links, pictures, videos, and in some cases instructions, to enhance the solution adoption. In the platform's back-office, Patient Innovation staff tags each post with relevant medical conditions, symptoms, parts of the body, functions offered, and the type of solution (device, digital, or service), so the impact transversality of each solution can be explored. The platform users can comment and indicate if they liked, copied, or purchased a specific solution. An effort has been made to provide the Patient Innovation platform in different languages to increase the sources of innovations from patient communities, and to expand its reach.

Patient Innovation is the largest concentrated venue of health innovation in Europe, (Oliveira and Pina e Cunha, 2021) with a community of 300 000 frequent users from over 100 countries and over 1.2 million visitors every year. Its innovator's community is constituted by 44% patients (those who develop solutions for themselves), 41% informal caregivers (those who develop solutions for loved ones), and 15% collaborators (those who develop solutions for someone outside their circle of family/friends with no intention to profit from it). 58% of the visitors are male and the most dominant age intervals are 25–34 and 35–44. In the beginning of 2023, 1826 solutions had been submitted, analyzed, approved, and published. From those, 593 (32.5% of the solutions approved) are being commercialized.

Patient Innovation later started to develop different activities to connect its innovative patient community with producer innovation value network agents, in order to encourage patients to innovate with healthcare industry actors and present them with tools and networks so that they can bring their innovations to the market. The Patient Innovation platform thus features different community activities, so it can link the patient innovators and their innovations with other potential users, either on or off-platform.

When patients find themselves struggling with a need related to the health condition that they face, their common approach is to first look for a solution in the market, mainly through recommendations from doctors and other healthcare professionals. In the case where that search is inconclusive or unsuccessful, some patients start thinking about possible solutions, and from those patients only a small amount will really work on it, designing a new product, developing its prototype, and testing it to diffuse it throughout the community. To diffuse their solution, innovators can either commercialize the product through already existing companies, create a new startup for that end, or just share it through peer-to-peer contact.

In order to ensure a complete and effective overview of the platform and activities development, the Patient Innovation team brings together complementary professional backgrounds such as medical, business, engineering, and social.

Innovation divergence: Contrasting user and producer networks in healthcare

Although new innovation networks are created, they usually disconnect users from the traditional R&D and producer innovation value network. Thus, users find difficulties bringing their innovations to the market, and the innovation creation potential gets bottlenecked.

Figure 1: Example of a solution submitted by a patient innovator, which was approved by the Patient Innovation Medical team and published in the Patient Innovation platform.

This leads to many good ideas and innovations ending up being only shared in local communities and may be lost for good, due to the insufficient sharing and capacity to bring them to market. For simple solutions, patient innovators might not know the appropriate and reliable place to share their innovations; for more complex solutions, most of the time, patients have a hard time connecting with innovation networks, since the implicit steps of the production process to turn the user ideas into products available in the market are absent and not clear in their environment. This happens as user innovation follows a different workflow and value chain compared to the innovation processes usually practiced by producers. The main difference between these two frameworks is the motivation to innovate: users aim to benefit from it, and traditional producers aim to profit (Boudreau and Jeppesen, 2015; von Hippel, 2017).

These two distinct innovation paradigms manifest themselves as different innovation value networks, taking into consideration the context in which the problem-solving and innovation processes take place: user- or produced-based (Christensen and Rosenbloom, 1995). Although both aim to solve a pressing problem, each value network presents a particular design that takes into consideration the stakeholders' roles and assets involved and the specific work flow process (Jacobides *et al.*, 2006). The value network design is resistant to quick change thanks to compatibility, interoperability, regulation, and existing preference matters (Ansari and Krop, 2012).

On one hand, the producer innovation value network improves its process to (i) be focused on research, (ii) achieve good production efficiency and viability, (iii) correspond to an accurate market value determination and get great product adoption, (iv) accomplish profit maximization and quick return of investment – cost-benefit and business plan analysis are relevant tools; it presents no or limited interaction with the user innovation value network (Baldwin and von Hippel, 2011). The traditional innovation value network is characterized as a classical linear logic chain, with well-defined stages with complementary features by specialized experts, with strong economic incentives, used to successfully take novel solutions to the healthcare market. Here, patients are faced as mere end-users by the end of the linear value chain that continuously delivers finished products; this approach limits the innovation search process, as it doesn't take into consideration the user's real needs.

On another hand, in the user innovation value network, value is measured as the perception and benefit of solving a personal burden, without a necessary reflection on the solution's economic impact as returns of investment, and innovators put in little to no effort to enhance product diffusion and adoption. The user/patient innovation value network processes feedback loops through the community, characterized by: (i) informal and peer-to-peer informal exchange, (ii) great personal need-related knowledge, (iii) lack of resources to develop and disseminate their novel solutions, (iv) and personal benefit from solving pressing problems or altruism as the main incentives for the innovative process, instead of the effort investment.

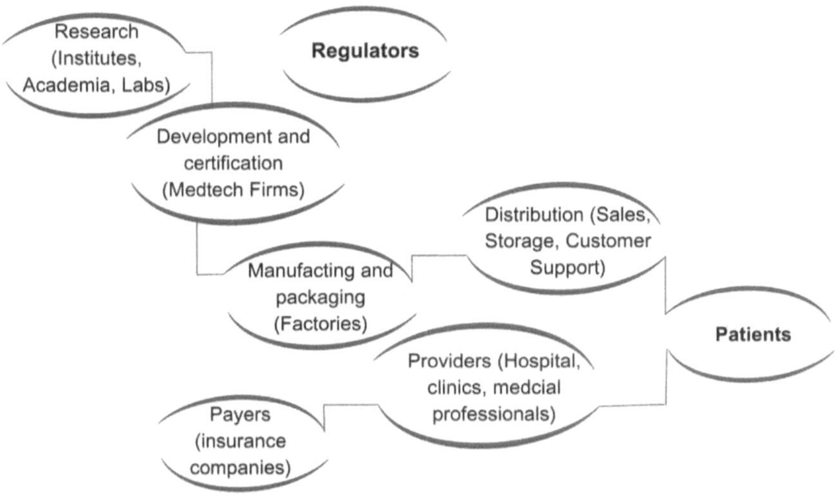

Figure 2: Producer Innovation Value Network (Cennamo et al., 2022).

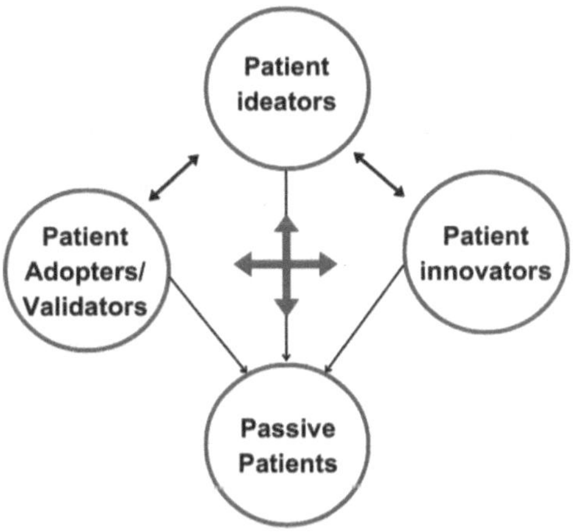

Figure 3: User Innovation Value Network (Cennamo et al., 2022).

Thus, the design and internal processes of both innovation value networks are different and mismatched, as both innovation paradigms exist in parallel. Taking as an example Michael Sers' case, an ostomized patient who created a novel ostomy bag sensor digitally connected with the patient's smartphone, to let him know when the bag was getting full and needed to be replaced, also sending real-time information to the doctor (Sers, 2018). As Michael never found a corporate partner to scale-up the dissemination of his *ostom-i-alert* sensor, he decided to bring his product to the market by creating his own venture. It is thus clear that sometimes innovation bottlenecks occur due to this disconnection and lack of coordination between the actors involved, whose motivations are limited by the innovation value network where they are framed and not aware of the final customers' needs (Adner and Kappor, 2010; Masucci *et al.*, 2020; Ozcan and Hannah, 2020). Very few patients are able to develop a novel solution for their own use and bring it to the market through an agreement with an established healthcare industry partner. Catherine Patton and her novel invention *I-Port* is a clear example of that. She was diagnosed with diabetes type 1 during her pregnancy in 2001. As she was scared of needle sticks, and there was no valid solution for this in the market, she invented the *I-Port*, a discreet injection delivery device used in conjunction with a syringe or pen that allows for multiple daily injections without repeated skin punctures. She founded her own company, Patton Medical Devices, in 2004 and later found an agreement with Medtronic for its large-scale distribution (Patton, 2014).

If on one hand patients and caregivers had proven really high innovative potential, the fact that the producer and the user innovation value networks are mostly disconnected, it might appear as a treat that blocks the impact of several valid innovations, that have been developed for true unmet needs. There is a clear need to connect the two innovation value networks through a win-win approach, where the intellectual property of the innovators (from whether innovation value network the innovation comes from) is respected and assured: traditional producers will save money by stopping to launch non-effective solutions, and patient innovators will find supportive partners who can help in the scaleup and implementation stages, where patients are usually less familiar with and traditional producers have great experience backgrounds.

Based on this framework, in this chapter, Patient Innovation will be analyzed as a potential tool that can not only scale-up the innovative potential of patients and caregivers but also connect the two value innovation networks to further promote its impact.

Analysis: Patient innovation as a multi-sided platform case-study

Multisided platforms: Integrating user and producer innovations in healthcare

One recent tool that appears as a possible solution to connect the producer and user innovation value networks, empower patients as innovators and bring solutions to the market by and for patients, are Multisided Platforms (MSPs). MSPs are new digital organizational setups that provide a proper environment to directly exchange value interactions between different types of platform users (e.g., service providers and users) (Hagiu and Spulber, 2013). These digital manager marketplaces are directed by a controlling entity responsible for setting the interaction rules within the platform and, in case of interest, coordinate transactions between the different platform users (supply and demand sides) and thus lead economic activity in and across sectors (Jacobides *et al.*, 2020; Hagiu and Wright, 2015; Parker and Van Alstyne, 2005). This coordination might therefore be faced as a platform orchestration, translated into the development of several processes that aim to increase the platform value to its users, by developing specific activities among the platform users (Dhanaraj and Parkhe, 2006). Most common MSPs explore pricing strategies that are common in several sectors, such as hospitality (e.g., Booking.com) or food (e.g., Uber Eats), where the product or service is provided as an option for free to the end-user, while the provider is charged 'on the other side' so it can be a displayed option to the final user.

MSPs can thus be faced as a reasonable solution to connect user and producer innovation value networks by putting them in contact and coordinating the different agents involved to meet each other and scale up solutions developed by patients. However, it is important to keep in mind that, unlike other areas where MSPs are getting more and more popular, healthcare solutions can't be freely traded as some are complex, involve different parts of their value chain, and imply regulatory approvals during their development process. Also, some of the involved parts are off-platform, as they are not framed in either demand or supply sides, but still need to be engaged in order to contribute to the process of transforming solutions created by patients into valuable commercial solutions. Orchestration activities thus imply more complex activities than just simply putting users of different sides of the platform in contact. It is expected that, when working in such heavily regulated industry, the platform provides activities and tools so that the involved agents can find motivations to produce and feel empowered by witnessing a clear solution for the innovation and value creation process bottlenecks, and a well-defined way to involve the external associated factors as healthcare regulatory framework. When considering solutions developed by patients, it is important to note that these people may miss the tools and know-how to develop, validate and increase its adoption. Additionally, since these innovations came up as solutions for personal needs related to the health conditions they face, the innovators can face other constrains and have limited access to resources/ incentives to dedicate themselves to bring those novel solutions to the market.

Patient innovation platform – a good MSP example

Although Patient Innovation started as an academic repository of solutions developed by patients and caregivers for their own needs, the development of new activities associated with its mission has slowly transformed Patient Innovation as MSP, orchestrating relationships with the patient community (innovators and passive adopters), and the traditional innovation value network.

Patient Innovation, an award-winning project, orchestrates itself in modules to enhance the connection between patients and the producer innovation value network, by providing different options for innovative solutions created by patients. In order to identify and facilitate the development, dissemination and scaleup of innovations created by patients through different pathways to be shared with the patient community and/or reach the market, Patient Innovation acts through the orchestration of activities framed in three different roles: **community organizer**, **market matchmaker** and **innovation manager** (Cennamo *et al.*, 2022). These three different roles, while working synchronously, link the generated ideas that came out from the platform user patient community, with innovation production and commercialization processes and agents from the well-established producer innovation value network. This implies a connection between on- and off-platform to reveal and direct the innovation process by patients. It is important to highlight that the platform's orchestration roles predominance depends on the solution's features and its risk class (e.g., medical device classes).

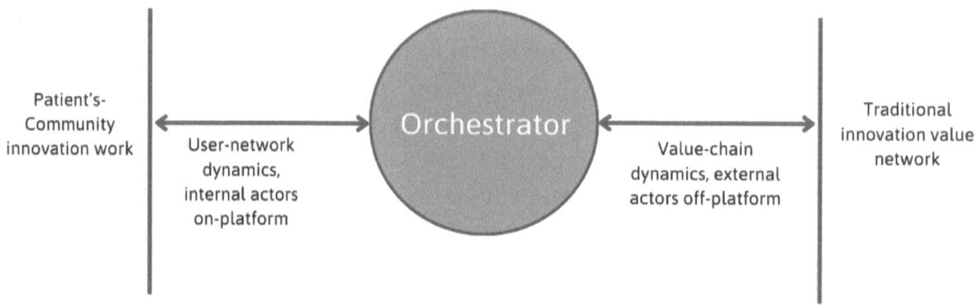

Figure 4: Patient Innovation as an MSP in the healthcare innovation landscape (Cennamo et al., 2022).

Until 2019, the Patient Innovation platform was mainly focused on the free sharing of solutions developed by patients to solve their own needs. Since 2020, the Patient Innovation started to create new activities, such as leading the Patient Innovation Bootcamp, and collaborating in other European Institute and Technology (EIT) Health's activities to help patient innovators bring their novel solutions to the market through the creation of new startups. Other recent activities, such as Demo Days and showrooms (a refined list of solutions that answer to a specific interest of implemented firms), were also recently developed to connect the innovators with existing companies and promote product commercialization through them. Activities like the Patient Innovation Awards – a ceremony always framed in big audience events (like Web Summit, EIT Health Summit and Estoril Conferences) – aim to recognize and congratulate high impact innovators, and motivate others to pursue their innovative potential, also aim to disseminate and scale-up the reach of solutions developed by patients and caregivers for their own needs. It is thus clear that the orchestrated activities are significantly different from other MSPs that coordinate buyers and sellers (as Amazon, Airbnb or Appstore).

The described activities maintain the user and producer innovation value networks separated so the platform's internal dynamics can work spontaneously. Still, both innovation value networks are sufficiently connected to facilitate their potential collaboration, thus converting the dual user-producer paradigm of innovation into an innovation individuality – a true innovation value shaper.

That connection must include the internalization into the user value network of externalities of the traditional producer-centered value network, as relationships with regulatory institutions, and steer the process so that these valuable innovations can be implemented in the market. This coordination aims to stimulate collaborations and contribute to the shape of the innovation ecosystem (Leten *et al.*, 2013). To do that, it must, at the same time, (i) assure the trust of the user innovation community as an organizer and demonstrate coherence to enhance the interest and dedication of the patient community, and (ii) create and maintain an innovation discovery channel reputation within the traditional value network agents, demonstrating tangible outputs and meaningful value to these players.

The community organizer role

In most common MSPs, its usual activities to manage the community comply with identity verification and exchange of information between the buyers and suppliers, to ease the desired economic transaction. In the case of Patient Innovation, the MSP community organizer role first relies on *knowledge exchange facilitation* as a platform orchestration activity to solve the knowledge fragmentation innovation bottleneck. This activity implies the provision of a proper setup where platform users can exchange their knowledge among their peers by submitting their novel innovations and/or providing feedback to solutions developed by others, which will consequently enhance the innovation and diffusion process of the new solutions developed by patients.

As discussed previously, since the Patient Innovation platform deals with healthcare solutions, a medical team evaluation step was established during the solutions submission process so it can answer to platform users' safety concerns and give them trust regarding the published solutions. Patient Innovation medical teams thus perform an *information certifier* activity, validating the proposed innovation and assuring its quality for the safety of the platform's users. This information filter process provides trust to the platform user community and enhances value creation as users' attention and development efforts will be focused on solutions with great potential that truly solve a specific need and don't represent a safety threat. Also, when browsing published solutions, a platform user who hasn't yet considered innovating, might better understand what a patient innovation is and get inspired to share and/or develop his/her own ideas for their personal needs. As the number of approved and published solutions increases, and consequently the awareness of patient innovations features, the amount of rejected solutions has decreased as the platform users learn what is, and what is not, suitable for publication.

The Patient Innovation platform also stimulates knowledge exchange between peers and links users working on similar solutions or solutions for similar needs. This 'get together' might help to solve some of the innovation challenges that these innovators often face while prototyping and producing their solutions. This *engagement manager* activity is thus focused on directing platform users' focal attention to a solution that requires support from the community, either engaging other users to support the innovator and/or motivating other patients to adopt the developed solution.

Together, these three roles increase the access to valuable innovative solutions to more potential users, by showing innovations that answer to different diseases and needs that were not fully addressed by the solutions available in the market. This leads to more and better innovations in both user and producer innovation value networks through an MSP approach.

The market matchmaker role

Most solutions published in the Patient Innovation platform are simple and low-risk products and services, easy to describe, that are not medical devices. More complex solutions are framed into class II and III categories, and some might present potential great market fit. From the pool of medically approved and published solutions in the Patient Innovation platform, around 68% are class I, 30% class II and only 2% class III. To bring these solutions to the market, it is necessary to involve producer innovation value network agents that have the know-how in manufacturing and commercial tools.

To promote the full potential of these more complex solutions, Patient Innovation must connect the innovators with off-platform agents that can support them in the product development and commercialization processes – another MSP feature. This matchmaking role implies that the platform works as an intermediary between the patient innovators and producers that present tools, skills and interest in bringing new solutions to the healthcare market. To do that, *information amplifier* activities are key, as the orchestrator aims to increase the information reach, overcoming information asymmetry problems between the patient innovators, the established firms in the traditional production chain, and the healthcare professionals who will adopt it. Activities like the Patient Innovation Awards – an event that happens every 2 years where platform users that presented great potential and impact solutions to the community are highlighted – help to promote and amplify the solution's reach.

The platform can also match innovative solutions with firms or other institutions interested in developing them into technical and economically viable products. This

MSP *value networks bridging* activity aims to put in contact the Patient Innovation disconnected innovation value networks, connecting innovators to relevant agents in the healthcare innovation value network. To do that, Patient Innovation promotes innovation contests, as the Patient Innovation Bootcamp DemoDay, where participating teams present their work to off-platform healthcare references, and expose these startups to the EIT Health network, composed of over 150 European members that include medical and pharmaceutical companies, universities, R&D labs and regulators.

These two types of activities screen innovative products based on their potential and aim to increase their market value by facilitating selective contact with possible buyers. Without it, the ability of those market players to properly evaluate the value of these innovations would be lower. One successful example is Lisa Crites, founder of *The Shower Shirt*, who benefited in terms of global advertising from being one of the winners of the Patient Innovation Awards, and improved its commercial efforts in the Middle East and Portugal while The Shower Shirt was showcased at the World Government Summit 2016 in Dubai and other initiatives by the Patient Innovation team.

Through this market matchmaker role, the Patient Innovation helps to improve the value of the solutions submitted by innovative patients, potentially improving its market availability, affordability, quality, safety, efficiency, and delivery through strategic connections between the patient innovator and established value chain agents. All sides will benefit from this matchmaking: (i) the traditional producer innovation value network will get more customers, when working as providers of part of the process, or an improved portfolio, when acquiring or collaborating with the innovators; (ii) patients will have better, safer, and potentially more affordable novel solutions in the market.

The innovation manager role

Patient innovators most of the time lack the knowledge and resources needed to develop and scale-up the solutions that they have created, transforming the initial idea into a prototype, and then finally to a functional and viable product with regulatory approval and produced at a large scale. The MSP innovation manager role implies the creation of innovation ecosystems that cover the complex healthcare externalities (as the need for regulatory approvals is typically required for class II and III medical devices before bringing the product to the market) by involving specialized agents for the different steps involved in the innovation and development processes.

One of its most important activities is *knowledge integrator*, which implies the selection and delivery of relevant knowledge to and from multiple actors involved in the innovation development processes. One clear example is the Patient Innovation Bootcamp – the first ever accelerator program focused on supporting patients and informal caregivers to develop and scale-up the solutions that they have created for their own needs. This program, supported by EIT Health, was created and designed by the Patient Innovation team in partnership with reference European institutions such as Copenhagen Business School, IESE Business School, Universidade NOVA de Lisboa, Biocat, and has recently started to count with the support of MIT and Harvard Medical School Bootcamps. The program includes personalized mentorship, and covers relevant topics for product development and implementation, such as technology and market validation, team building, and MedTech marketing. One practical example is Biel Digital Glasses, a company founded by Jaume Puig who decided to create novel high-tech eyeglasses to help his son Biel, who suffers from low vision. Biel Digital Glasses participated in the 1st Patient Innovation Bootcamp edition in 2020, where they learned about all the relevant steps of the entrepreneurial journey (product design and validation, product development, business model creation, pricing, negotiation, funding, among other topics); after their participation in the Patient Innovation Bootcamp, the team won the EIT Health pitch competition in the same year, and since then the team has participated in several follow-up activities, as project-based learning with students from European universities (Copenhagen Business School, Nova SBE) that aim to help the startup with challenges that they might lack knowledge to solve during their entrepreneurial journey. They have also received a lot of valuable insights regarding new markets, as the Danish one, which they have defined as one of the go-to-market strategy priorities.

Another relevant activity within this role is *the innovation system integrator*. These activities get together specialized agents within the innovation production process to develop structural roles and activities to cover specific development steps. This activity is more specialized than knowledge integrator ones, as it focuses on different innovation sub-tasks to be allocated to proper actors. An example of this activity is the Patient Innovation ecosystem, where bootcamp alumni and other companies created by patients and caregivers, are welcome to join and benefit from the support of specific experts, who partnered with Patient Innovation, regarding relevant topics for their entrepreneurial development, as lawyers for intellectual property protection or data privacy management.

The platform's innovation manager role thus enhances the value and benefit of patient innovations, as (i) the innovators benefit from an easier development process with skills and resources of specialized agents, increasing their chances and potential to bring a successful product into the market, (ii) end-users benefit of new and specific solutions for their problems, and (iii) society benefits of improved healthcare and quality of life, and enhanced economic activity.

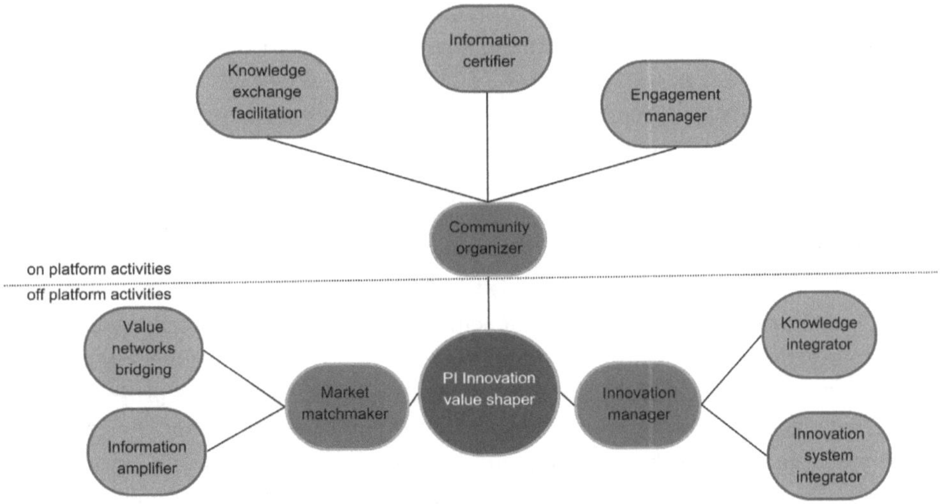

Figure 5: Patient Innovation MSP roles and correspondent activities, on and off-platform.

Discussion/conclusion

The 3-roles impact

Solutions developed by patients for their own needs can't always achieve their full potential impact on their own. Although the ease of **sharing in a safe, easy access and trustworthy venue**, where those who have novel ideas can share them with the community, and those who have unmet needs can search for a solution, it doesn't ensure, by itself, that these innovations will reach their full diffusion potential. To do that, the solutions need to be validated, improved where necessary, answer to regulatory requirements and find their way in the healthcare supply chain. The path to patient innovation product **commercialization can follow two directions: through existing well-established companies in the traditional producer innovation value network, or by creating a new firm through user entrepreneurship** (Block et al., 2016). When the platform offers the necessary links between the user and the traditional producer value networks, the platform acts as a value shaper. The singularity of Patient Innovation is that, to perform the discussed roles, it implies processes on-platform within the platform user patient community, and other off-platform processes that involve external platform agents (e.g., MDs, regulators, specialists, manufacturers). This raises some challenges for the platform provider, as it will be necessary to manage the potential tensions, lack of resources and organizational issues that might emerge when involving different audiences on- and off-platform.

The roles described shouldn't be mutually exclusive. The most benefit will arise from it if they work in parallel, leading to a tripartite role of Patient Innovation as an innovation value shaper.

As Patient Innovation coordinates the patient innovation community and connects the user and producer innovation value networks, either through market matchmaking or innovation management, the platform thus works as a tripartite innovation value shaper agent, guiding value creation and development through user orientation through more effective innovation pathways that include specialized actors in the healthcare value chain. This role is achieved by giving the patient innovators well-defined options to either freely share or commercialize their solutions, providing clear directions on how to move between the two innovation value networks, and getting together all relevant agents to easily bring those solutions to the market. By doing this, the project aims to unlock the innovation potential in healthcare that comes from patients and their personal daily needs. As an **inspiring patient innovation example** to the readers, who explore different roles of Patient Innovation project, we can explore the case of Raul Dorado, a patient who received a cardiac implant support and has created a chest protector for people like him to practice sports or other daily activities feeling safe from any chest physical impacts (Raúl Dorado, 2021). Raul worked on his 'Daiprox' prototype, and submitted his innovation on the Patient Innovation platform, which was validated by the Patient Innovation medical team and published. He later applied to Patient Innovation Bootcamp 2021 and got accepted into the program. A few months later, he managed to start 'Daiprox' at a large-scale production and commercialization.

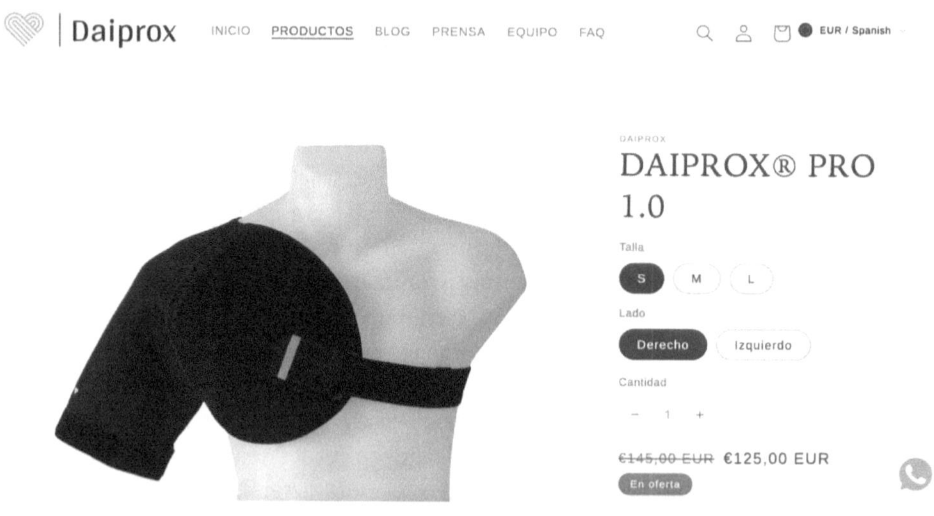

Figure 6: Daiprox, a product developed by Raul Dorado, a patient who submitted his innovation on Patient Innovation platform and participated in the Patient Innovation Bootcamp 2021, which helped him create his own company and produce and sell his product at a large scale.

Through the development of the activities and roles described, Patient Innovation has learned several lessons and fine-tuned its activities design and development based on that. Although the traditional innovation value network agents have become aware of the user innovation potential, their support to be part of an inclusive healthcare environment, where user and producer innovation value networks meet and collaborate, is still highly dependent on high level or mediatic references, or through a first partnership with a patient innovator "champion" who can work as a proof of concept. There is thus a need to measure patient innovations impact, so it becomes undeniable that patients and caregivers can (and they already do) create valuable solutions for real needs, which will improve healthcare systems' effectiveness and, consequently, sustainability. With that, the effort to join all healthcare stakeholders' voices will not only depend on patients, caregivers and other patient led institutions and NGOs, but also on the healthcare industry, established innovators, healthcare systems and policy makers. In the case of Patient Innovation, although the platform metrics are easy to measure and follow (number of users, users' profiles, number of solutions submitted, published and rejected, number of page views, etc.), the tangible impact of solutions created by patients and caregivers for their own needs, and brought into the market either by establishing their own venture or licensing to corporate, is much more difficult to measure. This impact works as a sum of the value/benefit that all those solutions bring to the world (patients, healthcare systems and societies where they are framed), which is not easy to measure or follow. The better connection with more patient and caregiver innovators, is also a constant working topic that, although it has been well achieved through connections with patient associations and communications in different types of events (scientific, societal, corporate, etc.), it can still be further improved so everyone can feel empowered to innovate and solve real daily unmet needs.

The increasing amount of innovators' contacts and data collected from the Patient Innovation platform and project activities, provide a valuable source of information that is continuously monitored for research purposes, through different angles and perspectives: the innovator profile and motivation, the need who motivated the innovative process, common ground for specific medical specialties or conditions, the innovators' entrepreneurial profile, etc.

References

Andrei Hagiu and Daniel Spulber, "First-Party Content and Coordination in Two-Sided Markets," Management Science, 59/4 (April 2013): 933–949.
Andrei Hagiu and Julian Wright, "Multi-Sided Platforms," International Journal of Industrial Organization, 43 (November 2015): 162–174;

Bart Leten, Wim Vanhaverbeke, Nadine Roijakkers, André Clerix, and Johan Van Helleputte, "IP Models to Orchestrate Innovation Ecosystems: IMEC, a Public Research Institute in Nano-Electronics," California Management Review, 55/4 (Summer 2013): 51–64, doi:10.1525/cmr.2013.55.4.51

Carliss Y. Baldwin and Eric von Hippel "Modeling a Paradigm Shift: From Producer Innovation to User and Open Collaborative Innovation." Organization Science, 22/6 (November/December 2011): 1399–1417

Carmelo Cennamo, Pedro Oliveira, & Leid Zejnilovic (2022). Unlocking Innovation in Healthcare: The Case of the Patient Innovation Platform. California Management Review, 64(4), 47–77. https://doi.org/10.1177/00081256221101657

Catherine Patton, "i-Port—Medication Delivery Device," https://patient-innovation.com/post/444 (2014)

Charles Dhanaraj and Arvind Parkhe, "Orchestrating Innovation Networks," Academy of Management Review, 31/3 (2006): 659–669.

Clayton M. Christensen and Richard S. Rosenbloom, "Explaining the Attacker's Advantage: Technological Paradigms, Organizational Dynamics, and the Value Network," Research Policy, 24/2 (March 1995): 233–257.

Eric von Hippel, The Sources of Innovation (London, UK: Oxford University Press, 1988).

Eric von Hippel, Jeroen P. J. de Jong, and Steven Flowers, "Comparing Business and Household Sector Innovation in Consumer Products: Findings from a Representative Study in the United Kingdom," Management Science, 58/9 (September 2012): 1669–1681, doi:10.1287/mnsc.1110.1508

Eric von Hippel, Free Innovation (Cambridge, MA: MIT Press, 2017).

Geoffrey Parker and Marshall Van Alstyne, "Two-Sided Network Effects: A Theory of Information Product Design," Management Science, 51/10 (October 2005): 1494–1504. https://www.jacobides.com/_files/ugd/0b15b1_7e0678d2815541bb920c77ec41e4d305.pdf

Harry DeMonaco, Pedro Oliveira, Andrew Torrance, Christiana von Hippel, and Eric von Hippel, "When Patients become Innovators," MIT Sloan Management Review, 60/3 (Spring 2019): 81–88.

Jeroen P. J. de Jong, Eric von Hippel, Fred Gault, Jari Kuusisto, and Christina Raasch, "Market Failure in the Diffusion of Consumer-Developed Innovations: Patterns in Finland," Research Policy, 44/10 (December 2015): 1856–1865.

Jörn Block, Joachim Henkel, Tim Schweisfurth, and Anika Stiegler, "Commercializing User Innovations by Vertical Diversification: The User-Manufacturer Innovator," Research Policy, 45/1 (February 2016): 244–259.

Kevin J. Boudreau and Lars B. Jeppesen, "Unpaid Crowd Complementors: The Platform Network Effect Mirage," Strategic Management Journal, 36/12 (December 2015): 1761–1777, doi:10.1002/smj.2324

Michael G. Jacobides, Thorbjørn Knudsen, and Mie Augier, "Benefiting from Innovation: Value Creation, Value Appropriation and the Role of Industry Architectures," Research Policy, 35/8 (October 2006): 1200–1221

Michael G. Jacobides, Carmelo Cennamo, and Annabella Gawer, "Distinguishing between Platforms and Ecosystems: Complementarities, Value Creation, and Coordination Mechanisms," working paper, 2020

Michael Seres, "From Patient to Patient-Entrepreneur: Development of an Ostomy Bag Sensor," The American Journal of Gastroenterology, 113/1 (January 2018): 8–10

Monica Masucci, Stefano Brusoni, and Carmelo Cennamo, "Removing Bottlenecks in Business Ecosystems: The Strategic Role of Outbound Open Innovation," Research Policy, 49/1 (February 2020): 103823

Pedro Oliveira, Leid Zejnilovic, Helena Canhão, and Eric von Hippel, "Innovation by Patients with Rare Diseases and Chronic Needs," Orphanet Journal of Rare Diseases, 10 (2015): 41;

Pedro Oliveira, Leid Zejnilovic, Salomé Azevedo, Ana M. Rodrigues, and Helena Canhão, "Peer-Adoption and Development of Health Innovations by Patients: A National Representative Study of 6204 Citizens," Journal of Medical Internet Research, 21/3 (March 2019): e11726.

Pedro Oliveira and Miguel Pina e Cunha, “Centralized Decentralization, or Distributed Leadership as Paradox: The Case of the Patient Innovation’s COVID-19 Portal,” Journal of Change Management, 21/2 (2021): 203–221, doi:10.1080/14697017.2021.1917493.

Pinar Ozcan and Douglas Hannah, “Forced Ecosystems and Digital Stepchildren: Reconfiguring Advertising Suppliers to Realize Disruptive Social Media Technology,” Strategy Science, 5/3 (September 2020): 193–217, doi:10.1287/stsc.2020.1366.

Raul Dorado, “Daiprox is a CE mark registered protection for pacemaker and defibrillator patients”, https://patient-innovation.com/post/4063 (2021)

Ron Adner and Rahul Kapoor, “Value Creation in Innovation Ecosystems: How the Structure of Technological Interdependence Affects Firm Performance in New Technology Generations,” Strategic Management Journal, 31/3 (March 2010): 306–333, doi:10.1002/smj.821

Shahzad (Shaz) Ansari and Pieter Krop, “Incumbent Performance in the Face of a Radical Innovation: Towards a Framework for Incumbent Challenger Dynamics,” Research Policy, 41/8 (October 2012): 1357–1374.

Youngbae Kim, “Consumer User Innovation in Korea: An International Comparison and Policy Implications,” Asian Journal of Technology Innovation, 23/1 (2015): 69–86, doi:10.1080/19761597.2015.1015672

Misha Gipsman, Denis Yagodin, Ilia Rozovskii

Crisis entrepreneurship: To be a robust link in the chain

Abstract: Social initiatives mobilised to respond to the humanitarian crisis of the Russian invasion of Ukraine are explored in this study. It focuses on exceptional direct communication with beneficiaries using social media and chatbots. It highlights the significance of volunteers and former aid recipients who can become contributors. The paper introduces the "link in the chain" principle, emphasising enhanced specialisation and tasks distribution among stakeholders. It also defines the long-term essential "360-degree care" principle, ensuring the sustained, comprehensive well-being of teams observed in all enduring projects. Furthermore, the study addresses the challenges of security, integration of innovations and the role of platforms. Findings contribute to effective strategies for responsible entrepreneurship and disaster management.

But Moses' father-in-law said to him, "The thing you are doing is not right; you will surely wear yourself out, and these people as well. For the task is too heavy for you; you cannot do it alone."
Exodus 18:17–18

Introduction

Responsible entrepreneurship is vital in addressing urgent social needs in all kinds of disasters, even more so during military conflict when state force is heightened with reduced social function. It is particularly evident in response to the Ukraine conflict, where many humanitarian initiatives have emerged. They have driven by a social-entrepreneurial revolution, that took place to solve medical, physical and mental health issues. Their guiding aspiration is succinctly captured in the phrase: "Our purpose is to make our activities no longer necessary".

However, the war has led to the failure of many projects and significant business damage (Audretsch, 2023). This situation underscores the necessity for consistent interaction with beneficiaries and diverse stakeholders to provide tangible and lasting help. The ongoing conflict has highlighted the importance of adopting previously underutilised innovative technological solutions, such as online document flow, messaging applications, automated chatbots, digital security and video conferencing tools,

Note: We are grateful to "Reshim.org" and "Teplitsa – Technologies for Social Good" for their assistance.

Misha Gipsman, Ariel University, Israel
Denis Yagodin, Teplitsa – Technologies for Social Good
Ilia Rozovskii, Fancy.global Agency, Germany

https://doi.org/10.1515/9783111241036-011

to provide much-needed assistance, including medical and psychological care. Entrepreneurship's role in disasters requires academic attention despite its obvious importance, as noted by Akinboye & Morrish (2022).

The research explores the initiatives' survival practices and effectiveness insights during the Ukrainian humanitarian crisis and post-soviet social disaster. The research reviewed initiatives responding to war-related challenges, mostly focusing on health issues. A review is conducted of organisations and initiatives that persist after a year-and-a-half and demonstrate varying productivity. The research aimed to capture insights by analysing projects' experience and interaction with beneficiaries and stakeholders.

Our research indicates that social projects in crises can initiate operations independently, circumventing traditional customer development or market research in contrast to commercial enterprises. They focused on direct assistance to those affected by the conflict here and now. Initiators found new seriousness in addressing security for themselves, their representatives, and beneficiaries. The initiatives showcased pronounced adaptability to the environment's fluid changes and a lack of resources and infrastructure. Most of these initiatives commenced operations swiftly, in a "burning as launch" regime, without comprehensive preparatory phases, and later encountered the need for strategic realignment. This approach often brought a clear understanding of the objectives ("what" needs to be done) but left ambiguity regarding the methods ("how possible" or "how better" to accomplish these goals). The primary development driver in these scenarios was not formalised contact or research but rather direct and meaningful dialogue with all stakeholders. Significantly, beneficiaries who transitioned into contributor roles initiated many innovations within these projects, while many others were implemented in collaboration with qualified partners.

Thus, the research identifies two key principles in successful initiatives. The first, which we term "the link in the chain," involves a focused increase in the specialisation of assistance throughout the entire journey of the beneficiary and network inclusion of stakeholders with complementary skills. Omitting the obvious dependence on resources, the second principle, "robustness," achieved through "360-degree care," ensures comprehensive support for teams, beneficiaries, and partners. Those principles were a common feature in the projects that endured and thrived.

Since Russia annexed Crimea in 2014, the post-Soviet geopolitical landscape has undergone significant shifts, marked by escalating tensions and a decline in state-mediated social functions (Oleinik, 2018; Benevolensky, 2019). The Russian invasion of Ukraine in 2022 has caused extensive infrastructure damage, leading to shortages of essential goods such as medical care, electricity, and heating and an increase in mental health issues and psychiatric disorders. The increasing need for social services both within and outside Ukraine, coupled with the state's focus on military and infrastructure challenges, has emphasized the important role of the public and non-profit sectors. Ukrainians and supporters initiated countless projects at the beginning of the war. Russian civil society has faced governmental restrictions, impacting liberties, health, lives, and suppressing liberal groups and cancelling in a migration (Darieva et al., 2023; Fomina, 2023; Terekhov, 2023). Many projects have been established to assist with relocations and security, notably supporting the Ukrainian people.

Responsible entrepreneurship with social initiatives has become crucial in responding to these challenges and recovery. Only on the 'Reshim.org' platform are more than ninety projects dedicated to mental health among Ukrainians presented, and on the "World Map" by 'Ok Russian', over two hundred anti-war projects and communities are presented.

Method

Our review methodology is grounded in the PMI Guides, enriched by elements from Holacracy and Lean Startup frameworks, as internationally accepted standards (Project Management Institute, 2021; Ries 2017; Robertson, 2021). The timeframe for this study was defined by the onset of the war to September 2023. We were focusing on the objectives and outcomes of the initiatives under review. This paper uses the term 'project' as an organised managerial synonym for 'initiative' to ensure readability. The terms 'crisis' and 'disaster' are used interchangeably, but with the understanding that the case refers to a continuing period of time with varying characteristics.

Our study employed a multichannel approach to recruit projects, utilising public emails, Telegram contacts, and partnerships with organisations like 'Reshim.org' and 'Teplitsa'. The research evaluated 25 initiatives and non-profit organisations, all consented to processing their information. Our data collection included 17 completed questionnaires and 10 semi-structured interviews, with 2 projects participating in both. While the interviews mirrored the structure of the questionnaires, they provided more in-depth content and involved a diverse range of projects most pertinent to our research theme. The research excluded 5 respondents who were either spearheaded by individual activists or did not fully align with pro-Ukrainian or Russian anti-war themes.

To verify the insights, we conducted subsequent interviews with project presenters to discuss the validity or falsification of our hypotheses derived from the preview meetings. In this research, we also directed specific formal additional inquiries to 14 projects via email or Telegram. Before conducting the interviews and following the completion of the questionnaires, we executed a critical analysis of the public information and digital communications of all the projects under study, including websites, chats, bots, and social media, to construct a profile of each project. In finalising our conclusions, we re-examined and sought corroboration by revisiting the public information of all the projects. The development paths of 12 projects were partly elucidated due to the additional opinions provided by 'Teplitsa' and partners with experience in interactions with them.

Team sizes across the studied projects varied. According to our information, the core of teams ranges from 3 to 20 members, with an average of 7. However, it suffers from significant variations in roles, engagement, and volunteer involvement, rendering it unreliable as a comprehensive representation. Apart from a few local projects, most have remote teams. Most reviewed projects, members, or agents were located at the same time inside and outside Ukraine or Russia. The scope of the projects very conditionally spanned various geographical locations, including Ukraine (The Center for Civil Liberties, Teenergizer), Israel (Wild Walks, AVAMind), Russia, Lithuania (Helpdesk), Georgia (The Ark, Tbilisi shelters), Slovakia (Nezábudka), Poland (WFU), Canada, Germany, Moldova, and the Netherlands. The list of projects includes psychological chatbots, medical and psychological platforms, refugees and rehabilitation centres, aggregators, informational coordination services, evacuation, human rights, and youth organisations. All the projects, permanent or regular, assist with health-related issues. Most of the projects include Ukrainian or Russian members affected by war. To provide a more comprehensive overview, we also mention some projects below that were not included in our data but serve as typical examples of initiatives to address the issues related to the crises.

Our questionnaire covered project aspects, including product, results, processes, and stakeholder communication. It included recurring questions from the initiation phase to the present, assessing implementation challenges, adaptation, and alignment of expectations. We asked how much information from stakeholders influenced the development and what feedback was received at each stage. Future plans were also discussed. The average interview lasts 1.5 hours. We have reserved the option to answer additional questions.

Most projects demonstrate depressive resource endowment at the time of research, except a few of those with direct support from large funds. By lexical and frequency analysis, the tone of voice in both the written responses and interviews was predominantly neutral, with optimistic attitudes and self-reflection expressions. Frequent use of the word 'team' indicates a collaborative organisational culture.

It revealed a statistically significant correlation ($r = 0.729$) between the alignment of management vision at inception and expectations for the next five years, suggesting a link between realistic initial vision and long-term optimism. Notably, projects in the 'Crisis / Stagnation' stage reported a lower level of alignment and were more pessimistic about their prospects. Another correlation ($r = 0.738$) was identified between the influence of stakeholder information during initial phases and the adaptability of projects, highlighting the importance of receptiveness to external input.

A comparative analysis revealed that "Ukrainian" projects, compared to "Russian", demonstrated a higher degree of alignment between initial expectations with a mean difference of 1.67 and actuality and displayed greater optimism regarding the upcoming year with a mean difference of 1.69. Dialogues with the other projects also confirm this tendency.

In this study, anonymity was an option. Most of the projects restricted direct quotes, and 16 chose to omit project names.

The study has some limitations. The greater preference for anonymity among Ukrainian projects might have been influenced by the declared war-related risks and the authors' Russian background. This paper potentially introduces subjectivity, further compounded by citation restrictions and the authors' personal experiential biases. The authors were absent from Ukraine or Russia during the study period. Despite email, no projects from the European Union responded to our questionnaire in English; responses were only from projects with Ukrainian or Russian website versions and filled out in these languages. Additionally, there was a notable limitation in data collection from unsuccessful projects. The project sample does not represent a comprehensive cross-section of the entire set.

From aid recipients to contributors

In periods of disaster, the experiences of aid recipients markedly differ from those of regular consumers or users. Faced with urgent needs, individuals, turned to relatives, online searches, digital groups, and chats. Often, they were initially hesitant to request help publicly. However, this situation improved as influencers and social media regularly published and updated lists of aid sources. Public organisations and leaders formed online groups to facilitate mutual support, making it easier for people to ask for and receive help.

The severity of the disaster led to the establishment of particular needs among the affected. The extent of these needs forced individuals to communicate all their requests to the limited aid providers, primarily through messengers. For instance, a family required evacuation. But in practice, it always had a wider list: medications, clothing, psychological support, and some unexpected things, such as assistance for distant elderly relatives in another city.

Regardless of physical distance and urgency, direct communication between the affected and benefactors is crucial to avoid misleading judgments and stereotyping. In a general sense, neither the benefactor nor this family initially really knows the whole process. They had only their naive conceptions. Through dialogue, both parties find and implement a solution in real time without pride. For instance, what transportation is required, where to purchase it, and how many items to bring with is possible, what kind, how much coordinator required time to organise it, and so forth. Consequently, because of such contact the initiatives could provide only the feasible specific assistance that was requested.

The initial months and subsequent events led to an inundation of requests, overwhelming the initiatives and causing delays. In response to the need for initial assessments and basic coordination protocols, many initiatives have adopted the use of chatbots. Telegram's popularity in Eastern Europe, along with its technical advantages, has facilitated the widespread implementation of chatbots in most projects. In fact, chatbots are now more commonly used in these projects than in government or insurance services.

People who formerly received aid became experienced and influential beacons within their social circles. Assuming the role of 'evangelists,' they disseminated information about the projects within their networks and aided in mobilising resources. It is not uncommon for ex-beneficiaries to start actively contributing or even joining teams as members.

Direct communication enabled benefactors to share their limitations and difficulties openly. Online communities have the power to provide necessary supplementation or compensation for deficiencies in knowledge, abilities, and networks for those who are stuck. Furthermore, chats under the projects' umbrella and moderation are not just tools for announcements; they are also sources of valuable information and spaces for the exchange of trustworthy and diverse mutual support. This environment enables people to stay informed and regularly participate in activities. Consequently, these groups cultivate an organisational culture that can sustain projects over time, contributing to their longevity and efficiency.

Over time of crisis, organically, public attention towards problems and initiatives generally diminishes. Instead, they shift to focus more on media rather than engagement. Despite the absence of a quantitative analysis capable of quantifying, our observations and the responses from those surveyed suggest the emergence of a contrarian clustering phenomenon. Projects with vibrant social media and open chats become integral to the identities of a significant number of individuals. They feel involved and empathic with those who remove "pain" or some lack of peace. Moreover, this is reinforced by a real opportunity to chat and participate. Any project would be appreciated if the ex-recipient recovers and suggests taking on some responsibility, such as a job. Someone who understands what suffering is, and especially those who have received help, are more likely to be happy to assist in eliminating it and preventing bad. In contrast to community development approaches in business, as described by Cyron et al. (2023), these projects often extended their communication beyond resolving immediate needs.

The solidarity strengthened the support ecosystem, enhancing the visibility and reach of the initiatives, thereby fostering a productive relationship.

Social throttle without reconnaissance

Comprehensive services, typically anticipated in commercial contexts, are notably absent in disasters. Many initiatives emerged rapidly in the immediate aftermath of the war, addressing evident public needs. These initiatives did not follow traditional processes or require extensive planning; instead, they used a grassroots approach to provide direct aid, which contrasted sharply with conventional corporate methodologies.

Our analysis shows that these projects were effective due to the transition without delay from idea to assistance.

Aid provision often surpassed formal requirements in response to extraordinary circumstances. Numerous medical consulting platforms were established without certification, and equipment procurement often occurred beyond the oversight of licensing authorities. These practices, circumventing bureaucratic and corruption barriers, were deemed positive.

In disaster, a specific type of leadership emerges, which we call 'crisis entrepreneurship'. These leaders, often not traditional businessmen but ex-managers, lawyers, and activists, focused on tangible impacts and networks rather than market competition. They entered the fray without prior experience in the specific assistance they offered. While, we are constants that experienced managers were better equipped to navigate these challenges than less seasoned individuals, who often required guidance from more knowledgeable stakeholders. Lack of skill frequently leads to reduced clarity in structure, which causes internal tensions. At the outset of the conflict, mostly directly affected or connected to the crisis initiated diverse, often repetitive and immature, volunteer initiatives. Pragmatic entrepreneurship involves the establishment of clear objectives and missions, adapting to new circumstances, and managing volunteer engagement in order to ensure a project's viability. To compare social initiatives with business resilience in this context, see Halonen (2023).

Collaboration and professional communication were often more crucial than direct experience in urgent social work, as Stepaniuk (2022) points out. Networks such as Ukrainian activists or the Russian political opposition played extensive roles in reserving talent, resources, and contacts. The presence of a supportive and professional network proved pivotal at the inception stage of major initiatives. They often originated from posts on the founders' social media pages or within active online communities, outlining objectives and required skill sets.

Consequently, social networks facilitated the identification of those in need and necessary partners, circumventing governmental involvement. An illustrative case is a small travel agency from East Ukraine that transformed because of requests from former clients. They started organising evacuation and humanitarian aid logistics. Afterwards, ex-clients developed digital automation tools for them. This shift was largely due to the social capital demonstrating the role of existing networks in crisis response. Similarly, the founders of 'WFU' utilised its audience network effectively, transitioning from activism to fundraising and equipment purchase. Although, they searched for partners for each step, logistics, legal NGO, negotiations, and technical expertise. Later, 'WFU' began to assist mainly with the participation of local stakeholders for efficiency.

Horizontal publicity evolved into a routine. Sharing and amplifying each other's calls became a common practice among partners. Project leaders unanimously reported that they are monitoring social media, and frequently interacting with the community. It assists them in receiving feedback and valuable insights in real time.

Through this communication, it is often possible to find solutions and implement many small but significant innovations. A concise overview of collective action in social media in actual context is offered by Ronzhyn et al. (2023).

The problem of reaching a client in business is usually a challenge; however, in a crisis, it is essential to optimise communication with the needy and make it more concise and informative.

Illustrative cases

The psychological impact of war is profound. In this study, we categorised psychological initiatives based on their foundational decisions into three distinct groups, a classification applicable to medical services and others. Our division categorises projects are resembled the "established-new" parameter of the disaster entrepreneurship typology provided by Linnenluecke & McKnight (2017).

The first category consists of new community initiatives. Psychologist communities, acting as primary stakeholders, initiated services to connect clients with specialists or provide first recommendations swiftly. It varies from grassroots efforts to expansive associations, including state-backed NGOs. A notable example is the chatbot 'Faino', started by a small group. Initially, these communities faced a lack of external competencies: technology, marketing, or specific disorder expertise. However, they overcame these through the attraction of partners with expertise.

The second group features strategic reorientations. 'AVAMind', for instance, shifted its focus from a commercial product to addressing PTSD. Services like 'Epicur' also adapted to war-induced needs by integrating reputable guidelines. Additionally, the 'Friend First Aid Bot', initially developed for COVID-19, was repurposed in 2022 to aid victims. 'AVAMind' underwent a rapid transformation, commencing content development in March 2022 and assembling a volunteer team at the Israeli hackathon #Code4Ukraine in April. The project evolved into a specialised chatbot with plans for an advanced AI application. The expanding team of volunteers, benefiting from support from friendly researchers, academics, and public policy and business experts, provided pro bono consultancy for its development. But at the moment of February 2024 it was not realised, because of the lack of the resources.

The third category includes expanding services. Mature platforms like 'VOS' and 'BetterMe' swiftly offered Ukrainian free services, adding sections with emergency guidance for common war-induced symptoms. Some add-ons were built in cooperation with entities like 'WHO' or psychological societies. Notably, government bodies and media significantly promoted these services. Many big associations and tech companies used the opportunity to fundraise.

These cases illustrate the rapid initiation of projects to address urgent needs, emphasising swift mobilisation and the inclusion of complementary stakeholders.

Take one burden, give the rest to your stakeholders

One project leader insightfully remarked, “In the face of a catastrophe, there is a burning urge to address every issue.” A common pitfall leading to project failures is the inability to maintain focus, often caused by the ambition to tackle multiple issues simultaneously.

Our analysis suggests that initiatives, spreading their efforts too thin without concentrating on a specific task, tend to face premature termination. Essential, akin to a link in a chain, is the maturation of specialisation and operational processes. Alternatively, it could be described as finding and identifying project strengths. It appears that a successful practice involves leaders assertively deciding the focus of efforts, rather than striving for an unattainable full consensus of a team.

Effective assistance was achieved through delegation to partners, facilitating a significant increase in the division of labour among projects over beneficiaries’ tracks. The chain allows for faster and easier spread of innovation due to the simpler, which means lower cost of implementation and increased number of teachable cases. Adherence to link status involves referring unsuitable requests to stakeholders rather than managing them in-house. A key characteristic of successful projects is their ability to specialise and cultivate a constructive network. Here are some illustrative examples:

- A team developed a free chatbot to connect clients with psychologists. After several tries to deal with all the tasks, they focused on enhancing its technical aspects and user interaction. Marketing, clinical content, and selection of psychologists were successfully outsourced to partners, including international entities.
- A shelter (rehabilitation centre) adopted a structured approach. After many inconveniences, they formalised client agreements for a predefined set of services within specified program dates. Logistics, arrivals and departures, trips and a major portion of medical services were outsourced.
- A volunteer consortium dedicated to fundraising and equipment donations formed collaborations with partners responsible for legal entities, accounting, and those involved in logistics.

Within successful projects, emerging work areas typically evolve into distinct organisations or expand autonomously yet retain alignment with the parent initiative’s ethos.

On the other hand, projects with conceptual fuzzy goals survive less. Though some exist, with significant support from the government, grants, or extraordinary founders’ social capital.

Apportioning responsibility is not enough. It is no less important to remain open to feedback and heed the advice from stakeholders. Moreover, as the data shows projects that incorporate external messages at the beginning are more likely to be more agile and long-lasting.

Volunteers driven

Volunteers are the cornerstone of these crisis response initiatives. Most projects begin as entirely volunteer-driven endeavours, gradually shifting to a hybrid model of volunteer and paid labour as they secure external funding through avenues like grants and crowdfunding (Kotelevets, 2022). The capacity of a project to attract and retain volunteers is closely linked to its long-term success. Long-term success is often connected with a project's ability to attract and retain volunteers. According to the Sociological Group "Rating", in March 2022, 80% of Ukrainian respondents assisted in Ukraine's defence, with 39% volunteering. By June 2023, occasional volunteering decreased to 43%, with regular volunteering at 6%. According to "OutRush", approximately 39% of Russian migrants donated or aided Ukrainians, while 46–49% provided support to other Russian migrants (Kamalov et al. 2023).

The management of volunteers, with their varied motivations and expectations, is a pivotal task for leaders, necessitating the creation of environments conducive to skill development and strong team bonds.

Maintaining an appropriate level of volunteer engagement is critical. Low engagement levels risk losing the sense of community and connection, while excessive demands can lead to volunteer burnout. Successful projects find a balance by offering volunteers opportunities to encourage personal and professional growth, thus integrating them more deeply into the team's fabric. An illustrative example is a project that enlisted volunteers from around the world and different time zones for 24/7 support, effectively managing a surge in requests and establishing systematic processes.

During our research for this work, we observed a notable emerging trend: a new wave of volunteers. Regardless of physical and psychological state, numerous ex-military personnel, especially those with professional skills, are looking for chances to continue contributing to society.

By 2024, another phenomenon had also emerged. Some commercial businessmen who previously lacked the capacity to offer assistance, over time, either established their businesses in migration or adapted to the more stable conditions within Ukraine. As a result, they got a surplus and have begun providing financial and resource support to what are now professional benefactors. There are very few who are fortunate enough to find and match with such helpers. It typically does not cover basic needs, but compensates somewhat for the decline in common involvement on "the market of resilience".

From benefactor to tribune of people

Projects that have amassed notable audiences and established effective operations over one and a half or two years are now assuming a new role. They help their own kind. Particularly in response to injustice, barriers, and officialdom, these organisations are increasingly advocating for their beneficiaries or stakeholders. This shift is driven by the same logic prevalent at the beginning of the war: the need is evident. And now, organisations possess not only latent social capital but also the authority to influence their loyal audience. This applies to projects both outside and inside Ukraine, including those run by migrants. It illustrates the transition from direct aid provider to lobbyist on one hand, and from a needy society to a civilian society on the other.

Self-care: A prerequisite for effective altruism

All initiatives underscored significant psychological struggles during their development. Respondents identified mental health crises occurring at specific intervals: the initial weeks, two to three months in, and around the one-year mark. The sustainability of the projects relied on implementing what we termed a '360-degree care' principle, prioritising the well-being of the entire team and surrounded people.

Benefactors, in their dedication to helping others, often overlook their well-being, with the repercussions becoming apparent only after substantial time has elapsed. Furthermore, they frequently work with individuals who are distressed, conflicted and traumatised. This drive to relieve others' distress can inadvertently lead to self-neglect, detrimentally impacting their health and long-term ability to provide aid. For example, psychologists in Eastern Ukraine required forced hospitalisation for care after continuous work without breaks, which led to severe hallucinations symptoms.

Prevalent anxiety, exacerbated by the conflict's duration and uncertain outcomes, was observed among Ukrainians, refugees, and initiative members alike. This condition often leads to burnout or compensatory behaviours. Projects had to continuously evolve and respond to fluctuating demands in an unpredictable context, complicating decision-making processes. Challenges such as deciding how to allocate resources between a suffering family and an organisational partner, or balancing the safety of employees with life-saving measures, can greatly add to the stress experienced by those involved in humanitarian work.

The term 'war-life balance' has become part of the vocabulary of many volunteers. It highlights the importance of well-being even in crisis. Like rescuers or psychologists needing supervision, social entrepreneurs and aid workers also require support mechanisms to maintain their effectiveness and optimism.

All successful initiatives of the study implemented efforts, such as psychotherapy, support groups, clearly defined work-life boundaries, and therapeutic and art training. Some organisations partnered with specialists to offer retreats. Moreover, a rehabilitation service provider noted that disengaging from social activities following rehabilitation is a positive outcome.

To ensure the viability of projects, it is vital to prioritise providing comprehensive care. It should include the psychological and physical well-being of team members, stakeholders, and beneficiaries.

Security: Critical yet neglected

The significance of implementing digital security measures has been rising considerably compared to the recent past. Especially with inadequate or antagonistic government backing, such as regions near the frontlines. Risky initiatives require the implementation of behaviour protocols, the use of anonymous phone numbers, and the establishment of rigorous verification processes. Projects dealing with people's live risk implement data obfuscation and anonymisation to reduce exposure. Secure messaging platforms such as Signal, Element, Session, and Simplex Chat, along with self-hosted data solutions like Rocket Chat and Nextcloud, are employed to protect sensitive information. This level of caution is critical for projects that might face physical inspections. For instance, organisations rescuing politically persecuted individuals operate with heightened security, often anonymously, and employ hierarchical data systems.

Security protocols have become a fundamental component of most organisations operating in occupied territories, frequently as a response to previous oversights. However, our analysis identified several challenges:

- There is a pronounced scarcity of specialists in social project security.
- Access to these experts is limited for many projects.
- Comprehensive security integration, beyond basic consultation, is often prohibitively expensive.
- Many projects fail to dedicate adequate resources to security, regardless of the awareness of the importance.
- The lack of sharing experiences related to security.

It emphasizes the crucial importance of consulting organisations in ensuring the success of various projects. Without expert involvement, there is a significant risk to the safety and effectiveness of these projects.

Main barriers

The most consistent theme in respondent challenges is the existing resource shortfalls. Fundraising emerges as the predominant challenge for all initiatives. The issue arises because individuals who require services cannot afford to pay for them. At the same time, there has been a decrease in public interest and financial backing over a while. And the mass requests have not disappeared. However, small non-governmental groups have no sources to be paid, which means projects with a high social impact cannot be sustained. Additionally, navigating relationships with government bodies and grant providers adds complexity, often requiring initiatives to sacrificially establish credibility and reputation without resources before receiving support. The cancellation further complicates the landscape for Russian initiatives.

Grant funding accessibility poses significant challenges, especially for new or unregistered organisations. Genuinely innovative technological solutions, such as PTSD applications, drones for emergency medical assistance, or matching platforms for connecting those in need with benefactors (Airbnb-like platforms providing housing for refugees), require substantial R&D investment and labour costs amounting to tens of thousands of dollars per month. Although these sums are unachievable for most non-corrupted or elite founders. Meanwhile, investing in impact ideas can lead to drastic transformative changes of all the crises.

All interviewed projects underline the importance of personal connections in overcoming bureaucratic and operational hurdles. They face opaque funding sources and stringent application requirements. Notable cases illustrate the mismatch between carved-out grant models and local aid realities. It underscores the need for grantors to empathise with the unique circumstances of impact organisations. Support policies like small cash grants or hackathons often fail to address this issue. Transitioning to startup ecosystem strategies could provide clearer growth pathways and more comprehensive support systems, but they are unsuitable for major projects.

Security considerations, particularly in data management and communication, are critical. However, initiatives mostly ignore secure, messengers and self-hosted data solutions to protect sensitive information.

Despite the reliance on volunteers, many initiatives struggle with long-term viability. An insane focus on aid results may bias leaders to be conservative. For most of them, it is more important to help someone else than to implement serious reform or develop innovations. In most cases, optimisation decisions were forced only when their social mission was in danger. Beyond the initial and vitally necessary innovations, the active exchange of innovations among projects is almost non-existent without the involvement of various organisations that provide a platform and encourage the sharing of innovative practices, as in the case of security.

The research findings underscore the vital role of intermediary aggregators in the crisis aid provider market. These aggregators can function as advisory partners and fundraising coordinators, bridging the gap between social initiatives and potential donors. It is evident that governmental bodies have limited effectiveness in roles beyond financing, presenting an opportunity for organisations to step in and ensure the longevity and effectiveness of social initiatives in crises. Additionally, it is important for these organisations to provide long-term legal, accounting, and managerial mentorship, going beyond just financial aid. Such comprehensive support can help ensure the sustainability and success of social impact projects.

Conclusions

The disaster has highlighted the critical importance of crisis entrepreneurship and effective communication, akin to the modern teal style. Extraordinary circumstances necessitate exceptional leaders capable of mobilising and developing social capital. Messenger technologies gave opportunities for the automation of interactions. Direct contact with beneficiaries unlocked true needs, vital innovations, and effective organisation of help. Whenever someone reached out for assistance, they could contribute and even take responsibility for a leadership role; in other words, to become a crisis entrepreneur. The close collaboration of the benefactors and the beneficiaries has proved its creative reasonableness.

Unfortunately, numerous projects have failed. Those who have survived have been particularly adept at defining their specialisation and mission. This focus has enabled them to be frugal with resources and practical in their efforts to provide assistance. The most successful projects have consciously limited their scope of responsibilities, thereby enhancing the division of labour and responsibilities among stakeholders. As a result, millions have received and continue to receive support through networks of complementary and cooperative projects.

Echoing Lee, Y. et al. (2023), the future research prospects into the networks of responsible initiatives during crises appear promising. Investigating the personal transition from beneficiary to social entrepreneur or contributor presents a particularly fascinating research path. Analyse crisis entrepreneurship intention and decision-making can expand this paper and provide valuable insights for public policymakers and health management. Such research can shape our understanding of effective disaster response strategies.

Literature

Akinboye, A. K., & Morrish, S. C. (2022). Conceptualizing post-disaster entrepreneurial decision-making: prediction and control under extreme environmental uncertainty. International Journal of Disaster Risk Reduction, 68, 102703.

Audretsch, D.B., Momtaz, P.P., Motuzenko, H., Vismara, S. (2023). The Economic Costs of the Russia-Ukraine War: A Synthetic Control Study of (Lost) Entrepreneurship. http://dx.doi.org/10.2139/ssrn.4378827.

Benevolensky V.B., Ivanov, V. A., Ivanova N. V., et al. (2019). The role of volunteerism and charity in Russian society and the tasks of national development. (Russian: Волонтерство и благотворительность в России и задачи национального развития). High School of Economics. Retrieved 11-03-2023, from https://publications.hse.ru/en/books/263487997.

Community of Change z.s. (2022). Reshim.org List Of Projects. Retrieved 11-03-2023, from https://reshim.org/ru/projects.

Cyron, T., Garz, M. & Steigenberger, N. (2023). Beware the community type: engagement and growth in core vs. open online communities. Small Bus Econ. https://doi.org/10.1007/s11187-023-00821-y.

Darieva, T., Golova T., Skibo D. (2023). Russian Migrants in Georgia and Germany: Activism in the Context of Russia's War against Ukraine. ZOiS Report 3 / 2023, Centre for East European and International Studies (ZOiS) gGmbH . Retrieved 11-02-2023, from https://en.zois-berlin.de/filead-min/media/Dateien/3-Publika-tionen/ZOiS_Reports/2023/ZOiS_Report_3_2023.pdf.
Fomina. J. (2023). Supporting Russian Human Rights Defenders in Exile: Best Practices, Current Challenges. WOT Foundation (Fundacja WOT) & U.S.-Russia Foundation.
Halonen, S. (2023). Entrepreneurial Resilience in the Micro and Small Business Context – Systematic Literature Review. American Journal of Management.
Havadzyn, N., & Kritsak, Y. (2022). Fundraising In War-Time Conditions. Pričornomors'kì Ekonomìčnì Studìï, 74. https://doi.org/10.32843/bses.74-27.
Kamalov, E., Kostenko, V., Sergeeva, I., Zavadskaya, M. (2023). New Russian migrants against the war: political action in Russia and abroad. Friedrich-Ebert-Stiftung. Retrieved 25-02-2023, from https://www.outrush.io/eng.
Kotelevets, A. (2022). Research Of Volunteer Activities During The Russian-Ukrainian War. 2022–6, 123–131. https://doi.org/10.51706/2707-3076-2022-6-15.
Lee, Y., Kim, J., Mah, S. & Karr, A. (2023). Entrepreneurship in Times of Crisis: A Comprehensive Review with Future Directions. Entrepreneurship Research Journal. https://doi.org/10.1515/erj-2022-0366.
Linnenluecke, M.K. and McKnight, B. (2017), "Community resilience to natural disasters: the role of disaster entrepreneurship", Journal of Enterprising Communities: People and Places in the Global Economy, Vol. 11 No. 1, pp. 166-185. https://doi.org/10.1108/JEC-01-2015-0005.
Media Freedom Rapid Response. (2023). Relocation of journalists in distress in the European Union. Retrieved 11-03-2023, from https://www.mfrr.eu/relocation-of-journalists-in-distress-in-the-european-union/.
Noda.Community. (2022). Map of Peace. Retrieved 11-03-2023, from https://mapofpeace.org/.
Oleinik, A. (2018). Volunteers in Ukraine: From Provision Of Services To State And Nation-Building. Journal of Civil Society, pp. 14, 364–385.
Project Management Institute. (2021). A Guide to the Project Management Body of Knowledge (PMBOK® Guide).
Rating Research Group. (2022). Assessment Of The Situation In Ukraine. Retrieved 11-03-2023, from https://ratinggroup.ua/en/research/ukraine/ocenka_situacii_v_ukraine_8-9_marta_2022.html.
Rating Research Group. (2023). Ukraine's Resilience Formula: The Essential Components During War And Post-War. Retrieved 11-03-2023, from https://ratinggroup.ua/en/research/ukraine/ukraine_s_resilience_formula_the_essential_components_during_war_and_post-war_6_11_june_2023.html.
Ries, E. (2017). The Lean Startup: How Today's Entrepreneurs Use Continuous Innovation to Create Radically Successful Businesses. Currency.
Ronzhyn, A., Cardenal, A.S., & Batlle, A. (2023). Collective Action on Facebook and Telegram During the Russia–Ukraine War. European Conference on Social Media.
Ries, E. (2017). The Lean Startup: How Today's Entrepreneurs Use Continuous Innovation to Create Radically Successful Businesses. Currency.
Robertson, B. (2021). Holacracy Constitution Version 5.0. HolacracyOne, LLC. Retrieved 12-03-2023, from https://www.holacracy.org/constitution/5-0/.
Stepaniuk, N. (2022). Wartime Civilian Mobilization: Demographic Profile, Motivations, and Pathways to Volunteer Engagement Amidst the Donbas War in Ukraine. Nationalities Papers.
Terekhov, Y. (2023). A Survey of Russian Grassroots Anti-War Resistance. Kennan Cable. 84. Retrieved 11-03-2023, from https://www.wilsoncenter.org/publication/kennan-cable-no-84-survey-russian-grassroots-anti-war-resistance?collection=32543.

Kristian Eiken, Elin M. Oftedal

Superpower or kryptonite?

To innovate by involving users

Abstract: The study investigates the role of user involvement in the innovation process within the health technology sector, aiming to understand how companies integrate user feedback into product development. A grounded theory approach with a phenomenological perspective was utilized, centering on qualitative, in-depth interviews with six companies engaged in digital health innovations. The findings reveal that user involvement provides essential insights for refining products and aligning them with market needs but also introduces complexities such as increased costs, time, and potential biases in decision-making. Companies experience a range of benefits from improved product alignment to challenges in managing diverse user expectations. The research underscores the importance of user involvement in the early stages of innovation, where it significantly shapes the development trajectory of health technologies. However, it also highlights the need for companies to balance the openness to user input with strategic decision-making to manage the increased complexity and ensure the innovation process remains focused. This study contributes to innovation management discourse by emphasizing the nuanced role of user involvement in health technology, offering practical insights for companies to effectively navigate its complexities.

1 Introduction

Considerable attention has been devoted to user inclusion in innovation (von Hippel, 1986; Chesbrough, 2003; Prahaland and Ramaswaymy, 2004; O'Hern and Rindfleisch, 2010, Füller, 2010).

User inclusion in firm's innovative endeavors is particularly crucial when developing health technology, considering specific market for these products. Often, these markets are primarily state-run, especially across Europe, where the public sector often acts as the primary customer for such technologies. The actual end-users include patients, next of kin, or healthcare professionals. This market constellation creates a significant power asymmetry, marked by a high difference in resources, interests, and influence between the public sector entities and the individuals who ultimately use the technology (Iakovleva, Oftedal, & Bessant, 2019). Consequently, overlooking user involvement or insufficient or tokenistic inclusion in the innovation process can result in technologies that fail to meet user needs (Fischer, Peine, & Östlund, 2020), Greenalgh et al., 2017; Scarbrough, & Kyratsis, 2022 Van Leersum et al., 2022; Ambrosini et al., 2019).

https://doi.org/10.1515/9783111241036-012

Although user involvement is highly recommended and beneficial, it's important to acknowledge the complexities it introduces. Mierlo et al. (2020) provide critical insights into the "opening" of the innovation process. He underlines that user-involvement doesn't automatically resolve underlying challenges or research choices. Moreover, inclusion of diverse stakeholders does not always lead to more effective solutions than those derived from expert analyses. The complexity of addressing end-user needs, further complicates the development of effective technological solutions (Von Hippel, 2005). Nevertheless, opening up the development process to user input do inevitably broaden the scope and complexity of the issues at hand, increasing the chance of adding valuable dimensions to the solutions developed (Mierlo et al., 2020, p. 362). Therefore, engaging in a process of learning and adapting through active user inclusion is often regarded as a foundational aspect of innovation within health technology (Greenalgh et al., 2017; Scarbrough, & Kyratsis, 2022)

Moreover, while the literature provides examples of good results from of user inclusion, it is difficult to find evidence of how companies actually experience and experiment with it; it might not be carefully explored or might be spread across a wide range of more specific case studies, industry reports, and empirical research articles that are less visible in the broader theoretical discourse.

Therefore, the aim of this study is to investigate companies' perspectives on the implementation of user involvement. To clarify companies' experiences and gain insights into the outcomes of user involvement, this research seeks to address the following question: *How can we understand firms' experience with involving users in the innovation process?*

This study contributes to the literature around user involvement by collecting data from six companies' that are at the forefront of innovation in the digital health sector focusing on their experiences involving users' inclusion. The study focuses upon the experiences of the companies and will provide insight by exploring their thoughts and reflections and what gains or challenges they have experienced from user involvement. At the same time, this study will focus on how user involvement affected their product and further development process.

The role of user involvement in firms' innovation process

Innovation, despite being associated with creativity, often unfolds as a meticulously planned sequence of experiments designed to introduce variation, select promising ideas, and implement innovative solutions (Tidd & Bessant, 2014, p. 12). Schreiner et al. (2016) advocate for the significance of the early phase in the innovation process (Schreiner et al., 2016, p. 996). This phase, often referred to as the "front end innovation" (FEI) or "fuzzy front end" (FFE), encompasses the pre-development stages of new product development, occurring before the actual development commences (Schreiner et al., 2016, p. 997). FFE spans from the initial analysis of possibilities to the clarification of ideas, involving various activities such as idea generation, screening, market and technical evaluations, concept definition, development, testing, and evaluation (Schreiner et al., 2016, p. 996).

Companies are often critiqued for opening up the innovation process too late- and it is advocated for opening up the FFE to inform the innovation process with rich information needed to make the correct assessment later on. in practice, users are typically included late in the innovation process, reacting to near-finished products which cannot be substantially modified (Knight-Davidson, Lane, and McVicar 2020; Silva et al. 2019). Such practices can have negative consequences for the innovation process. (Supple et al. 2015). Similarly, if users are included too late in the process, the product or service may not be malleable enough to account for their input, making it unusable (Fischer, Peine, and Östlund 2020; Iakovleva, Oftedal, and Bessant 2019). As such, it is an important aim for innovators in healthcare to ensure user participation with real influence.

Briones (2012) holds that organizations should adopt a system that emphasizes the uncertainty levels early in the process and the use of appropriate analysis tools at each stage when the uncertainty drops. This approach allows for iterative cycles of customer evaluation, market analysis, and business development, enabling rapid prototyping and efficient resource allocation. pThis model depends on rich information in the FFE. One way to achieve this is to open up the innovation process to stakeholders to broaden options and prevent dominant interests from overshadowing the process by shedding light on silenced voices, uncertainties, and overlooked issues (Mierloxxx; Stirling, 2008).

Companies can gain valuable insights into the specific needs and challenges faced by end users through accumulated product knowledge and experience (Antorini & Muñiz, 2013, p. 24;Christensen & Raynor, 2003, pp. 119–120). By incorporating input from various user groups, decision-making processes can become more open and participatory. This inclusivity fosters the emergence of new perspectives, questions, and dilemmas, thereby enriching collective considerations of what is deemed significant (Iakovleva et al., 2020, p. 5).

However, Voβ, Bauknecht, and Kemp (2006) claim that while there are several advantages of opening up, increasing openness in discussions and considering a broader set of factors can lead to challenges in decision-making and action. User involvement will often lead to increased costs and time spent. The funds are directed towards acquiring competent people to participate in the process, and it also requires time to involve users in an innovation process. Increased time can also occur when different users hold conflicting thoughts and visions, which can make the decision-making process longer, and thus affect the innovation process (Iakovleva et al., 2020, p. 5). The prolonged time will be incorporated into product development, but will help develop alternative solutions (Ovesen, 2014, p. 88). One must be conscious and willing to pay the investment costs and then recoup any gains at a later stage in the innovation process (Ovesen, 2014, p. 88).

Moreover, Malterud & Elvbakken (2021) argue that there is no guarantee that an extensive user involvement process will result in new and useful knowledge. Boote, Telford & Cooper (2002) also highlights the challenge of including a representative sample of users in testing. They point out that often resourceful people are recruited for research projects which may lead to biases and inaccuracy in actual users need (Solvang & Feiring, 2021, pp. 71–72). This highlights the need to balance between opening up and closing down to effectively navigate the complexities of innovation and achieve sustainable development goals and of finding a balance between maintaining openness and reducing it to facilitate decision-making and action.

Thus, the as the critical role of early-phase innovation management in driving success in product development processes. opening up the innovation process early, particularly in the fuzzy front end (FFE) phase, which spans from idea generation to concept definition. Opening up the FFE allows for the incorporation of rich information, iterative cycles of evaluation, and efficient resource allocation.

By involving various user groups, decision-making processes become more open and participatory, leading to the emergence of new perspectives and enriching collective considerations.

However, increasing openness in discussions and considering a broader set of factors can lead to challenges in decision-making and action, as it may result in increased costs and time spent. Additionally, there is no guarantee that extensive user involvement will always result in new and useful knowledge, and recruiting resourceful people for research projects may lead to biases.

2 Method

As the study seek to understand the "how" to include users in the innovation process, the research design was originally sought to have a phenomenological approach (Creswell, 2007, p. 57). At the same time, it was natural to formulate the findings in metaphors, comparisons whilst also illustrate the finding through models. Therefore, the choice of research design fell upon grounded theory with a phenomenological approach.

In the phenomenological research design, it is desirable to explore the subjective perception and different perspectives from applying the practice of user involvement and the significance for the respondents' life experiences (Biemel & Spiegelberg, 2023). Grounded theory advances from description and moves in the direction of generating or developing an overall theoretical explanation. Here, grounded theory helps to analyze and evaluate data and construct theory through the analysis of data (PEDIAA, 2022).

This study does not at the same time have as many respondents to reach the saturation point that grounded theory usually requires. This study will then scrape the surface for different experiences, but at the same time apply the same inductive approach (Creswell & Poth, 2018, p. 82). Following, this study uses qualitative, in-depth interviews to capture the meanings and experiences that is not accessible through numbers or measures (Dalland, 2017, pp. 52–53).

2.1 Data setup

To obtain data, this study was written with access to the contacts of Norwegian Smart Care Lab (NSCL) for selection of respondents. NSCL have delivered various test services to different companies where user involvement has been used by most companies to obtain feedback. These companies are typical cases, but they have different target groups to their solution. In that way it was possible to explore a variety of perspectives on user involvement in encounters with a variety of users, relatives, customers and test partners that one can find in the health industry.

Based on the contacts of NSCL, six companies were chosen to participate. Five companies had previous experience in collaborating with NSCL, while NSCL had a separate arrangement with the last company in the spring of 2023. The new company was invited to participate in a pilot project in relation to the involvement of the user panel associated with NSCL where the company would present a concept and the user panel were to give feedback.

2.2 Inclusion criteria

The chosen companies were primarily selected because they all have been through a form of development process with NSCL where user involvement has been a methodology. In this way we were able to ensure that the data collected has been characterized by the same type of service delivery.

Our goal was not to retrieve information of user participation from one certain phase, but rather understand how companies experience user innovation. The selected companies have been through different processes of user involvement. By having diversity in time perspective and in different business areas, we were able to receive reflections based upon a broad form of experiences and consequences in both a short-term and a long-term perspective when involving users in the innovation process.

Six different interviews were conducted, each with a representative from a different company. Therefore, it can be specified in the text that six companies were interviewed, with one interview conducted with a person from each company (or however it can be presented most effectively).

Additionally, interviews were scheduled for approximately one hour each, with two lasting around 40–45 minutes, two lasting approximately one hour, and one lasting about 1 hour and 10 minutes.

To de-identify the companies, the companies´ names were replaced with letters from the Greek alphabet. The companies are hereby referred to as Alpha, Beta, Delta, Gamma, Delta, Epsilon and Zeta with further description below Table 1:

Table 1: Overview over business cases.

Nr.	Name	Workspace	Previous experience with user involvement	Wordcount/ pages
1	Alpha	Digital motivation and activation	Early phase involvement in real environments, pilot testing, focus groups and clinical trials	4443 words
2	Beta	Ergonomic aid	Functional tests and pilot testing	5958 words
3	Gamma	Sensors for measuring health data	Prototype test on device, focus groups and full-scale pilot test	7153 words
4	Delta	Digital skills training	User café, prototype test	8288 words
5	Epsilon	Medical technical equipment	Usability test and prototype test	8113 words
6	Zeta	Bathroom solutions	Project groups, research projects, pilot tests, functional tests and user café	3197 words

2.3 Analysis

This study will employ inductive empirical coding by analyzing the transcription from the interviews to the different respondents. Open coding will also be used, which takes a sentence, phrase, statement or paragraph and makes codes for what is in the transcription (Tjora, 2021, pp. 218–219). Here, the goal is to extract the essence from the empirical material, reduce the volume of the material and facilitate idea generation based on details in the empirical data (Tjora, 2021, p. 218). In this way, the coding will help ensure that the empirical reading contributes to as inductive a first phase of the analysis as possible. When using the inductive empirical coding, the coding is characterized by being very close to the empirical data and often using concepts that already exist in the data material (Tjora, 2021, p. 218).

Subsequently, the individual codes have been gathered into 20 different code groups which are: general experiences around user involvement, user competence in-house, involvement of different user groups, representativeness in recruitment, scope of the project, understanding of the user's needs and problems, clarification of expectations for participation in tests, testing of product, feedback, practical framework around the product, user-friendliness, outlining of priorities and schedule, changes in the development process, approach to the market, involvement after launch, importance of neutrality in test, insight for further development, cost/benefit assessment, the gift of hindsight and value as a result of involvement. From these categories we synthesize the findings presented in section 3.

3 Findings

3.1 The blindfolded explanation of an elephant

One thing apparent in the studies is that the companies have unique assessments and experiences related to the process of involving a variety of different user groups. In the meeting point between the user groups, there will be different needs, perspectives, and a diversity of important matters that the company encounters when developing a product. In this context, the company has the opportunity to capture accumulated product knowledge and experience about the precise needs and problems experienced by customers, consumers and end users (Antorini & Muñiz, 2013, pp. 22–23). At the same time, it appears that by involving different user groups, user involvement can also be compared to the old parable of the blind men explaining an elephant, all with different explanation depending on which side of the elephant they touch (Saxe, 1873).

Figuratively, as one gathers accumulated product knowledge and experience about precise needs, the different user groups will carry with them different aspects from their everyday lives, which in turn will have an influence on how they describe the product and what it can help solve. The companies must therefore be aware of the different needs in the market and involve the right users accordingly to the current need. Here, Epsilon highlights the importance of painpoints:

> *Where does the problem exist? It's incredibly valuable. It is perhaps one of the most valuable that we can get from a user because then we see a problem and try to solve it . . . Talking to a customer and hearing what is their problem and what are we willing to do, what problem do they have that they want solved? And what are they willing to get fixed? There are many people who accept that they have problems and that things don't work optimally, but it's not big enough pain that they're willing to dedicate resources to it. . . . And identifying painpoints that, overlap with our product, allows us to tailor use cases to exactly those scenarios.*

Several companies highlight the challenge of involving the voice of those who would otherwise not be asked. Delta and Gamma tell of some users who either don't feel qualified to have an opinion, or who felt stupid. Users react by saying, "*don't listen to me*" or "*listen to what the other smart ones are saying.*" In this way, user involvement can be perceived as demanding when one has to face the users on their uncertainty and lack of mastery in a test situation. In addition, it can seem frustrating when the company sees the importance of users' input, but that users downgrade their own opinions.

In addition, Alfa problematize representativeness by pointing out that those who want to get involved are usually more technologically advanced then the average person from the target group. Thus, the users involved can create a false image of what they need from the product. This highlights the challenge to connect with the majority of the users, the silent crowd, that the company originally need to involve.

Alfa highlights at the same time the importance of not falling in love with your own solution. One must listen to what the user groups describe as needs and familiarize oneself with their understanding of what lies behind various problems. In this way, user involvement works by both weeding out speculation about what is actually the problem, but also by getting input on whether the product adds value or adds a non-existent problem to the workplace.

Like those who describe the elephant, there is a need for the various user groups to speak out and describe their situation. In this way, they can help shed light on the product's quality and the desired effect from all the different angles. Then it's their job as testers to report back to the company that then gets the job of weaving together the feedback in the best possible way. In this extension, it will be important to have a bird's-eye view of the process of involving users in an innovation process.

3.2 Finding a superpower or kryptonite?

Most companies presented user involvement as a necessity when developing their product. Several of the companies comment that there have been generally positive experiences or exclusively positive experiences with involving users. Delta goes on to describe user involvement as a "superpower" and "the way to find solutions":

> *In another way, it's a whole field of study, so you have to have a lot of respect for reaching out, tests and quantity training and getting sort of your finger on the pulse yourself to be able to know how to make things better. And that it's kind of like, a superpower.*

> *Then we believe that the solution or way to find the solution is to involve the users themselves. Also, it is the way you involve them, that you have to see the problem from all sides of the table and then have to involve the users themselves, right.*

In other words, user involvement is not only understood as a key element but can work in the form of powerful forces that opens for creative processes that are not possible to access outside of involving users.

At the same time, several of the companies mention that there are several negative aspects of involving users. Originally it was a stressful for Beta to involve users. It was also expressed difficulties related to accessing users and evaluating if there has been recruited enough to represent the user group. Another challenge highlighted by the companies is to carry out tests with quality by weeding out practical aspects that can lead to invalid responses, filtering feedback, and facilitating neutrality in testing. At the same time, several companies elevate the financial costs as well as the time spent on involvement associated with the multifaceted costs related to testing and user involvement. The expenses incurred in conducting tests encompass resource utilization, impeding the innovation process, and prolonging product development due to the frequent necessity for revisions. The costs linked with testing involve facilitation, hiring third-party services, engaging institutions, and collaborating with other pertinent stakeholders, all of which commonly entail associated expenses."

However, Beta saw the benefit of involving users by acknowledging that there was a gap between what they thought was logical and the actual use of the product.

Several companies also mention that user involvement becomes part of the company's culture and influence the companies´ attitudes towards approaching an issue. This indicates that user involvement is seen as a working methodology that involves some challenges, equally to other work methods. Eventually, Zeta points out what many of the companies were experiencing:

> *We think to ourselves: we should never do this again. But then one forgets it out and does it anyway*

It points out that their reflections are negatively charged in the process, but the remaining experience of user involvement and gained understanding of improvement potential remains positive. This becomes visible when one sees the value of what user involvement has added to the product. Thus, it may indicate that it would be disadvantageous not to involve users, even though it may sting a bit during the process. Therefore, it seems that many of the challenges and difficulties are hidden behind the positive experiences associated with the final product when the focus is on the importance of user involvement.

3.3 The bird's eye view

When different user groups are involved, it emerges that it can be challenging to filter out what is useful feedback and what not beneficial to develop further. Thus, it is important that while the company is able to receive the feedback, they also have an overall bird's eye view of where the company is and where they want to end up. Delta comments that:

> *We're going to have that bird's-eye view and see all the needs and then create the solution across that.*

The companies' shares experiences of wanting to be able to offer a product that can solve many of the users´ needs. Here it becomes important to stick to the core function of the product so that the product is not stretched in many directions. Gamma comments that they have become steadier on the core function of the product that allows them to be tougher in meeting users and test partners by standing their ground and say:

> This is where we are, yes, we listen to what you say and we bring it to later, but now we have to deal with where we are.

When involving users, one must filter the feedback from users, in the event that feedback either does not fit with the core function of the product or is too narrow to benefit several user groups. In this context, Zeta points out that the product should not reach all the needs of the population:

> *After all, it is not possible to create a product that can cover 100% of the needs of 100% of the population. It's just not possible, no matter how much you try. So, we've kind of been aware of that all along, but we put ourselves so close on top of them so that the product covers 80% of the needs of 100% of the population. Then there will always be some groups that have a complete, very special need. And then there may be other products that fit better.*

3.4 The X marks the spot

In the same way that "x" marks the treasure on a map, user involvement can help mark where the x should be on the market map. At the start of a treasure hunt, there is more uncertainty about what lies ahead. User involvement can then be a great way to start the journey as companies move into uncharted territory. Here users can help point out the direction in the meeting for where they are going. Here again, it will be important to either include many users to get a good idea of where to start looking for the treasure or know that the users with whom one is involved knows where the treasure is. In other words, they must be representative for the user group. Similarly, it will be important to get feedback in order to narrow down the direction of the project and look at what the intended use should be. Here, users can help control the direction according to existing needs in the market.

Alfa points out the importance of being corrected early, so that one does not head out for the north when one is actually going west. By disproving hypotheses, it will also be a victory if one does not have to spend time and energy on something that would not have worked. This gives one the opportunity to weed out all unnecessary thoughts so that one does not chase after the wrong "x".

Once the journey is set, the boat is ready to sail, and the product is "up-to-speed", users can help correct the direction of the road. Coherently, it will be important to make a priority list for the journey based on available resources and the product pipeline. Here, Epsilon highlights the role of users in shaping the priority list based on various functions that will be implemented in the service at some point. The conclusion will be the same, but users can give their opinion on what is important to focus on at the moment. In this way, user involvement is experienced as a method for mapping further action and an opportunity to gain insight into what is important to focus on.

In addition, user involvement is understood as a separate market approach. Here, both Gamma and Zeta point out that the product is anchored by a certainty that there is a real need in the market for the product that is launched:

> *Then you get a completely different anchoring in the market rather than if you just come up with something that you are going to sell. So, we have tested this with users before we even started selling it. We know this works, we've mapped out, we've done studies, we've had feedback, we've made changes along the way, we've prepared reports. So, we can cover, we have the backing of everything that we have, with the users. We know there is a need!*

When the starting point is to involve users to map the journey, instead of plowing yourself through the jungle, cutting down every tree in your way, one can rather gain insight on how to navigate the jungle so that one does not need to use force to find the treasure. In other words, there will be no need to hammer the product into the market in order to make a sale. Gamma points out that one may succeed in getting through some sales with the right customers without testing in advance, but one will not manage sales on a large scale. In this sense, user involvement can be understood as means of maneuvering and navigating through the unknown market terrain by pointing out where to move in order to reach the goal. When the treasure is found, one will find the product in its final form, the form of a need in the market.

3.5 User inconsistency

User involvement is perceived as varying in the feedback that the company receives. Here, Gamma says that they experienced inconsistency when they monitored the users' activity in tests by using camera to film their reaction and what they did on the computer. The users said that the solution was good, but the camera showed the actual confusion when they tested the app for the company. At the same time, Delta says that users are not supposed to agree with the solution and that you cannot bring "your mother" in for tests that only say that "that's great".

At the same time, there is a balancing act between the fact that one can always test more to get greater representativeness, but also involve users in the crucial aspects in the development process that provide the most value for further development. In this case, Delta comments how they administered the testing:

> *Yes, it's definitely demanding. So, you also need to know that you are testing the right things. Break things down into small enough pieces that you can test it and get something of value that you can iterate on and provide feedback and then work on.*

In product development, it can be challenging to be accountable to the users for whom one develops the solution. Gamma states that when the company asks for feedback, they must be willing to make changes with the product. They also need to be able to take the consequences of the input that is gathered, rather than prioritizing the easiest or fastest way to develop a product. If one does not want or is not ready to make changes, Gamma believes that one should not start either.

In addition, there are several companies that have reflected and experienced that they would like to maintain a steadier course from an early phase of the innovation process. In this way, user involvement can be perceived as alluring and unsteady, where the boundaries are reined, and the basic function of the product is challenged.

Still, Delta argues that users' job is to provide insight, and that the company's job is to develop a good product from the insights that emerge. At the same time, users do not have direct influence in decision-making processes, but it is nevertheless their input that forms the basis for further development and thus plays an important role in the exchange of opinions.

In this context, Zeta emphasizes that if there are different needs from different user groups, the company must have the ability to compromise. In those cases, it will be important to take into account the different needs but consider the needs in relation to the core function of the product and what is appropriate to do. Nevertheless, it is important to be flexible to make changes if needed. In this process, there will be many practical factors that go into how the product works in reality.

Further, user involvement appears to be something that must be arranged for so that everyone can participate by weeding out all practicalities that could spoil the test. Delta shares experiences of seniors forgetting their glasses which makes that person unable to see the screen properly, or that users forget to show up or that they cannot find the venue. In this way, user involvement takes a human form with the fact that even the simplest errors can result in the form of invalid data or test results.

The value of testing with users and pivoting the solution

There may be a gap in product development between the intention of the developer and the practical execution in everyday life. In this case, it seems that users may be revealing hidden factors and difficulties that make the product work or not. Therefore, Gamma and Zeta justify that it is through user involvement that one succeeds in the market. Precisely because one closes that gap between what works on paper and what works in real life. The hidden world of users does not have to be complicated processes or intellectual levels to be considered. Nevertheless, Alfa points out that there are various forms of knowledge that were previously unknown, but have now emerged:

> *We think that it is not unusual, ofc, but it was just not knowledge that were not accessible for us. That was something that we did not know in advance. So, these, we think, typical examples, offer things that you would discover that you were not aware of, which, you then need to address.*

This is done by gaining insight into a world that one does not have access to. A world of different practical challenges that the users face, it will affect how one uses the product. In this way, the product can close the gap by gathering input on where knots can arise in the workflow and illuminating practical frameworks that affect the product in real environments. The practical framework can be in the form of work routines around the product, the users´ habits and actions, communication processes or other factors that influence how well the product hits the ecosystem of practicalities. Here, Epsilon cites the example of their own practice where they rely on their product to interact with external systems.

> *The challenge is often to consider workflow and not necessarily functionality needs. So, yes, we can think of a product that fits well into the home care services, but if we get there and then it turns out that the most used information channel goes through a link that we haven't thought of, so suddenly our tool can't be used without us making some changes.*

Therefore, there is a need for Epsilon to gain insight into each stage of a process in order to adapt the product to the market. Here it will also be relevant to use the testing's feedback to find the treasure.

4 Discussion

4.1 Assumptions vs. Testing

In the Fuzzy Front End, the company is in a position where there are many assumptions about the product and an openness to go in several directions. As companies find themselves in the situation where they have tested and developed the product over a long period of time, the knowledge and insight from users will sharpen.

When you have come a long way with product development and have been through a test run, factors such as commercialization and scaling will work as a motivation for launching the final product. In that process, the threshold becomes higher and the resistance stronger to continue with user testing to gain insight into smaller and more specific elements of the product, even if there is a testing need for the company. This is illustrated in Figure 1.

This emerges from, among other things, Beta who say that they actually need more testing of the product after they launched in the market. Despite the need, the threshold has become very high for testing as the testing will have a direct consequence for further sales. The result is that they are not able to be as free of bias in testing, but rather use all feedback that comes from customers to make further improvements to the product.

With a high threshold for testing and strong incentives for launch, user involvement seems to help companies to see if they have tested enough through valid feedback to see if the product has "the finishing touch" in order to meet the needs of the

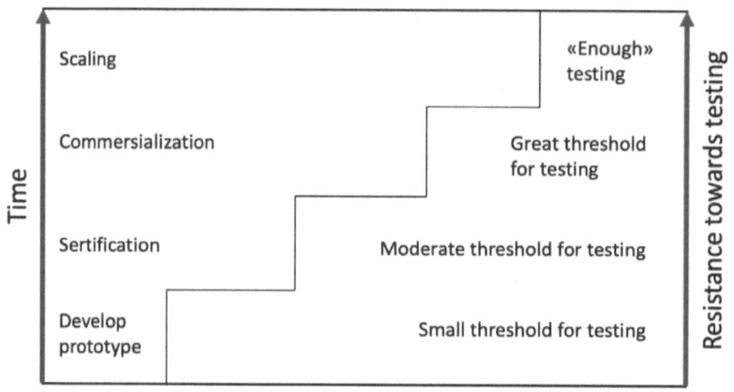

Figure 1: Threshold for testing.

users. This will help to create anchorage in the market as the solution is tailored to the relevant user group.

At the same time, Gamma argues that one must be patient by making all changes before commercialization. By valuing patience, the company has the opportunity to test each stage as needed before launching the product. Because if the customer is satisfied with the product at the time of testing, one can proceed directly to sales. Still, Zeta highlights that at some point, the product needs to be good enough to start selling. It is not profitable to test for ages. Thus, one can assess through user involvement whether one is approaching the point of "enough testing", or whether there is a need to test more features.

At some point, Alfa confirms that one will get to "the point of no return". At some point, it will be too late to turn back, or that changes later in the race will come with huge costs. Alfa thus goes on to argue that the cost and benefit of testing would be in favor of testing as early as possible. The significance of user involvement in the interaction between cost and benefit assessment in testing.

If the threshold for testing is high and the commitment to selling comes quickly, you risk missing out on the full potential of the product. In addition, most companies said they looked back wanting both to start testing as early as possible and that they had conducted more testing along the way. Thus, user involvement became more important than originally intended.

On the other hand, Zeta says it will be an ongoing effort to process feedback, even after launch. There will always be some childhood diseases that no one else has thought of before. As a result, good procedures must be established to receive the feedback and pivot. In this way, user involvement can be viewed as a recurring spiral.

4.2 Recurrent cycle

In order to achieve the greatest possible effect from user involvement, involvement cannot be perceived as a tool that one inserts into a specific point such as a checklist. Rather, user involvement seems to be understood as a recurring spiral between testing and development, as illustrated in Figure 2. This can be found to be particularly beneficial in the Fuzzy Front End when there is an interaction between many complex processes that are progressing, continuous testing and acquisition of feedback that will become an important argument for figuring out which direction to proceed in (Schreiner et al, 2016, p. 997).

In this extension, there will also be different elements in the various processes of the development process that one needs feedback on. Therefore, there will be a need to get feedback on incremental or major changes to know if the changes made are consistent with the intention behind the change. Thus, user involvement becomes a recurrent force for getting feedback on what has been further developed.

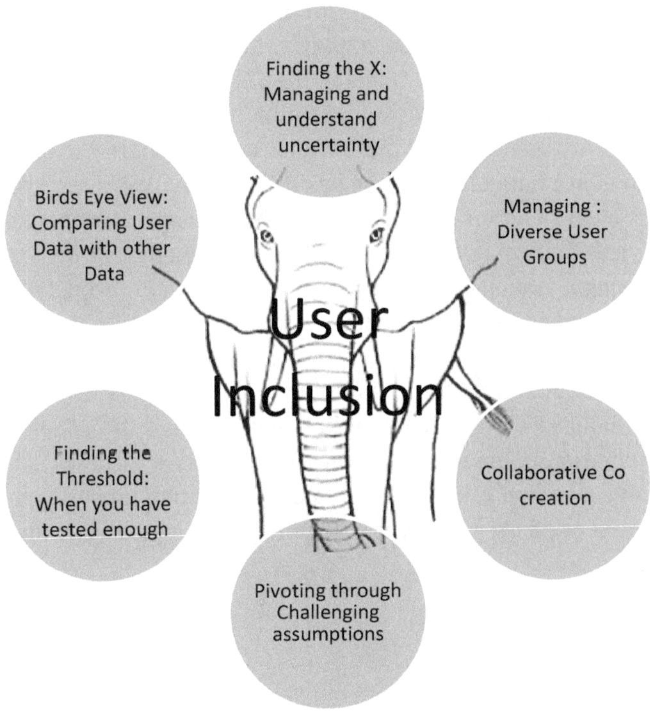

Figure 2: Finding the Elephant – Model of User Inclusion.

The model of user inclusion depicted in Figure 2 delineates a comprehensive framework for integrating diverse user perspectives into the innovation process. At its core lies the concept of "User Inclusion," symbolized by an elephant, denoting the central role of incorporating varied user insights.

Surrounding this central theme are six key areas, each contributing to the facilitation and enhancement of user inclusion within innovation endeavors. "*Managing and Understanding Uncertainty*" underscores the importance of navigating and comprehending uncertainty throughout the innovation journey. This involves developing strategies to effectively manage ambiguity and adapt to evolving circumstances to foster innovation. Understanding the uncertainty is highest in the start of the innovation process is important here. "*Managing Diverse User Groups*" highlights the significance of incorporating a wide array of user demographics into the innovation process. By considering diverse user backgrounds, preferences, and behaviors, innovators can better understand and address the varied needs and experiences of their target audience. "*Pivoting through Challenging Assumptions*" emphasizes the critical examination of underlying assumptions within the innovation process. By questioning and challenging assumptions, innovators can mitigate biases and foster a more open and innovative environment. "*Collaborative Co-Creation*" highlights the value of collaborative efforts between users and innovators in developing solutions. Through co-creating products with users, innovators can leverage their expertise and insights to produce solutions that are more relevant and impactful. "*Finding the Threshold*" involves recognizing the moment when it's appropriate to stop pursuing further development. Continual testing and feedback are essential, yet there comes a point where the marginal gains from modifications are outweighed by their costs. Beyond this juncture, it's advisable to shift focus towards minor enhancements and perhaps concentrate more on enhancing the services that complement the technology. Finally, "*Bird's Eye View*" advocates for maintaining a strategic perspective on user inclusion throughout the innovation process. This involves balancing openness to user input with a focus on actionable insights, ensuring that the innovation process remains aligned with overarching goals and objectives. Additionally, it should be noted that this model is intended to be iterative, symbolized by its circular shape, emphasizing the ongoing and cyclical nature of user inclusion in the innovation process.Collectively, these components form a comprehensive model of user inclusion in the innovation process, emphasizing the active involvement of users at every stage to drive meaningful and impactful innovation outcomes.

5 Conclusion

Throughout this study, we introduce experiences from companies, particularly within the health technology sector, regarding the inclusion of users in the innovation process. Our insights build on practical application of theoretical frameworks and stem from empirical observations of companies' experiences. We do not propose a generalization of our findings, but rather we suggest a model that may be explored in future research.

As such, we provide real – life examples from companies' experiences, bridging the gap between abstract theoretical discussions and real-world practices. The metaphor of the "blindfolded explanation of an elephant" vividly illustrates the diversity of user perspectives and the challenge of effectively integrating them into the innovation process.

Further, we explore the complexity and paradox of user involvement, highlighting its importance in tailoring products to meet user needs while also acknowledging the challenges of managing diverse opinions and power dynamics in addition to the variety and sometimes also paradoxical feedback from users.

We also advocate for a bird's eye view – a strategic approach to managing user involvement, emphasizing the need for a balanced perspective that opens up the innovation process to user input while focusing on actionable insights. This strategic framework helps companies navigate the complexities of user inclusion effectively. Finally, we discuss the concept of user involvement as a recurring spiral, particularly in the Fuzzy Front End of innovation. Continuous adaptation and integration of user feedback are highlighted as crucial for innovation success.

By focusing specifically on the health technology sector, we shed light on the unique dynamics of user inclusion in an industry characterized by significant power imbalances and the key role of technology in health outcomes. This industry-specific perspective adds depth and relevance to the discussion.

In summary, our contributions lie in the empirical grounding of user inclusion, nuanced exploration of complexities of user inclusion, strategic insights into managing user involvement, and our understanding of individual companies in the health technology sector. These contributions enrich the discourse on innovation management and offer valuable guidance for practitioners navigating the challenges and opportunities of user inclusion.

References

Agarwal, R., Gao, G., DesRoches, C., & Jha, A. K. (2010). Research Commentary – The Digital Transformation of Healthcare: Current Status and the Road Ahead. Information Systems Research, 21(4), 796–809.

Ambrosini, A., Quinlivan, R., Sansone, V.A. *et al.* "Be an ambassador for change that you would like to see": a call to action to all stakeholders for co-creation in healthcare and medical research to improve quality of life of people with a neuromuscular disease. *Orphanet J Rare Dis* 14, 126 (2019). https://doi-org.ezproxy.uis.no/10.1186/s13023-019-1103-8

Andreassen, T. A. (2018). Service user involvement and repositioning of healthcare professionals: A framework for examining implications of different forms of involvement. Nordisk Välfärdsforskning | Nordic Welfare Research, 3(1), 58–69. https://doi.org/10.18261/ISSN.2464-4161-2018-01-06AA

Antorini, Y. M., & Muñiz Jr, A. M. (2013). The Benefits and Challenges of Collaborating With User Communities. Research-Technology Management, 56(3), 21–28. https://doi.org/10.5437/08956308X5603931

Biemel, W., & Spiegelberg, H. (2023, May 26). Phenomenology. Encyclopedia Britannica. https://www.britannica.com/topic/phenomenology

Björn Fischer, Alexander Peine, Britt Östlund (2020 October). The Importance of User Involvement: A Systematic Review of Involving Older Users in Technology Design, *The Gerontologist*, Volume 60, Issue 7, e513–e523, https://doi-org.ezproxy.uis.no/10.1093/geront/gnz163

Boote, J., Telford, R., & Cooper, C. (2002). Consumer involvement in health research: A review and research agenda. *Health Policy*, 61(2), 213–236. https://doi.org/10.1016/s0168-8510(01)00214-7

Briones, J. A. (2012, March 19). A New Approach to Manage Disruptive Innovation in an Environment of High Uncertainty. Innovation Management. Retrieved from https://innovationmanagement.se/2012/03/19/a-new-approach-to-manage-disruptive-innovation-in-an-environment-of-high-uncertainty/

Carman, K. L., Dardess, P., Maurer, M., Sofaer, S., Adams, K., Bechtel, C., & Sweeney, J. (2013). Patient and family engagement: a framework for understanding the elements and developing interventions and policies. Health Affairs, 32(2), 223–231.

Chesbrough, H. (2003). Open innovation: The new imperative for creating and profiting from technology. Harvard Business School Press.

Christensen, C. M., & Raynor, M. E. (2003). The innovator 's solution: Creating and sustaining successful growth (1st ed.). Harvard Business School Press.

Creswell, J. W. (2007). Qualitative Inquiry & Research Design: Choosing Among Five Approaches (2nd ed.). Sage Publications.

Creswell, J. W., & Poth, C. N. (2018). Qualitative inquiry & research design: Choosing among Five approaches (4th ed.). Sage Publications.

Dalland, O. (2017). Method and thesis writing (6th ed.). Gyldendal.

Füller, J. (2010). Refining virtual co-creation from a consumer perspective. California Management Review, 52(2), 98–122.

Forshaug, A. K. (2015). User involvement in design of health care services. Department of Product Design, Norwegian University of Science and Technology.

Greenhalgh, T., Wherton, J., Papoutsi, C., Lynch, J., Hughes, G., A'Court, C., Hinder, S., Fahy, N., Procter, R., & Shaw, S. (2017). Beyond adoption: A new framework for theorizing and evaluating nonadoption, abandonment, and challenges to the scale-up, spread, and sustainability of health and care technologies. Journal of Medical Internet Research, 19(11), e367.

Iakovleva, T., Oftedal, E. M., & Bessant, J. (2020). Changing Role of Users – Innovating Responsibility in Digital Health. ResearchGate, Preprint, 1–22. http://doi.org/10.20944/preprints202011.0007.v1

Knight-Davidson, P., Lane, P., and McVicar, A.J. (2020)Methods for co-creating with older adults in living lab-oratories: a scoping review. Health and Technology, 10,997–1009 *(16) (PDF) Inclusion of elderly users via virtual spaces in the early stages of the innovation process*. Available from: https://www.researchgate.net/publication/362256064_Inclusion_of_elderly_users_via_virtual_spaces_in_the_early_stages_of_the_innovation_process [accessed Jul 04 2024].

Kvalvåg, S. H. (2023, Feb. 02). We have to keep our heads and bodies in shape so we can manage self. Stavanger Aftenblad: Local. https://www.aftenbladet.no/lokalt/i/RGOeBW/vi-maa-holde-baade-hodet-og-kroppen-i-form-saa-vi-kan-klare-oss-selv

Lynch, P., & O'Toole, T. (2003). After von Hippel: The State of User Involvement Research in New Product Development. ResearchGate. https://www.researchgate.net/publication/255668394

Malterud, K., and K. T. Elvebakken. 2019. "Patients Participating in Health Research: A Systematic Review of Outcomes and Experiences." Scandinavian Journal of Public Health 1–12. doi:10.1177/1403494819863514.

Mierlo, B. V., Beers, P. J., & Hoes, A-C. (2020). Inclusion in responsible innovation: revisiting the desirability of opening up. Journal Of Responsible Innovation, 7(3), 361–383. https://doi.org/10.1080/23299460.2020.1780409

Mohn, K. (2022, October 15). The challenges in the health sector will mount in the years to come. Kkrono. https://khrono.no/utfordringane-i-helsesektoren-vil-tarne-seg-opp-i-ara-som-kjem/724704

NOU 2023: 4. (2023). Time for action: the personnel in a sustainable health and Ministering. Ministry https://www.regjeringen.no/contentassets/337fef958f2148bebd326f0749a1213d/no/pdfs/nou202320230004000dddpdfs.pdf

O'Hern, M. S., & Rindfleisch, A. (2010). Customer co-creation. In N. K. Malhotra (Ed.), *Review of Marketing Research* (Vol. 6, pp. 84–106). Emerald Group Publishing Limited. https://doi.org/10.1108/S1548-6435(2009)0000006008

Oftedal, E. M., Foss, L., & Iakovleva, T. (2019). Responsible for Responsibility? A Study of Digital E-health Startups. Sustainability, 11(19), 1–21. https://doi.org/10.3390/su11195433

Oliveira, P., Zejnilovic, L., Canhâo, H., & Hippel, E. V. (2014). Innovation by patients with rare diseases and chronic needs. Orphanet Journal of Rare Diseases, 10(41), 1–9. http://doi.org/10.1186/s13023-015-0257-2

Ovesen, J. (2014). FFO and involvement in the health service. In T. A. Andreassen (Ed.), User involvement in the health services: work in user committees and others Participation processes (3rd ed., pp. 78–88).

Prahalad, C. K., & Ramaswamy, V. (2004). Co-creating unique value with customers. *Strategy & Leadership*, *32*(3), 4-9. https://doi.org/10.1108/10878570410699249

PEDIAA. (2022, April 27). What is the difference between phenomenology and grounded Theory. Education. https://pediaa.com/what-is-the-difference-between-phenomenology-and-grounded-theory/

Saxe, J. G. (1873). The Blind Men and the Elephant.

Scarbrough, H., & Kyratsis, Y. (2022). From spreading to embedding innovation in health care: Implications for theory and practice. *Health Care Management Review*, *47*(3), 236–244. https://doi.org/10.1097/HMR.0000000000000323

Schreiner, L., Thomas, M., & Nascimento, P. T. de S. (2016, 04–08. September). Fuzzy Front-End integration: Describing roles and defining boundaries on multi companies [Paper presentation]. Portland International Conference on Management of Engineering and Technology/ PICMET, Honolulu, USA. DOI:

Solvang, P. K., & Feiring, M. (2021). User participation in research: in a sociology of knowledge perspective. In E. Skjeldal (Ed.), Critical perspectives on User interaction (1st ed., pp. 65–78). University Press.

Stirling, A. (2008). "Opening Up" and "Closing Down": Power, Participation, and Pluralism in the Social Appraisal of Technology. *Science, Technology, & Human Values*, *33*(2), 262-294. https://doi.org/10.1177/0162243907311265

Supple, D., et al and on behalf of the U-BIOPRED PIP group (2015) From tokenism to meaningful engagement: best practices in patient involvement in an EU project, Research Involvement and Engagement, 1.5.

SurveyMonkey. (n.d.). Exploratory research: what is it? (And 4 ways to implement it into your research!). Retrieved May 11, June 2023, from https://www.surveymonkey.com/mp/exploratory-research/

Tidd, J., & Bessant, J. (2014). Strategic innovation management (1st ed.). Wiley.

Tjora, A. (2021). Qualitative research methods: in practice (4th ed.). Gyldendal Publishing House.

United Nations, Department of Economic and Social Affairs, Population Division. (2021). World Population Ageing 2020 Highlights (ST/ESA/SER.A/451). United Nations.

Voß, J.-P., Kemp, R., & Bauknecht, D. (2006). *Reflexive governance: A view on an emerging path.* Edward Elgar Publishing.

von Hippel, E. (1986). Lead users: A source of novel product concepts. *Management Science*, *32*(7), 791–805.

Von hippel 2005: von Hippel, E. (2005). *Democratizing Innovation.* MIT Press.

Anna Szopa

The impact of users on the development of Morphic auto personalization

Abstract: As the digital landscape evolves, the demand for personalized user experiences continues to grow. This chapter investigates the role of users in shaping the development of Morphic Auto Personalization, a cutting-edge technology designed to enhance user interfaces by dynamically adapting to individual preferences. The research incorporates user feedback, behavioral analysis, and usability testing to assess the effectiveness of Morphic Auto Personalization. By examining user interactions, preferences, and perceptions, this study seeks to elucidate the impact of user input on refining and optimizing the software auto personalization. The findings shed light on the challenges and successes encountered during the development process, highlighting the relationship between user engagement and technological advancement. Ultimately, this research contributes to the broader discourse on responsible innovation and the role users play in shaping the trajectory of emerging technologies. The insights gained from this study can inform future developments in Morphic Auto Personalization and serve as a model for the collaborative development of user-centric technologies across diverse digital platforms. Through a combination of user engagement approaches, Morphic aims to create a seamless and tailored digital environment. Morphic auto-personalization integrates users' past, present, and future actions, identified through a user experience study. This approach uncovers usage issues, allowing the team to enhance the product for better alignment with user needs. Leveraging participants' knowledge leads to additive effects, resulting in highly personalized and accessible assistive technology.

Introduction

The increasing ubiquity of information technologies brings to the forefront the growing challenges of accessibility for individuals with disabilities. As information technology advances in sophistication, the hurdles faced by users with disabilities become more pronounced. According to the World Health Organization, a substantial segment of the global population, comprising 1.3 billion individuals or 16%, encounters significant disabilities and requires assistance to attain a decent quality of life. Full participation in social and economic life on an equal basis with others is contingent upon addressing the accessibility barriers faced by people with disabilities (WHO, 2023). The pervasive integration of information and communication technologies (ICTs) in society underscores the imperative to make these technologies universally accessible. Mainstream ICTs are now designed with inclusivity in mind, aiming to accommodate

https://doi.org/10.1515/9783111241036-013

the widest range of users, thereby enabling independence and active engagement for individuals with disabilities. Design approaches such as Inclusive Design (ID), Universal Design (UD), Design for All (DfA), User-Sensitive Inclusive Design (USID), and Ability-Based Design (ABD) converge with the common objective of enhancing technology accessibility, however. there remains a gap in knowledge regarding effectively involving users in the development of assistive technologies. Therefore, the chapter aims to outline diverse strategies employed to engage a wide array of users in the research and development of the Morphic auto personalization software while also delving into the challenges encountered by the team during this process. The overarching goal is to contribute to the ongoing discourse on inclusive technology design and accessibility. The software Morphic auto personalization stands as a transformative technology with a dedicated focus on enhancing the computer experience for users of assistive technology. Its primary function lies in facilitating a seamless transition of assistive technology and interface adaptations across diverse devices. This software is designed to augment accessibility features in a user-friendly manner, providing essential tools that significantly improve both computer visibility and usability. Commitment to open-source principles not only aligns with Morphic's ethos of inclusivity but also promotes widespread access to assistive technologies, fostering a more equitable digital landscape (morphic.org). This innovative approach not only enhances user experience but also holds significant implications for responsible innovation.

Responsible Innovation represents a strategic paradigm shift in the field of technological advancement, embodying a deliberate and conscientious integration of ethical, social, and cultural dimensions into the fabric of innovation processes. This approach signifies a departure from traditional models solely focused on economic gains, seeking instead a harmonious synthesis of economic progress with societal well-being. At its core, Responsible Innovation adopts a comprehensive viewpoint, transcending narrow economic considerations. It underscores the need to anticipate and address potential ramifications of emerging technologies, products, or services, extending its purview to encompass the multifaceted impacts on human life and the environment. By prioritizing ethical considerations alongside technological advancements, responsible innovation endeavors to foster a balanced and sustainable innovation ecosystem that not only propels economic development but also contributes positively to the broader welfare of society (Stilgoe et.al, 2013, von Schomberg, R. 2013, Owen et. al, 2013, Bessant et. al, 2019). Transparency and accountability are paramount principles in the realm of responsible innovation, shaping the ethical development and deployment of emerging technologies. This paradigm underscores the necessity of explicit and comprehensive communication regarding the objectives, methodologies, and potential ramifications of innovative endeavors. By fostering transparency, responsible innovation seeks to bridge the information gap between developers and the broader society, fostering informed decision-making and public engagement. Equally crucial is the emphasis on accountability, whereby innovators are held responsible for the outcomes, whether positive or adverse, resulting from their creations. This accountability extends beyond the immediate development phase to encompass the entire life cycle of the technology, reinforcing the ethical imperative for continuous assessment and mitigation of potential risks. In essence, the intersection of transparency and accountability forms the cornerstone of responsible innovation, contributing to a technologically advanced landscape that is not only progressive but also ethically grounded and socially responsible (von Schomberg, R., 2011). This multifaceted process involves a comprehensive assessment of potential risks, encompassing not only the immediate impact on individuals and society but also potential long-term consequences. Privacy and security, integral components of ethical discourse, demand meticulous attention to safeguard against any encroachments or vulnerabilities arising from innovative solutions. Furthermore, Responsible Innovation obliges a proactive stance in addressing ethical dilemmas that may emerge during the development, deployment, or utilization phases. This proactive engagement with ethical concerns ensures that the innovation aligns with societal values and norms. Ultimately, by weaving ethical considerations into the fabric of innovation, responsible practices strive to create a technological landscape that not only advances progress but also upholds a robust ethical framework, promoting trust and social well-being (Hankins & Schomberg, 2019, Hellström, 2003). User involvement stands as a pivotal element in the realm of responsible innovation practices. The active engagement of end-users and stakeholders throughout the innovation process serves as a foundational principle, fostering inclusivity and diversity of perspectives. By incorporating the insights and feedback of those who will ultimately interact with the innovation, a more comprehensive understanding of the diverse needs and expectations of the intended beneficiaries is achieved. This multifaceted involvement not only enhances the ethical dimension of the innovation process but also significantly increases the likelihood that the resulting innovations will be more attuned to the real-world requirements of the target audience. In essence, user involvement is not merely a procedural step but an ethical imperative that ensures the responsible and responsive evolution of innovations, thereby promoting a more inclusive and user-centric approach to technological advancement (Hankins & Schomberg, 2019, Bauer et al., 2021, Bessant, 2013) Advocating for meaningful involvement of a diverse range of stakeholders, particularly those representing broader societal interests, in the decision-making processes of technological change and innovation embodies a perspective firmly grounded in principles of inclusivity, equity, and responsible governance. This approach recognizes the multifaceted impacts that technological advancements can have on various segments of society and seeks to ensure that decision-making reflects the interests and concerns of a wide spectrum of stakeholders. By actively involving individuals from different backgrounds, professions, and communities, this perspective aims to mitigate potential biases and power imbalances inherent in the innovation process. In doing so, it contributes to the creation of technology that not only addresses the needs of a more comprehensive user base but also aligns with ethical considerations and societal values. Ultimately, this commitment to inclusivity and equity fosters a more democratic and socially responsible approach to technological change, emphasizing the importance of shared decision-making and the collective shaping of our technological future (Iakovleva et al., 2021, Lubberink et al., 2019)

Morphic auto personalization as a living innovation

Morphic auto personalization has been a dynamic and continuing process. It is a product of the evolution of the Trace Research and Development Center located at the University of Maryland, the College of Information Studies. The history of the Trace starts in 1971 when Gregg Vanderheiden, a student pursuing an undergraduate degree in Electrical Engineering and working as a technician in the Behavioral Cybernetics Lab at the University of Wisconsin-Madison, created a ground-breaking product called an auto-monitoring communication board, that helped disabled boy communicate with the use of technology.

The achievements and impact of the Trace Center are attributable to the collaborative efforts of numerous individuals. Over the course of 50 years, more than 400 students, faculty, and staff dedicated their time and expertise to contribute to the center's accomplishments. While not directly affiliated with Trace, some individuals played crucial roles in supporting its early stages, either by allocating time from their careers or deviating from conventional expectations to foster the development of Trace Center as an undergraduate student initiative. The center also received substantial assistance from individuals within our university, colleagues, and partners in our field, as well as various companies and organizations that provided support and expertise. People with disabilities, along with professionals, family, and friends, shared valuable insights and experiences that contributed to the center's growth. Additionally, government agencies and other entities played a pivotal role by providing essential funding.

By actively shaping industry and policy standards and engaging in innovative research and development initiatives, Trace has played a pivotal role in enabling millions of individuals to interact with the world using ubiquitous everyday devices such as telephones and computers. The tools and accessibility features developed by Trace through research have become integral components in billions of devices used by individuals with disabilities worldwide. These innovations are prevalent in every computer and mobile device operating on Windows, MacOS, iOS, and Android systems. Moreover, they have been seamlessly integrated into international accessibility standards, making a significant impact on enhancing inclusivity.

Throughout its evolution, Trace Center has expanded its focus to encompass all forms of disabilities and has adapted to integrate emerging and evolving technologies. Notably, the center pioneered the development of initial computer and software accessibility guidelines, a pivotal achievement in establishing standards for inclusive technology. Furthermore, it spearheaded the creation of the first consumer access guidelines, ensuring broader accessibility considerations. Additionally, the center played a leading role in formulating the inaugural Web accessibility guidelines, laying the groundwork for enhancing inclusivity and usability in the digital domain. Significant innovations include cross-disability-accessible ATMs and web kiosks. In the 2000s, the team began exploring cloud-based accessibility solutions, and in the 2010s, efforts were initiated to establish global infrastructures supporting inclusive information systems on a worldwide scale. The team undertook leadership roles in two extensive projects in Europe, bringing together over 50 groups and companies from the United States, Canada, and Europe. These efforts resulted in the creation of the Unified Listing and the DeveloperSpace. The Unified Listing serves as a global repository of products aimed at enhancing accessibility in communication, computing, and digital devices, consolidating data on Information and Communication Technologies (ICT) accessibility from 12 diverse databases spanning Europe, the United States, and Australia. The platform offers various search methods, including guided and power searching, accommodating individuals with differing levels of knowledge and search proficiency, thus facilitating the discovery of products that meet their needs. The DeveloperSpace provides a platform for discovering materials, elements, and individuals to generate, assess, and promote novel accessibility solutions. Both projects were funded by the European Union's Seventh Framework Program for research, technological development, and demonstration (Vanderheiden et al., 2023)

The latest innovation created by the Center unveiled in 2021, is Morphic auto personalization—an innovative technology aimed at augmenting the user experience of computing devices, with a specific focus on accommodating assistive technology users. Morphic auto personalization represents a pioneering approach toward ensuring a seamless integration of assistive technology functionalities and interface customizations across a spectrum of devices. Functioning as software, Morphic auto personalization serves to streamline the accessibility features within an intuitive user interface. At its core, Morphic furnishes users with a suite of indispensable tools engineered to enhance computer visibility and usability. Among its basic features are provisions for adjusting text dimensions, leveraging a magnification tool, enabling text-to-speech functionality for selected content, capturing and excerpting information for integration into reports or emails, optimizing contrast levels, mitigating glare, and furnishing filters tailored for individuals with color vision deficiencies. The accompanying image, labeled as Picture 1, illustrates the MorphicBar.

The implementation of Morphic Plus introduces a novel dimension to user customization through the provision of personalized MorphicBars. By leveraging the MorphicBar customization tool, which is conveniently accessible online, users are afforded the capacity to craft, adapt, and sustain MorphicBars from any web-enabled browser. An inherent attribute of this tool lies in its seamless synchronization functionality, whereby alterations effected therein are instantaneously propagated to other Morphic-enabled computing devices, irrespective of geographical dispersion. Moreover, the Morphic Enterprise framework extends the ambit of inclusivity within organizational settings, thereby engendering enhanced opportunities for stakeholders. Diverging from the capabilities inherent in Morphic Plus, Morphic Enterprise furnishes organizations with the capacity to integrate up to three alternate custom buttons onto the standard MorphicBar. This augmentation serves to accommodate a spectrum of user requirements, thereby fortifying the platform's versatility and adaptability. Furthermore, the scalability of Morphic lends itself to expeditious deployment across a substantial subset or entirety of an organization's computing infrastructure. This streamlined deployment facilitates the optimization of accessibility and usability paradigms across both on-site and remote operational milieus, thereby redounding to the overall efficiency and efficacy of organizational computing environments. (morphic, 2023).

Figure 1: MorphicBar.

Furthermore, Morphic facilitates the effortless integration of assistive technologies and necessary accessibility features for individuals. These elements seamlessly activate, install and adjust automatically on any computer the user employs. Importantly, these functionalities discreetly disappear once the user completes their tasks and logs off, safeguarding privacy. The synergy with Assistive Technology on Demand (AToD) enhances Morphic's capabilities. Given Morphic's open-source nature, allowing free installation on any computer, this amalgamation significantly improves accessibility and user-friendliness (Vanderheiden et al., 2023). Notably, Morphic has been implemented on shared computers in various universities and libraries throughout the United States and Canada.

Users' engagement in designing Morphic auto personalization

Designing effective assistive technologies necessitates a profound understanding of users' behaviors, lifestyles, and their daily interactions with technology. Recognizing this imperative, the Morphic team has conscientiously engaged users at every stage of the design process. By actively involving users, the team seeks to gain insights into the nuanced ways in which individuals incorporate technology into their daily lives, as well as the specific challenges they face. This user-centric approach ensures that the design of assistive technologies aligns closely with the needs and preferences of the intended users.

Years of research and the problem statement

Before the release of Morphic auto personalization in 2021, the research and development endeavor spanned over a decade. Originating from a focus on aiding users of assistive technology facing hurdles in computer usage, the project's scope expanded as the research team unearthed broader challenges encountered by individuals not proficient in personal computer operation. This shift in focus underscored the significance of addressing usability and accessibility issues inherent in computer interfaces.

Recognizing the potential for improvement in user experiences, the team embarked on a journey to delve deeper into computer functionalities and raise awareness regarding the array of built-in accessibility features within operating systems. Moreover, they observed that even among individuals cognizant of these features, difficulties persisted in their discovery and utilization (Vanderheiden & Jordan, 2021).

Identification, recruitment, and active user community creation

The research, user testing, and development of the Morphic platform were conducted within a framework of collaboration with a selection of prominent institutions across the United States. These institutions, encompassing public libraries, job centers, community colleges, and universities, were strategically chosen due to their multifaceted societal roles and extensive reach within diverse communities. The selected institutions were recognized for their pivotal contributions to society, offering an array of essential services and resources to a broad demographic spectrum. Their functions include facilitating access to a diverse array of informational materials, delivering educational programming, and serving as invaluable repositories of knowledge. Additionally, these institutions serve as vital community hubs, hosting a variety of meetings, events, and training sessions that foster social cohesion and knowledge dissemination. Moreover, public libraries, job centers, community colleges, and universities function as integral components of the educational landscape, effectively extending the reach of formal education systems and providing accessible points for the delivery of public services. Within these institutions, a palpable ethos of professional dedication to public service is often observed, with many actively participating in initiatives aimed at fostering accessibility and inclusion. Notably, several libraries and related organizations have demonstrated proactive engagement in initiatives promoting accessibility and inclusivity. Furthermore, adherence to policies concerning the provision of services for individuals with disabilities is a hallmark of these institutions, underscored by their commitment to integrating assistive technologies into their facilities and service offerings. This adherence not only reflects a legal and ethical imperative but also aligns with broader societal imperatives toward fostering equitable access to resources and opportunities for all members of the community. In summary, the collaboration with public libraries, job centers, community colleges, and universities in the United States provided a robust foundation for the research, user testing, and development of the Morphic platform. Through their multifaceted roles, these institutions not only served as testing grounds for the platform but also exemplified a commitment to accessibility, inclusion, and the provision of essential services to diverse populations. (American Library Association, 2023; American Job Centers, n.d.; U.S. Department of Education, 2022). Due to its extensive 50-year history of providing support to individuals with disabilities, the Trace Center was able to draw upon the resources and expertise of the community throughout the phases of research and testing.

The study comprised two sequential phases: identification and user testing. It adhered to the guidelines stipulated by the Institutional Review Board, ensuring ethical compliance, with participants providing informed consent prior to engagement. Collaborative efforts with institutions involved in the pilot phase facilitated participant selection. The needs analysis phase encompassed engagement with staff members alongside end users, encompassing individuals with disabilities, the elderly, those with limited literacy, non-native English speakers, and individuals with restricted computer navigation proficiency. Subsequently, the user testing phase exclusively involved end users.

Needs analysis

The process of needs analysis commenced with qualitative research conducted across public libraries, job centers, community colleges, and universities in the United States spanning from 2018 to 2020. Utilizing semi-structured interviews with personnel from these institutions, including librarians, job center staff, and school employees, the research aimed to gather insights on computer-related challenges and assess perceptions regarding a prototype of the Morphic system. The outcomes of this investigation contributed to a deeper understanding of the potential benefits of such a system for individuals, streamlining tasks for employees, and impacting institutional performance positively.

In the initial phase of the study, the research team focused on examining the viewpoints and perspectives of staff members within these institutions, to gain comprehensive insights. Semi-structured interviews were chosen for their adaptability and suitability for small-scale research endeavors. A series of key questions were formulated by the team to guide the exploration process, followed by systematic categorization and analysis of data collected during the interviews. The interview methodology involved initiating discussions with broad questions to capture a wide range of information, gradually narrowing the focus to specific issues of interest as conversations progressed. The format of the interviews remained flexible, allowing staff members to elaborate on their views freely and encouraging the emergence of novel concepts. Questions posed were open-ended, fostering an informal conversational atmosphere conducive to obtaining meaningful insights into various aspects of participants' experiences and the challenges they encountered.

Throughout the interviews, the research team delved into the day-to-day experiences of staff members in assisting users with computer usage, including demonstrations of the prototype Morphic system. Participants were queried about the features of Morphic available at the time and asked to identify the most significant features in their opinion. Staff members from libraries and job centers frequently mentioned assisting users in navigating and comprehending information on computers. Common challenges faced by users included difficulties in tasks such as double-clicking a mouse, accurately pointing to specific locations, accessing USB drives, and resolving printing-related issues. Moreover, a subset of patrons struggled with Microsoft Word or found its functionalities overly complex. Staff also reported instances where patrons encountered difficulties logging into email and social media accounts due to forgotten passwords, as well as language barriers, particularly with non-English speaking patrons. Requests for assistance in enlarging on-screen content for improved visibility were also frequently encountered by staff members.

User testing

User testing was integral to the developmental stages of Morphic, commencing before the completion of its prototype between 2017 and 2018. This initial exploratory phase aimed to gauge user perceptions of the software. Subsequent testing occurred upon the prototype's completion, spanning 2019 and 2020, focusing on evaluating the software's efficacy. Additionally, testing was conducted immediately before the product's release in 2021 to validate its functionality. Presently, as Morphic is deployed across numerous organizations, remote usability testing is ongoing to solicit user feedback and accommodate evolving user needs. Furthermore, after adjustments in Morphic's settings, users are invited to retest the software to verify the efficacy of the alterations in addressing issues identified during initial testing.

The overarching objectives of the user testing phase were delineated as evaluation criteria:

Ease of Learning: Assessing users' ability to complete tasks successfully and the speed at which tasks are performed.

Efficiency: Determining users' capacity to independently locate requisite information to accomplish tasks and whether tasks can be completed within predefined timeframes.

Reliability: Identifying instances of errors encountered by users and the timing of such errors.

Satisfaction: Gleaning insights from users' feedback to ascertain the overall user experience.

User testing took place within designated rooms at pilot institutions, involving individual sessions lasting approximately 30 minutes. Participants engaged in various tasks using MorphicBar and provided feedback. The testing approach was informal, encouraging an exploratory demeanor among users to assess usability. Feedback was acquired through observation of participants' interactions with computers and Morphic, attending to nonverbal cues and verbalized thoughts during tasks, and responses to open-ended questionnaire items. Task analysis facilitated the identification of user challenges, preferences for Morphic features, and areas requiring further development.

Initial testing revealed a lack of awareness among users regarding features such as screen scaling for content enlargement without scrolling, contrast modification, and the existence of accessibility and usability features. Common feedback expressed surprise at the computer's capabilities when demonstrated at libraries and community colleges. Moreover, a considerable portion of users exhibited apprehension and superstitious behaviors in their computer usage.

The synthesized results informed a comprehensive report containing recommendations for product enhancement. Morphic was described by first-time users as "a smart way to reach out . . . in one toolbar," "a shortcut for all the settings," and "something intuitive," signifying an empowering experience in navigating computer usage (Szopa et al., 2019).

Participants played a collaborative role in software development, contributing not only to usability studies but also providing feedback through interviews and focus groups, thereby aiding in the identification of new features and emerging needs.

The feedback from the research

The research findings exerted a substantial impact on the technical decision-making processes throughout the software development cycle. Valuable input garnered from both internal staff members and external individuals regarding the prototype version of Morphic led to notable advancements in Morphic's evolution. The team implemented novel mouse settings seamlessly integrated into the Morphic interface, encompassing options for modifying mouse speed, facilitating smoother double-click actions, enlarging the visual size of the mouse pointer, and enabling users to switch the primary mouse button. Furthermore, a new feature dubbed the "open USB" button was integrated, allowing users to effortlessly access the contents of a USB drive with a single click. The streamlining of the Microsoft Office button now empowers users to customize and generate new menus, thereby augmenting accessibility to diverse functionalities. Additionally, the introduction of a Screen Capture button permits users to capture the entire screen, a specific window, or a user-defined area. Acknowledging the significance of linguistic diversity, the team introduced a document translation feature to aid users encountering language barriers, thereby facilitating access to additional cloud services capable of real-time translation across a wider spectrum of document types. The research also led to the introduction of a highly impactful function, Assistive Technology on Demand (AToD), in 2023, which enables users to access requisite assistive technologies on any computer, irrespective of location or time. This advancement was made possible through collaboration with assistive technology vendors, who stand to benefit from exposure to a broader audience.

From a technical standpoint, user testing facilitated comprehensive analysis of user behavior, enabling software developers to gain insights into usage patterns and identify areas for refinement or enhancement. Given that personalization is a key attribute of Morphic, feedback from users and the testing phase facilitated the customization of the system to meet individual needs, thereby enhancing software quality through the incorporation of more precise user requirements. During the user testing phase, users provided valuable feedback regarding software bugs, which played a pivotal role in the software development process. Users also assessed the compatibility of the new software with a diverse array of devices, aiding in anticipation of future challenges and opportunities.

From a market perspective, early-stage user testing ensured that the software delivered meaningful value to customers. Users who participated across all phases of software development emerged as expert users, serving as ambassadors for Morphic and demonstrating its efficacy in simplifying computer usage to others. Additionally, early testing helped minimize development costs by eliminating non-essential expenditures.

Challenges in research and software development

Similarly, to most of the research in the field of assistive technologies where the issues are complex and heterogeneous, the Morphic team faced the following challenges (Johnston et al., 2009)

- Complexity – certain activities focus on health or physiological processes. Alternatively, some involvements address skills, emotions, or conduct, while others target elements of the social or physical environment that impose restrictions on individuals with disabilities.
- Less rigorous research methods- research, testing, and implementing stages entail a dedication to an inclusive method, involving individuals with disabilities as active decision-makers. This approach necessitates research designs and methodologies that enable meaningful participation. While crucial for ensuring the research's relevance to the experiences and principles of people with disabilities, these activities might be perceived as rigorous as the standard research methods.
- Small sample- despite the widespread prevalence of disabilities, they exhibit significant diversity. Effective interventions often require a high degree of customization, focusing on individual needs and adapting to specific impairments or personal and contextual factors. The requirement for personalized approaches

contributes to the frequently observed limitation of small sample sizes in conducted studies. The Morphic research team continuously changes this situation and at this moment the feedback is collected constantly from the software users.

- Defining an ethical and practical control- Randomized Controlled Trials represent a relatively recent addition to research and development in disabilities, there is unease among practitioners and individuals with disabilities regarding the withholding of services for control groups in RCTs.
- Funding- The complexity of research and development in assistive technologies is often intertwined with issues related to clinical service delivery and advocacy, rather than solely concentrating on research and development concerns. Consequently, funding for in-depth scientific investigations involving comprehensive multisite activities is frequently inadequate.
- Need to address issues within a large social context- dealing with problems in systems involves considering the social, physical, and economic aspects of the environment. Many major issues, such as universal design, accessibility, public attitudes, legal rights, cultural effects, and economic factors, relate to extensive social systems.

Furthermore, in conducted user testing, many of the users did not have, training on the devices they used, and some of them had a perception of no need to use computers, felt fear of dependence on the technology, or even embarrassment. Some participants did not receive prior training on the devices they were asked to use. This could impact their ability to navigate and use the technology effectively. Few struggled with basic functionalities, leading to suboptimal user experiences. Some participants expressed a perception that they don't see a significant need for using computers. This could be due to a lack of awareness of the potential benefits or relevance of technology in their context. The fear of dependence on technology was a common concern. This fear could stem from worries about the complexity of technology or concerns about overreliance on digital solutions. Users felt embarrassed about their lack of familiarity or proficiency with technology. This emotional barrier could impact their willingness to engage with digital devices.

In addition, the team faced challenges related to implementing innovative ICT solutions. New IT systems may have vulnerabilities that could be exploited by hackers, leading to data breaches. Innovative technology that could be exploited by malicious actors. These vulnerabilities might be unintentional and arise from coding errors, misconfigurations, or other oversights during the development or deployment process. Furthermore, hackers might attempt to compromise the security of a system. They could exploit vulnerabilities to gain unauthorized access, manipulate data, disrupt services, or achieve other malicious objectives. Data breaches could include personal data, intellectual property, or any other information that the organization considers valuable.

In addition, in some instances, the software did not integrate well with existing systems. Different systems might use incompatible technologies or programming languages, making it challenging to establish seamless communication and divergent data formats and structures between systems can impede the smooth exchange of information.

Actions taken by the research team to address the challenges.

- Advocating for the importance of creating and testing new interventions using rigorous methods when they are deemed appropriate. Analyzing best practices in the field of assistive technologies to identify effective strategies, approaches, and techniques.
- Creating collaborative networks (enterprises, universities, research institutes, government organizations, and intermediaries) to combine ideas and knowledge, harness collective knowledge for problem-solving and ideas exchange, and foster a shared culture and disability awareness among stakeholders.
- Building trust in technologies- making the technology understandable and easy to use. This includes showing the technology itself, how it works, and engaging users in software development. Providing customized experience. Providing suitable training and guidance for adoption. The open-source model and accessible algorithms contribute to Morphic's transparency. Morphic is available on any computer free of charge.
- Understanding and addressing the psychological and emotional aspects of user interaction. Creating a supportive and non-judgmental environment during training or introducing user-friendly interfaces helped alleviate embarrassment and encourage users to explore technology without hesitation.
- Establishing data privacy- Morphic gathers anonymous data on the utilization of our product features to enhance the quality of our software and services. Morphic team assures users that their data will never be tracked, shared, or sold for advertising, marketing, targeting, or any other purposes. Personal information is only collected if users opt for Morphic Plus. Additionally, Morphic adheres to FERPA compliance and has implemented rigorous protocols and tools to prevent unauthorized access or disclosures.
- Establishing a new privacy model. This included establishing an external Council for Privacy and Data Ethics, comprised of global privacy and security advocates and experts. This council is responsible for supervising all privacy policies and procedures at Morphic.
- Financial diversification and sustainability- Morphic is the result of the following grants to the Trace Center grant from the Rehabilitation Services Administration of the U.S. Dept. of Education, a grant from the National Institute on Disability, Independent Living and Rehabilitation Research, Administration for Community Living, U.S. Dept. of Health & Human Services, The European Union's Seventh Framework Programme and other.
- Creating a system architecture that can work with different operating systems- Morphic software developers ensure that Morphic can run seamlessly within the environment provided by the different operating systems. Among various activities, the team studies and analyses features and guidelines selects a programming language that is supported by the targeted operating system, is aware of system variations between operating systems, uses relative paths to handle file system dif-

ferences, matches the look of the target operating system, tests Morphic on various operating systems to ensure compatibility, and implements robust error handling.

Summary

The development team's overarching objective was to create a highly flexible product that could practically accommodate diverse users and usage scenarios, as articulated by Vanderheiden in 2000. This aspiration materialized through the implementation of personalization, with a particular emphasis on auto-personalization—an instantaneous and automated adaptation of the interface to align with individual needs and preferences. The concept of Morphic extended beyond mere personalization, incorporating a layered complexity to the process. The team introduced various capacities, including facilitating the discovery of accessibility and usability features, auto personalization, Installation on Demand (IoD), and custom, ultra-simple, one-click interfaces, as highlighted by Vanderheiden and Jordan in 2021.

The importance of user engagement throughout the design process was underscored by research findings, emphasizing its crucial role in assistive technology creation and development. By aligning past, present, and future user actions, the design team effectively connected with users' experiences. User experience studies played a pivotal role in uncovering usage issues, and informing iterative product development to better suit user needs. Participants' in-depth knowledge about their computer-related challenges and daily experiences contributed synergistically, resulting in more personalized assistive technology. Leveraging personal expertise, collective skills, and knowledge, the Morphic team successfully crafted software that is not only accessible and user-friendly but also enhances users' performance in their everyday lives. This user-centered design philosophy, marked by iterative and collaborative approaches, reflects a dedication to inclusivity, recognizing that the effectiveness of assistive technologies hinges on a profound understanding of the users they aim to serve.

The manifestation of user engagement in Morphic development is intricately entwined with the acknowledgment of responsible innovation, a concept that conscientiously integrates ethical, social, and environmental considerations into the fabric of technological progress. The process of innovation, in this context, has been conducted with a sense of responsibility and has yielded positive outcomes for user engagement, primarily through the adoption of User-Centric Design principles. Throughout the innovation journey, users perceived that their needs, preferences, and concerns were not only acknowledged but actively considered, fostering a greater inclination to engage with the final product. Their active participation and interaction with these innovations were marked by a heightened awareness of the environmental and social impact of the software. Users, understanding of the alignment of innovations with their input, demonstrated a greater propensity to engage. Responsible innovation, thus, played a pivotal role as a facilitator of augmented user engagement, creating a symbiotic relationship between technological progress and user satisfaction.

References

About idea. Individuals with Disabilities Education Act. (2022, November 7). https://sites.ed.gov/idea/about-idea/

American Job Centers. DOL. (n.d.). https://www.dol.gov/general/topic/training/onestop

American Library Association. (2020, September 25). Services to people with disabilities: An interpretation of the library bill of rights. Advocacy, Legislation & Issues. https://www.ala.org/advocacy/intfreedom/librarybill/interpretations/servicespeopledisabilities

Bauer, A., Bogner, A., & Fuchs, D. (2021). Rethinking societal engagement under the heading of Responsible Research and Innovation: (novel) requirements and challenges. Journal of Responsible Innovation, 8(3), 342–363. https://doi.org/10.1080/23299460.2021.1909812

Berliss-Vincent, J. (2022a, June 7). Morphic makes computers easier to use. Morphic. (2024, May 9). https://morphic.org/

Bessant J. (2013) Innovation in the Twenty-First Century In Owen, R., Bessant, J., & Heintz, M. (Eds.). (2013). Responsible Innovation: Managing the Responsible Emergence of Science and Innovation in Society. John Wiley & Sons. https://doi.org/10.1002/9781118551424

Bessant, J., Iakovleva, T., & Oftedal, E. (2019). Chapter 15: The Future of Responsible Innovation. In Responsible Innovation in Digital Health Empowering the Patient (pp.232–250). Edward Elgar Publishing

Gregg Vanderheiden Trace Research and Development Center, Vanderheiden, G., Center, T. R. and D., Ito, D., Hawthorne, I. R., & amp; Metrics, O. M. A. (2000, November 1). Fundamental principles and priority setting for Universal Usability: Proceedings on the 2000 Conference on Universal Usability. ACM Conferences. https://dl.acm.org/doi/abs/10.1145/355460.355469

Hankins, J., & Schomberg, R. von. (2019). International Handbook on Responsible Innovation: A Global Resource. Edward Elgar Publishing.

Hellström, T. (2003). Systemic innovation and risk: Technology assessment and the challenge of responsible innovation. Technology in Society, 25(3), 369–384. https://doi.org/10.1016/s0160-791x(03)00041-1

Iakovleva, T., Oftedal, E., & Bessant, J. (2021). Changing role of users – innovating responsibly in Digital Health. Sustainability, 13(4), 1616. https://doi.org/10.3390/su13041616

Johnston, M.V., Vanderheiden, G.C., Farkas, M., Rogers, E.S., Summers, J.A., & Westbrook, J.D. (2009). The Challenge of Evidence in Disability and Rehabilitation Research and Practice: A Position Paper.

Lubberink, R., Blok, V., van Ophem, J., & Omta, O. (2019). Responsible innovation by social entrepreneurs: An exploratory study of Values Integration in Innovations. Journal of Responsible Innovation, 6(2), 179–210. https://doi.org/10.1080/23299460.2019.1572374

Morphic Organization, https://morphic.org/

Multi-part document BS 7000 – Design Management Systems. BS 7000 – Design management systems. (n. d.). https://landingpage.bsigroup.com/LandingPage/Series?UPI=BS+7000

Owen, R., Stilgoe, J., Macnaghten, P., Gorman, M., Fisher, E., & Guston, D. (2013). A framework for responsible innovation. In Responsible Innovation (pp. 27–50). John Wiley & Sons

Stilgoe, J., Owen, R., & Macnaghten, P. (2013). Developing a framework for responsible innovation. Research Policy, 42(9), 1568–1580.

Szopa, A. M., Jordan, J. B., Folmar, D. J., &Vanderheiden, G. C. (2019). The auto-personalization computing project in libraries. Advances in Intelligent Systems and Computing, 802–812. https://doi.org/10.1007/978-3-030-19135-1_78

Vanderheiden, G. C., Lazar, J., Lazar, A., Kacorri, H., & amp; Jordan, J. B. (2023). Technology and Disability: 50 Years of Trace R&D Center Contributions and Lessons Learned. Springer.

Vanderheiden, G., & Jordan, J. B. (2021). An open-source tool for simplifying computer and assistive technology use. The 23rd International ACM SIGACCESS Conference on Computers and Accessibility. https://doi.org/10.1145/3441852.3476554

Von Schomberg, R. (2011). Towards responsible research and innovation in the information and communication technologies and security technologies fields. Proceedings of the European Conference on ICT for Sustainability, 1–9.

von Schomberg, R. (2013). A vision of responsible research and innovation. In Responsible Innovation (pp. 51–74). Springer.

World Health Organization. (n.d.). Disability. World Health Organization. https://www.who.int/health-topics/disability

Thomas Laudal

The dilemma of achieving responsible innovation in regulated markets

Case: Equipment for the home care sector

Abstract: This chapter addresses the challenge of fostering responsible innovation in the home care sector, particularly within regulated markets that involve public authorities subsidizing and distributing home care equipment. It explores the PPPI (Public Provision of Private Innovations) dilemma, which concerns the tension between ensuring availability and affordability through public provision and maintaining the quality and innovation of privately produced equipment.

The analysis involves a review of existing literature and case studies from various countries to understand how public authorities manage the provision of home care equipment. The study also assesses the regulatory frameworks governing this sector across four Northern European countries.

The findings indicate that public provision of subsidized goods typically involves a significant go-between role of public authorities, which often restricts direct interaction between end users and equipment providers. Due to the intention to ensure that essential home care equipment remains affordable and accessible, this tends to limit market competition and innovation.

The PPPI dilemma is evident as public authorities' involvement in equipment provision can hinder the responsiveness and adaptability of the market to user needs. While public oversight is crucial for ensuring that vulnerable populations have access to necessary equipment, it also creates barriers to feedback and innovation. The PPPI-dilemma may be solved if users are incentivized to give feedback to innovators, and the innovators are incentivized to adapt their offerings to this feedback. However, this seems hard to accomplish as part of a national healthcare scheme. But it is argued that the dilemma may be solved if the state supports a systematic use of user-cafés and living labs, and acted on the feedback from these events. The state may then stimulate the dialogue between users and innovators despite the go between role of public authorities. Thus, the dilemma identified at the macro scale may be overcome by measures at the micro scale.

This study highlights the need for a balanced approach that accommodates both public welfare goals and the dynamic benefits of market-driven innovation.

https://doi.org/10.1515/9783111241036-014

Introduction

There seems to be a challenge related to innovation when public authorities subsidise and distribute goods to end users. The components of responsible research and innovation (RRI), commonly referred to as “anticipation”, “reflexivity”, “inclusion”, and “responsiveness” (Stilgoe et al., 2013), require a dialogue between users and innovators. But a well-functioning dialogue along the supply chain is difficult to achieve, given the trend towards increasing division and specialisation of labour. The division of labour leads to a marginalization of the non-specialists in innovation processes. Today, non-specialist with no formal competences in technologies involved in the innovation, but with relevant user-experiences, rarely have a formal role in innovation projects. The challenge of expanding the number of participants in the innovation processes in an economy increasingly dominated by specialists, is referred to as the “innovation paradox” by John Bessant (1997). Recent studies indicate that this paradox may be partly overcome in the health sector due to the patients’ inherent motivation to solve their own medical problems (Cennamo et al. 2022).

User participation is included in a growing number of healthcare studies the last two decades (e.g. Bar & Riis, 2000, McNichol, 2012, Kushniruk & Nøhr, 2016, Ghasemzadeh, 2022). In a literature study of IoT-solutions adapted to home care services it was found that 80 percent of the articles referred to some kind of user participation (Podesta et al., 2018). And the potential of user involvement in the health sector was the focus of an international research project on how patients engage in innovation processes (Iakovleva et al., 2019). One of the assumptions was that patients’ and next of kin’s insights and feedback represent an untapped potential for hospitals. However, to include patients in the innovation process seems difficult when healthcare providers traditionally rely on a “patient centred service”[1] where patients are seen as a source for improving their own treatment, but not as a source for improving any *category* of patient with similar symptoms and needs (Laudal & Iakovleva 2019). It is observed that the role of users is viewed as only advisory in most academic studies. We assume that “user-centred design” is the typical option for adapting equipment delivered by private suppliers to the elderly as part of a public scheme for home care. “User-centred design” is considered a less user-dominated model than “co-operative designs” and “user-driven innovation” (Kushniruk & Nøhr, 2016).

Improving the innovation processes may be linked to the feedback from users to innovators and suppliers. When users in the health sector and innovators/suppliers are not co-located, this dialogue may be demanding. We see this in the case of home care services for the elderly. The dialogue between the elderly and the innovators

---

1 The Norwegian Ministry of Health (2020) defines ‘patient centered health services’ as; «.. services where patients and relatives are seen and listened to – with words they understand. Shared decision-making is the norm, residents can communicate with the service digitally, and users have a say in the development of the healthcare service.»

may be impaired not only by the increasing division and specialisation of labour, but also by the go-between role of public authorities to ensure availability and affordability of equipment demanded by the elderly (see Figure 1). In many countries the critical importance of home care goods and services, and the limited purchasing powers of the target group, seems to have motivated a particular go-between role and subsidy function of the government. This has led to a dilemma between the need for user-feedback to support innovations and fulfilling the components of RRI, and the need for subsidies and a go-between role for the public sector. We refer to this as the dilemma of public provision of private innovations, hereafter referred to as the PPPI-dilemma.

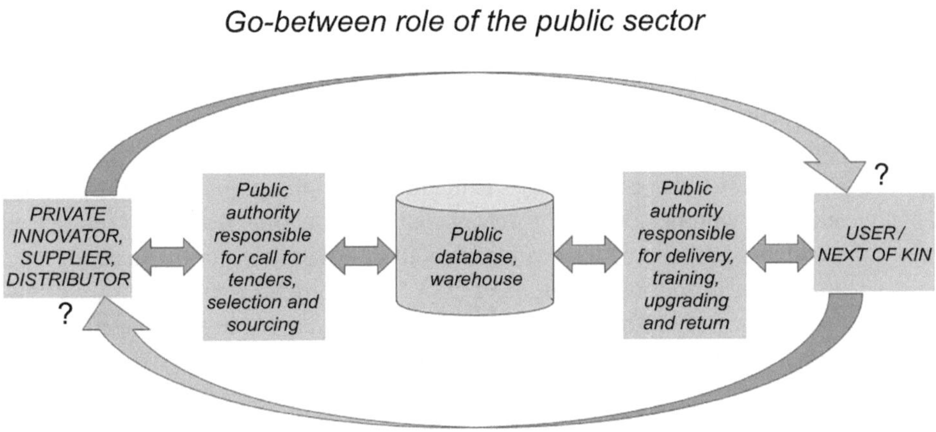

Figure 1: The go-between role of public authorities in the provision of equipment to the elderly.

The rationale for the public sector to be involved in the distribution of equipment for home care, is similar to the rationale for "services of general economic interest" (SGEI) from the competition regulations in the EU (Treaty on the Functioning of the European Union, TFEU, articles 14 and 106–2). The reference to SGEI in the EU Treaty indicates that services of this nature are only subject to competition law as long as this does not obstruct the performance of the tasks assigned to them. This reference is seen as a justification of the restrictions of competition where non-economic values are being promoted. Or in positive terms; the exemption justifies state intervention in the economy for the provision of SGEI to accommodate non-economic values in competitive markets (Zhu, 2020). The PPPI-dilemma seems also to be based on non-economic values as it concerns critical needs of individuals that belong to a vulnerable group in our society.

The market for subsidised equipment for the elderly illustrates the PPPI-dilemma. Public authorities at the local, regional and national level, pick suppliers and products to be included in the public offering of home care equipment. There is a dilemma between

- the need for a dialogue between the users and next of kin, and the suppliers and innovators, and
- the need for a go-between role for public authorities to ensure availability and affordability for all users.

Figure 1 shows that the go-between role may cover three functions. A procurement function, a display function, and a delivery and follow-up function. A direct dialogue between the innovator and the user is difficult under these circumstances. We will return to the actual go-between role of public authorities in four Northern European countries.

The PPPI-dilemma suggests there may be a limit to how responsible the innovation can be in regulated markets. The main theme of this chapter is to consider this claim. The approach is two-fold: After considering how we may stimulate innovation in regulated markets in general, we examine whether it is common for the public sector to have a go-between role to support the allocation of equipment to the elderly. Then we examine whether the PPPI is recognized as a dilemma. Do we see references to tensions related to the need for availability and affordability, and the need for user feedbacks to inspire product development? If a PPPI dilemma is recognized, we consider whether there are efforts to overcome the dilemma. We begin by considering how we may stimulate innovation in regulated markets in general.

Stimulating innovation in regulated markets

Several factors are critical if one wants to stimulate innovation in regulated markets. A well-functioning market feeds on the free flow of information, we need to design environments that spurs innovations, and durable goods need to be linked to follow-up services.

Free flow of information

According to textbook economics the price in a well-functioning market economy signals where the profit margins are, and a market analysis may tell us where we should invest in research and development projects. However, these “truths” may be complicated by the fact that free markets – with a free flow of goods and with no actor commanding substantial market power – are rare. But it is not only a well-functioning market that counts. The mere *threat* of new entrants may also discipline market behaviour. The threat of a new competitive product may enforce behaviour very similar to the pattern we expect under conditions of perfect competition, according to Schumpeter 1942:85). This threat may supplement a classical equilibrium model with the idea of a "transient order", according to Bloch & Metcalfe (2018). But the assumption that credible threats of new entrants leads to efficient markets, is based on the premise that potential suppliers are able to offer their product on the market. If the market only includes products that are listed in public framework agreements, neither the conditions for an equilibrium model nor for a transient order may be in place, and we would expect less innovation and a less efficient market.

- According to Moors & Lukkien (2014:287), "adequate linkages between users and producers seem to be important for emerging healthcare innovations."
- And Bessant (2005) and Hippel (2017) show that both innovators, producers and end-users benefit from a well-functioning dialogue along the supply chain, starting with innovators that are responsive to user needs.

The question here is if such linkages, or a well-functioning dialogue, is in place in the home care sector.

Designing a market space that stimulates innovation

To ensure that the products and the on-going product development meet the demand, the producer needs to engage with users and adapt to their needs. This may be referred to as the innovation space. Seebode et al. (2012) describes an innovation space as any innovation context – from incremental to radical,[2] with or without environments, that are purposely designed to stimulate innovation. Without such a designed environment the innovation space may be referred to as a 'business as usual' space. If we design an environment that encourages innovation, this may be referred to as *reframing* the innovation when it applies to incremental innovations. When this is done to stimulate radical innovations, it will often involve a process of *co-evolution* where there are no clear starting- or ending points (Seebode et al., 2012:198).

When participants in a particular marketplace at a given location stimulate the innovation processes, this may be referred to as a "boundary innovation space". Boundary innovation spaces have two defining characteristics. They

- incentivizes stakeholders, and in particular end users, to engage in the development of products, and
- incentivizes producers and innovators to seek feedback from stakeholders.

The boundary innovation space may be created at the micro scale between innovators and producers by organizing *user-cafés* where innovators and users meet and ex-

2 Here Seebode et al. (2012) refers to the four-cell matrix of Henderson & Clark (1990).

change experiences, or by organizing *living labs* where users are included in the value-creation process, or research experiment, which could include sensing, prototyping, validating and refining solutions in multiple real-life contexts (Eriksson et al., 2005).[3] But boundary innovation spaces may also be created at the macro scale when state schemes at the national level are designed to stimulate innovation. In this chapter the initial focus is on the macro scale and the challenges of public provision of private innovations (the PPP-dilemma).

The provision of durable goods

Many products require maintenance and training to be utilised. These products are referred to as durable goods. Much of the equipment delivered to the elderly as part of a home care scheme, will be durable goods and demand follow-up services. In these cases we see that the go-between role of public authorities is not only conditioned on the goal of accomplishing availability and affordability for all, but also on the need for a wide range of services. These services are frequently referred to as "extended producer responsibility" (Gupt & Sahay, 2015, Huang et al, 2019, Huang et al., 2019, and Alev et al., 2020). In our context of home care for the elderly, this implies that the go-between role of the public healthcare units, or of charities, should also include follow-up services.

Questions raised in this chapter

Based on how we stimulate innovations in regulated markets by ensuring free flow of information, we question how subsidised products are offered in regulated markets. We consider two questions in this chapter:

- Is the go-between role of public authorities (see Figure 1) common in Northern European countries and how does it vary?
- Is the PPPI-dilemma recognized in the market for equipment for the elderly? And if so, do we see attempts to overcome this dilemma?

The first question concerns the design of the provision scheme for equipment to the elderly. The second question concerns the relevance of the PPPI-dilemma. Is the PPPI-

3 There are many definitions of «living labs». Nele De Witte, a specialist on the use of living labs in different settings – and a contributor to this book – defines living labs as an open innovation systems where end users and other stakeholders are involved in the exploration, co-creation and evaluation of solutions in realistic circumstances.

dilemma addressed and acknowledged? Do we see efforts to mitigate this? We will address these questions in turn.

This chapter builds on secondary sources as studies published by state authorities and studies funded by state authorities published by private institutions. The data on national schemes included in this chapter is not sufficient to validate the findings, but they improve our understand of the go-between role of public authorities varies, the nature of the PPPI-dilemma, and actions aiming to mitigate this dilemma.

In Scandinavia and England the state plays a more dominant role in the health-care system than in most other European countries. In Scandinavia the share of elderly (75 +) using home care services is between 60 and 80 percent while the average in the EU for this group is 52 percent (Eurostat, 2022). The selection of countries seems therefore fit to consider the PPPI-dilemma.

Home care services and equipment for the elderly

The go-between role of public authorities in four North-European countries

The dilemma of public provision of private innovations are brought to the forefront in the market for equipment for the elderly. In many countries we find policies and regulations to ensure that critical equipment for the elderly is available and affordable for all entitled users. Due to the increasing population of elderly people in most developed countries, the market for adapted equipment is growing. World-wide it is estimated that the "disabled and elderly assistive technologies market" will grow from around $ 27 billion in 2021 to $49 billion in 2030 (Nextmsc, 2022). In the UK it was forecasted that the market for home care equipment will double between 2021 and 2027 (Grand View Research, 2022).

Before we describe the go-between role of public authorities in the four countries, we distinguish between three go-between functions (see Figure 1):

- *Purchasing function*
  Responsible for tender announcements, supplier selection and contract models.
- *Display function*
  Responsible for maintenance of the database displaying the equipment, prices, and setting the conditions for eligibility.
- *Delivery and follow-up function*
  Responsible for delivering the required product to the elderly, and for training, upgrading and for the return of the product when it is no longer in use.

We will consider the presence of these functions in each country.

Norway

In Norway the *purchasing function* is carried out by the municipalities (356) (on their own and in collaboration) and by the national public authority NAV, including the regional units (hjelpemiddelsentraler) operated by NAV. Municipalities offer equipment to more than 200,000 elderly (SSB, 2022). The equipment which is most in demand are wheelchairs and stove guards. These are borrowed by the elderly from the municipality. To be entitled to equipment directly from NAV you must have a significantly reduced functional ability that is believed to last for a minimum of two years.

The go-between role in Norway is underscored by the fact that 90% of the suppliers of equipment in this scheme have NAV as their only customer. 40 percent of the suppliers report that no innovation of their products is going on in Norway (Oslo Economics, 2016). Thus, most equipment provided by the public sector in Norway is not offered on the private market. This seems to be a unique feature of the Norwegian home care sector.

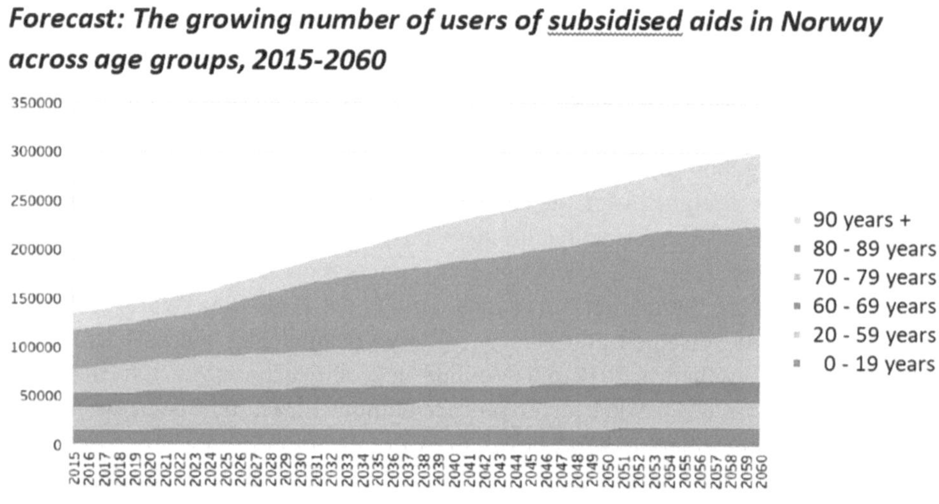

Figure 2: Forecast of the number of users of subsidised equipment in Norway.
Source: Agenda Kaupang (2017).

The national database run by NAV (hjelpemiddeldatabasen) handles the *display function* and the equipment is distributed by twelve regional distribution centres (hjelpemiddelsentraler). The national database include approximately 200 suppliers and 4,000 products. But only a bit over 100 suppliers have signed framework contracts with NAV for delivery of subsidised products to entitled users in Norway (osloeconomics, 2016). Several sources report that applying for equipment from the hjelpemiddelsentral is complicated. Users need assistance of social care workers to search and to apply for equipment (NSCC, 2016, and NAV-Hjelpemidler, 2022). The equipment provided by the municipality is free of charge or subsidised with an amount relative to the private means available to the user.

The home care units of the municipality are responsible for the *delivery and follow-up function*. If needed, they may request assistance from a state hospital unit. The state subsidies for equipment for all eligible groups (elderly, sick, and disabled) is estimated to be 89 euro per capita (MedTekNorge, 2016). The number of users is estimated to double before 2060 (see Figure 2).

Sweden

In Sweden both the municipalities (290) and the regions (21) are responsible for the *purchasing function* for equipment to the elderly. The provision schemes and the assortment vary significantly among the 21 regions, according to a green paper (SOU, 2017, p. 124/146). An indication of this is that the percentage of elderly (80 +) receiving home care services varies between 24 percent to 35 percent among Swedish regions (Socialstyrelsen, 2022).

The region is responsible for the *display function*, but only some regions display all equipment in a shared database, as we see in Norway. Most regions display equipment in regional or local databases. If the local case manager considers an elderly entitled to the equipment, the equipment is normally provided free of charge.

The "Hemtjänst" in the municipality is responsible for the *delivery and follow-up function*. In some regions users can choose between receiving equipment from the municipality (lending the equipment) or buying equipment on the market as long as the user pays the difference between the sales price and the subsidy given for a product (referred to as "fritt val"). For some equipment the elderly may also be assisted by a polyclinical unit (Vårdcentral – there are approximately 1000 in Sweden) where there are more specialized medical competencies. Subsidies per capita for equipment in Sweden (elderly and disabled persons) is calculated to 87 euro/capita (SOU 2017:43).

Denmark

In Denmark municipalities (98) are responsible for the *purchasing function*. They coordinate this purchasing function by linking the offered products to a common database for equipment for the elderly and the disabled (Hjælpemiddeldatabasen). This database is operated by the governmental Board of Social Services (Socialstyrelsen). For certain products (e.g. hearing aids) the regions are responsible for the purchasing function.

The *display function* is taken care of by municipalities and regions (5). They operate a central database that includes 1,300 suppliers and 90,000 equipment categories (Social- og Boligstyrelsen, 2022). No approval is required from the suppliers to advertise their products in this database. The user is assigned a piece of equipment within a price limit and may choose a product offered in the market, or borrow it (only a narrow product range) from the municipality. If the user buys the equipment the user must cover the difference between the market price and the price estimated by the state/municipality (Borger.dk, 2022).

The *delivery and follow-up function* is the responsibility of the Hjemmehjælp unit in the municipality. Subsidies per capita for equipment in Denmark (for elderly and disabled persons) is calculated to 56 euro per capita (Socialstyrelsen, 2014).

England

In England there are two markets for home care and therefore two sectors responsible for the *purchasing function* for equipment for the elderly. The publicly funded market, in which local authorities are the main purchasers, and the self-funder market where you may be eligible for direct payments to compensate for part of the cost. (King's Fund, 2018). The local councils in England (333) are responsible for the quality control and funding of the majority of the home care services and care for 350,000 older people whereby 257,000 were paid for by their local authority (King's Fund, 2018). The quality of home care services has been criticized due to low staffing and low wages. According to one study 90 percent of care workers were paid less than the real living wage (Age UK and Home care Association, 2021). 30 percent of the elderly self-fund home care services, compared to 25 percent in Scotland and 21 percent in Wales (Home care Association, 2020).

The *display function* – both for subsidised and non-subsidized equipment – is a shared responsibility between the government (NHS) and private providers. An important element is the database "Living Made Easy", offered by the charity DLF. This includes advisory information and a presentation of more than 10,000 products with links to around 1,000 suppliers (Living made easy, 2022). To receive home care services and equipment a "need assessment" is required by the council (NHS, "Getting a need assessment", 2022).

The *delivery and follow-up function* is shared by private (85%) and not-for-profit (12.5%) home care services in England (Home care Association, 2020). Elderly who are not able to get the help they need from the local council or the NHS, can apply for a grant from private charities to help with the costs (NHS, "Household gadgets and equipment to make life easier", 2022). Most users must pay privately for personal alarms and monitoring systems based on GPS. One exception is "community alarms" which users may apply for in certain regions (NHS, Personal alarms, 2022). The subsidies per capita for home care and equipment to the elderly and disabled in England is calculated to 51 euro/capita (Home care Association, 2020).

Summing up

In *Norway* and *Denmark*, the display function is taken care of by a national database and websites offering advisory services linked to this database. The national database displays subsidised equipment that are covered by public framework contracts but also products that are advertised by suppliers without being covered by framework contracts. In *Sweden* the regions are responsible for the display function and the design of the provision scheme for equipment for the elderly. In *England* the display function is shared by a charity (database) and the councils. The delivery and follow-up function in England is based on several thousands of independent and affiliated home care providers.

The go-between role of public authorities in the home care sector in the four countries is summarized in Table 1.

Table 1: Summarizing the elements relevant for the go-between role of the state. (Sources of quantified information is included in the paragraphs above.).

Go-between role issue	NORWAY (Pop. 5.4 mill.)	SWEDEN (Pop. 10.4 mill.)	DENMARK (Pop. 5.8 mill.)	ENGLAND (Pop. 56 mill.)
Average pop. Municipality **Average pop. region**	15 k 450 k	36 k 495 k	59 k 1,160 k	168 k (Council) -
Responsible for purchasing function	State/ Municipal authorities	Regional authorities	State/ Municipal authorities	Private/Charity home care services
Responsible for displaying available equipment	National level (4.000 products)	Regional level	National level (90.000 products)	Private charities (10.000 products)
Warehouse function of subsidised equipment	State/ Municipalities	Regional level + municipalities	Municipalities	Private and non-profit
Delivery and follow-up function	Municipality	Municipality	Municipality	Council, private and non-profit
User may buy private and be compensated	No	Yes (some)	Yes (most)	Yes (low/none compensation)
Home care expenditures per capita (subsidy costs)	89 euro/cap	87 euro/cap.	56 euro/cap.	51 euro/cap.

We see that the expenditures linked to the go-between role varies considerably between the countries: In Norway and Sweden the home care expenditures per capita is much higher than in Denmark and in England. In Denmark the distribution costs are probably lower due to lower costs levels in a country with relative high population density compared to Norway and Sweden. In England the public sector covers a lesser portion of the user's costs compared to the Scandinavian countries.

The main differences of the go-between role of public authorities is illustrated in Figure 3.

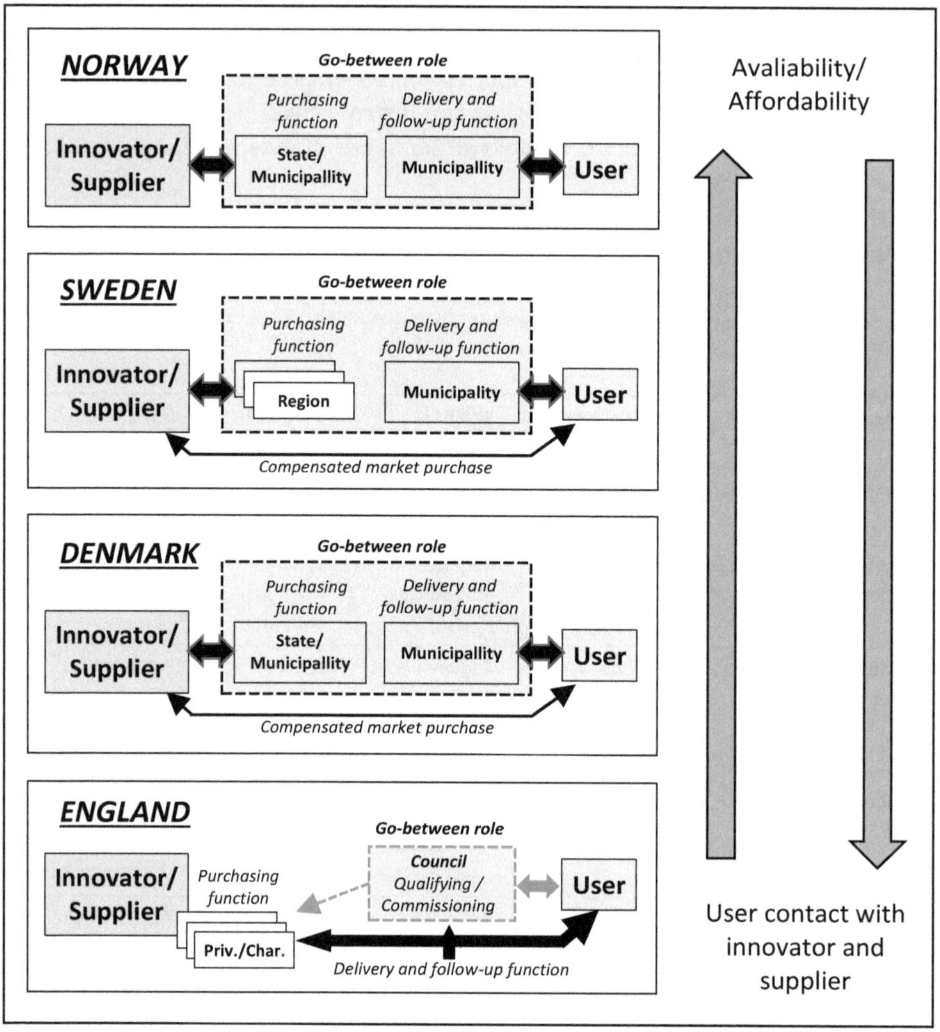

Figure 3: Illustration of differences in the go-between role of public authorities and private corporations and charities.

The barrier for contact between innovators and users is strongest in Norway and weakest in England. Sweden and Denmark allow users to purchase equipment (certain products in certain contexts) in the private sector and be compensated by an amount equivalent to the price offered through the public scheme.

When it comes to affordability and availability, we see an opposite ranking compared to the go-between role (see Figure 3). In England the compensation of equipment to the elderly does not cover the market prices in many situations, or the product category may not be subsidised at all. There are different local practices and support levels and no standard prices because the private sector is partly responsible for the delivery function. The user may either purchase the equipment directly from the private sector, or the equipment is commissioned by the Council. The elderly must often cover the full market price themselves, except for the equipment categories that the Council lends to the elderly. In Norway and Sweden, in contrast, all equipment available from the municipality and from the regional distribution centres are provided free of charge, or for only a minor fee. And the range of equipment is standardized by including all products in the national database used by case handlers in both municipalities and the regional distribution centres.

We can also assume that the ranking of "well-functioning market" is opposite to the order of the go-between role (see Figure 3). Where the go-between role is least dominant (in England), we expect the best functioning market. This is in line with claims in a study by European Observatory/World Health Organization where the "extent to which a home care market exists" was considered "high" in England and "low" or "medium" in the Scandinavian countries (Genet et al., 2012:74–75).

Recognition of the PPPI-dilemma

The evidence above shows how the go-between role of public authorities varies in the home care sector. The next question is whether the PPPI-dilemma is recognized by healthcare professionals and stakeholders, and if so; if we see attempts to mitigate this dilemma.

There is rich evidence that the home care sector recognizes the importance of the user voice. Textbox 1 shows examples of actions highlighting the importance of users when home care services are designed and when equipment is selected. There are also several studies showing that healthcare professionals want to be involved when managers in the local authority introduces new welfare technology in the home care sector (e.g. Vécha & Kandusová, 2018, and Glomsås et al., 2020).

Most of the examples and research findings in this area focus on the contact between users and employees in the health sector. We found only *one* example suggesting that the contact between users and the private sector (suppliers and innovators) should be strengthened (SOU, 2017, p. 190.). However, the emphasis here was only on the advantages for users. Opportunities for businesses was not discussed. And there is no mentioning of the potential business benefits related to user feedback in any of the legal acts requiring local authorities to provide home care.[4]

Textbox 1: Initiatives with the potential to mitigate the PPPI-dilemma

INITIATIVES WITH THE POTENTIAL TO MITIGATE THE PPPI-DILEMMA (HIGHLIGHTING THE NEED TO LISTEN TO USERS.)

Norway

Representatives of user-groups are appointed to review the practices of the regional distribution centres – hjelpemiddelsentralene (Arbeids- og sosialdepartementet, 2017, p. 64).

A government committee concluded that user interests should be emphasized more when the state and the municipalities develop home care services (NOU, 2010).

Sweden

Patient contracts (patientkontrakt) are established as a non-binding mutual agreement between the patient and the caretaker. The aim of the agreement is to involve the users in how their home care service is to be designed. (SKR, 2018).

The Swedish Standards Institute (2017) has issued a quality standard for home care services (SS875200:2015, see point 5.3.2.). This demands that care workers allow the elderly to influence the selection of aids as much as possible.

A law introduced in 2014 (Patientlagen), demands that home care users should have a free choice of aids. A green paper points out that the freedom of choice depends on the availability of alternative aids in the regional assortment. If the range of aids offered by the region is very narrow, the freedom of choice will no longer exist (SOU, 2017, p. 194–195). The same green paper states that the system for compensating suppliers of the home care sector have no incentives for cost reduction or innovation (SOU, 2017, p. 262).

Denmark

Users may log on to the "Idea and debate forum" in the national database for aids (Hjelpemiddeldatabasen) and suggest and discuss changes of any kind to this scheme.

The aim of the Center for Velfærdsteknologi is to support the distribution of welfare technologies and facilitate knowledge sharing among municipalities and other stakeholder. (Arbeids- og Sosialdepartementet, 2017, 5.1.5.)

A study of home care services finds that the elderly do not believe they have sufficient influence on the services they receive (Danmarks Statistik, 2021).

Sweden (two regions) and Denmark (most municipalities)

A "free choice" regulation for certain aids, allow users to purchase the aid from the private market as long as they cover the difference between the market price and the subsidised price.

England

The department of Health argues that incentivising innovation by third sector providers, possibly through grant funding and improving local authority's own commissioning practices, would lead to better and more relevant home care services (Department of Health, 2014).

Guidelines for employees responsible for home care services highlights the need for taking users' needs into account (SCIE, 2014.). A study commissioned by the Local Government Association in 2017

4 The legal acts: England: National Health Service and Community Care Act. Denmark; Serviceloven. Sweden; Socialtjänstlagen. Norway; Helse- og omsorgstjenesteloven.

emphasized the need for user-tests before new products were introduced (Local Government Association, 2017).

According to a King Fund report, hightech is not that much in demand in the home care service. Home care providers state that users lack the competence of utilising many digital technologies and that high-tech will not solve the immediate problems in this sector (Kings Fund, 2018:34).

Europe

One finding in a large EU-study published in 2020 on innovations related to home care services, was that "voices of the end users often were neglected". The project did not recommend any specific mitigating action (HoCare, 2020:30).

Is there a limit to how responsible innovations can be in regulated markets?

Though we see little or no explicit recognition of the PPPI-dilemma in policy documents, academic studies and relevant legislation, there are plenty of examples and many research findings indicating that the dilemma exists. The account of the role of government in Scandinavia and England in the home care sector support that such a dilemma exist. We also see that the stakeholders recognize the importance of listening to user voices. The missing component that would mitigate the PPPI-dilemma seems to be the voice of users, including user experiences for specific products and allowing users to decide which of the available products on the market they want to purchase (see Figure 1). Today the goals seem to be restricted to allow user-feedback to healthcare professionals.

According to Stilgoe et al. (2013) "inclusivity" and "responsiveness" is associated with user-driven, open, and participatory innovation processes, and a capacity to change shape or direction in response to stakeholder feedback and changing circumstances. The innovation of equipment for the home care sector – a sector serving more than 60 percent of the elderly (75+) with a market value expected to double the next decade – do not permit a free flow of information to allow for inclusion and responsiveness. The PPPI-dilemma arises as markets need free flow of information while users at the same time need public authorities in a go-between role to ensure affordability and availability.

Does the PPPI-dilemma mean that there are limits to how responsible innovation may be in regulated markets of this kind? Does increasing the user-feedback to the market need to be at the expense of affordability and availability? One may imagine, everything else being equal, a reform that incentivised users to give feedback to suppliers and suppliers to adopt their offering to feedback. Both incentives would depend on giving eligible users a free choice among a group of approved equipment. And this would require a market platform with an interface and functionality that is accessible for all (Cennamo et al., 2022). However, at a national scale it would be challenging to engage user and innovators without face-to-face contact in a physical location. Incentives would have to rely on formal regulations and procedures and platform interfaces. The boundary space established by this platform would resemble a public good: It would be open to all (non excludable), and the benefits would be shared by all (non-rivalrous). But, as with any pure public good, it would be challenging to incentivise users to engage when there are no immediate private benefits involved.

However, if innovators, users, and other stakeholders would meet face-to-face in settings where they are introduced to the technological options and the individual needs of potential users, the incentives for engagement would likely be greater. User-cafés and living labs meet these requirements. Thus, a challenge identified in the health sector at the macro scale – the PPPI-dilemma, may be mitigated by user-cafés and living labs at the micro scale. If any of the four countries studied above, launched a nation-wide network where users, innovators, and actors mediating the contact between these two, the PPPI-dilemma might be overcome. User-cafés and living labs could enable a dialogue and a mutual understanding between users and innovators without challenging the availability or affordability of the equipment for the elderly. If this micro level action is to mitigate the PPPI-dilemma, it requires the public authorities in charge of the purchasing function, the display function, and the delivery function, to act on the feedback they get from user cafés, living labs and directly from users. It is this feedback, not the personal preferences of any public official, that ought to decide the specifications in the tender documents.

Conclusion

This chapter examines the home care sector and the conditions for responsible innovation of equipment for the elderly in regulated markets. The evidence from Norway, Sweden, Denmark, and England show that these countries have two related challenges in common: the go-between role of public authorities in the market for equipment, and related to this; the lack of feedback from the users of equipment to the innovators and suppliers. Taken together, these challenges appear as a dilemma. There are two conflicting aims:

- The aim of available and affordable products is ensured by the public authorities' go-between role. This is not compatible with a free flow of user feedback to the market.
- The aim of responsible innovations is ensured by the free flow of user feedback to the market (innovators). But this is not compatible with a go-between role for public authorities.

This dilemma is referred to as the "public provision of private innovations" dilemma (PPPI-dilemma). We find evidence of this dilemma in all the four countries examined.

There are interesting national differences. We find the most well-functioning market in England where the funding level is lowest, and the national coordination of the delivery function is weakest. In Norway all equipment is provided by the municipality or by the regional distribution centres, with a relative high level of funding. Most users need assistance from a case-handler to apply for equipment through the national platform. The scheme in Norway seems to restrict users' freedom the most. The schemes in Sweden and Denmark includes a free-choice option for certain equipment in certain contexts.

Is there a limit to how responsible the innovation can be in regulated markets? If the PPPI-dilemma is overcome, it would stimulate responsible innovation and improve the offering, and likely also the demand, of home care equipment for the elderly. We find that the PPPI-dilemma may be solved if users are incentivized to give feedback to suppliers, and the suppliers are incentivized to adapt their offerings to this feedback. However, this seems hard to accomplish in a national healthcare scheme. But if the state launched a program supporting user-cafés and living labs, and acted on the feedback from these activities, the dilemma identified at the macro scale might be overcome by measures at the micro scale.

Literature

Age UK and Home care Association ()2021). *What if you need care at home and there's no one to provide it?* Downloaded in December 2021: https://www.ageuk.org.uk/globalassets/age-uk/documents/reports-and-publications/reports-and-briefings/home care/home care-report-age-uk-home care-association.pdf

Agenda Kaupang (2017). "Gjennomgang av hjelpemiddelformidlingen" Report commissioned by the Ministry of labour and social affairs. Downloaded, December 2022: https://www.agendakaupang.no/wp-content/uploads/2020/08/Rapport_ASD-Gjennomgang-av-hjelpemiddelformidlingen_AK.pdf

Alev, I., Agrawal, V. V., & Atasu, A. (2020). Extended producer responsibility for durable products. *Manufacturing & Service Operations Management*, 22(2), 364–382.

Arbeids- og sosialdepartementet (2017). *En mer effektiv og fremtidsrettet hjelpemiddelformidling – for økt deltakelse og mestring*. Report from expert committee. Downloaded in December 2022: https://www.regjeringen.no/contentassets/869af6e38d594020a851ace0b11dc12e/en-mer-effektiv-og-fremtidsrettet-hjelpemiddelformidling.pdf

Bar, F., & Riis, A. M. (2000). Tapping user-driven innovation: A new rationale for universal service. *The Information Society*, 16(2), 99–108.

Bessant, J. R. (1997). *High-involvement innovation: Building and sustaining competitive advantage through continuous change*. John Wiley & Sons Incorporated.

Bessant, J. (2005). Enabling continuous and discontinuous innovation: Learning from the private sector. Public Money and Management, 25(1), 35–42.

Bloch, H., & Metcalfe, S. (2018). Innovation, creative destruction, and price theory. *Industrial and Corporate Change*, 27(1), 1–13.

Borger.dk (2022). Website administered by the Danish state, informing users about huma care and aids. Downloaded in December 2022: https://www.borger.dk/handicap/Hjaelp-i-hverdagen/Hjaelpemidler-og-forbrugsgoder

Cennamo, C., Oliveira, P., & Zejnilovic, L. (2022). Unlocking Innovation in Healthcare: The Case of the Patient Innovation Platform. *California Management Review*, 64(4), 47–77.

Danmarks statistic (2021). *Undersøgelse om hjemmehjælp. Report, 89 pages. Downloaded in December 2022*: https://www.aeldresagen.dk/presse/viden-om-aeldre/analyser-og-undersoegelser/2021-analyse-hjemmehjaelp-071221

Department of Health (2014). "Care and Support Statutory Guidance." Downloaded in December 2022: https://assets.publishing.service.gov.uk/government/uploads/system/uploads/attachment_data/file/315993/Care-Act-Guidance.pdf

Eriksson, M., Niitamo, V. P., & Kulkki, S. (2005). State-of-the-art in utilizing Living Labs approach to user-centric ICT innovation-a European approach. Lulea: Center for Distance-spanning Technology. Lulea University of Technology Sweden: Lulea. Downloaded in May 2023: https://d1wqtxts1xzle7.cloudfront.net/50573062/stateoftheart_livinglabs_eriksson2005-libre.pdf?1480261949=&response-content-disposition=inline%3B+filename%3DState_of_the_art_in_utilizing_Living_Lab.pdf&Expires=1685099282&Signature=RLdYF27WnzIguyQOMUBR~v2lYi1mcivG9zYUyH5LIU3MtyBFZzOwZ1veFIVsgfPCVY~YkINP3lgZWuddJ~ob0UQpnbVvx2ZlCYh7SVqCm2y87ij~o1XQNaq4FGPnWUvFmLEtSut0RzklLg2gomkREymmwsW1xS0bgAfuAj61RGIlFZeua1uGXQM9K4qE3Q7dVS3pWcrRu4rBHRaOtyClo3F0zuhpXLqHzctS8ZMY56z-wusN0QIxCLCbWAk0nYL~TEPC1S4xT4uRx5GYtpFx5CP9C8utvyFhJ-VJWNYLjvqypzgTf0jJQZqaRB0bpPGfFO3TNuHtDqDiXDZR7uk1Uw__&Key-Pair-Id=APKAJLOHF5GGSLRBV4ZA

Eurostat (2022). *Self-reported use of home care services by people with severe difficulty in personal care activities by age and household type*. Online data code: HLTH_EHIS_AM7SH. Downloaded in December 2022: https://ec.europa.eu/eurostat/databrowser/view/hlth_ehis_am7sh/default/bar?lang=en

Ghasemzadeh, K., Escobar, O., Yordanova, Z., & Villasalero, M. (2022). User innovation rings the bell for new horizons in e-health: a bibliometric analysis. *European Journal of Innovation Management*. 25(6), 656–686.

Genet, N., Boerma, W., Kroneman, M., Hutchinson, A., Saltman, R. B., & World Health Organization. (2012). *Home care across Europe: current structure and future challenges*. European Observatory and World Health Organization. Regional Office for Europe. Downloaded in December 2022: https://apps.who.int/iris/handle/10665/327948

Glomsås, H. S., Knutsen, I. R., Fossum, M., & Halvorsen, K. (2020). User involvement in the implementation of welfare technology in home care services: The experience of health professionals—A qualitative study. *Journal of clinical nursing*, 29(21–22), 4007–4019.

Grand View Research (2022). *Europe Home Care Market Size, Share & Trends Analysis Report by Component*. Figures highlighted from their consultancy report. Downloaded in December 2022: https://www.grandviewresearch.com/industry-analysis/europe-home care-market

Gupt, Y., & Sahay, S. (2015). Review of extended producer responsibility: A case study approach. *Waste Management & Research*, 33(7), 595–611.

HoCare (2020). *Innovations in home care – bringing innovative home care solutions quicker to the market by using quadruple-helix approach.* A joint thematic study, published 31st of March 2020 as part of an Interreg Europe and funded by the European Regional Development Fund. The report was downloaded in December 2022: https://keep.eu/projects/18778/Delivery-of-Innovative-solu-EN/

Henderson, R. M., & Clark, K. B. (1990). Architectural innovation: The reconfiguration of existing product technologies and the failure of established firms. *Administrative science quarterly*, 35, 9–30.

Home care Association (2020). "An Overview of the UK Home care Market". Downloaded in December 2022:https://www.home.careassociation.org.uk/asset/F8E900CF-C19F-46D5-A90A7018F5980DB4/

Huang, X., Atasu, A., & Toktay, L. B. (2019). Design implications of extended producer responsibility for durable products. *Management Science*, 65(6), 2573–2590.

Iakovleva, T., Oftedal, E. M., & Bessant, J. (2019). *Responsible innovation in digital health*. Edward Elgar Publishing.

King's Fund (2018). *Home care in England. Views from commissioners and providers*. Downloaded in December 2022: https://www.kingsfund.org.uk/sites/default/files/2018-12/Home.care-in-England-report.pdf

Kushniruk, A., & Nøhr, C. (2016). Participatory design, user involvement and health IT evaluation. *Stud Health Technol Inform*, 222, 139–151.

Laudal, T., & Iakovleva, T. (2019). *Patient-initiated innovation-evidence and research agenda*. In Iakovleva, T., Oftedal, E. M., Bessant, J.. "Responsible Innovation in Digital Health". Edward Elgar Publishing.

Living made easy (2022). A database provided by the charity DLF. Accessed in December 2022: https://livingmadeeasy.org.uk/DLF-about-us

Local Government Association (2017). *A smarter approach to digital transformation.* Reported on the website of the association 13th of July 2017. Downloaded in December 2022. https://www.local.gov.uk/case-studies/smarter-approach-digital-transformation

McNichol, E. (2012). Patient-led innovation in healthcare: The value of the 'user'perspective. *International Journal of Healthcare Management*, 5(4), 216–222.

MedTekNorge (2016). "Hjelpemiddelformidling i Norge". Report. Downloaded in December 2022: https://melanor.overcastcdn.com/documents/Hjelpemiddelformidling-i-Norge-publikasjon-april-2016.pdf

Moors, E., Lukkien, D. R., Michalek, T., Hebáková, L., Hennen, L., Scherz, C., Nierling, L., Hahn, J. (2014). Healthcare innovations in an ageing society. *Technology Assessement and Policy Areas of Great Transitions*, 281–288. Proceedings from the PACITA 2013 Conference in Prague.

NAV-Hjelpemidler. Website recommending help for applications. Downloaded in December 2022 from here.

Nextmsc (2022). *Disabled and elderly assistive technologies market.* Figures belong to consultancy report issued by Next Move Strategy Consulting. Downloaded in December 2022: https://www.nextmsc.com/report/disabled-and-elderly-assistive-technologies-market

NHS website: "Getting a need assessment". Downloaded in December 2022:https://www.nhs.uk/conditions/social-care-and-support-guide/help-from-social-services-and-charities/getting-a-needs-assessment/

NHS website: "Household gadgets and equipment to make life easier". Downloaded in December 2022: https://www.nhs.uk/conditions/social-care-and-support-guide/care-services-equipment-and-care-homes/household-gadgets-and-equipment-to-make-life-easier/

NHS website: "Personal alarms, monitoring systems (telecare) and key safes." Downloaded in December 2022 from: https://www.nhs.uk/conditions/social-care-and-support-guide/care-services-equipment-and-care-homes/personal-alarms-security-systems-and-keysafes/

Norges Offentlige Utredninger NOU (2010). *Aktiv deltakelse,likeverd og inkludering. Et helhetlig hjelpemiddeltilbud*. Downloaded in December 2022: https://www.regjeringen.no/contentassets/30d5513459a347718706b98b9f028bf4/no/pdfs/nou201020100005000dddpdfs.pdf

Norwegian Ministry of Health and Care Services (2020). "National Health and Hospital Plan 2020–2023." Downloaded in December 2022: https://www.regjeringen.no/contentassets/95eec808f0434acf942fca449ca35386/en-gb/pdfs/stm201920200007000engpdfs.pdf

Norwegian Smart Care Cluster – NSCC (2016). "Morgendagens hjemmeomsorg. TJenesteforeløpet. Rreise 6.». Downloaded in December 2022 from here.

Oslo Economics (2016). "Vurdering av praksis for offentlige anskaffelser av tekniske hjelpemidler." Downloaded in December 2022. https://www.regjeringen.no/contentassets/2f3ae6c7a2dd4adbae2c2e152af97c3e/rapport-oslo-economics.pdf

Podestá Gaspar, R. D., Bonacin, R., & Gonçalves, V. P. (2018, July). Designing IoT solutions for elderly home care: a systematic study of participatory design, personas and semiotics. *International Conference on Universal Access in Human-Computer Interaction* (pp. 226–245). Springer, Cham.

Schumpeter, J. A. (1942). "Capitalism, Socialism and Democracy". London and New Yorik. Routledge, 5th edition.

Seebode, D., Jeanrenaud, S., & Bessant, J. (2012). Managing innovation for sustainability. *R&d Management*, 42(3), 195–206.

SKR (2018). *Patientkontrakt. Slutrapport. Samarbetsprojekt I tre landsting/regioner.* Region- og Landsting-rapport. Downloaded in December 2022: https://skr.se/download/18.1f376ad3177c89481f745b33/1615362686662/Patientkontrakt_slutrapport_2018-02-14.pdf

Social Care Institute of Excellence (SCIE), 2014. "Commissioning home care for older people". Guide 54. Downloaded in December 2022: https://www.scie.org.uk/publications/guides/guide54/what-older-people-want.asp

Socialstyrelsen in Denmark (2014) *Formidling af hjælpemidler til voksne borgere*. Downloaded in December 2022:https://socialstyrelsen.dk/udgivelser/formidling-af-hjaelpemidler-til-voksne-borgere/@@download/publication

Socialstyrelsen in Sweden (2022). *Statistikdatabas för äldreomsorg*. Downloaded in December 2022: https://sdb.socialstyrelsen.se/if_ald/

Social- og Boligstyrelsen in Denmark (2022). *Hjælpemiddelbasens indhold*. Website text describing the database for aids. Downoladed in December 2022: https://hmi-basen.dk/news.asp?newsid=10689&x_newstype=29

Statens Offentliga Utredningar (SOU) 43. "På lika villkor! Delaktighet, jämlikhet och effektivitet i hjälpmedelsförsörjningen". Green paper published by the Swedish Government. Downloaded in December 2022: https://www.regeringen.se/49c8c5/contentassets/09ba8e1b70554a88a21c6450cc10af8e/sou-2017_43_webb_ta.pdf

Statistisk Sentralbyrå, SSB in Norway (2022). *Sjukeheimar, heimetenester og andre omsorgstenester.* Statistics on home care in Norway. https://www.ssb.no/helse/helsetjenester/statistikk/sjukeheimar-heimetenester-og-andre-omsorgstenester

Stilgoe, J., Owen, R., & Macnaghten, P. (2013). "Developing a framework for responsible innovation." *Research Policy* 42 (9), 1568–1580.

Statens Offentliga Utredningar, SOU in Sweden (2017). *På lika villkor! Delaktighet, jämlikhet och effektivitet i hjälpmedelsförsörjningen.* Green paper commissioned by the Swedish government. Downloaded in December 2022: https://www.regeringen.se/49c8c5/contentassets/09ba8e1b70554a88a21c6450cc10af8e/sou-2017_43_webb_ta.pdf

Swedish Standards Institute, SS 872500:2015 (2017). *Quality of care, service, nursing and rehabilitation for elderly people with extensive needs in ordinary and residential care facilities*. Downloaded in December 2022: http://sfamportal.s3.amazonaws.com/files/5ad0afa39bc2570500fc036a/SS%20872500_2015.pdf

Vácha, T., & Kandusová, V. (2018, May). Making innovation in elderly care possible using participatory design: the smart home-care project in Prague. *In 2018 Smart City Symposium Prague* (SCSP) (pp. 1–6). IEEE.

Von Hippel, E. (2017). Free Innovation by Consumers—How Producers Can Benefit: Consumers' free innovations represent a potentially valuable resource for industrial innovators. *Research-Technology Management*, 60(1), 39–42.

Zhu, L. (2020). *Services of General Economic Interest in EU Competition Law*. T.M.C. Asser Press; 1st ed.

Elin M. Oftedal, Tatiana Iakovleva, John Bessant

Navigating towards improved user engagement in healthcare innovation – releasing the power of users

Abstract: This chapter synthesizes key findings from various studies within the book, emphasizing the pivotal role of boundary innovation spaces—such as living labs and collaborative online platforms—in fostering user inclusion in healthcare innovation processes. These spaces are crucial for enhancing user engagement and aligning innovations with real-world needs through co-creation.

The research highlights that successful boundary innovation spaces are not merely supportive environments but are central to the innovation process, acting as catalysts for user inclusion and adoption of healthcare innovations. These community settings significantly enhance the relevance and applicability of innovations by aligning them more closely with user needs.

Effective management and strategic engagement within these communities are essential for maximizing the potential of user insights and contributions. This chapter advocates for a shift towards more inclusive, community-oriented innovation practices, which are foundational for developing sustainable and user-centered healthcare solutions.

Additionally, the chapter provides comprehensive guidance for policymakers and innovation managers on developing strategies that foster community-driven innovation processes. It underscores the importance of environments that support experimental and non-routine interactions, and the need for tools, methods, leadership, and facilitation that enable these innovative activities.

By integrating these elements, the chapter contributes significantly to the field of healthcare innovation, offering actionable insights that promote inclusive and effective user involvement, thereby ensuring the long-term success of innovation initiatives in healthcare.

Introduction

Users matter in innovation. There is ample evidence that users can contribute at the ideation phase, and that their unique perspective and access to tacit knowledge offers new insights which are hard for non-users to access or generate. In addition, their involvement means that problems around ensuring compatibility of innovations with their adopting populations can be avoided since user inputs help identify and resolve

https://doi.org/10.1515/9783111241036-015

issues of fit. Put simply, user innovation can enhance successful creation and scaling of new products, services, or processes.

Our earlier work also strongly highlighted that users need to be involved in any innovation process which considers itself 'responsible' (Iakovleva et al. 2019; Iakovleva et al. 2021). Inclusion of user perspectives means that their concerns as well as their insights are explored and resolved and enhances the chance of successful adoption and diffusion. This is particularly relevant as we week to exploit powerful opportunities opened up by new technologies in the digital space; without user inclusion we might end up with technology that does not solve and may even amplify the problems they purport to solve.

The challenge comes because not every user is an active innovator; indeed the participation of users in the innovation process can be seen as distributed along a spectrum from passive recipients of innovation through to active 'hero' innovators prepared to engage fully with creating and developing innovations (Bessant et al. 2019). This spectrum serves as a map and our attention is particularly drawn to those positioned on the left-hand side of this spectrum—users whose potential influence remains untapped, whose voices are waiting to be amplified.

This endeavor requires us to rethink our approach to user engagement, to devise methods that not only invite but also valorize user participation. It compels us to ask: How can we more effectively **articulate** the insights of users, ensuring their voices are not just heard but heeded? How can we **amplify** their contributions, ensuring they resonate throughout the innovation ecosystem? And ultimately, how can we **act** upon these insights, co-creating with users in a manner that harnesses their full potential and propels innovation forward?

Boundary innovation spaces

It's not just a question of asking users for their opinions. User engagement is a process and we have been particularly interested in the role of environments to enable this, places where the innovation conversation takes place and where co-creation amongst stakeholders can happen. We call these *'boundary innovation spaces'* and they encompass a wide array of environments from tangible, physical locations to transient gatherings like hackathons, and extends into the realms of online and virtual reality spaces. These diverse settings are unified by their foundational purpose: to furnish space, alongside facilitating processes and tools, that nurture dialogue and collaborative creation.

In this landscape, a myriad of innovators and researchers are pioneering varied approaches to engage participants within collaborative spaces like fab labs, open labs, studios, and notably, living labs. These environments bridge organizational divides, fostering collaboration among diverse actors to co-create groundbreaking solutions

(Caccamo, 2020; Fritzsche, 2018). Since their rise in popularity in the early 2000s, living labs have been distinguished for their immersion in real-world contexts, their openness, and their commitment to user-driven innovation (Almirall et al., 2012; Leminen et al., 2011; Leminen & Westerlund, 2019). They are designed to prioritize the user experience, promote the exchange of knowledge, and tackle intricate issues in technology and society, such as sustainability, head-on.

As the concept of boundary spaces matures, there is an evolving discourse and accumulating experience regarding the various ways these environments can be structured and managed. Physical and virtual spaces go beyond serving as mere venues, platforms, and frameworks for collaborative research and development and innovation efforts. They crucially mold the cognitive processes of participants engaged in innovation, impacting how collaboration is facilitated and new knowledge is created (Clark, 2008; Fundneider and Peschl, 2012). These environments play a pivotal role in the innovation journey, influencing the generation, development, and exchange of ideas among collaborators. Boundary spaces should be more than physical confines sometimes decorated with unique architecture and artifacts; they, in fact, embody multifaceted dimensions including space, time, and a place where trust – relations are built and explored.

There is an emerging understanding that the efficacy of boundary spaces is linked to their evolution and capability to foster conversations and co-creation, underpinned by ongoing reflection and development. Living Labs exemplify this, drawing on decades of experience to underscore the significance of a well-established platform. Amidst the current surge in the establishment of Innovation Labs, there's a cautionary note against their potential to devolve into mere symbols of "innovation theatre," transiently existing as fashionable embellishments rather than enduring instruments of innovation.

Luckly, recently, the places and spaces where innovation activities unfold have emerged as significant subjects of academic inquiry (Leminen et al., 2016, 2020). These diverse environments—spanning physical, virtual, and cognitive realms—provide fertile ground for citizens and various stakeholders to collaborate and co-create innovative solutions. Leminen et al. (2024) introduce a matrix to analyze innovation spaces, categorizing them by two distinct dimensions: their *type* of physical contra virtual space and the *nature of collaboration* they facilitate, distinguished by group or community.

Type of collaboration

These spaces, whether physical or virtual, significantly influence the dynamics and success of collaborative efforts. Physical environments are lauded for encouraging direct interaction and creativity, vital for accommodating diverse participant needs (Oksanen and Ståhle, 2013). Virtual spaces, contrastingly, offer flexibility and support for dispersed teams, differentiating between emergent spaces that develop organically and designed spaces that are purpose-built (Leminen et al., 2021; Leminen et al., 2020). These environments are instrumental in fostering user engagement and scaling collaboration (Füller et al., 2007; Enkel et al., 2020).

Extending this line of thinking and based on our observations of empirical settings in the chapters of this book, we suggest that the spectrum of spaces can be more nuanced in relation to their type, stretching from physical, to blended, to fully virtual. During the COVID-19 pandemic, many boundary spaces began to incorporate user involvement through digital platforms and the application of digital tools. What remains post-COVID is that blended methods have become the new norm, as evidenced by our case studies of the Norwegian Smart Care Lab (Chapter 4) and LiCallab (Chapter 3). Furthermore, in the case of the Digital Futures Lab (Chapter 8), it is evident that digital technologies, which are tested and experimented with, reinforce this blending of both physical spaces and the utilization of virtual tools. Similarly, in the chapters describing firms' practices in user involvement, such as the Morphic case (Chapter 13) and Norwegian Healthtech firms (Chapter 12), user interaction also occurred through both physical interactions and digital platforms.

Collaboration dynamics

The second dimension, *collaboration dynamics*, according to Leminen et al. (2001), distinguishes between group-level and community-level collaborative innovation. Group-level collaboration involves small teams focusing on interactions that streamline decision-making (Leminen et al., 2021). Community-level collaboration, on the other hand, encompasses larger groups or ecosystems, fostering a wide idea range and collective ownership by integrating diverse perspectives (Nyström et al., 2014; Leminen et al., 2017a, 2020). This spectrum allows for varying depths of collaboration, from intimate groups to expansive communities.

Throughout the examples in this book, we can see the role of communities in successful user inclusion process, both for boundary innovation spaces as well as for the individual companies. Crucially, the success of inclusion valuable inputs from users is contingent upon their integration with the broader ecosystem, moving beyond the confines of isolated, "island" – environments. A key element in this appears to be the idea of building wider communities within which the boundary space can operate. Research by Von Hippel (2005) and colleagues (Jeppesen and Molin, 2003) has shed light on innovation communities, emphasizing the significance of user involvement as a core source of innovation. Such communities, defined by Von Hippel as networks of individuals or firms linked by information transfer, whether through face-to-face or electronic means, play a crucial role in the innovation process. These communities are not necessarily formal membership groups but are characterized by their continuity and the free exchange of innovative ideas, which others find valuable.

This approach to innovation highlights the concept of "sticky information" — the idea that knowledge about user needs and manufacturer capabilities is highly contextual and challenging to transfer (Von Hippel, 1998, 2005). Innovation communities serve as a solution to this problem by creating a platform for the free flow of information, thereby aligning the interests of users and producers in a mutually beneficial manner.

Heiskanen (2010) discusses how the literature on communities of practice (CoP) further enriches our understanding of how such communities operate, with the knowledge created within these communities being deeply embedded and shared through continuous practice (Wenger, 1998; Lave & Wenger, 1991). Heiskanen (2010) unwraps four types of user communities ranging from

1. **Local or Neighborhood-based Communities (Type 1):** Focuses on specific local issues or interests, often within a localized setting such as a specific neighborhood, or user group.
2. **Stakeholder-driven Communities (Type 2):** Comprises various parties with a vested interest in particular outcomes, emphasizing collaboration among diverse stakeholders, including large and small retailers, NGOs, experts, and consumers
3. **User-centric Communities (Type 3):** Where the innovation or service directly involves or affects the users, such as patients and caregivers in healthcare innovation. he innovation directly involves users (healthcare professionals) who are integral to the design and implementation process, focusing on their specific needs and experiences.
4. **Transdisciplinary Communities (Type 4):** a broader ambition of some projects, where innovation crosses traditional boundaries. Cross traditional boundaries to include diverse expertise and perspectives for innovation, facilitating collaborative ecosystems that serve as idea incubators at the crossroads of diverse fields like healthcare, technology, and social sciences. Transdisciplinary communities aim to merge diverse expertise across fields to tackle complex problems holistically. For addressing issues like climate change and public health that might sometimes be required. Success requires creating common spaces for dialogue, institutional support for cross-disciplinary work, effective leadership to manage diversity, and flexible approaches to integrate varied contributions. Examples include multidisciplinary research initiatives and innovation hubs that demonstrate the potential for transdisciplinary efforts to produce innovative, comprehensive solutions. Despite challenges, these communities represent a promising frontier for advancing knowledge and addressing global challenges.

We adopted the useful typology suggested by Heiskanen (2010) to enhance the contingency of the collaboration dynamic offered by Lemening et al (2021). In our chapters, we present illustrative examples for the four types of collaboration in figure 1. Two chapters in our book, based on the case of Citizen Lab in the Netherlands, clearly can be categorized as neighborhood engagement communities. Chapter 5, "Age-Friendly

Living," utilizes citizen science to engage older adults in the Dutch neighbourhood of Schelhorst, focusing on creating age-friendly living conditions in that particular neighbourhood. The project evolved around a shared community feeling that Schelhorst is a very pleasant neighbourhood to live in. However, there were complaints about the fences and the lack of plants in the streets, as illustrated by one user's citation: *"It doesn't look good, I'm ashamed of the street when my family comes to visit."* Similarly, some of the projects described in Chapter 7, "TopFit Citizen Lab," also refer to neighbourhood communities.

Furthermore, several chapters illustrate a stakeholder-driven approach. For instance, the NSCL, as detailed in Chapter 4, is organized by regional stakeholders such as the county, University of Stavanger, and Stavanger Hospital. It was initiated to enhance the role of regional actors in digital health innovations. Another example is the virtual platforms organized as an urgent response to help Ukrainian refugees. These platforms are either user-community driven or stakeholder-community driven and often include individuals who can utilize technologies to foster problem-solving in crisis situations. This research interestingly emphasizes that stakeholder-driven platforms have a better chance of success compared to purely user-driven ones, as they rely on a broader inclusion of relevant competencies.

Perhaps the majority of our cases can be classified into user-centric communities. Starting from a very fascinating patient-driven innovation platform that was started in in Portugal but become truly international with user innovations from over 100 different countries (Chapter 11), through firm-related cases like Morphic (Chapter 13) and Norwegian Healthtechs (Chapter 12), which primarily focus on user inclusion in the innovation process on the firm level. As pointed out by one of the informants in the study of Norwegian high-tech firms, *"we believe that the solution, or the way to find the solution, is to involve the users themselves. It is also about how you involve them; you have to see the problem from all sides of the table and then involve the users themselves, right."* This category also includes a study of the innovation hub in a UK hospital (Chapter 9), where the users were healthcare professionals themselves, as well as LiCalab (Chapter 3), which developed a truly user-centric approach with a strong panel of users (over 1000 users).

Finally, we placed Chapter 2, which provides a historical overview of innovations in the health sector, into the category of transdisciplinary communities, as these often span across various fields. Additionally, Chapter 6 falls into this type as well; in this chapter, citizens were asked to fulfill the role of experts in conducting research, necessitating a transdisciplinary approach.

The alignment of interests between users and producers within these different communities is not always straightforward, as highlighted by various studies (Namioka and Schuler, 1993). Whilst the members of community may not participate in every project they represent the diverse population who can feed the innovation process. As many of our examples demonstrate a wider community provides the supporting context for effective boundary spaces. In many cases the physical nature of the

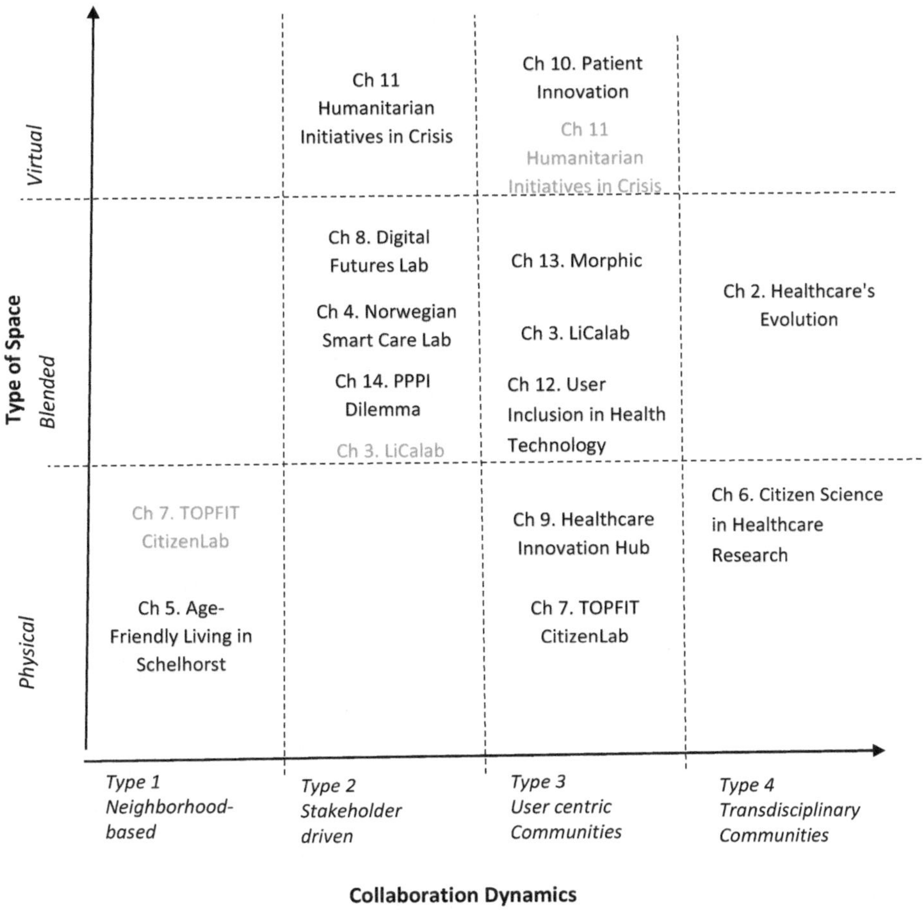

Figure 1: Boundary Innovation Space and Community Typology.

boundary space was of low importance – they could even be temporary in nature as long as they served the function of providing a node around which conversations and co-creation could take place.

We need to understand more about how such communities are formed, how they are focused on a shared purpose (communities of practice) and the varieties of relationship which can emerge to co-create innovation – even, at the limit, without the focus of a physical boundary space.

In summary, the discourse on boundary innovation spaces and user-inclusive innovation communities underlines the need for a deeper understanding of community formation, shared goals, and the multifaceted relationships that can foster innovation. Our finding are in line with previous research, including works by Von Hippel (2005),

Jeppesen and Molin (2003), and others, highlighting the complex interplay between physical spaces, community dynamics, and the iterative process of innovation.

Take aways: how to enhance user inclusion in healthcare innovations

We can summarize a few key take aways of user empowerment in healthcare innovations. First, we underscore the impotence of the community building. While a boundary innovation space might provide the infrastructure for innovation, it's the community within that drives progress. Focused projects serve as a catalyst for collaboration, bringing together individuals around shared objectives. However, it's essential to distinguish that a lab facilitates projects but doesn't equate to the community itself. Based on this we can draw some conclusions:

Highlighting diversity in community engagement: Our framework showcases the wide range of community types involved in healthcare innovation, from local neighborhood-based groups to transdisciplinary communities. This diversity underscores the multifaceted nature of user involvement and the need for approaches that are flexible and adaptive to different community contexts.

Empowering users through active participation: Across the various types of communities, a common theme is the empowerment of users—whether they are patients, caregivers, healthcare professionals, or residents. By actively involving users in the innovation process, from ideation to implementation, these communities help ensure that the resulting products and services are more attuned to real-world needs and challenges, thereby increasing their effectiveness and acceptance.

Ensuring continuity: Balancing the temporary with the long-term. Navigating the balance between temporary initiatives and long-term strategies is crucial for the sustainability of the innovation space. While short-term projects can generate immediate impacts, a long-term vision is necessary for enduring change and strategic growth within the ecosystem. In summary, an effective boundary innovation space transcends the conventional, fostering an environment that encourages experimentation, supports robust collaboration, and nurtures a vibrant community committed to innovation. Through strategic commitment, the right mix of tools, and an inclusive approach, these spaces can become powerhouses of creativity and innovation, driving advancements that are both meaningful and impactful.

Demonstrating the value of cross-disciplinary collaboration: The chapters that focus on transdisciplinary communities (Type 4) particularly underscore the importance of bringing together diverse fields—such as technology, healthcare, social sciences, and design—to foster innovative solutions. These boundary innovation spaces are crucial for nurturing creativity, enabling rapid feedback, and incorporating user-centric design principles, thereby driving responsible and inclusive innovation practices.

Challenges and barriers of user inclusion

We have identified that several chapters include resource constraints, complex stakeholder dynamics, ethical and privacy concerns, difficulties in measuring the impact of user-driven innovations, and challenges in integrating user feedback and ensuring inclusivity and diversity. These challenges underscore the multifaceted nature of integrating user perspectives into the traditional innovation process and highlight the necessity of navigating these obstacles to foster inclusive, effective, and sustainable innovation practices.

In healthcare and technology, user-driven innovation faces significant *barriers* due to resource constraints, stakeholder dynamics, ethics, and evaluation challenges. Smaller organizations struggle to allocate the necessary resources for comprehensive user testing, recruitment, and sustaining diverse user panels, exacerbating the difficulty of engaging users effectively. Balancing the needs and interests of various stakeholders, including patients, caregivers, clinicians, industry representatives, and regulatory authorities, presents a complex task that can impede innovation trajectories if misaligned.

A significant focus is placed on the *ethical imperative of user inclusion* in digital health technology development. This approach aims to tailor solutions to meet the actual needs of stakeholders like patients and caregivers, despite the challenges in integrating these innovations into healthcare and technology sectors. The influence of regulations on fostering or hindering innovation is also discussed, emphasizing the need for strategic resource allocation to support user-centric and responsible innovation practices. *Ethical considerations and compassion*, ensure that technology serves to enhance rather than detract from the human elements of healthcare. This ethical lens is further applied in discussions around responsible innovation, where the potential repercussions of technological advancements are scrutinized, committing to innovations that contribute positively to societal well-being.

In chapter 2 we suggested a pragmatic view of Responsible Innovation, to navigate the real-world complexities of technological advancement, market pressures, and regulatory landscapes. We also underscore the importance of the ethics of care and capability approach to healthcare. This approach extends beyond critiquing traditional idealistic perspectives on responsible innovation, which can pose challenges for firms. It encourages firms to explore various avenues for user inclusion while also prioritizing methods that align with their unique needs and capabilities.

The chapter focusing on the living labs, such as the Citizen Lab, Licalab, Norwegian Smart Care Lab and also the Patient Innovation initiative embody the concept of PRI through their emphasis on helping the firms reach the users through their user focused activities.

The experiences of creating and sustaining boundary innovation spaces in the UK, as well as the challenges and solutions proposed in the Laudal chapter for home care equipment innovation, further illustrate PRI's application. These examples showcase the necessity of dialogue, flexibility, and adaptability in nurturing inclusive and empathetic innovation environments, and the strategic integration of responsible innovation practices to balance public provision with user-driven innovation needs.

In essence, Pragmatic Responsible Innovation champions a methodical, inclusive approach to technological development. It positions ethical foresight, stakeholder engagement, and interdisciplinary dialogue at the core of crafting innovations that are technologically effective, ethically responsible, and socially attuned. Through its practical application across diverse contexts—from participatory labs and MSPs to boundary innovation spaces—PRI underscores the vital role of placing users at the heart of innovation, ensuring that new technologies are developed with a deep respect for societal values and needs.

Looking to the future

We've tried in this book to reflect experience in exploring different ways in which such user voices can be ***articulated, amplified, and used*** in the co-creation process around user innovation. But there remain a few questions which would benefit from further research.

Motivation and the 'free innovation' challenge for firms?

Users are only one part of the innovation development system; there is a need also to reflect on the co-creation opportunities opened up to firms if they draw in the valuable insights and ideas from this community. The growing literature on user innovation and particularly the 'free innovation' model (Von Hippel, 2016) shows the potential but also raises a challenge. In principle there are significant advantages to companies to engage with it – it provides low risk inputs to the front end of innovation in terms of novel ideas, tested prototypes, and access to a community of early adopters and lead users with whom further development work is possible. And it assures faster and more effective diffusion of innovations downstream because questions of compatibility can be resolved through including user insights ('sticky' tacit knowledge) about the context into which the innovation will fit. Additionally, the role of user innovators as influencers helps deal with the 'homophily' challenge identified by Rogers – we are more likely to adopt innovations when they are offered to us by people like us (Rogers, 2003)

Yet there appears to be resistance and reluctance on the part of companies to this offer. Of course, 'free innovation' is not really that; engagement with users will require time and opportunity cost and potentially slow down decision-making processes. But we need to understand further the problem around this – what might affect motivation to adopt such an approach? Boundary spaces, especially neutral shared facilities like Living Labs, Smart Care Cluster, etc., can provide an enabling context for such a process but what else is needed? Why do companies use such facilities and what has their experience been? What else would be needed to enable the more extensive operation of the free innovation approach?

Emotional barriers to user involvement – how to make safe spaces?

One of the big challenges we have tried to explore is the 'how' question around releasing the power of users. We've explored mechanisms which can help articulate, amplify and enable co-creation and draw in a wider pool of users than those who are active 'hero' innovators operating at the extreme end of our spectrum. But there remain questions around participation which we need to explore further. Providing enabling tools and methods in a supporting environment is clearly not sufficient and there is a need to explore further some of the affective dimensions of user participation.

For example a key feature of a laboratory environment is that it offers a 'safe' space within which to experiment. But translating this concept of safety to user perceptions of the value of participation might be important as a future research direction. What are the anxieties which potential user innovators may feel and how might these be addressed in the design of future arrangements to enable co-creation?

Multi-layer markets – who are users and their role in decision-making?

Healthcare is among several sectors where the process of making decisions about innovation is notably complex. Whereas consumer goods and business-to-business innovation usually involves clearly identifiable end-users who have decision making power this is often not the case in social markets. Instead, they represent what could be called multi-layer markets in which the purchasing decision and the resource commitment decision making are often distributed across different players – there are multiple target markets and there may be very different value propositions associated with each layer. This is a challenge in many public sector activities where adoption is by key agents who are not the end user (Gray and Bessant, 2024). An educational innovation, for example, may have impact on the learning of the student but the adoption decision will be made (or at least influenced) by procurement agencies inside ministries of education, local school leaders and teachers – all of whom have 'user voices' which could shape the innovation in the ways we have been describing in the book. How to work with all of these users – and especially the end user who is often a passive recipient is a key challenge. It is faced by humanitarian and development agencies where there is growing concern that innovation still has an element of '*we know best*' and that end user voices are not being heard.

This multi-layer dimension is explicitly address in chapter 14 written by Thomas Laudal, where he underlines complexity of interactions and challenges inherent in public-private partnerships, particularly in how these relationships manage to balance public interests with private investment objectives." (cross reference Thomas Laudal). This is also an interesting avenue for further research.

Peer to peer learning in communities and labs?

Boundary spaces like Living Labs are not a new concept even if the label is. Some have been operating for decades and we have managed to capture some of the rich experience in this book which highlights common practices, shared tools and other valuable routines derived from this experience. As the concept of boundary spaces becomes more popular and there is continuing experimentation it becomes important to recognise the value of such peer-to-peer learning. Boundary spaces focused on challenges like healthcare offer rich opportunities for mobilising an effective community of practice which can accelerate the learning and sharing of good practice, amplify the possibilities of shared experimentation.

Communities of practice, like the European Network of Living Labs, act as catalysts for the broader adoption of the boundary space model to boost user involvement in innovation. This book aims to nurture and spread understanding of fostering boundary innovation spaces, and to highlight the primary challenges and support their growth. Delving deeper into the formation of such communities and the acceleration of their operational routines, particularly in shared experimentation and the creation of innovative working methods, would be beneficial.

Conclusion

Addressing societal needs is not just the responsibility of the market or individual entities but requires collective action. This involves collaboration between governments, non-profit organizations, communities, and businesses. The cost of user inclusion can therefore perhaps be reduced by awareness of the concept of responsibility. The concept of training all members of society to take responsibility for societal welfare is a profound and crucial idea, particularly in the context of our rapidly evolving world. This notion underscores the belief that every individual, regardless of their role or position, has a part to play in shaping and maintaining the health and well-being of their community and society at large. The importance of this training and awareness encompasses several key aspects:

- Cultivating a sense of community and shared responsibility: Training all societal actors to be responsible citizens fosters a sense of community and collective re-

sponsibility. It emphasizes that the actions of each individual can have a significant impact on the broader society. This awareness encourages people to act ethically and considerately, not just for personal gain but for the common good.
- Empowering individuals to make positive changes: Educating and empowering every member of society with the skills and knowledge to contribute positively can lead to widespread social improvements. People are more likely to take initiative and engage in actions that benefit others, such as participating in community service, being environmentally conscious, or advocating for social justice.
- Enabling resilience in times of crisis: Societies where members are trained to be responsible and proactive are better equipped to handle crises. People are more likely to come together, support each other, and find innovative solutions to challenges.

In summary, training all actors of society to take responsibility is not just about creating a more ethical and conscientious population; it's about building the foundation for a more resilient, inclusive, and sustainable society. This approach equips individuals with the mindset and tools necessary to contribute positively to their communities and the world at large.

References

Almirall, E., Lee, M., & Wareham, J. (2012). Mapping Living Labs in the Landscape of Innovation Methodologies. *Technology Innovation Management Review*, *2*(9), 12–18. DOI: 10.22215/timreview/603

Bessant, J., Maher, L., 2009. Developing radical service innovations in healthcare: the role of design methods. Int. J. Innov. Manag. 13, 555–568.

Bessant, J., Iakovleva, T., & Oftedal, E. M. (2019). Chapter 15: The Future of Responsible Innovation. In J. Bessant, T. Iakovleva, & E. M. Oftedal (Eds.), *Responsible Innovation in Digital Health Empowering the Patient* (pp. 232/250). Edward Elgar Publishing.

Caccamo, M. (2020). Leveraging innovation spaces to foster collaborative innovation. *Creativity and Innovation Management*, *29*(3). DOI: 10.1111/caim.12357

Clark, A. (2008). Supersizing The Mind: Embodiment, Action, and Cognitive Extension. Oxford University Press, USA. DOI: 10.1093/acprof:oso/9780195333213.001.0001

Enkel, E., Gassmann, O., Chesbrough, H., 2020. Open R&D and open innovation: exploring the phenomenon. R&D Management 50, 175–184.

Fritzsche, H., Barbazzeni, B., Mahmeen, M., Haider, S., & Friebe, M. (2021). A structured pathway toward disruption: A novel HealthTec innovation design curriculum with entrepreneurship in mind. *Frontiers in Public Health*, *9*, Article 715768. https://doi.org/10.3389/fpubh.2021.715768

Fritzsche, A., Jonas, J., Roth, A., Moeslein, K., 2020. Innovating in the open lab: The new potential for interactive value creation across organizational boundaries. Oldenbourg: De Gruyter.

Füller, J., Jawecki, G., Mühlbacher, H., 2007. Innovation creation by online basketball communities. J. Bus. Res. 60, 60–71.

Fundneider, T., & Peschl, M. F. (2012). Enabling Spaces. Space impacts organization and vice versa. In S. Jeschke, F. Hees, A. Richert, & S. Trantow (Eds.), *Prethinking Work. Insights on the future of work* (pp. 73ff). Berlin, Zurich: Lit Verlag.

Heiskanen, E., Hyysalo, S., Kotro, T., & Repo, P. (2010). Constructing innovative users and user-inclusive innovation communities. *Technology Analysis and Strategic Management*, *22*(4), 495–511. DOI: 10.1080/09537321003714568

Iakovleva, T., Bessant, J., Oftedal, E.M., 2019. Responsible innovation in digital health. Edward Elgar Publishing.

Iakovleva, T., Oftedal, E., & Bessant, J. (2021). Changing Role of Users – Innovating Responsibly in Digital Health. Sustainability, 13(4), 1616.

Ian Gray and John Bessant, 2024, 'The scaling value playbook', de Gruyter, Berlin

Jeppesen, L. B., & Molin, M. J. (2003). Consumers as co-developers: Learning and innovation outside the firm. *Technology Analysis & Strategic Management*, *15*(3), 363–383.

Lave, J., & Wenger, E. (1991). Lave, J., & Wenger, E. (1991) Situated Learning: Legitimate Peripheral Participation. Cambridge: Cambridge University Press. http://dx.doi.org/10.1017/CBO9780511815355

Leminen, S., De Vita, K., Westerlund, M., & Ritala, P. (2024). Places and spaces of collaborative R&D and innovation: navigating the role of physical and virtual contexts. *R&D Management*, *54*(2), 201–213

Leminen, S., Westerlund, M., & Nyström, A.-G. (2012). Living Labs as open-innovation networks. *Technology Innovation Management Review*, *2*(9), 6–11.

Leminen, S., & Westerlund, M. (2019). Living labs: From scattered initiatives to a global movement. *Creativity and Innovation Management*. Advance online publication. https://doi.org/10.1111/caim.12310

Leminen, S., Westerlund, M., Nyström, A.-G., 2011. Living labs as open innovation networks. Technol. Innov. Manag. Rev. 1, 20–26.

Leminen, S., Nyström, A. G., Westerlund, M., & Kortelainen, M. J. (2016). The effect of network structure on radical innovation in living labs. *Journal of Business & Industrial Marketing*, *31*(6), 743–757.

Leminen, S., Rajahonka, M., & Westerlund, M. (2017) Towards Third-Generation Living Lab Networks in Cities. Technology Innovation Management Review, 7(11): 21–35. URL: http://doi.org/10.22215/timreview/1118

Leminen, S., Rajahonka, M., Wendelin, R., & Westerlund, M. (2020). Industrial Internet of Things Business Models in the Machine-to-Machine Context. *Industrial Marketing Management*, *84*, 298–311.

Leminen, S., Nyström, A.-G., & Westerlund, M. (2021). Change processes in open innovation networks – Exploring living labs. *Industrial Marketing Management*, *91*, 701–718. https://doi.org/10.xxxxx/yyyy

Nyström, A.-G., Leminen, S., & Westerlund, M. (2014). Actor roles and role patterns influencing innovation in living labs. *European Journal of Innovation Management*, *17*(4), 480–499. European Journal of Innovation Management.

Oksanen, K., & Ståhle, P. (2013). Physical environment as a source for innovation: Investigating the attributes of innovative space. *Journal of Knowledge Management*, *17*(7), 815–827. https://doi.org/10.1108/JKM-04-2013-0136

Rogers, E. M. (2003). *Diffusion of innovation*. Free Press.

Schuler, D., & Namioka, A. (Eds.). (1993). *Participatory design: Principles and practices*. Lawrence Erlbaum Associates, Inc.

Von Hippel, E. (1998). Economics of product development by users: The impact of "sticky" local information. *Management Science*, *44*(5), 629–644.

Von Hippel, E. (2005). Democratizing innovation: The evolving phenomenon of user innovation. *JfB*, *55*, 63–78. https://doi.org/10.1007/s11301-004-0002-8

von Hippel, E. (2016). Free Innovation The MIT Press. https://doi.org/10.7551/mitpress/9780262035217.001.0001

Wenger, E. (1998). *Communities of Practice: Learning, Meaning, and Identity*. Cambridge: Cambridge University Press.

List of contributors

Ingrid Adriaensen holds master's degrees in business management and communication. Throughout her career, she built a large experience in (international) sales, with a focus on business development, strategy and communication. At Thomas More University of Applied Sciences, Ingrid lectured in the business management program. At the research group/living lab LiCalab, Ingrid consults businesses and organisations about innovation projects in healthcare and facilitates the collaboration with and between companies, care organisations, knowledge institutes/academia, end users and other actors. This role also includes the management of (international) projects. Her motivation is making the right fit between healthcare solutions and citizens and care providers, ensuring full inclusion, for both digital skills and accessible communication.

Joana Afonso is a Registered Nurse in Portugal, with professional experience in both palliative care and thoracic vascular surgery at Centro Hospitalar Lisboa Central. In 2018, she founded Careceiver, a platform dedicated to providing care management, training, and information for informal caregivers. Recognizing the potential of technology to enhance patient care and streamline healthcare processes, Joana explores intersections of technology and entrepreneurship within the nursing field. Apart from her clinical and entrepreneurial activities, Joana is involved in research and education serving as a Scientific Reviewer for the Journal of Nursing: Projetar Enfermagem and is currently pursuing a nursing specialty and master's degree in Rehabilitation Nursing at Escola Superior de Saúde Egas Moniz. Understanding the significance of research, Joana has also enrolled in the Clinical Investigator Education program offered by the Association for Professional Training and Research of the University of Aveiro and NOVA Medical School. Currently, Joana is also a research fellow at Nova SBE for the Open and User Innovation Knowledge center, where she collaborates with Patient Innovation Association, gaining valuable experience in user innovation in healthcare. Through this program, Joana deepened her understanding of clinical research methodologies and applied them to help develop novel solutions that address the evolving needs of patients and caregivers.

John Bessant, Originally a chemical engineer, has been active in the field of research and consultancy in technology and innovation management for over 40 years. He is Emeritus Professor of Innovation and Entrepreneurship at the University of Exeter and also has visiting appointments at the universities of Stavanger, Norway and the Friedrich-Alexander University at Erlangen-Nürnberg, Germany. He has acted as advisor to various national governments, to international bodies including the United Nations, The World Bank and the OECD and to a wide range of companies. He is the author of over 40 books and monographs and many articles on the topic; the most recent including Managing innovation (now in its 8th edition), Creativity for innovation management (2023, Routledge, 2nd edition) and Scaling value (2023, De Gruyter).

Leen Broeckx holds a master's degree in communication science and a master's degree in Cultural Studies. In 2013, Leen joined the LiCalab team at Thomas More University of Applied Sciences as panel manager. Her role within the team is to manage and guide the panel of more than 350 citizens, care organisations and caregivers. She supervises the living lab activities: from recruitment, scenario writing, guiding group discussions and real life tests through the processing the results. Leen champions Human Centered Design and she strongly believes in the participatory approach to healthcare innovation.

https://doi.org/10.1515/9783111241036-016

Helena Canhão is the Dean of NOVA Medical School, Universidade Nova de Lisboa. She is a Full Professor of Medicine, Coordinator of the Research Unit Comprehensive Health Research Center (CHRC), and Head of the Associated Laboratory REAL. She is the President of the Portuguese Medical Schools' Council (CEMP) for 2023-2024. She is Chair of the Advisory Council of AICIB and Chair of the Advisory Council of the Collaborative Laboratory Value for Health. Helena Canhão is also Senior Rheumatology Consultant, Head of the Rheumatology Unit at CHULC- Hospital Santo Antonio dos Capuchos, Lisboa. She is Portuguese Society of Rheumatology president, and co-leader and Chief Medical Officer at Patient Innovation.

Helena holds an MD, PhD and Habillitation in Medicine (Rheumatology) from Faculdade de Medicina, Universidade de Lisboa. She is also Master in Medical Sciences (Clinical Research) by Harvard Medical School, University of Harvard, Boston, USA.

She supervised 16 PhD students and 4 post-doc researchers. She is PI of several international and national funded research projects. She is the author and co-author of various books and book chapters and more than 200 research papers indexed in PubMed/Medline. She is member of different international and national networks, acts as reviewer and associate editor of international journals. She was awarded by several distinctions such as Prize Clinical Medicine Bial 2008, Harvard Portugal Program senior clinical researcher award 2009, Grand Prize Bial 2016, and she is one of the female scientists in the book "100 women in science", Ciência Viva, and elected for Mediterranean Science Team 2023. Her research interests are related with epidemiology, implementation research, health innovation, digital health, ageing and rheumatic diseases.

Luís Correia is a second-year student in Biomedical Technology at Instituto Politécnico de Setúbal interned at Nova SBE for the Open and User Innovation Knowledge center, collaborating with the Patient Innovation Association, contributed to promoting and invigorating of the Patient Innovation Bootcamp initiative.

Outside of his academic and professional pursuits, Luís volunteers his time as an ambulance crew member, lifeguard, and firefighter, reflecting his commitment to community service and making a positive impact beyond the academic and professional spheres. With a passion for leveraging technology to enhance patient care and a dedication to serving his community.

Annouck De Cat holds a master's degree in rehabilitation sciences and physiotherapy and a master's degree in health care management and policy. She joined the LiCalab team at Thomas More University of Applied Sciences in early 2023 as panel manager. She is passionate about design thinking, innovation, and the living lab approach. Her experience in health care, education and business analysis is an asset in managing the LiCalab panel database and in setting up living lab activities. Together with the team, she submits ethical applications for studies, drafts protocols, does recruitment for activities and conducts co-creation sessions, real life testing, human factor studies and surveys. Finally, she engages in reporting on these activities.

Nele A. J. De Witte works at the Centre of Expertise Care and Well-being at Thomas More University of Applied Sciences. She holds a PhD in Psychology and has over 10 years of research experience, mostly in practice-oriented research. She is the scientific coordinator of LiCalab - which uses living lab research to support companies and organisations in the health and care sector to co-create, evaluate and test innovative solutions with users in their own living and working environment. At LiCalab, Dr. De Witte is committed to the scientific valorization of living lab methodologies and supports the design of user research. She is also a senior researcher in the research line Psychology and Technology, with specialization in digital mental health, attitudes towards technology, and implementation. Additionally, Dr. De Witte coordinates the course on Digital Psychology in the department of Applied Psychology at Thomas More.

Kristian Eiken holds a master's degree in change management from the University of Stavanger where he graduated in 2023. During his tenure at the master's program, he became a part of Norwegian Smart Care Lab with responsibility for further development of the user panel. In addition, he has a passion for renewal and for finding the gold in situations, people, processes and products. This led to him focusing upon innovation in addition to how people perceive and experience the innovative mechanisms within start-ups. Currently, he works as a consultant in Capgemini Invent where he is a part of the Workforce & Organisation department.

Misha Gipsman Zeldin is a researcher, lecturer and manager with degrees in business administration, psychology, economics, and management.

Dr. Matthew Halkes provides clinical leadership for innovation and digital transformation at Torbay and South Devon NHS Foundation Trust, an integrated provider of health and social care serving the population of Torbay and South Devon, UK. His role supports the creation of organisational culture and adoption of innovation best practice that enables the Trust to achieve its strategic objective of continuously improving the delivery of care. His particular focus has been on digital healthcare and the development and scaling of digital technologies that empower patients to self-manage and monitor their health conditions (Health and Care Video Library and the CONNECTPlus app). This has been achieved through working in partnership with Health and Care Innovations Ltd. Dr. Halkes also acts as Clinical Director for the company, providing useful insight into interaction between the public and private sector. Alongside colleagues, he has also been instrumental in supporting the creation of the Digital Futures. This incubator hub brings together clinical teams, academia, industry and patients in order to explore the role of digital technologies in the delivery of healthcare.

Judy Hong Huang is a PhD candidate at the University of Stavanger School of Business and Law. With master's degrees in business administration specializing in Innovation, as well as Mass Communications, Judy is currently working on a research project titled 'Releasing the Power of Users-articulating user interests to accelerate new innovative pathways in digital health and welfare sector' funded by the Research Council of Norway. Her research delves into user involvement in collaborative innovation spaces, particularly focusing on living labs. Additionally, she shares her knowledge and insights by teaching master's degree courses in business innovation and entrepreneurship at the University of Stavanger. Prior to her doctoral studies, she gained experience in product innovation within the marketing department of a multinational company.

Denis Iagodin since 2021 at Teplitsa of Social Technologies, previously engaged in healthcare innovation and political activism in Eastern Europe. His work focuses on civil society, leveraging big data for project development. He uses a practical approach to enhance societal outcomes through strategic analysis and implementation. His background includes significant roles in initiating and guiding projects, combining analytical skills with practical solutions for community improvement.

Tatiana Iakovleva is a distinguished Professor of Entrepreneurship at Stavanger Business School, Norway. She earned her Ph.D. in Entrepreneurship from Bode Graduate School of Business in 2008. Dr. Iakovleva's research focuses on entrepreneurial intentions, gender dynamics in entrepreneurship, social responsibility in business, and the impact of digitalization on opportunity recognition. She has authored two influential books: one in 2019 on inclusive entrepreneurship in digital health across seven countries, and another in 2022 on the role of entrepreneurial universities in European regional development. Dr. Iakovleva has over 55 publications in international peer-reviewed journals and leads the Responsible Innovation Special Interest Group at the Society for Professional Innovation Management (ISPIM) and is a member of the Norwegian Network for Responsible Innovation. She is currently leading the “Releasing the Power of Users” project, which focuses on responsible innovation in digital health across seven countries, underscoring her dedication to advancing this critical field.

Maria João Jacinto is the Executive Director of Patient Innovation and Nova SBE Open & User Innovation Knowledge Center. She is also a researcher at Nova School of Business and Economics with focus on ‘Healthcare Innovation and Entrepreneurship for Impact: Creating a Resilient, Safe and Crowd-based Innovation System’. She has previously worked as bionanotechnology R&D lead for Biotrend and as post-doc researcher at Universidade Católica Portuguesa. Maria João Jacinto received her Ph.D. degree in Bioengineering framed in MIT Portugal program, and her MSc in Biological Engineering from Instituto Superior Técnico.

Maria João had different international collaboration and research experiences as her master thesis in University of Ghent, in European research projects, part of her PhD thesis in University of Houston, Texas, USA, and as Patient Innovation Bootcamp program director since 2020.

Her ‘hands-on’ experience in applied healthcare science provided her the opportunity to contribute to several teaching modules in different schools, either as teaching assistant, invited lecture or responsible teacher.

Kornelia E. Konrad is Associate Professor of Anticipation and Assessment of Emerging Technologies at the Knowledge, Transformation and Society (KiTeS) research group at the University of Twente in the Netherlands. Her research interests include the role of socio-technical futures in innovation, the role of users in innovation and how users integrate eHealth and other sensoring devices in their social practices, as well as approaches for embedding societal considerations early on into research and innovation, such as Constructive Technology Assessment and Responsible Research and Innovation. She has been one of the PIs forming the TopFit Citizenlab in Twente.

Thomas Laudal is an associate professor at the UiS Business School in Stavanger Norway. He has four years of experience from the Ministry of Industry in Norway, and 13 years of experience in different consultancy roles in the Norwegian government and in the Norwegian oil and gas industry. Laudal holds a PhD in Change Management and has 14 years of research experience as a faculty member teaching courses on institutional economics and sustainable business practices. His research experience includes several projects focusing on innovation processes linked to digitalization in the health sector. Laudal has authored/edited seven books on sustainable business practices and innovation, and published twelve articles in peer-reviewed journals.

Dr. Katherine (Katie) Neary is a Lecturer in International Business Management at Liverpool Business School, Liverpool John Moores University. She holds a PhD in Management from The University of Liverpool, which focused on Health Innovation as part of an ESRC Funded Studentship. Her PhD research incorporated the broader management themes of collaboration, process, people management and organisational culture. Her main research interests are in the areas of Healthcare Innovation, Strategic Management, Social Responsibility and Sustainability. She is particularly interested in exploring the role of collaborative networks in supporting her ongoing research. She is currently involved in research projects which contribute to the teaching and learning, research and civic agendas of Liverpool John Moores University, building on her emerging interest in experiential learning and action research.

Elin Merethe Oftedal serves as a professor specializing in Change Management and Innovation at the University of Stavanger's Institute of Media and Social Sciences. She is also a member of the AFINO network, aimed at promoting innovation for a just, inclusive, and sustainable Norway and her research spans sustainable and responsible innovation, entrepreneurship, institutional change, and cultural entrepreneurship, among other areas. Oftedal's work includes leading and contributing to significant projects on academic entrepreneurship, responsible innovation, and sustainable business practices, notably in digital health, welfare services, and CO2 utilization strategies.

Margarida Almeida Oliveira works as a Digital Communications Officer at Patient Innovation. She is currently getting her International Master's in Management from Nova School of Business and Economics and also holds a Bachelor's degree in Business Administration and Digital Management from Copenhagen Business School.

Pedro Oliveira is Dean and Calouste Gulbenkian Chair Professor at Nova School of Business and Economics (NovaSBE).

He is also Professor MSO at Copenhagen Business School; the Founder and President of Patient Innovation (www.patient-innovation.com); Academic Fellow at the Cornell Institute for Healthy Futures at Cornell University; co-founder of PPL Crowdfunding; member of the Environment and Sustainability Board of Energias de Portugal – EDP and Principal Investigator of several research grants.

Previously he was Professor at Católica-Lisbon School of Business and Economics, where he served as Senior Associate Dean for Faculty and Research, Academic Director of the Lisbon MBA (a partnership between NovaSBE, Católica-Lisbon and MIT Sloan School of Management), and Director of the doctoral program in Technology Change and Entrepreneurship (jointly offered by IST, Católica-Lisbon and Carnegie Melon University). He was also an International Faculty Fellow at MIT Sloan School of Management and Advisor to the Portuguese Ministry of Science, Technology and Higher Education.

His research has been published at Production and Operations Management (POM), Research Policy, Organizational Research Methods, Journal of Product Innovation Management (JPIM), Sloan Management Review (SMR), California Management Review (CMR), Orphanet, New England Journal of Medicine – Catalyst, Technological Forecasting and Social Change, among others.

He received his PhD in Operations, Technology and Innovation Management from the University of North Carolina at Chapel Hill; his M.Sc. in Operations Research and Systems Engineering; and his Bachelor's Degree in Naval Engineering from Instituto Superior Técnico (IST) in Portugal. He also completed some advanced training at Harvard Business School and Northwestern University's Kellogg School of Management.

Nick Peres is the Programme Director of Innovation and Transformation at Torbay and South Devon NHS Foundation Trust. He is an innovator and researcher in the digital healthcare field, with experience in broadcast media and the NHS for the last 12 years. He has created cutting-edge projects for virtual reality (VR) healthcare solutions and pursued a PhD focusing on compassionate behaviour in VR. During that period, Nick has developed, executed, and overseen various XR-based projects, such as the nationally recognised NHSE-supported VR Lab. Nick is the founder of PatientVR, a project designed to educate healthcare workers on non-technical skills through immersive patient perspective scenarios. He currently co-leads the Digital Futures programme at Torbay and South Devon NHS Foundation Trust, which is nominated for a parliamentary award. The programme supports research and development projects, digital health fellowships, and digital literacy initiatives in XR and other emerging technologies. Nick has provided guidance to NHS organisations on implementing XR technologies and holds advisory positions for NHS England and the University of Plymouth. Nick has an honorary research position with Transtechnology Research at Plymouth University and is a TEDx speaker specialising in humanities perspectives on technology in healthcare.

Ilya Rozovskii is an entrepreneur and digital communications consultant and think-tank. He has developed educational programs and lectured at the British Higher School of Design, various universities, and at events such as Impact Demhack. He is also a co-founder of the digital agency Fancy Interactive and a partner in the relocation service Intermigro. He has co-authored more than 200 projects in communications and digital for leading international companies and is a populariser of cutting-edge innovations.

Dr. Anna Szopa is currently working as an Associate Lecturer at the University of Central Florida. With over 15 years of dedicated experience in both teaching and conducting extensive research. Her primary research interests revolve around understanding and enhancing the intersection of innovation and technology management, with a focus on how these dynamics can be leveraged to develop assistive technologies. Additionally, her expertise extends to the application of design thinking methodologies in solving complex problems and fostering creative solutions. She is an author of numerous books, book chapters, and journal articles, each offering valuable insights derived from her extensive research endeavors.

Gemma Tria specialized in Social and Cultural Anthropology along with advanced studies in Social Integration. Gemma has been actively engaged with vulnerable groups, including refugees, offering Spanish language and literacy instruction to newly arrived non-speakers, alongside assistance with bureaucracy. Additionally, she has provided support to people with disabilities, guided by the principles of the Independent Life movement. Gemma took courses on personal assistance for individuals with physical and cognitive disabilities to better understand their challenges. Currently, during her scholarship at Nova SBE as a research and technical assistant for the Open and User Innovation Knowledge center, she collaborates with Patient Innovation, gaining valuable experience in the field of user innovation in the healthcare realm. Gemma's motivation lies in fostering a better alignment between communities' interests and policies, with a special focus on promoting development. She strives to ensure that innovations are tailored to community needs, aiming for impactful change and increased community involvement.

Vicky Van der Auwera holds a master's degree in Engineering Sciences from Brussels University Belgium, where she graduated as civil mechanical-electrical engineer. She built up her expertise in Research and Development within the private sector in the area of mechanical engineering, machine construction, mechatronics and semiconductor industry. At Thomas More University of Applied Sciences, she started working at the tech transfer office and the unit Research & Innovation. She is one of the team members that started up LiCalab in 2012, in close collaboration with the City of Turnhout. She is the research manager of LiCalab, responsible for the daily management of the research group, the quality of the research activities, the strategic goals and she leads EU-projects as well as private assignments.

Johan van der Zwart has a background in Architecture (MSc, 2001), Healthcare Real Estate Management (PhD, 2014) and Healthcare Management (MSc, 2015). He worked as assistant professor in landscape architecture at Delft University of Technology, postdoc researcher *Smart Hospital Architecture* at the Norwegian University of Science and Technology (NTNU) and as postdoc researcher for *responsible innovation in healthcare technology* at the department of Science, Technology and Policy Studies (STePS) of the University of Twente in the Netherlands. His research focus is on the interaction between technology, people, practices, and place. His distinct contribution to projects is based on his holistic, transdisciplinary approach, connecting different disciplines from an in-depth understanding of scientific research and design of healthcare service systems. He is the author of several journal articles, books and book chapters in the fields of healthcare architecture and landscape architecture.

Dr. Catharina van Leersum is working as a postdoctoral researcher at the Open University of the Netherlands on the topic of artificial intelligence (AI), in particular AI and aging and AI in healthcare. Among other things, Catharina's research is influenced by explainability of AI and how AI shapes and is shaped by new forms of practicing health, caregiving, and staying socially connected as we age. Before joining the Open University in 2023, Catharina has been working as a postdoc at the University of Twente for 2,5 years. As part of TOPFIT Citizenlab, her research focussed on investigating citizen science methodologies and exploring how various groups of citizens integrate innovations and new forms of information and data into their daily lives. These citizen science methodologies remain part of her current work. Catharina has two master's degrees in Technical Medicine, and Philosophy of Science, Technology and Society, and during her PhD, she worked with clients in long-term care to develop the website "What matters to me" that helped to articulate preferences of clients regarding their care and lives.

Hilde Vandenhoudt works at the Centre of Expertise Care and Well-being of Thomas More University of Applied Sciences in Geel, Belgium. She graduated in 1989 as a general practitioner at KU Leuven and attained additional degrees in tropical disease management, public health, epidemiology, and business and innovation. She worked in primary health care and prevention for many years in sub-Saharan Africa before moving back to Belgium, where she became a lecturer in nursing, midwifery, and health care management until 2020. Her fields of interest are prevention, integrated primary health care, health and digital literacy, transmural care, self-management support, and caring technology. At LiCalab she is project manager and researcher and focuses on technology use in primary care and prevention through new collaborative models. She currently co-coordinates the learning community of the 8 Caring Technology Principles and a learning community on heart failure care.

Sascha Vermeylen holds a Master's degree in social economic sciences from University of Antwerp. Since 2018, she's a panelmanager and researcher at LiCalab (living and care lab) at Thomas More University of Applied Sciences in Belgium. LiCalab focuses on health technology and new collaborative models in health by applying user-centric research. Sascha manages the LiCalab panel of testers/volunteers and maintains the panel database, following GDPR. This panel consists of citizens, patients, caregivers and care organizations. In addition, she is responsible for the operational side of the living lab activities, such as setting up co-creation sessions, real life testing, human factor studies and surveys.

List of figures

Introduction: Meeting the inclusion challenge in innovation

Figure 1 Spectrum of User Innovation Behaviour. Adapted from Bessant et al. 2019 —— **7**

Back to the future: Reflection on healthcare's past to understand its future

Figure 1 Philosophical Perspective for the Future of Healthcare —— **30**

Sustainable user involvement: Building a user community and fostering high-quality research

Figure 1 Schematic overview illustrating the steps for building a user community as well as executing specific user research activities —— **37**
Figure 2 Development of the LiCalab user community over time —— **40**
Figure 3 Overview of the activities of LiCalab in 2022 —— **42**
Figure 4 The Moonbird breath pacer —— **54**
Figure 5 Schematic representation of the 'Welgerust' (well-rested) trajectory according to the four phases of the SHINE methodology —— **55**

The emergence of a boundary innovation space – the case of Norwegian Smart Care Lab

Figure 1 Timeline of NSCC development —— **67**
Figure 2 Evolution and strategic positioning of NSCL —— **76**

The creation of a community to engage in innovation processes and citizen science

Figure 1 An empty flower as part of the flower association exercise. The co-researchers were asked to think about their role within a project —— **88**

https://doi.org/10.1515/9783111241036-017

Ageing in your place: Envisioning healthy, happy, and safe ageing in a neighbourhood with citizen science methods

Figure 1 First page of the living and environment factsheet that was shared with the citizens to discuss the statistical health data of their neighbourhood — **112**
Figure 2 Holistic approach towards age-friendly living — **115**

Climbing the citizen science ladder: Juxtaposing citizens' levels of participation and influence in research analysis and dissemination

Figure 1 Level of participation in research activities and citizens' influence on results — **135**
Figure 2 Cross-project analysis of research activities and citizens' influence on results — **136**
Figure 3 Juxtaposing levels of participation and influence in research — **138**
Figure 4 Citizen science ladder — **140**

Patient innovation as a case-study example of a multisided platform for involving patients in the social innovation process

Figure 1 Example of a solution submitted by a patient innovator, which was approved by the Patient Innovation Medical team and published in the Patient Innovation platform — **177**
Figure 2 Producer Innovation Value Network (Cennamo et al., 2022) — **179**
Figure 3 User Innovation Value Network (Cennamo et al., 2022) — **179**
Figure 4 Patient Innovation as an MSP in the healthcare innovation landscape (Cennamo et al., 2022) — **182**
Figure 5 Patient Innovation MSP roles and correspondent activities, on and off-platform — **187**
Figure 6 Daiprox, a product developed by Raul Dorado, a patient who submitted his innovation on Patient Innovation platform and participated in the Patient Innovation Bootcamp 2021, which helped him create his own company and produce and sell his product at a large scale — **188**

Superpower or kryptonite?

Figure 1 Threshold for testing — **222**
Figure 2 Finding the Elephant – Model of User Inclusion — **223**

The impact of users on the development of Morphic auto personalization

Figure 1 MorphicBar — **234**

The dilemma of achieving responsible innovation in regulated markets

Figure 1 The go-between role of public authorities in the provision of equipment to the elderly — **247**
Figure 2 Forecast of the number of users of subsidised equipment in Norway. Source: Agenda Kaupang (2017) — **252**
Figure 3 Illustration of differences in the go-between role of public authorities and private corporations and charities — **256**

Navigating towards improved user engagement in healthcare innovation – releasing the power of users

Figure 1 Boundary Innovation Space and Community Typology — **271**

List of tables

Introduction: Meeting the inclusion challenge in innovation

Table 1 Overview of the book —— **16**

Back to the future: Reflection on healthcare's past to understand its future

Table 1 Main historical developments of technological and human advancements and their pivoting points —— **25**

Sustainable user involvement: Building a user community and fostering high-quality research

Table 1 Relevant features of a software tool for managing the community —— **43**
Table 2 Criteria for sample size selection for qualitative research, based on an integration of the guidelines based on Morse (2000), Guest et al. (2017), and Visileiou et al. (2018) —— **48**
Table 3 Overview of the SHINE methodology —— **52**

The emergence of a boundary innovation space – the case of Norwegian Smart Care Lab

Table 1 Summary of interviews —— **66**
Table 2 User Cafés with NSCL —— **71**

The creation of a community to engage in innovation processes and citizen science

Table 1 Ten principles of citizen science [Robinson et al. 2018] —— **84**
Table 2 Ten principles of citizen science [Robinson et al. 2018] and links between these and the four common aspects (recognizing and acknowledging each other's capacities, acknowledging different goals, building a relationship of trust, or creating a learning environment) —— **97**

https://doi.org/10.1515/9783111241036-018

Ageing in your place: Envisioning healthy, happy, and safe ageing in a neighbourhood with citizen science methods

Table 1 Socio-demographic information of the 39 citizens involved in the project — **104**

Climbing the citizen science ladder: Juxtaposing citizens' levels of participation and influence in research analysis and dissemination

Table 1 Three perspectives on citizen science as analytical frame — **125**
Table 2 Applied methods to include citizens in research activities — **127**
Table 3 Summary of level of participation and influence on results per research activities in the projects — **133**
Table 4 Three perspectives on citizen science as analytical frame — **140**

Superpower or kryptonite?

Table 1 Overview over business cases — **214**

The dilemma of achieving responsible innovation in regulated markets

Table 1 Summarizing the elements relevant for the go-between role of the state. (Sources of quantified information is included in the paragraphs above.) — **255**

Index

Ageing 12, 101–102
Analysis: Patient Innovation As A Multi-Sided Platform Case-Study 180

Bounded innovation space 63
breath pacer 52–54

Citizen science 84, 86, 95, 102–103, 121, 123, 125
Citizenlab 12, 83, 85–96, 101, 103, 121–122, 125, 132, 139
Communication 75, 95, 156, 233
Community 39, 43–44, 241, 258, 268
Co-researcher 89, 131, 135

Delivery and follow-up function 251
Diabetes 135
Disability 241
Discussion/conclusion 187
Display function 251

Ethical 49–50, 53, 63, 273
Ethical considerations 273
expectation 143, 146, 151, 153, 155–156
Experimental research 48

Health 1, 36, 50, 66, 68–69, 74–75, 83, 129, 143, 166–167, 169, 182, 185, 229, 241, 246, 257–258
Hub environment 147, 149, 158
Hub staff 143, 146–152, 157–158

Inclusive 11, 230
informed patient 7, 39
Innovation 1–3, 6, 9, 11, 13, 15, 36–37, 61–64, 66, 68–70, 122, 143, 148, 154, 158, 164, 166, 169, 173–176, 180–189, 210, 230, 267, 269, 273–274
Innovation Divergence: Contrasting User and Producer Networks in Healthcare 176
innovative patient 174, 176, 185
Introduction 173
involved patient 39, 135

Living labs 13, 36, 38

moral agency 21
Morphic 14, 229–230, 232–242, 268, 270
Multisided platforms (MSP) 173, 181, 183–185
Multisided Platforms: Integrating User and Producer Innovations in Healthcare 180

Panel manager 40–41
Participation 132
Patient innovation 174
Patient Innovation – a project to revolutionize healthcare through user innovation 175
Patient Innovation as a case-study example of a Multisided Platform for involving patients in the social innovation process 173
Patient Innovation platform – a good MSP example 181
Patient innovators 185
Patients as a great source of valuable innovation 174
PPPI-dilemma 245, 247–248, 250–251, 257, 259–261
Purchasing function 251

Qualitative research 47

Responsible innovation 243

Sample sizes 48
Scenario-building workshop 102, 107
Space 70, 144–145
Stakeholders 146, 201

technological determinism 4, 21
The 3-roles impact 187
The community organizer role 183
The innovation manager role 185
The market matchmaker role 184

Usability research 48
User engagement 63, 266
User experience 50, 242
User testing 237–238
Users 4, 7, 68, 144–148, 150–151, 154, 156, 158, 215, 234, 239–240, 242, 252, 265, 274

https://doi.org/10.1515/9783111241036-019